THE YIELD

MERIDIAN

Crossing Aesthetics

Werner Hamacher

Editor

*Stanford
University
Press*

———————

*Stanford
California
2015*

THE YIELD

Kafka's Atheological Reformation

Paul North

Stanford University Press
Stanford, California

Printed in the United States of America

Library of Congress Cataloging-in-Publication Data

North, Paul, 1971– author.
The yield : Kafka's atheological reformation / Paul North.
pages cm
Includes bibliographical references.
ISBN 978-0-8047-9445-9 (cloth : alk. paper)
ISBN 978-0-8047-9659-0 (pbk.   )
1. Kafka, Franz, 1883–1924—Philosophy.
2. Philosophical theology. I. Title.
PT2621.A26Z8114 2015
833'.912—dc23
2015007376

ISBN 978-0-8047-9669-9 (electronic)

for caro

He strained my faith—
Did he find it supple?
Shook my strong trust—
Did it then—yield?

        —Emily Dickinson

Contents

xi

Conversations

I'd like to thank Jeffrey Cassvan's father, whom I haven't met. If he hadn't handed Jeff a volume of Kafka with the nerve that only a parent has vis-à-vis a child to transmit the most vexed and troublesome gifts, and if Jeff had not been daring enough to whisper "Kafka" to me one night on the street in Queens in a tone reserved for a god no one remembered, I would never have started reading. I would never have started thinking had I not found myself in a seminar on Kafka and Nietzsche taught by Peter Fenves at Northwestern University in 2003. My engagement with Kafka continues to be driven by the dialectic laid out there. Some of this book is Peter's ground; I hope to have planted a few creepers in it. In the summer of 2012, Werner Hamacher got up from his table in Frankfurt and disappeared into his labyrinthine library. He returned, face shining, with the passage on the illuminated corpse from a letter by Kafka. Our subsequent dialogue about Rosenzweig's nothing and its basis in Cohen's *Infinitesimallehre* added themselves to the continuous seminar that Hamacher has been holding in my thoughts for many years. I am thankful for his mentorship and his remarkable essays. The book also benefited greatly from his proposals. I am grateful as always for the ongoing intellectual agon with Anthony Adler, from whom in our cantankerous exchanges I keep experiencing what thinking can possibly be. He read parts of the book with the courage he always has to point out the broadest conceptual frame. Around Rüdiger Campe and his students at Yale an international Kafka workshop formed that raised crucial questions about the structure of address in Kafka's writings. I am also obliged to Rüdiger for his patient responses to my speculations at lunches in New

Haven. Thanks to the faculty of the Yale German Department for their support and to a Morse Junior Faculty Grant from Yale for the time to write. Parts of the book were presented at the Yale Whitney Humanities Center, Tufts University, the University of Zürich, and the University of Tel Aviv. Gratitude is owing to Margaret Czepiel of the Bodleian Library at Oxford for facilitating work with the manuscripts and to Hans-Gerd Koch for sharing a draft of the 1918–20 volume of Kafka's *Briefe* before funds were found to publish it. Finally, a host of encounters and exchanges with some of the most interesting people on the planet brought many thoughts to formulation and many to the scrap heap. I am profoundly beholden to Carolina Baffi, Andrew Libby, Eyal Peretz, Yue Zhuo, Roshen Hendrickson, Demetra Kasimis, Friese Undine, Anna Glazova, John Whalen, Katrin Trüstedt, Paul Grimstad, Carol Jacobs, Michael Levine, Henry Sussman, Thomas Schestag, Jacques Lezra, Paul Fleming, Kirk Wetters, Vivian Liska, Avital Ronell, Hindy Najman, Eckart Goebel, Rainer Nägele, Michel Chaouli, Paul Franks, and Liliane Weissberg for the generous exchange of so many sentences. Thomas Stachel's careful and precise editing of translations and his fact-checking for the final revision were invaluable. The final revision happened within the penumbra of David Farrell Krell, who read the manuscript afternoons on a Greek isle and gave it the kind of epimethean shock treatment without which such a promethean venture would surely not have survived. He noticed that the pivot point of my argument and Kafka's movement of thought was, whether I knew it or not, the concept of eternal recurrence, and this enabled me suddenly to see the book as it should have been. You will, however, read the present version of it, in which I have only briefly sketched out this relation. The real book will come in the next revision, the one after this one, the one after the last—

Preface

To understand how Kafka, working through some theological issues, came to a peculiar conclusion about the good, the true, and the being-ground of everything, you will first, I think, have to accept a peculiar idea. You will have to be willing to accept a replete universe, everything together at once in a cosmos in which there is absolutely no room to breathe or move or change, no chance to be anything other than you are at this very instant. Such a universe is saturated with itself, chaotic maybe, but still all is there, filling every corner. This peculiar idea has serious repercussions: the only creation in this kind of universe is de-creation, the only possible addition is subtraction, the only movement is pause, the only freedom is a species of bondage, and, yes, the only production is the production of inequality. This last corollary will take some time to explain.

Who would desire such a universe? No one would like to live there, or even be able to imagine it: everything packed into the pleroma that no one can see. Inside it, an entity or an event only happens when someone or something steps back, makes room. Making room is the only real act in such a cosmos.

A minor motif in Genesis, a tale ancillary to the story of creation but important for it too, may make this packed universe seem less peculiar an idea. It is a motif of making room, of yielding. The motif is remarkably consistent across the P and J sources for Genesis. It appears at three pivotal moments: the Garden of Eden, the forming of Adam, and the initial gestures of creation. Reading backward, God planted a garden (Gen. 2:8), God formed human being from earth (2:7), and God began to create the all (1:1). Reading forward, creation happens to an "unformed" earth. The earth "brings forth" vegetation (1:11, 1:12). Soon all living creatures emerge from it (1:24). Then the human being is formed out of earth, a geolassic creature before it is a pneumomorphic one. God needs earth. Why? The earth *lets him* do what he wants to do; it has give. The same give of the earth makes for the creation of the world, the creation of the model human, and the creation of the Garden, and in the Garden, also by grace of earth, come all the growths and especially the two trees, of life and of moral judgment.

No doubt earth's give is a minor issue when compared with God's great feats and disasters in those early years. Yet if creation is formation, something needs to be formless, and what's more, it also needs to be form*able*. We can imagine a medium that is formless but *cannot take a form*. Water is like this, and that is why when heaven and earth are created the waters are immediately separated off. What is needed is something *tohu wa-bohu*, "shapeless and formless," that gives just enough, and earth has the precisely needed give—not too much, not too little. Earth responds to forming forces by receding a bit, and after it does this, through no force of its own, life comes forth out of it, though not from it. Earth has give;[1] earth yields so that there can be a yield. The replete cosmos in which things happen only after something makes room is thus there "in the beginning"; it is not so peculiar, or at least not all that new.

In a sense this book is about gardening. On one hand, I try to chronicle a highly theoretical Franz Kafka who prunes back the theological growths of a couple millennia, back to the branches, to the stalks, then to the roots, and in some cases all the way back to the earth, finding evidence of an originary yielding. He illuminates many motifs in Genesis and liberates some peculiar ideas within the major stories that have become justifications for all sorts of ideological forcings and transplantations throughout Europe and its domains. On the other hand, I also report on a highly practical Franz Kafka who soon after harvesting this crop of "thoughts" enrolled in an anti-ideological course of study at the Pomologisches Institut, where he learned "fruitology," the art of cultivating orchards, political gardening, that is, the art of provisioning the masses. Kafka has both a theoretical and a practical interest in the earth's "give": earth is a model for and an essential instance of a medium whose activity is to yield.

Gardens have a rich history as more than pastimes in modern Europe. One of the few, I think, to see the gift of a garden as the "give" of the earth was Friedrich Hölderlin, for whom *Gärten* echoed with another verb *gären*, to ferment but also to decay. Anthony Adler brings this near pun to light in his book on Hölderlin's *Hyperion*: "The garden is life in the middle, the life of plants in collaboration with man. The ferment, in contrast, is life in its extremity; life in its distance from the origin—an over-ripeness that falls backward to the place from whence it sprang— and also life in its under-ripeness, its barely organic origins in mulch and decay."[2] Fermenting (*gären*) names the natural yielding back of the fruit, the yielding of the yield, the return of what has already come to fruition to the heterogeneous humus. Kafka thinks through the backward tendency in a slightly different manner. His version of the retreat of the completed does not emphasize excess, overabundance or overripeness, hyperbole, bubbling. His garden is subject to evanescence rather than effervescence, evaporation rather than frothing and leavening, debasement without sublimation into wine; that is, his is not a dialectical garden.

Kafka's thought bears comparison to another somewhat repugnant, also not dialectical thought. Yet no one whispers "yield" in your ear the way Nietzsche's demon whispers the news of the eternal return of the same into his. "This life as you now live it and have lived it you will have to live once again and innumerable times again."[3] So runs the heaviest thought, according to Nietzsche. Nietzsche's heaviest thought, Kafka's fullest universe. What do these two superlatives have in common?

There is a remarkable similarity of effect: Nietzsche's heaviest thought leads you to . . . do nothing, at least at first. And the fullest world likewise leads you to . . . do nothing. Then we ask: are the two resulting non-actions, are these two nothings really commensurable? Heaviest thought, fullest world. A preliminary response would be: yes. They are both monstrous and nearly total negations. If we follow the work of the negative, each of these thoughts says "no" to an unheard-of degree, no, as Nietzsche writes "to everything to which up to now people had said yes."[4] The negations then are similar in their all-encompassing scope. Yet beyond the similarity in scope we are bound to say: no. The two negations are commensurate in neither kind nor effect. Although he bears the heaviest thought, Zarathustra nevertheless pole-vaults over "no" to "yes." He is the "yessayingest" despite his monstrous "no." The word most used to describe the hero's disposition in *Thus Spoke Zarathustra* is in fact "despite" (*trotz*). And then, Nietzsche reflects on Zarathustra in *Ecce Homo*, "that everything decisive emerges 'nevertheless' [*dass alles Entscheidende* '*trotzdem' entsteht*]"[5] is the mark of one who takes all oppositions into himself and overcomes them on behalf of a new world. He has thought the most abyssal thought and *trotzdem* finds that there has been no ill effect on his existence, no ill effect even if he has to repeat that same existence to infinity. Despite the heaviest thought he discovers he has the artist's power to "create"—*schaffen*—and he can exercise it more strongly and more broadly than anyone on earth; he can even exercise his power on the past; he can recreate everything about which we say "it was" thus and so—*alles "Es war" umzuschaffen*—as a product of his own will. And then he can announce: "That's the way I wanted it! [*So wollte ich es!*],"[6] and everything to which he said "No, thank you" appears now to have been created by him. The heaviest thought is a means to power. The thought is heavy, but it can be lifted.

Perhaps we don't even need to say how different Zarathustra's heaviest thought, his defiance (*Trotz*), and the rhetorical overcoming of opposites (*trotzdem* . . .) are from Kafka's replete cosmos with no room for action. Kafka's quintessential negative adverb indicates that there are conditions for overcoming but they have not yet been met. Rather than *trotz*, his characteristic adverb is *erst*—"not until." And his brands of non-act—secession, surrender, the yield—are alternatives to power. Overcoming on the one hand, yielding on the other. The protagonists in the texts by Kafka discussed below, if there are any, decline to use power, dismiss the *Übermensch*, and would rather stay under the thumb of a master than become one.

A Note on References

The small notebooks that Kafka wrote in during fall, winter, and early spring of 1917 and 1918, called by the editors of the historical-critical edition *Oktavhefte G* and *H,* are referred to throughout the book as "the Treatise" or "Kafka's *pensées,*" rather than by their conventional title, the *Zürau Aphorisms.* The reasoning for these names will become clear in the course of reading. The majority of quotations in this book are taken from these notebooks. Some, however, are taken from the fair copy Kafka wrote sometime later onto small slips of paper, called by the editors *Zettel.* Citations that refer to *Zettel* refer to these slips and the numbers Kafka wrote on them.

Abbreviations

GA   Martin Heidegger, *Gesamtausgabe*. 102 vols. Frankfurt am Main: Vittorio Klostermann, 1976–2011.

GS   Walter Benjamin, *Gesammelte Schriften*. Edited by Rolf Tiedemann and Hermann Schweppenhäuser. 17 vols. Frankfurt am Main: Suhrkamp, 1972–89.

FKA   Franz Kafka, *Historisch-kritische Franz-Kafka-Ausgabe*. 8 vols. and 4 supplements. Edited by Roland Reuß and Peter Staengle. Basel: Stroemfeld, 1995.

KSA   Friedrich Nietzsche, *Sämtliche Werke: Kritische Studienausgabe*. 15 vols. Edited by Giorgio Colli and Mazino Montinari. Berlin: De Gruyter, 1988.

NS   Franz Kafka, *Nachgelassene Schriften und Fragmente*. Edited by Malcolm Pasley. 2 vols. Frankfurt am Main: S. Fischer, 1992–93.

SW   *Selected Writings.*

§ Introduction

1. Atheology

When a historical category loses its meaning and threatens to disappear, an opportunity arises that has a strange consequence. The category "Jew" in middle Europe during the first quarter of the twentieth century is an example of such a threatened category with its strange consequence. While the term "Jew" certainly continued to refer to a group of living individuals and was used by lovers and haters of them alike, its meaning, for many complex reasons, had for some time—since the Jewish Enlightenment at least—been becoming too diverse to signify one thing. All sides clung to the category with renewed force, however, despite or perhaps because of its splintering meaning. In what David Suchoff has recently called "the hidden openness of the tradition," the strange consequence was that it also became possible to reinterpret the category altogether.[1] Since "Judaism" in Central Europe had become hard to parse, and many Jews who held on to the category often had, in point of fact, little or no experience with Judaism, their interpretations of it were precisely not grounded in the tradition. These Judaisms were not wholly, and often not even necessarily, "Jewish."

Some got their Judaism from books, some from personal experience of particular sects, and some, or so it seems now, got it largely from their imaginations. Franz Rosenzweig was in part such a figure: he "converted" to Judaism from assimilation, and his conversion involved inventing a highly elaborate theological system with no real precedent in Jewish history so that he could go back to "his" religion via an imaginative re-

I

construction of some thought complexes from German idealism. Consciously or not, for some of these figures, the tradition became available all of a sudden as source material for recreating what never was, and the montage work of putting it together also often brought other traditions, other doctrines, even ones that had previously been sworn enemies, back onto the drawing board.

Rosenzweig is a conspicuous example of what you do in the strange event of historical weakenings and emptyings of categories, in this case the category "religion." He ultimately rescues and reinvents a kind of religious practice by means of a highly formalized theology. We may find that all monotheisms contain somewhere within them a logic or logos of the divine, an attempt to justify by means of arguments or formulas the existence or preeminence of one God. Yet theology is a very technical activity, which is not always well developed and is hardly important at all moments. Theology, however it is construed, happily takes a back seat to practices, stories, political maneuvers, institutional habits, affective or mystical events, and so forth. Attempting to save religion or a religion, or secularity for that matter, from transformation or disappearance by means of theology is not a universal gesture; it has its own history, which is at key moments intertwined with the history of philosophy. To speak very generally, the first half of this history, which we might call "absolute theology," begins with Aristotle and ends with medieval Aristotelianism—with many exceptions, of course—and the second half, in which theology became an attempt to salvage religious hopes by transforming them, often beyond recognition, begins with Luther and the Reformation, transits through Spinoza, the Enlightenment, and Kant, and issues into the early twentieth century where theological thinking, poorly disguised in Heidegger, toyed with in Walter Benjamin, and systematized in Rosenzweig, could seem the only salvation for a tradition—here, peculiarly, the tradition of secular philosophy—perceived as irrecoverable.

In this epoch, in the years when Heidegger was reading Saint Augustine, Benjamin was in conversation with Gershom Scholem, Rosenzweig was corresponding with his cousin Eugen Rosenstock-Huessy, and Carl Schmitt was calling for a recognition of the theological underpinnings of the modern state—Franz Kafka, responding to some of the same philosophical, cultural, and social forces, was planning a different reformation, this time not using theology to save religion or, conversely, to reformulate and re-entrench a set of nominally secular beliefs about power, existence, language, or history. Kafka sketched out a reformation of the theo-logic—not Judaic and not not Judaic—on which these activities depended.

We are used to classifying Kafka either as an extremely peculiar person or as a quintessentially literary writer or both. Literary writer par excellence was a post he held for the twentieth century's foremost thinker of "the literary," Maurice Blanchot. More than this, Blanchot's Kafka was a writer of literature for whom literariness and writing were constant topics of concern. Even those critics who consider Kafka a "thinker" of this or that topic other than "writing" see his "thinking," about the law, say, to give one example, as interesting precisely because it presents a literary viewpoint and not a legal one. Only recently has the fact that Kafka was not only a lawyer but a legal theorist in his own right begun to be taken seriously. Reading his legal writings, we discover that the government agency where he worked called upon him not only to defend this or that worker or to process claims under this or that insurance law. While grumbling about the time stolen from his literary writing, he also wrote elaborate briefs about how workers' insurance laws should be conceived, written, and applied.

A handful of books and articles over the past two decades present the many spheres, law being only one, in which Kafka was thinking about something other than writing or his own personal life, and in a mode other than literature. Arnold Heidsieck, Barry Smith, Stanley Corngold, Benno Wagner, and Andreas Kilcher, among others, have contributed to this small library. To be sure, "other than literature" is a questionable phrase, especially given how many of these areas already involve literary strategies: law, phenomenology, Jewish thought, theology, and so forth. And yet in a few critical texts, like Heidsieck's relatively unknown study, the reverse turns out also to be true. It emerges that the "literary" for Kafka in point of fact already involved elements from these other spheres: ideas about perception and consciousness from Brentanian "descriptive psychology," recondite practices of language from jurisprudence, and from his theological reading concepts of time, being, the self, good and evil, and many others.

When Kafka began to think seriously about aspects of theology, in line with what some called Judaism, but few in his circle could define definitively,[2] with reference to what some would have considered to fall well outside Judaism, that is, nominally Christian theological motifs—two things made his thinking along the lines, along the fault lines, of theology unprecedented. First of all, he used theology neither to rescue religion nor to condemn it, and he didn't hope directly to improve anyone's life in the world by means of it, including that of the Jews.[3] From theology he sought a justification, not for changing the world, but for interpreting it differently, which, it seems to me now, he imagined would produce a much more fundamental shift than a revolution would have done. Unlike his friends, who found new justifications for action in religious motifs, Kafka was interested primarily in the *logos* of theology, which was interesting for him because it was flawed. So, secondly, Kafka engaged with theological themes, which included Jewish and non-Jewish, Christian, pagan, and animistic themes and other notions and scenarios, in order to demonstrate that what was called theology, which he believed was the main resource for our conceptual commitments, was precisely not logical; no divinely perfect logic stood behind it, and thus a stark opposition between the secular and the religious could not properly be asserted. In short, the prefix *a-* in "atheology" modified both *theos and logos*. He pursued this uncommon track, not because he believed that the secular was ultimately religious, although in many ways he might have agreed that it was, but because the only interesting thing about secular modernity was that its logic was a-logical in a variety of ways that could be explored, and exploited, and shown to correspond to theology, rightly understood.

We have an opportunity here to sketch out the parameters of a further possibility for theology that is neither its triumphant return nor its total demise at the hands of secular thought, that is, a path other than political theology (exemplified by Carl Schmitt) or theological politics (exemplified by Spinoza),[4] a path that comes to us from Kafka's writing of the late teens.[5] The path emerges from perhaps the one work by Kafka that calls for a complete reconstruction, although it has never had one.[6] In the winter of 1917–18, Kafka wrote more than three hundred *pensées* (he had read Pascal the summer before), which can be seen as "wisdom literature," provided one credits "wisdom" with the potential to reveal the inconsistencies in a world system, to present, very wisely indeed, a world "dysstem." In fact, these extensively small but intensively massive passages, often known as the *Zürau Aphorisms*, though they are better described as "thoughts" and not "aphorisms," constitute Kafka's only explicitly and thoroughly critical work, his "atheological-political treatise." They cover almost every significant theologoumenon in the history of European thought. Each individual "thought" in Kafka's treatise undertakes a complex linguistic and philosophical operation to reduce a theologoumenon to an original confusion, absurdity, inconsistency, or contradiction.[7] In this way atheology, the procedure he undertakes, brings to language a set of specific *alogoi* that animate Kafka's thinking work on the afterlife of the mono-god. In the Greek-derived terminology expressive of erudite scholarship, his atheology could be described as *alogotheic*.

It should go without saying that Kafka's atheologic and alogotheics can't be adjudged simply Jewish or Christian, pagan or animistic, although they draw into their fire elements that have been counted under each of these names at different historical moments. I make no attempt to class phenomena or doctrines rigorously under one or another such historical name.

Kafka's response to political theology, which insists that secular concepts are at base theological, would be substantially the same as his response to theo-politics, which insists that theological concepts are at base all-too-human, interested, and political.[8] He shows that the concept of theology—itself not theic but fallen—out of which both develop their arguments is ambiguous and frequently self-contradictory, and so it can neither become a foundation for thought and action, nor be criticized and negated as the basis for yet another God-free logic.[9] Theology's ambiguities are undoubtedly endemic to "Europe." Kafka's "thoughts" thus respond to the question "What to do?" in a Europe with ambiguous foundations and no pure "theology," in which neither theism nor atheism are coherent options, when neither can be thoroughly negated or completely affirmed. What to do? Kafka's response is summed up in the word "yield," the central concept animating both his so-called aphorisms and this book. In this seemingly untenable situation, you might do nothing—or, in fact, less than nothing.

The mode and manner of "yielding," a word that has no single German correlative, I describe as "atheological" in a special sense. I am not the first to use the term "atheology," of course; it is being used increasingly often these days. Unlike "theology," it has not, however, become a technical term; it does not name a body of argument that we could refer to and no branch of learning corresponds to it. The word appears early in a still not well-understood gesture by Georges Bataille—*the title of* whose projected series of five volumes, *La somme athéologique* (*The Atheological Summa*), was meant to signal, with no little irony, the conviction motivating a highly unsystematic corpus of writings. Bataille's conviction was that lived experience had to be valued for itself, on the basis of the impossible. We might sum up theology—unfairly, no doubt, but not without some truth—by saying that it works to make transcendence acceptable to reason by means of reason. That is, from the perspective of human thought, theology makes God seem at least possible (that is, not contradictory) and at most real. Bataillean atheology does the converse: it works to make transcendence seem impossible, by means of non-knowledge. Non-knowledge is the proper attitude toward the impossible, and both correspond to life insofar as it is made up of chance occurrences and profanities such as bodily excretions—which break the frame of theology. At one point Bataille gives what he calls a "definition" of atheology: "the science of the death or destruction of God."[10] This shows in some sense why religion was crucial for Bataille to achieve his Nietzschean objective: because Abrahamic religions were the ones that paid serious attention to the profanities that hindered the progress of the faithful toward transcendence. Profanities offered perfect absurdities on the basis of which experience could, on good grounds, abandon anything higher or more explanatory than itself. God is dead already in flesh, for example, and more than "dead" in flesh's putrid decay and waste, which makes spirit indeed seem ridiculous. "Atheology" was the name Bataille gave to the special non-science with special methods that described risible things such as waste, chance, laughter, and other phenomena.

Jean-Luc Nancy resurrects the word "atheological" in a project he calls the "auto-deconstruction of Christianity";[11] Nancy expects from this word a rise in respect for the "nothing" that Christianity brings into the center of "the world." "Nothing" here takes the place of Bataille's "impossible." It is a Bataillean project; Nancy gives it this label himself. Yet unlike Bataille, Nancy believes that non-knowledge emerges within Christianity and has a special status there. Within nominally Christian theologoumena, Nancy finds an atheological moment, a moment in which one concept or another—faith, eternal life, the mono-god, messianism—is not only not affirmed but in fact turns out to be essentially nothing. From this essential nothing, Nancy wants to show, furthermore, that atheism is an essential component of mono-theism, or at a minimum that the two are mythical twins born from the same parent. When the capricious, humanoid, and plural gods of Greece are reduced to one, the divine effectively disappears. It vanishes behind all the new strategies that are suddenly needed in order to make a one—that may be an abstraction, a force, a principle, a unity, an alpha or an omega or both—thinkable. The way of this new singular god-principle, this first of firsts, is precisely to vanish behind the world, nature, knowledge, and so forth. For Nancy, atheism and theism operate within the same "horizon of a subtraction, of a retreat, an absence," the primary phenomenological event of a nothing that makes both logics possible.[12] And yet, this phenomenological "atheology" is quite reasonable; Nancy shows that the operations of the non-God are consistent, even in his retreat. Nancy's conception is *a-theos*, and yet he seems to avoid anything too *a-logos*.

One of the most compelling "auto-deconstructions" Nancy discovers is that of the concept "faith." The theologoumenon is special to Kafka as well. To Nancy faith is special because it preserves a conspicuous nothing at its core, a nothing that, furthermore, is not nihilistic. Nothing does not come from nothing, but we are surprised to discover that everything does. Nancy writes in the essay "Atheism and Monotheism," translated and reproduced in *Dis-Enclosure: The Deconstruction of Christianity*: "That 'God' himself may be the fruit of faith, which at the same time depends only on his grace (that is, exempts itself from necessity and obligation), is a thought profoundly foreign—perhaps it is the most foreign—to the theism/atheism pair."[13] This sentence is a lesson in Nancy's method and a clue to his hopes for atheology. He seeks to move beyond the theism/atheism pair by uncovering an identical moment in each of their structures. The reciprocal production of God by faith and of faith by God is the moment when both atheism and theism are born from nothing. The pivot on which everything turns is faith. "But faith?" he writes in the introduction, "Should it not form the necessary relation to the nothing: in such a way that we understand that there are no buffers, no halting points, no markers, no undeconstructible terms, and that disenclosure never stops opening what it opens ('Europe,' metaphysics, knowledge, the self, form, sense, religion itself)?"[14] This list must go on, perhaps to infinity. Everything, in this new kind of genesis, derives from faith, which means that it is "grounded on nothing." This idea of a generative and almost infinitely productive nothing whose conduit is faith,[15] it should be said, is echoed *avant la lettre* in a theopolitical book by Kafka's bosom friend Felix Weltsch: "Faith overcomes itself, by creating. For as soon as something is actually believed, it is no longer the case that: it is because it is believed; rather, it is believed because it is."[16] Faith is its own miracle: it reverses the order of things and makes an absolute out of a relative and an objective out of a subjective act. Weltsch does not say, as Nancy does, that with the act of faith, a nothing irrupts into perhaps the most meaningful modern moment, but he does, like Nancy, associate the moment of faith with a pure, incorrigible human freedom, the hope that I take it stands behind Nancy's use of the same verb, "create." In his book *Gnade und Freiheit (Grace and Freedom),* Weltsch calls the source of faith "creative freedom" (*schöpferische Freiheit*), and also "freedom with respect to grounds" (*Freiheit zum Grund*).[17] The positive reference points in Weltsch's argument are Jakob Böhme and Friedrich Schelling.[18] For this reason, the similarity with Nancy is not fortuitous. In the era of neo-Kantianism and phenomenology, with his late work still largely unexplored, Schelling became an almost irresistible figure for Weltsch, not to mention for Rosenzweig, and soon also for Heidegger, whose Schellingian view of human freedom, sometimes called *Freiheit zum Grund,* resounds throughout Nancy's work.[19]

Let us mark out Nancy's Heideggerian-Schellingian position clearly so that we can see where it differs from Kafka's, and how this difference might affect our understanding of the non-term and un-field "atheology." In the middle of what is arguably the most important modern theologoumenon—faith, *fides, Glaube,* and *Glauben*—Nancy identifies an exclusive, necessary, foundational point of access to the "nothing" upon which all the European institutions of knowledge, politics, and so forth—what he often calls "the world"—are founded. It is a foundational nothing, a huge nothing, a substantial nothing, a nothing that makes everything possible—this is what is designated by the *a-* in Nancyan "atheology." On a side note, a nothing by which one effectively obtains everything is not totally dissimilar to the way Luther describes faith in "The Freedom of a Christian," or the way Kierkegaard follows suit in *Fear and Trembling.*

Kafka is perhaps closer to Bataille; indeed, he could be said to develop something like a system of non-knowledge, albeit without any knowledge of Bataille. Like Nancy, Kafka is attracted to the faith idea as somehow key to what we do beyond theism and its atheological converse, and yet he is unwilling to appropriate faith and accept its by now traditional powers, or by means of a nothing that is really something to exercise a great world-opening power and gain everything. He likes neither the possessiveness of "everything" nor the total productiveness of "nothing." So, what then is faith? One of the thoughts in Kafka's treatise indicates an answer: *Faith means: emancipating the indestructible* [das Unzerstörbare] *within oneself or better: emancipating oneself or better: being indestructible or better: being.*[20] We notice right away in this thought that faith does not contribute to a deconstruction; it does not open a pathway to the nothing that decloses the world or lead us to its limits. Quite the contrary, here faith is a relation to what cannot be destroyed, to the impregnable fortress of being. The correct atheological account of faith is being.

Kafka is concerned with what the word "faith" conceals, with the commitments it causes to arise in us through its subterfuge, and with the subterfuge itself, through which being disguises itself as faith. This and other "thoughts" in Kafka's atheological summa are supposed to help us in the end abandon certain words because of the hold they have on our imaginations. Belief (*Glauben*) is one such word.

We shouldn't neglect the vocabulary of the schoolroom employed here. "More correct," *richtiger*, is what a teacher tells a student. Our conceptual health improves as we read the sentence—our concepts get better and better, less and less deceptive. Faith is not a relation to nothing, but means "being," not absence but full powerful presence and fullness—a theologoumenon that Kafka attacks mercilessly in an array of "thoughts"—and both these cornerstones of European self-confidence—faith and being—originate in a kind of freedom different from the Schelling-Heidegger-Nancy kind. Elsewhere in the treatise, the figure that Kafka associates with the indestructible (*das Unzerstörbare*) is "paradise." Faith does not liberate us for the world or liberate the world for us, as Nancy and Weltsch believe: rather, it sets a paradise free within us (since we can't find one on earth, or so the story goes), and chains us to this imaginary Eden for the duration of what Kafka calls "life."

Freedom is a good point of difference between the two atheologies. In Nancy's atheology, faith frees us *from* God *for* the nothing at the root of the world. He quotes Meister Eckhart approvingly, "I pray to God that he make me free of God,"[21] and deduces from a strange phrase in the Epistle of James that faith proceeds according to a "law of freedom."[22] The law of freedom is, in Nancy's reading of James, the necessity of the incommensurability of faith with its object, and thus the freedom of the faithful is freedom from *parousia*, freedom from the presence of God, freedom from being.²³ In brief, what many of Nancy's formulations show is a great belief in "faith" as the route to freedom, power, world-destruction, and ultimately to world-creation. In Kafkan atheology, faith does not defer the *parousia*; quite the contrary, the parousia is simply waiting for faith in order to get started. Faith liberates being in our most intimate interior and leaves us no escape from it.

*Faith means: emancipating the indestructible within oneself or better: emancipating oneself or better: being indestructible or better: being.*²⁴ We cannot yet imagine a freedom, Kafka seems to be saying—and he corroborates this in other thoughts—that does not transplant the distant God into our innermost selves. This is what faith means: an interior, ownmost, incorruptible, paradisal fortress so deeply identified with its bearers that we cannot conceive of ourselves without it. Instead of asking about that-toward-which one has faith (God, world, soul), Kafka becomes suspicious about the apparent "nothing" out of which so powerful a capacity as faith could arise.

Other "thoughts" corroborate this line of argument. *The human being cannot live without an enduring trust in* [Vertrauen zu] *something indestructible within himself, whereby the indestructible thing as well as the trust can remain enduringly hidden from him.*²⁵ You learn that the indestructible, standing between faith and being, is not valuable in and for itself. You don't love paradise for paradise's sake. You love it for what it gives you, for the permanence it lends to the intentional act of trust. Faith frees up the indestructible within you—be it a soul, a mind, a capacity, a "nature," a language—so that you can then borrow permanence from it for yourself in the form of the capacity to trust.²⁶ This feedback loop, what Hegel would call a *Reflexionsbestimmung*, gives faith a "lunatic strength" to go on even in the face of its total negation, even when it is properly "nothing."

A dialogical thought informs us of this:

> "No one can say we lack faith. The simple fact alone of our life can in no way have its faith-value used up."
> "There is a faith-value here? But no one can not-live."
> "Precisely in this "no one can not" hides the lunatic strength of faith; in this negation it gets its contour."²⁷

You could say that the thoughts in Kafka's *summa atheologica*—almost all of them—are attempts to find moments in everyday practices, in idioms of language, in concepts that hold us, and in everyday thoughts where faith falters, weakens, loses some of its power. This thought is no exception. Here he presents a conversation in which a troublesome obstacle appears that could derail his own project of disempowering faith. Even life, even basic, sensorial, bodily, empirical non-theological experiences— like the ones Bataille holds up as an antidote to transcendence—depend on faith. In them its "lunatic strength" reveals itself, because once God withdraws, once the nothing or the impossible is exposed as the basis of all things, faith shifts its attention to sex, shit, and dirt, the imperfect, the low, the fallen—to God's residue, if you will. Bataille intuits this in a note he makes under the rubric "execration": "there might even be a systematic 'experience,' but this experience has only one end, the liquidation of experience, of all systematic experience. From this a taciturn valorization—without literature—of nonsystematic experience. Without any other literature than the construction in the human mind of atheological renunciation."[28] In his brief dialogue, Kafka reaches the limits of a systematically unsystematic experience like that proposed here by Bataille. Whatever would be achieved by "atheological renunciation" remains in the end still a valorization, and this belies a stubborn faith and an ongoing faith in that faith; no matter how taciturn one is with respect to the valorization, faith still affirms a total fact, itself included. In the Kafkan scene, two atheists are sitting and talking. One says faith no longer operates in the unsystematic sphere called "life"; the other reminds him that commitment to this sphere is also an act of faith.

There is, nonetheless, another kind of faith. Kafka imagines a faith thin enough that it could negate itself. *A faith like a guillotine, so heavy, so light.*[29] The blade of this guillotine would be a hairline trust in faith's opposite. Kafka lets the blade fall in several places. *Whoever has faith cannot experience a miracle. By day one sees no stars.*[30] Let us understand by this that Kafka is not only calling for the darkest night of unbelief, but he is also claiming—a proposition that requires faith, it is true, but an infinitely thin one that cuts itself off, a self-severing faith—that faith merely punctuates a milieu in which faith no longer makes sense. Wherever faith implies the power to overcome negativity or to put it to use in the service of transcendence or immanence, fallenness or world, Kafka imagines powerlessness in its place. Or better: in place of nothing, the impossible and the fact of life, which remain powerful, Kafka imagines a field of weaknesses that cannot be converted into power. Or better:

he rejects the hopes that underpin the free opening of worlds, rejects *Freiheit zum Grunde* (one imagines, with respect to this phrase, secret alliances between Schellingian/Heideggerian/Nancyan philosophy and some iterations of "Zionism," political, territorial, cultural, and theological). It is time, rather, for much more humble prerogatives. One quick example of this: in response to grandiose plans to settle Palestine or build a Jewish state, it was in the summer after writing down these thoughts that Kafka went to the *Pomologisches Insitut* to learn gardening.[31] We can only speculate as to what attracted Kafka to tending the earth; maybe it was the way soil, contrary to its political reputation, freely abandons its consistency, the way soil yields itself to alien growths.

2. Thoughts

One of the humble prerogatives that arises out of the weak new milieu of faithlessness is Kafka's atheological-political treatise itself. That the small texts that make up the treatise, over three hundred scrawled in small notebooks, are thoughts in the style of Pascal's *Pensées* means first and foremost that they are neither parts of something larger, fragments, say, nor stand-alone wholes such as aphorisms, the genre for which they are most frequently taken. Fragments and aphorisms are mirror images, both defined by the question of independence and completeness. If it is complete and independent, it is an aphorism; if incomplete and dependent, it is a fragment. These qualities, completion and independence, are precisely what are at risk and in question in atheology, and so Kafka's thoughts are suitably skeptical of or even indifferent to both qualities. As thoughts, his texts are no more or less complete or independent than any thought may ever be considered to be.[32] Thoughts are either the fallout from thinking, or better, as the unorthodox psychoanalyst W. R. Bion put it in 1962, thinking is a post-hoc maneuver for overcoming and domesticating the disturbances that are thoughts.[33] In this light, the small passages are thoughts before the coming of a thinking that would tame them—and any attempt to reconsider them is fated to remain a contingent response that may be a thinking alongside, but never a thinking through, or better: a commentary on thoughts without thinking.

Even if we don't accept that thinking is a silent conversation in the soul, we can, without any residual Platonism, recognize the conversational aspects of Kafka's *pensées*. They call to one another, and to further unwritten passages, in the manner of a conversation, or rather several at once, a polylogue spoken from multiple positions, including—and this is perhaps the most important mode of positioning—the position from after a thought. Thoughts and afterthoughts, we could call them, insofar as when a word or question occurs in one, it often recurs in a later thought, with implicit reference to the former. We might guess that this is why Kafka left the small passages in the order in which he jotted them down when he selected a little more than one hundred of them and made a fair copy on slips of paper the editors call *Zettel*.[34] The task of coming to terms with these thoughts, of thinking them—after the fact, in the manner of a synthesis that is not in them but in the posthumous thinking of them—is to bring out the conversation, the implicit inter-references, the calls and responses, without losing the shifts of intention, vocabulary, and context, through which a rich view of European intellectual and political history in all its contradictoriness is achieved.[35] There is a whole here: it is the whole of the wholly scattered and contingent intellectual commitments that motivate the animal and human communities in their attitudes and behavior toward themselves and one another. It is a whole, the whole of Europe you might say, flawed as it is, whose flaws these thoughts set out to dramatize.

For the purposes of this book I don't distinguish absolutely between thoughts from the "fair copy" and thoughts from the notebooks. This is not because I discount authorial intention, but rather because I prefer one of Kafka's intentions to the other. The project of catching thoughts, writing them as they came, keeping them in the order of their occurrence is more important for us now, I would contend, than the effort to reshape their genesis, to remove some (but not all) traces of their occurrence, and, as with many of Kafka's emendations in his fictions, to subtract the more obvious associations. Kafka's self-editing is a complex topic, given his extremely conservative views about the quality of his own works. In short, a story had to be perfect, and perfection consisted of two requirements. A story had to be written in "a breath" and without what he called "errors." These thoughts would seem to fulfill the first requirement but not the second. In fact, they fulfill the second, too, though in a different way. They came as they came, without second thoughts, as it were, and they correct themselves, but over the course of further thoughts, afterthoughts—and so in some way they are all "second" thoughts. Indeed, they arrive in a second coming, and this means they are not measured against any standard outside themselves.[36] They come back and renew themselves; they become what they are. Thus the polylogue of thoughts and afterthoughts is not only best in the notebooks, it is also best when it includes the thoughts unchosen by Kafka. The fair copy and the notebooks are of course in conversation in a way that enriches the commentary and contributes to the reconstruction. Yet in effect I am taking the notebooks as my source text, in all their contradictions, revisions and re-revisions, with reference to the fair copy where helpful. A book like this could not be written either by one who believed that these were fragments or aphorisms or by one who believed that the final version was a whole unto itself. It could only be written by one convinced that the real story was the atheological reduction of "secular modernity" to original ambiguities that had to be written outside its major forms and logics, also between singular thoughts, in their progressive intrasyntagmatic distances, and in the reformulations, re-evaluations, and frequent contradictions that plague them.

Three moments of occurrence are reflected in the collection at the Bodleian Library in Oxford, or perhaps four, depending on how you count. As I've said, the original "composition" was not continuous or uniform; it was not a composition (like the legal writings) or a communication (like the letters), or even a daily writing practice (like the diaries), but a game of catch with thoughts as they happened to occur.[37] Kafka dated many of the notebook entries and this gives them some relationship to calendric time. For one thing, we can say pretty accurately that they were written down between October 17, 1917, and the very end of February or the beginning of March 1918. This counts as one moment of their occurrence, a series of days and dates. Then at some point, either in the spring of 1918 or when he returned to work over the thoughts again in 1920, Kafka selected individual entries to copy onto small, numbered slips, the *Zettel*. And finally a typescript was made from these—it is not clear when or by whom—numbered in the same order as the slips. A further moment was the addition of lines to the notebooks separating "thoughts" and diagonal lines crossing out individual thoughts and at times whole pages. Even Roland Reuß, one of the meticulous editors of the historical-critical edition of Kafka's writings, admits that the material evidence does not allow us to decide exactly when the dividing lines were inscribed: immediately after writing down one or more thoughts, or later as part of the selection procedure.[38] What is clear is that the numbers printed with every edition were added at the time of the *Zettel*, but it is important to note that the numbers still express the exact order of occurrence in the notebooks, even though in the slips the majority of thoughts have been edited out.[39] Thus this book is not only a reconstruction but also a restoration of the plurality in the original.

We can only speculate why Kafka recorded thoughts in this manner, at this time, and in secret. He tells his closest friend, Max Brod, in a letter that he is not writing at all.[40] This deflection is telling. It belongs to a strategy Kafka had developed for disentangling himself from his friend's grandiose expectations for his literary talent, which alternately uplifted and dismayed Kafka. On the other hand, it also gave him an opportunity to change his own expectations and commitments. "Writing" has a very different sense in these thoughts than it did in his literary endeavors to this point. He noted in 1913: "Everything that isn't related to literature I hate."[41] And the same year in a letter to Felice, there is the famous declaration: "I . . . am made of literature."[42] When he says in the fall of 1917 that he is "not writing at all," he brushes off Brod's insistence that he write fiction and also sets aside his own early and rather grandiose pronouncements about his writerly essence. And he has a third objective as well: to take a stand against Brod's current writing project. In fact, his best friends, Brod and Felix Weltsch, were both at work on theological-political treatises, each project closer to political theology than to a critique of religion. In Vienna at the time there was "a lively dominant interest in the epistemological and logical problems that are linked with the foundations of physics."[43] In Prague the interest was in the ethical, ontological, and political profit to be had from rethinking religion. It was a year of theological treatises elsewhere as well. Franz Rosenzweig was beginning his. Kafka knew that Weltsch was working on a treatise on religious ethics, and he read the manuscript at various stages of completion. It was Kafka who chided Weltsch that his apparently secular ethics had an obviously religious ground, so why should he hide it?[44] *Grace and Freedom (Gnade und Freiheit)* were the poles around which Weltsch organized his theological refurbishing of European ethics. His book by this title presents a dialectical argument with debts to Schelling, which develops through stages, reversals, and syntheses toward the "redemption of God through human beings."[45] Without knowing it Weltsch had come very close to Rosenzweig, who was revolutionizing the same theological narratives at almost exactly the same time, also out of sources in German idealism.

Weltsch says of himself that he is seeking to formulate the "fundamental principles of the being of human beings [*Urprinzipien menschlichen Seins*]."[46] Brod, in contrast, follows Max Weber in thinking of major religions as "thought systems." *Paganism, Christianity, and Judaism*—so goes the title of his treatise—in his estimation are the only thought systems worthy of the name. Yet they are permanently at war with one another, and this conflict is perpetuated by contemporary political and ethical conditions.[47] On a side note: the disparagement and dismissal of Islam in these "renewals" of theology are vehement, a tendency as prominent in Rosenzweig as it is in Brod. Brod thought of himself as adjudicating between the three warring factions in order to come up with a new mixture of ethical attitudes, drawn from the successes and failures of the latter two. Weltsch sees freedom, understood as decision or choice (*Entscheidung*), as the pivotal heroic concept of Abrahamic religions, whereas Brod chooses grace, by which he means, not the intervention of God, but a worldly accident. The differences aside, both champion the potential to act and criticize passivity, which they associate with Jewishness. Within this framework they produce sophisticated, historically focused, conceptual arguments for a new theological or religious foundation of ethical action. For Brod this culminates in an ethical world-nation based on the nation of the Jews. For Weltsch it issues in a religion of freedom (*Freiheitsreligion*) that inheres in the free decisions of individuals.

Kafka's "thoughts" differ from these treatises in form, obviously, but also in assumptions and objectives. Kafka read Pascal in the summer of 1917. His diaries say little about France's most negative theological thinker, and nothing on the subject shows up in his letters, but this is typical of Kafka. Nietzsche was the engine of his thinking from his teens on, and there is next to no mention of Nietzsche in the writings to which we currently have access. One could surmise that for Kafka the relationship of strongest attachment stands in inverse proportion to the number of explicit references. As a model for a method, Pascal is obviously more negative than either Brod or Weltsch. And Kafka's intention was very different from the Buber-inspired "renewal" that motivated the two friends to construct their respective theologically inspired systems. What Buber was to Brod and Weltsch, we can surmise, Pascal was to Kafka, yet Pascal's are systemless thoughts in view of the impossibility of a coherent ethical or ontological program. Thoughts occur in an unredeemed and unredeemable world. And yet, although the negativity for Pascal is not to be abrogated, it is also allegorical. Thought draws great power from the "end of life." "The order of thought is to begin with ourselves, and with our author and our end."[48] In this directive on the alpha and *archē* of thoughts, Pascal also differs from Kafka, who refutes the idea of individual finitude, through this refutation attempting to disempower death as the origin of thinking. For the finitude of each Pascalian thought and their collective disorderliness are signs of the theological order that they negatively represent, and death represents in an inversion its own overcoming. Kafka takes note of the impulse within this theory of finite thinking toward orderliness and transcendence, when he writes his one diary entry on Pascal: "Pascal tidies everything up [*macht . . . große Ordnung*] before the entrance of God, but there must be a deeper, more anxious skepsis than this skepsis of the human being ascending the throne, who, with a miraculous knife indeed, but still with the calm of a butcher, cuts himself to pieces. Whence this calm? Certitude in his command of the knife? Is God a theatrical triumph chariot that someone, notwithstanding all the toil and despair of the workers, draws from a distance onto the stage with ropes?"[49] We already hear a more anxious skepsis beginning to move through Kafka's own description of Pascal. Cutting himself up with a miraculous knife, Pascal finds that the more he cuts, the more the riven body of his intellect indicates the divine totality. Each shard offers an isolated, abandoned image, and the absoluteness of the higher unity is reflected virtually in the potential infinity of shards.

Kafka recognizes the comforting nature of each of Pascal's "thoughts," and also of the portrait of the thinker who cuts himself to pieces before the one, the whole, the end. For this self-immolating thinker "order" saves the day, order—which has to include the orderliness of the thoughts themselves. Pascal's *ordre*—a word that obsesses him in the *Pensées*—Kafka reads as *Ordnung machen,* cleaning up a mess. Pascalian skepsis is thus by Kafka's lights already quite a calm doubt, tranquil in view of the ultimate entrance of God.[50] Doubt is provisional uncertainty that is still certain about one thing: coming certainty—Kafka puts his finger on the residual Cartesianism here, which is as much in the idea as in the practice of Pascalian thoughts.[51] Kafka thus takes something from Pascal but leaves something else behind. Thoughts in the mysterious order of their occurrence will be his medium, or better, his experiment, though we must begin to use a different word than "order" for their arrangement. You can see in one *pensée* how Pascal hedges himself against too free a disposition of thoughts: "As if the same thoughts did not form a different form of discourse by being differently arranged, just as the same words make different thoughts by being differently arranged."[52] This implies that orderability is the substitute for system, for a sinuous whole, for an all of thought and being. A deeper, more anxious skepsis would produce a less comforting outcome. Bion is right: it is already apparent in Pascal that thoughts out of order, or thoughts whose main question is not their ultimate orderability, are so disturbing that they give rise to thinking as a way to restore calm.[53]

The present commentary does not so much give order to the thoughts as bring to words the concrete and specific disorder or anorder, the shifts and jumps in the conversation among them.[54] To this end I often pervert the order of occurrence and associate conversational sets—the calls and responses, echoes, stutters, repetitions, jokes, guesses and ripostes that crisscross the thoughts and that defy the march of calendric days over those few months.

Early in the experience of receiving these thoughts, Kafka thinks an astonishing question: *Is it possible to think something that does not console?*[55] It is a dire question, an anti-Pascalian question, a question about the effects of thinking, one that points toward the very deeper skepticism than the shallow one he resisted when reading Pascal; moreover, it implies a negative answer. Unconsoling thoughts, we have them all the time, don't we?—why did Kafka think they might not even be possible? This brief thought about the nature of thoughts stands like a preface to our reconstruction of his atheological polylogue.

When he writes down this question, Kafka may not yet know what he is saying, whether this thought should or can be continued, least of all whether it can become the test of a whole project. There is not yet any project. Like any true conversation, this one begins tentatively, without assurance that it will go on from where it has not begun. And like a true conversation, it often gives up and begins again from another point.[56] Anyone reading these thoughts has to remain sensitive to the unconscious, tentative, risky steps out of which it will ultimately have been made, with the frequent culs-de-sac. This early thought is no exception. Yet it is difficult not to see in it, however futureless it may have been in the moment of its occurrence, a primary provocation, a pinprick of desperation or a thin shadow of hope that may have pushed him into a cycle of responses. "Can I discover a thought that does not console?" One way to honor this accidental program is to consider each thought, on one hand, simultaneously the first in a series and potentially the last, and, on the other hand, as such also potentially only ever a middle, as calling up more accidents and yet another thought, whose coming was not at all assured and which might well revoke or worse partially revoke the previous one.

Is it possible to think something that does not console? Or rather something not-consoling without even a whiff of consolation [Trost]*?*[57] Kafka hits on a ruthless, one might even say reckless, possibility here: completely expunging consolation from thinking. We might notice that the term and concept "consolation" is at home in many nominally religious contexts and texts, but it also contains the seeds of a virulent atheism. In early days, Nietzsche imagined that his radically revised aesthetic religion would aim at "the art of comfort in this world."[58] Pascal thinks of this-worldly options as consolations as well: "The only thing that consoles us for our miseries is distraction, yet that is the greatest of our wretchednesses."[59] The dialectic of consolation shines in this thought. A distraction is still a distress, but, to Pascal, it transforms into a comfort when it is recognized as trivial, and this recognition happens in thought, in a thought, in this thought, where distraction is put in its place. The thought is the consolation for what is thought. Now, if any theologian teeters on the edge of the inconsolable, it is certainly Pascal. And this is for two reasons. To start with, the thought of the inconsolable, this extreme at which he several times almost arrives, also gives comfort. One soon realizes that in the *Pensées* everything distressing is converted to consolation through thinking. There is no human distress that cannot be overcome by the proper use of the method of having thoughts. At the same time, the *Pensées* as a whole completely neutralizes the effects of distress and suffering to the point at which there is nothing left to threaten us, nothing left to think—at least this is the project. And so it also moves past the need for thoughts, past the need for consolation, into a district in which consolation no longer has meaning—an atheological district. Secondly, even if one receives consolation by and through a negative movement such as Pascal's, wherever consolation is the immediate and overarching goal, it threatens to become theology's only justification. Consolation suspends the need for divinity, if momentarily. And so, while theological thoughts may console, theology and God also come to exist rather quickly in this light for the purposes of human consolation and only for those purposes. Through consolation, God comes to sit at man's feet.

The strong implication of Kafka's question is that even the thought of something that does not console us, by the very form of thinking, in the fact that we make a sentence about it or represent it to ourselves, provides solace. Even the thought of an unconsoling thought maintains a whiff of consolation insofar as it is a thought. We reach a limit here. It is not a limit to the content of thought, as though there were thinkable and unthinkable objects, as though we couldn't in fact think of everything that pertains to our world. Instead here we reach a limit of what thinking is for, what it means and what it does, because of the inescapable soothing effect of thoughts on the thinker. Thoughts always console, even if it is the thought of thoughts' own limits. What does not console would thus not be a thought. Everything that is "unthinkable" in Kafka comes from this insight into the limit of thought per se. To be sure, the main intuition of modern Europe, that there are limits to human thinking, has a comforting effect. If we can think the limit we cannot be surprised by the abyss beyond. Socrates is in this light a master consoler; Kant too, as well as Freud. In Pascal, the entire scope of the unknowable—the author and the end of thought—is contained and tamed in the miniscule thought that thoughts are inadequate, multiple, messy, temporal. This is the other sense in which thoughts console. They can embrace their own fallenness, imperfection, precarity, and the Pascalian word for this ability is *ordre*. Indeed all one has to do is think it consoles; if it thinks it, it does it. Possibility is actuality for thought when it comes to consolation. This is perhaps the greatest comfort, since nothing indeterminate, unactualized, unthinkable remains beyond its reach, even, as one can see, what is actually beyond it.

Consolation has been the center of the Western intellectualist project. One doesn't have to minister to the afflicted; before any such practical activity one merely gives one's attention to them, as Simone Weil recognized. Luther's text "Fourteen Consolations" is presented to the gravely ill Frederick the Wise for his "contemplation."[60] It introduces thoughts in order to cover over or draw the thinking being away from a situation that cannot be resolved through acts. Thoughts give momentary asylum in a world of suffering. Descartes points in this direction when he conflates the thinking being with the doubting being. The power he discovers in doubt *qua* thinking alleviates his own suffering over the suggestion that his childhood experience was untrustworthy and his sensual experience, like wax, is plastic, so that deformation is not an aberration of experience but the norm.

Kafka finds the heart of this dialectic with one further turn or half-turn. *A way out of this predicament could lie in the fact that knowing* [Erkennen] *as such is consolation.*[61] That is to say, apperceiving, attending to a fact—the fact of knowledge, the fact about knowledge that it is for the purposes of consolation—may open a route to a different mode. This, let's say, is the first thought in a Kafkan "new thinking." It should be rigorously distinguished from a fetishization of suffering, although it does aim to produce an experience that is inconsolable.[62] Without a remedy in thinking or in thoughts, suffering "as such" cannot be conceived; it loses its meaning when it loses hope of conversion in thought, as one Kafkan sentence puts it, *. . . in such a way that that which in this world is called suffering, in another world, unchanged and only freed from its opposite, is bliss.*[63] The opposite of suffering is consolation and a thought that does not console should indeed, by this logic, effect a happiness with no opposite. Kafka sometimes calls this beatitude (*Seligkeit*), a kind of holiness that we have to understand of course atheologically, and which it may well be the aim of the treatise to produce.

Possessed by the Pascalian paradigm, Kafka worries about the effects thoughts have on thinkers and on the world. There is scarcely an escape from the dialectic of consolation. Thoughts are those conversion loops in which the world becomes the sign of its ultimate unimportance, where what is distressing loses its value in comparison to the absolute and suffering becomes a comfort and a good through a gesture elsewhere. Consolation is a form of substitution: a thought for an experience, one thought for another, and at times one kind of thought for another kind of thought. Luther tells us the difference between the two kinds. How close his language is to the language of modern philosophy! True to the Augustinian presuppositions he shares with Pascal, Luther tells readers, and told them again and again through the many editions of this popular text, that consolation happens when the mind is diverted from the thing (*res*) that causes distress to another absent thing. What brings about this diversion is the word of God.[64] This supplementary movement beyond cognition, this replacement of the thing thought with another thing, which will remind us, perhaps, of other rationalist or quasi-rationalist activities of the mind, the imposition of concepts, say, on intuitions, as well as a certain interpretation of interpretation, the replacement of the foreign text with the historical text, the corrupted with the true, "paraperience" with "experience"—these are all analogous to the operation of consolation within thinking. And yet the effect of thinking should also bring about a new distress—yes, precisely when it impinges, as it does when its purpose or effect is consolation, on the relationship of thinking to truth, which, in order to be truth, cannot be conditioned by the need for consolation. Indeed if it is *for* consolation, thinking moves *away from* truth. This is made clear in a note Kafka made in 1920 to the effect that consolation is always judged on its effectiveness, not on its truth.[65]

Is it even possible to think something that does not console, and would that be called thinking? The act of thinking, this substituting of one thing for another, is structurally identical to consolation as Luther describes it. The first answer that Kafka gives is negative. By worldly means thinking builds a shell or a burrow against the world, and yet, as soon as this thought comes to you, one thing penetrates the shell, an image of thinking as no more than a shell, as merely protective, and thus as delusional, misleading, and so forth—as consolatory but not true. Thinking toward truth splits off from thinking toward consolation. Ostensibly, however, this division and categorization is also another thought, another protection, another wall around the burrow. The scramble to escape digs us in deeper, and this quicksand effect is indeed the effect of what Kafka calls thinking. *One could well think: you must do away with yourself, and still that you could, nevertheless, without faking this knowledge, derive comfort from the fact that you know it. But that really means pulling yourself up out of the swamp by your own hair.*[66] Thinking, even thinking without the consolation of a self, just here, where it imagines that it has escaped upward, sinks downward. Thinking is sinking. The precision of this "thought" is ferocious. As long as thinking means holding on to an image, a sentence, a formula, there is no "higher" thinking that transcends the lowly desire for comfort. The thought of another kind of thought is also comforting, and so on. And thus it is not our own personal limits that keep us from being able to pull ourselves out of the swamp. It is, rather, a fact of gravity, or the limits of a genre. In fact, moving toward truth is illusion: it really moves away. The more thought struggles toward truth, the more it consoles you with the thought that it is getting there. You can see this in Pascal: one simple thought—say that life ends—is not enough; soon he is buried under the weight of hundreds of them. Gravity is what Kafka calls the force that conditions us without our being able to claim that we ourselves set the ultimate condition. Thinking is sinking. And yet there may be a way of having thoughts, of letting them come without thinking them, where they do not accumulate, but, as it were, float in and float out, and away.

If we switch frames and imagine a world without conditions or with different conditions, the problem vanishes; for *what is laughable in the bodily world is possible in the spiritual. There the law of gravity is not in effect, (the angels do not fly, they have not suspended gravity, we observers from the earthly world only know no better way to think), which in any case is not imaginable for us, or only at a higher level.*[67] Angels do not think. That is, they need no consolation, they do not recognize burdens as burdens. A *consolatoria pro laborantibus et oneratis* would not be written by them.

Can one think without consolation? Can one be an angel? Here is a question that by its nature cannot console us; perhaps it cannot even distress us, once we understand that it shifts the frame of reference. So Kafka is not looking for an anxious mode, an inconsolable thinking, but an unconsolatory one, one outside the parameters of the consolation of philosophy. In 1920 Kafka returns to this issue with a surprising conclusion: the way out of consolation is directly through it. "No consolation can console him, precisely because it is consolation."[68] Kafka asks whether there could be a thinking absolutely removed from the goal of comfort and solace. The answer involves as thoroughgoing a negation of the precepts of European thought as can be imagined. The precepts are not consoling to the very extent that they console us, since consolation, if it is the final cause and goal of thinking, supersedes the reason it gives. Consolation is an end in itself and thus is the most terrifying fact. This is, to be sure, the hole in the bottom of the tradition—that thought is for consolation, not for truth, with consolation as a by-product of truth's abandonment. So thoughts console, but they can never truly console.

3. Four Circles

Kafka's theopolitical thoughts cut across four circles. The circles are not concentric; in some cases it is only Kafka's treatise that allows them to touch. In other cases the circles overlap historically or conceptually. First, the smallest circle: he writes within the most intimate combat with his friends Max Brod and Felix Weltsch (see §10, §12, §13, §18–§20, §22, §27,

§35), contesting their theological interventions in Zionism without ever confronting them about it in person. They never knew during his lifetime that he was writing his treatise while they were writing theirs. Second, a larger circle: he swims in the sea of Zionisms about which he reads almost daily in the Jewish journals (§5, §15, §18, §19, §32, §35). One can safely say that Kafka had read about and thought through a great number of the subtly different attitudes and possible solutions to the quandaries, real and perceived, of European Jews. Like Rosenzweig and many others, he was returning to a religion he had barely known, and this gave him the opportunity to make of it what he imagined it was, and, with and without a clear sense that he was doing this, also to make it what it never had been. Third, he opened a door that was not theo-politics in the pantheist tradition of Spinoza or the atheist tradition of Feuerbach, but was also not political theology in the sense that Carl Schmitt was developing it over the same span of years (§5, §6, §8, §17, §19, §20, §28, §39). We must place Kafka near the path leading from Spinoza to Schmitt and Rosenzweig in order to point out his deviation from it. And finally, the fourth circle: he is in conversation with, in the circle of but departing from Nietzsche and Kierkegaard. One can see the thoughts as an encounter between the long-standing Nietzschean pose of Kafka's thinking and the Kierkegaard that Brod coerced him into reading that fall. A battle between Nietzsche and Kierkegaard was in the air in those years. Brod favored Kierkegaard; Rosenzweig obviously did too. Kafka favors Nietzsche but undermines certain of his convictions. If Nietzsche was the last metaphysician, Kafka is the first post-metaphysician—which is to say, in some deep sense, just a physician. In this respect also he grazes very close to Heidegger's concerns, the early ontological ones in *Being and Time* and the ones Heidegger starts to discover in the 1930s after reading Nietzsche, by which I refer to the Heideggerian problematic of willing (§20, §28, §39).

You might worry that these circles are circles of hell, and that Kafka tries to make his way out of them with weak instruments and little chance of grace. But this is not quite right. If anything he creeps along their radials toward the centers in order to note down the formulas from which they generate themselves. And all four of his contexts, in one way or another, pivot around motifs from the Book of Genesis that permeate these thoughts.[69]

The battle or *Kampf* (a key Kafkan term with clear Nietzschean overtones) between Kafka and Max Brod is as old as their friendship, and it can be expressed as a staged battle between Nietzsche and Schopenhauer. They connected seriously for the first time on an evening when Brod, in a public speaking engagement, was supporting Schopenhauer against Nietzsche, and Kafka stood up to defend Nietzsche. Such an allegiance, between Kafka and Nietzsche, on the one hand, and Brod and Schopenhauer, on the other, and such a war, between Brod/Schopenhauer and Kafka/Nietzsche repeats itself in the period of the treatise. Kierkegaard is Brod's new Schopenhauer; the transcendental tenor is all too similar. In this way the first circle, the intimate sphere of friends and the fourth, intellectual-formative circle are overlapping. The overlap we could describe as a hangover from not yet finished, perhaps not yet fully started nineteenth-century political, religious, and philosophical shifts that broke up Europe's conceptual grounds, marooning some groups, such as the German-speaking Jews in Prague, raising some to mountaintops, such as Bismarck with his *Realpolitik* and his imperial welfare state, and, producing a Herzl, with his political solution for the future of the Jews. In his diary Kafka notes the "constant clamor" (*ewiges Geschrei*) at the Eleventh Zionist congress in Vienna, which he attended.[70] The only thing constant about the meeting was its Babelian hubbub. Of the Bismarckian legal framework for the welfare state, we know Kafka's opinion: he wrote official contributions to it in his day job and butchered it at night.

In the second circle belongs the larger event and wish and experience of a "return to Judaism," although some embarrassing matters have to be admitted right away. As I have begun to explain, it wasn't much of a "renewal," since many of the homecomers of the period, such as Kafka, Brod, Weltsch, and analogous figures outside his circle, most saliently Rosenzweig, and to be sure also Walter Benjamin, were from long-assimilated families. Brod and Weltsch for instance both had Catholic primary educations. In a sense it was a truly paradisal moment in the history of an idea: the Garden of Eden could be planted anywhere, since the memory of the original had become beclouded. Jewish things had to be sought and found, selected, adapted, tried on like costumes; indeed, in the most interesting cases, it had to be cut from whole cloth. There is little doubt that Rosenzweig did this. Buber was doing it too, with his mythico-ecstatic cultural ideas. Hermann Cohen likewise, with vastly different assumptions. Brod and Weltsch were each at work, as I have noted, on definitive statements of their respective theologically inflected world philosophies out of the sources of Judaism.

The third context ignores the personal motivations for writing (the outbreak of illness; the final breakup with Felice; a very bloody period in the war; the sharp rise of Czech nationalism; the Balfour Declaration, which was publicized in all the Jewish journals Kafka was reading)[71] and the genre (as if Kafka wrote "in genres," as an objective decision, committing to them beforehand, treating them as sets of rules). It does, however, take account of the procedure of the thoughts, the thoughts as subtle, sometimes ironic, but always logically rigorous demonstrations of confusions in the basic theologoumena underlying Europe's intellectual and practical commitments.[72] The history of theopolitical critiques is thus the third circle. Neither Kafka's treatise nor the letters and diary entries surrounding it, I must admit right from the start, mention Spinoza, Feuerbach, or Kant, let alone a contemporary like Cohen. Nevertheless the treatise contributes to this larger array of thoughts; it takes up the critique of the Hebrew bible from Spinoza; it concurs with Feuerbach that gods are images, even anthropomorphic ones, but it disagrees that revealing this will topple them from their false heights for the sake of an immanent divinity: the human being; it parallels Kant (and Nietzsche) in taking theology as in the service of morality.

Within each of these contexts the treatise has a singular position. Kafka is distant from and yet silently contesting his Zionist friends; he is reinventing Judaism without some of the traits that make it Jewish; he supports the critique of religion, yet he does not celebrate the coming of secularity or atheism. You will notice some tension, which perhaps approaches contradiction, in each of these positions. He is not and is not not a friend; he is not and is not not a theologian. Or as Kafka will put it about someone else a few years later, she is "not a Jew and not not a Jew." This "not and not-not" is a logical category peculiar to Kafka, or so I believe, a nondialectical self-relation that he develops across the thoughts as an instrument for cutting a pathway through theology and philosophy.

4. The Fourfold Atheological Analysis

The tradition, as Kafka embroiders his thoughts onto it, has as its main threads a set of four concepts, best presented as a parallelogram (see Fig. 1).

Such a diagram is obviously overly schematic but some basic relationships nevertheless become conspicuous in it. Being and time define the

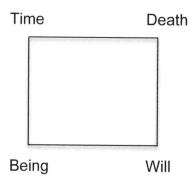

FIGURE I

pillar of the tradition. They are its main anchor points, but they also represent a tension. Time strains upward against the weight of being, threatening to uproot it, but also standing directly on being and extending out of it, just as in the same gesture being is a precipitate of time. That time and being are dependent on one another Kafka recognizes explicitly in the treatise. Two extremes that do not fall along the axis of being and time do however intersect with it and modify its tensed stability. Death does this: its line issues from time as the punctuating finitude of its infinity, at once threatening and aiding being in its claim to permanence and time in its claim to continuity. The line that joins being and time is transcendence. Being is no single being; it is eternal preservation, unchanging unity; time is no single instant; it is constant slipping away, perpetual motion. The key aspect of death, in contrast, is finitude, interruption, a direct challenge to perpetuity and eternity, on one hand, and the condition for transcendence on the other. Only insofar as beings and moments pass away can being and time be said to live on forever, to be deathless.

These knots in the philosophical and theological threads—being, time, and death—could also be called, respectively, God, world, and human being. Being/God, world/time, human being/death—these are often considered not only the major but also the only poles of European thought and practice. We name the pairs and hypostatize them, say that they are, are true, persist, and will continue to, and we orient ourselves by their light. Rosenzweig's star has them at three of its points.

In this picture, being and time are stable, though in tension, while death is the greatest threat to them as well as the means of their repeated overcoming. You can see how the three support each other in deflection; a dialectic forms by which death contributes to the unity of being and time. This is equivalent to the Hegelian dialectic. Yet in this diagram there is a fourth vector, a trajectory coming from much lower than death and breaking the synchrony of the trinity; this is will. If anything could disturb the machine of survival and eternity it has been thought, since Nietzsche at least, to be willing. Willing, however, is precisely what ends in individual death, and so even this monstrous power is mastered and contained by the parallelogram.

If we look at this chart, this x-ray of fundamental commitments, from another position, the skeleton of European thought and practice changes its aspect. For in fact, each of these topoi admits of interpretation. What we mean when we say "being" is on Kafka's mind in 1917–18, as is "our concept of time." And once these poles are interpreted by him, a different diagram emerges (see Fig. 2).

These new, translated terms are the result of procedures Kafka carries out on the parallelogram: as he writes down his thoughts, the basic precepts and their relationship are changed, dragging the parallelogram out of shape. From the perspective of the yield—which we still must explain—being comes to look like an act or activity of belonging, to someone or to some greater impersonal power. Belonging, the meaning of being, has several corollaries in English: having, possessing, and finally and most developed, property. Being results from an act of taking possession, but more than this, from the conceit that it is somehow justified by a force beyond the act, by a primordial vectoriality of weaker toward stronger things, in the mysticism of "belonging-to." Time, in turn, results from an act of faith, faith that . . . this or that will eventually come to belong (to me, to you, to him or her, or to Him). Faith positions an event of possession-taking in the future and projects a path along which it will be reached. Next, what had been the impediment to being and time, individual death, becomes, after Kafka's procedures, the highest artifice in a continuum of images whose origin is ultimately the Book of Genesis.[73] Human beings may have been created in God's image, but this means that they were created *as* an image. Finally, there is what I am calling "the yield."

In essence, the first three nodes or trajectories of Kafka's treatise are radical interpretations—being is interpreted as belonging, time as faith, and death as artifice—of the pillars of European intellectual history. All

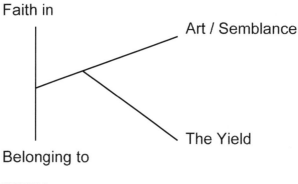

Faith in

Art / Semblance

The Yield

Belonging to

FIGURE 2

three, however, belong, forgive the tautology, to belonging. What counts as a being, in the most fundamental terms, is what belongs to some proprietor, be it you or me, the world, a god or God. Faith at first asserts a suspension of belonging in the absence of the proprietor; yet it only suspends in view of a fuller future possession. The images of art are what give us a sense of that future, although and because it is distant. The yield, in contrast, is the gesture by which belonging is both created and ultimately abandoned. Yielding denotes both giving up or giving in and giving something away or going away, the pull between withdrawing and producing—yielding a yield—such that anything or anyone could belong to anyone or anything. Something must be given up in order for it to be given to—in order for it to be taken and finally to be considered to belong. This fundamental inequality will concern us, the disproportion between giving and taking. Yield gives by giving up. It also gives itself up. That is, it abandons all claims to self-possession.

And so there is a process, arising from this gesture I am calling "the yield," by which it comes to look like what it isn't. This isn't sublimation; it isn't loss or "lost time." Rather, self-dispossession is a fact of yielding. Unlike being, yielding has zero staying power. It does not want or need to preserve itself. Indeed, its greatest tendency and its greatest danger to itself and its gift to the world is to give out.

And so, under the sign of yielding, belonging-to comes to seem like all there is. Being there, inert, preserved, identical with itself, independent— all aspects of entities and their relations appear, falsely, as prior to the yield. We have being when we don't have the yield, though, we should add, only when we have given yielding up by means of yielding's particular weakness. The next steps in the conceptual development of Europe follow from this one. Being is what "we have" when we are given up by the yield and when we give up yielding. Faith is then what we have when we recognize that we don't have all of being—the suspension of possession in view of future total possession. Time is the medium invented to illustrate a means of carrying out faith's promise, and it is also that which we are left with in our "secular" times, after faith has been discredited. So the yield yields itself and its opposite. This is worth remembering. In this light, "secular" means the concealment of an original moment of yielding that gives us both the theic and the atheic. The yield itself is pre- or a-theological. Walter Benjamin wrote in a note: "The relationship of three things, law–remembering–tradition, is to be explained. Kafka's work is probably made out of these three."[74] Let us add in the fourth thing that Benjamin was hesitant to include because of the foibles of critics in his day: theology. The time has come to reincorporate what was never excluded by Kafka, during or after 1917–18, although Benjamin was surely correct in saying that the "theology" of the early interpreters, Max Brod and Joachim Schoeps among others, was "shameless."[75]

PART I

Kafka's Being and Time

§   Refutation of What Being Never Was

5. Toward a General Echontology

We shall start with what will not yield and ask how it too can be a function of yielding. Being, which should be a result of divine creation or naturally enduring substance, change limited by a telos, genus of a species, formed matter, not-nothing, or one or another of the known determinations from the history of philosophy, will have to be shown, at base, to be marked or marred by an obdurate quality[1] in order to suggest its resistance and ultimate susceptibility to and emergence from yielding. Being is what will not yield. Yet the obdurateness that marks being will have had to "come into being" as well. And so, when we ask what gives being its obduracy and its ability to lend resistance and staying power to things and concepts, a response would account not only for the duration that being provides, the main characteristic it lends to things, but also for its ability to lend out, to give itself away, to transmit its highest characteristic to the largest variety of things, human beings, states of affairs, epochs, the world, and what's more, always to some and not to others, in short, what we might call in English being's "give." Being's take depends, we want to say, on its give.

For a thinker who avoids conscious references to philosophy, little could be odder than finding in Kafka a confrontation with a central philosophical concept or idea, in what might, in another thinker, seem like a step toward the development of an ontology.[2]

If you were writing a prolegomenon to a systematic theological politics, you would not ignore being, if for no other reason than that it has been

a stalwart of theological speculation since Aristotle. It is not every theo-
politics, however, that confronts the term; indeed, it seems anathema to
the idea of theopolitical critique. Ludwig Feuerbach, for instance, is determined to demonstrate that God is a projection by humans of human
characteristics onto a higher plane. God as the being-ground of nature,
however, Feuerbach doesn't address, and so nature and natural beings
take on, surreptitiously—as they do also at points in Marx, nature as the
self-producing thing—an aura of magic. What we could call the political economy of being's effects and meanings still needs to be brought to
light; we still need to explore how being lends or shares itself out, how
it circulates, and what sorts of limits it puts on thinking and speaking.
Marx declared the critique of religion in Germany finished, so that the
critique of thought could begin, but in fact, where Feuerbach transferred
a kind of divinity to humankind and to nature, albeit a diminished one,
Marx transferred it to the natural capacity for labor. Kafka takes issue
with this kind of transferal. He saw in words for and around "being" an
act by which ontological characteristics, through a theological gesture
that was sometimes hidden, sometimes overt, were transferred to this or
that. He sometimes called this transferal "building," especially when it
went on indefinitely or was destined to entrap its occupants.

The God of monotheism, as many scholastic philosophers recognized, is
not only the God of providence, the moral God, but also the essence of the
cosmos and the source of the perfection of beings, the highest being on the
scale. The characteristic of being that Kafka singles out and that is marked
by a relationship to "the yield" is the act or event of "belonging-to," the crux
at which the two conditions for "being" intersect, obdurateness and transferal. That is to say, being is conditioned. This is the first revelation. The
second revelation is that being is conditioned by a strange motility and something like a force, a force and an intention, the force of "belonging" and the
intention of "to." Belonging—*gehören*—gives being its obdurateness; belonging is the act or event that should maintain a thing in some way or other as
it is.[3] "To" names its transferability, and perhaps also gestures toward the
conflicts that can ensue over its meaning and place. If being is interpreted
as "belonging-to," all controversies about what being is and what counts as a
being become conflicts about who arrogates to herself the ability to dispose of
beings: human, thing, conceptual, imaginary, or otherwise.

From one perspective, belonging-to is all-too-human. It is human and
it is practical, as opposed to theoretical, divine, or juridical. We thus have

to distinguish it from thought, creation, and ownership, respectively—figures whose ideality is impossible to ignore. Belonging-to is closer to possession than to ownership, and closer to "having" than to possession; in fact, it is the objective correlate of the subjective "have." In English, one "takes possession," meaning that only once one has taken can one possess, although one can take without possessing. And while it might seem otherwise, taking and having are both accomplished on the basis of a prior belonging. World is what belongs to itself, worldly things what belong together. Where does "belonging" come from? We can suppose that it comes from something prior that belongs to no one and yields itself up for its opposite. For Feuerbach, a human power (*Macht*) gives God being.[4] In more modest terms, Kafka would later identify this as the strength (*Kraft*) to do something. Human being itself, its essence—human nature—is also subject to the pragmatics of "belonging-to," and thus human being arises in an initial taking and a subsequent prophylaxis against loss, a resistance against an ever-present potential, or rather de-potential, for giving itself away.

Marx was wrong: the critique of religion in Germany did not end with Feuerbach; in Kafka's day it still needed to be said that *das Wort "sein" bedeutet im Deutschen beides: Dasein und Ihm-gehören*. The German language holds onto a remainder of religious reasoning after the critique has concluded. *The word being/his/its* [sein] *in German means both things: existence* [Dasein] *and belonging to him/it* [Ihm-gehören].[5] In Kafka's "thoughts," the so-called Zürau Aphorisms, the coincidence of being (*Sein*) and "his, its" (*sein*) is no doubt deduced in a peculiar way, far from the grand critical gestures of Kant, Marx, or Nietzsche. His is a small deduction, a supposition of the meaning of being from a seeming triviality, a fluke of language, the fluke of a single language, and so at first glance it looks like anything but a universal matter.[6] The supposition of being as "belonging-to him/it" is inferred from a homonymy, a pun, or a mishearing, without any supporting argument. Although one could argue that the smallness of the evidence implies the importance of the insight, we shouldn't wish away the diminished form in which the co-occurrence of "being" and "his" or "its" appears. Doesn't the trivial way in which the possible identity of being and belonging to a "him" or an "it" makes itself known, in a pun, without philological support, which would anyway probably be spurious—couldn't the pun tell us something about being and reveal something hidden in its history?

Kafka hints that between what-is and "what belongs to him or it," there is some relationship beyond the pun. We ask first, in the spirit in which Kafka brings this up: what makes it a pun and not the same word? In a beginning German lesson the two are different words. Further, the category "homonym" suggests that there are not only two words but two separate things that accidentally overlap in their names. Behind a ruse of grammar, Kafka hints, these entities may in fact be confused or even the same; what appears to be a homonymy is in fact a mononymy naming a single entity or effect. Being and belonging-to converge at some point. It is true that at some point they diverged for speakers of many European languages. Several schemata immediately come to mind for ways in which being and "belonging to him/it" have been thought to be unrelated, though in fact they have been unthinkable apart from one another in European logics: the relationship of properties to substances in substance ontology; the relationship of concepts to intuitions in Kant; the relationship of creation to the monotheistic God in the *Tanakh*, seen from the perspective of created beings; and the relationship of the ecclesia to Christ in the New Testament. All these admit that when we say being we mean *belonging to him/it* (*Ihm-gehören*).

Athenian philosophical language about being is steeped in notions of belonging, and this first turns intense with Aristotle's *Categories*.[7] This text, while its doctrines may subsequently fade behind the hylomorphism of the *Metaphysics*, nevertheless had a huge impact on medieval philosophy. By translating Aristotelian *ousia* as *Anwesen* (or *Anwesenheit*), Heidegger made us aware that ontology's secret was that its highest concept was named after the common Attic word for "landed property."[8] Ontology, from this perspective, is the logos of property. Although Plato's *metechein* belongs to a lexicographically distinct set of words, they nonetheless also have to do with belonging.[9] The *echein* group has a range of interesting uses in the Homeric poems, from a gestural use for holding up the hands, to holding still, to, in the middle voice, holding something for oneself.[10] For our purposes the middle voice—holding for oneself—and the act of holding still or keeping some prior activity in check are both important. Being as having—*estin hē echein*—may correlate with a holding oneself in check, a self-restraint put on another more primal movement or process. From this we can begin to develop a general "echontology," a way of thinking that leads through having to holding back to the yield.

A general echontology—this would have had to have been developed in the schools of Plato and Aristotle[11] for Kafka not to have discovered the coincidence, if we can call it that, of being and belonging to him/it in a trivial similarity within the German language.[12] Make no mistake: there is nothing special in the history of German or in its specific morphology that makes it a privileged locus for this insight. It could have been overheard for a thousand years in Latinate philosophy, echoing in the technical ontological term, "properties." One thing is not fortuitous. Since it was so deeply buried on the surface of German, it most likely would have had to be found by accident *and* by a non-philosopher, someone with an ear to the language and a deep irreverence toward philosophy. Indeed, "having" has not often been heard from in philosophy. In 1933, Gabriel Marcel, himself no stranger to irreverence, had this insight: "We should first notice that the philosophers seem to have always shown a sort of implicit mistrust towards the notion of having (I say 'notion,' but we must ask whether this is a suitable expression, and I really think it is not). It almost looks as if the philosophers had on the whole turned away from having, as if it were an impure idea, essentially incapable of being made precise."[13]

We would like to know the history of this impure or imprecise idea. It appears at several moments in Aristotle. In the *Categories,* having gets a strong start, but is quickly marginalized. From this moment on, "having," as holding yielding in check, lives without revealing itself in the corpus of philosophy. We encounter again and again a strained combination of dependence on having and denial or outright rejection of having. Nowhere is this more prominent than in categorical thinking. This is perhaps because, once a plurality of aspects or genera are introduced into the perfect, one, whole sphere of being, one has to account for the necessary being together of the plurality; one has to account for the being-together of the categories and the being-in-categories of phenomena. Once more, the need for "belonging-to"/"having" and the need to exclude this disposition or activity from the highest genera seem to be a special feature of a thinking in which being is plural and needs to be brought together into one. We could formulate a rule that holds in most cases: wherever there are primary and derivative modes of being, such as *ousia* and *to on,* and wherever there are qualitatively irreconcilable modes of being, such as *aisthesis* and *noēsis*— to stay with the Aristotelian vocabulary—the originary bond between the modes becomes a primary preoccupation. At first this is a peculiarly Hellenic problem, which struck the fifth century as the waves of Pythagorean and, from another quarter, Elean speculation hit Athens. A uniform whole is unsatisfying to the extent that it is empty of differences, and at the same time, it is never empty enough; it leaves behind the puzzling remainder of appearance, "opinion," *doxa*, which itself constitutes a separate aspect that then has to be either excluded or reconciled. The suggestion that there is another, more fundamental feature of being—unity or oneness—may explain a lot, but it also adds yet another multiple, another aspect that then in another gesture itself has to be brought into the one so that it can be made, once again, whole. And the unity of unity with itself and with the other aspects of being cannot be talked about, except perhaps in the language of "belonging."[14]

As some ancient evidence of this, take an important operative term in Aristotle's logical and metaphysical writings that can mean "belong to." Let me note two instances of the word *hyparchein* to illustrate a possible reading, which still would have to be supported by a more careful and exhaustive investigation and a set of philological debates. For now, a hint: a look at chapter 5 of the *Categories* and then book Γ of the *Metaphysics* indicates the centrality of this word for achieving two Aristotelian objectives, on the one hand, for expressing the binding of the all together once it has been analyzed into aspects or parts (as well as for excluding what is contradictory to it), and, on the other hand, for helping to define contradiction.[15]

We can speak of predication, and this is how the Ackrill translation of the *Categories* renders the verb *katēgorein*,[16] but we can also recall that "predication" in this early Aristotelian text means "to be said of" something. Categorical activity is linguistic, and in this way: it is the way we speak when we attach two words, when we say one word about another, assigning a word its place. In one important case this happens when we assign the name of a secondary substance to the name of a primary substance. In this important case, which Aristotle discusses at length in his chapter 5, the act of categorizing a single individual, saying *anthrōpos* of a proper name, is a peculiar sticking point for the system, because a secondary substance (*anthrōpos*) cannot be considered a property of a primary substance (Socrates) in the way that a color can be said to be a property of a surface, say, or weight can be said to be a property of a body. The unique substance of a singular being can nevertheless be categorized, Aristotle argues. First of all we routinely say of Socrates that he is an *anthrōpos*. How to do this despite the difficulties Aristotle discusses at the beginning of chapter 5, and the verb that makes the relationship possible and intelligible is *hyparchein*. This verb explains how Socrates can be an *anthrōpos* without *anthrōpos* being inherent in him in the way that green is inherent in a spring leaf. Such a verb, it would seem, would conform to Aristotle's basic distinction in this text between two ways of going together: being in (inherence) and being said of (categorizing). Being in, *en estin*, and being said of, *katēgoreisthai*, are the technical concepts at issue for Aristotle. A color *is in* a body; "animal" *is said of anthrōpos* ("animal" is not in *anthrōpos*) because *anthrōpos* belongs to it.[17] These are the thematized relations that he discusses. It seems as though *hyparchein* comes to describe a relation of necessary inclusion and subordination where the metaphor of physical inclusion can't be used. An operative rather than a thematized concept, *hyparchein* comes from a general and diffuse discourse of belonging-to that is also in evidence in Plato.[18] Being nowhere identified as a technical term does not mean, however, that the effects of the concept are less pronounced, it only means that Aristotle doesn't discuss them, and one wonders if he could have discussed them and still maintained some of the other elements of his system.

It is perhaps intuitive to think of a property as "being in" a substrate, taking "in" as a physical term, just as dye is physically in a cloth or marbles are in a box. Already with the assertion that parts are "in" a whole, however, we have moved to a metaphysical or ontological register, and it is obviously not intuitive to speak in the same quasi-physicalizing terms about yet more abstract relations, such as genus and species. One Aristotelian innovation is to say that an important analogical sphere for the categories is language, in addition to space. Something is "said of" another thing. Yet here, in an early formulation, which gets worked out differently when it is revised in the *Metaphysics*, Aristotle struggles to articulate the difference between the two types of relation, language and space. The higher relation that unites them is another analogy, an analogy with the sphere of belonging. It is interesting that the category *anthrōpos*, according to the text, *belongs to* the singular human being. The order of belonging, we should note, is always unidirectional, but the direction is not always the same. Here belonging proceeds from *anthrōpos* to the primary substance; said in reverse, Socrates *has* what we might call "anthropicity." This is only to say that the two make sense, form a unit, can be said with respect to one another to the extent that belonging-to is operating on them both.

In this incomplete and philologically unrigorous survey, we stop next at *Metaphysics* Γ.[19] However fundamental you think the principle of non-contradiction is in Aristotelian logic and ontology, wherever it stands in his hierarchy of first principles, it articulates itself regularly through *hyparchein* with the dative. Contradiction means that what cannot belong does not belong; what a thing is and must be—as itself, without its negations—derives as a consequence from an assertion of self-belonging. For a thing to be a thing, to be itself, to be uncontradictory, powers of belonging must be operational. In one sense, the function of logic and of the "law" of non-contradiction is to police this more basic operation. Earlier in the book, Aristotle concludes that the one science, metaphysics or theology, that studies being *qua* being is also the one that studies *ta hyparchonta*. This word cannot mean just "beings," since he gives its contents: "those above named and what is prior and posterior, genus and species, whole and part, and the others of this sort."[20] So *ta hyparchonta* must mean something like what belong to something as its proper parts, even though partness is exactly what is in question. All those questions circle around this issue: is a whole a part of itself? are parts parts of themselves?—and so forth. That is to say: being *qua* being stops at belonging-to. It is a matter of whether and how all these characteristic ways of dividing being or saying being in multiple ways belong to each other and to a higher domain. And the principle of non-contradiction says something similar, though in a different way.

The formulation in *Metaphysics* Γ: "If it is impossible that contrary attributes should belong [*hyparchein*] at the same time to the same subject (the usual qualifications must be presupposed in this proposition too), and if an opinion which contradicts another is contrary to it, obviously it is impossible for the same man at the same time to believe the same thing to be and not to be; for if a man were mistaken in this point he would have contrary opinions at the same time. It is for this reason that all who are carrying out a demonstration refer it to this as an ultimate belief; for this is naturally the starting-point even for all the other axioms."[21] Let us hold onto this formulation: the belonging of being to itself and the belonging of proper attributes and the unbelonging of other attributes to a being is called here by Aristotle an "ultimate opinion," *eschatē doxa*.[22] This "ultimate" and finally also "primary" opinion is what Kafka identifies in the trivial German pun.

With this phrase belonging-to becomes the category of categories, and begins a career moving mutely through the story of ontology. Something like it, though changed, without the admission that it is opinion, shows up again in Kant's critical writings. This is no surprise, since for transcendental philosophy, pluralism always has to account for the ground of its plurality, for the unit of its manyness, in the same way that monism has to account for the inescapable appearance of plurality.

There is no category "having/belonging-to" in Kant's table of categories in the *Critique of Pure Reason,* and this difference from Aristotle deserves a treatment of its own. Still, a layer of belonging terms, not thematized as such but nevertheless in full view, appears throughout the *Critique of Pure Reason.* An entire field of cognitions "belong to" a science;[23] the predicate of a synthetic judgment is not contained in the subject—as it is with Leibniz's *inesse*—so it must in some other way "belong to" it.[24] Recourse to belonging-to is particularly prominent in the discussion of the synthetic unity of apperception. The ground for all understanding is the unity of apperception in me, and this means that the I and my unity must together transcend cognition. To be sure, one can think of a unity of understanding without an "I." If we can think backwards for a moment, we can see that asserting a transcendental unity addresses two basic fears. The first is the fear that the I is not unified, but let us concentrate on the second: the fear that experience is not "for me," not "mine," that there indeed may be a unity but that it does not ultimately belong to me. The "to-whom" of experience needs a grounding in necessity, and it gets this in the transcendental deduction of the categories. Before the analysis of categories, even before their deduction, a target *to whom they pertain* is needed. Next to this need, the need for a proprietor, unity ought to be secondary. Kant however insists that the opposite is true, that unity is more important than belonging. Let us cite a famous passage:

> The thought that these representations given in intuition all together belong to me [*gehören mir insgesamt zu*] means, accordingly, the same as that I unite them in a self-consciousness, or at least can unite them therein, and although it is itself not yet the consciousness of the synthesis of the representations, it still presupposes the possibility of the latter, i.e., only because I can comprehend their manifold in a consciousness do I call them all together my representations [*meine Vorstellungen*]; for otherwise I would have as multicolored, diverse a self as I have representations of which I am conscious.[25]

We recall how Kant says that the "unity" in the categories is subordinate to a higher unity, that which makes the cluster of categories into one. This will not be a meta-category, a highest kind. It will be, the passage says, self-consciousness, the proprietary field that, receiving itself in pure spontaneity, through self-affection lends synthesis to experience. This field is a unity "beyond all concepts of combination."[26] It makes up the identity of the subject, and that identity is immediately expressed in the to-which of belonging. What is so worrisome about the "diverse self" cannot, in other words, be merely the multiplicity whose emblem is the rainbow. Although Kant doesn't say this expressly, unity is presented as a function of belonging-to. The I must accompany all my representations, but the "mine" is the condition for both; representations and the I come together in "mine," which corresponds to the activity of "accompanying."[27]

In a surreptitious way, critical philosophy and specifically transcendental idealism continues the trend toward a primal narcissism of "being"— in evidence of course in Descartes' as well. The "mineness" that precedes the unity of experience is a feature of the apparently neutral form of the universal subject, even when Kant says "hands off" and restricts his claims to original apperception, excluding interested empirical consciousness. Belonging-to is not an empirical matter; it is not the result of an individual's interest or self-love or personal greed; yet this just makes the analogy to social relations all the more mysterious. What is the sociality of thinking such that it can be constituted on analogy with narcissistic taking and holding, forgetting the holding in check of the opposite, giving up, over, yielding to—? Ontological narcissism obviously cannot be ameliorated by "fair practices" or even by communism.

With the focus on consciousness in general as transcendental belonging-to, another possibility is locked out, precluded, and thus it is indicated negatively. This is the possibility that being is founded in an activity of group formation, that morals may be prior to knowledge, practical philosophy to theoretical philosophy, and that neither are pure, but rather both are perforated, not by desire or interest or errancy, but by another sense, a sense of what goes together and what does not, first among these a belonging-to that excludes its own contraries, the inappropriate, repulsive, improper, released, surrendered, the yield. Keep in mind that transcendental belonging-to differs from common possession in one significant way: it is not subject to privation. "Having," *ihm gehören*, "accompanying" cannot be taken away from your "I," because privation as a mode of negation always presupposes this belonging. To take something away, even transcendentally, that something has to be had.

One type of having does in fact become an Aristotelian category—
hexis. And yet *hexis* belongs to the categories in a somewhat peculiar way.
"Having" is the last category listed in Aristotle's text, and it is added with
no discussion of its relationship to the others. It later becomes important
for his moral philosophy of course. In the *Nicomachean Ethics* the virtues
are considered habitudes, *hexeis*.[28] And indeed already in the *Categories,*
hexis is used to talk of qualities like virtue and knowledge that, although
they are not part of us, are held by us "as things on a body."[29] This sort of
having is not "belonging" in the sense that the operative term *hyparchein*
expresses, but rather something like "mere possession." We can see here
that possession, for Aristotle, is lower than belonging on the metaphysical
scale of meaningful associations. *Hexis* is also said of personal property,
he notes, such as a house or a field. The relative unimportance of having
is indicated in the last line of the section: "Some further ways of having
might perhaps come to light, but we have made a pretty complete enu-
meration of those commonly spoken of."[30]

Further ways of having, yes, more fundamental than *hexeis*, and what's
more a sketch for a general echontology: this one could say is a project of
Heidegger's *Being and Time* and the writings of the 1930s that develop its
themes. *Sein "Da," eigentlich, Eigenheit, Jemeinigkeit, Ereignis, aneignen,
übereignen*—these terms and others fulfill Aristotle's casual suggestion
that there may be more versions of *hexis* that are not limited to habitude
and physical or legal possessions without reference to a higher justification for the having. Heidegger's own return to Aristotle stepped beyond
Brentano, and yet he nevertheless drew his inspiration for a philosophy
of being from Brentano.[31] As I've said, none of the four main senses of
Aristotelian being according to Brentano are "hexis," although Brentano
does occasionally mention the category. Heidegger can thus reinvent ontology by adding a fundamental existential category, "owning," an *Ex-
istenzial* more fundamental than *Rede (talk), Verstehen (understanding),*
and *Befindlichkeit (state of being or mood),* and he can avoid doing what
he does in most other cases with inherited concepts, namely, expose their
metaphysical provenance. Heidegger may destroy being, time, subject,
substance, and so forth, but "owning" and its correlates do not come
under his hammer. At a key moment, beings are even said to "belong-to"
Being.[32] This distinguishes Kafka's *Being and Time* from Heidegger's,
and it also by extension distinguishes Kafka's yield from Heidegger's
Gelassenheit.[33] The latter makes sense within a general logic of *Ereignis*, of

"enowning," which involves a claim, however abyssal and free, to something higher than possession, to "mineness," to the power and mystique, if not also the myth, of belonging and a privileged beneficiary of the belonging; the former, Kafka's yield, refuses this logic. With Kafka we step back from the *echontology* that never fully revealed itself in the history of philosophy but often pulled the strings.

A playful phrase, "properly speaking,"[34] dots Derrida's text on Heidegger's understanding of death—*Aporias*—in which Derrida gives a striking critique of the idea that one can claim an "own" and "proper" personal death. Death is the limit of all Heidegger's talk of properness, owning, and belonging-to, for Derrida, who reaches this conclusion in 1993, a little more than twenty years after he proposed, not quite publicly but somewhat reservedly, in a footnote, the project of catching Heidegger by his ownership fetish, the root -*eigen*- that cloaks itself in various prefixes and suffixes but always retains its peculiarly undeconstructable character. Perhaps Derrida did not know it would turn into a lifelong project, one that would come to own his thoughts, although it never owned his writing. One of Derrida's great abilities was to write without appropriating, allowing "his" language not to clutch what it purported to speak about. This is what got him into trouble, too, this terrible agility, the tendency his writing has to let go of things, and sometimes also of writing as we know it. This is also what makes any theoretical appropriation of Derrida faulty to the point of falsity, when it portrays him as a holder of beliefs, positions, or theses, as a producer of concepts or of philosophies, since this is what his style staunchly refused.

The project of catching Heidegger by the "proper" was announced in a footnote appended in 1972 to a reprint of the 1968 essay "La Différance," in which Derrida quotes from Heidegger's late lecture "Zeit und Sein": "The gift of presence is the property of Appropriating [*sic*] (*Die Gabe von Anwesen ist Eigentum des Ereignens*). ([Heidegger,] *On Time and Being*, 21–22)." Derrida then offers *différance* as an alternative to "appropriating." Keep in mind that this note answers a key question raised in Derrida's essay but not answered very well there, that is, the question how *différance* differs from Heidegger's ontic-ontological difference. Derrida writes in the note: "*Différance* is not a 'species' of the genus *ontological difference*. If the 'gift of presence is the property of Appropriating . . . *différance* is not a process of propriation in any sense whatever. It is neither position (appropriation) nor negation (expropriation), but rather other.'"[35]

Several things are being done and said in this footnote; let us remark on two of them. As an act, the note disclaims something, and this is not trivial. No matter how Heideggerian the concept of *différance* may be, and no matter how much Derrida continues to "appropriate" the Heideggerian transcendental method, the one gift Derrida simply will not accept from Heidegger is the "proper" and the "appropriative." And another thing: he will not accept, as a way to be rid of them, their mere privation, but only, as he says, what is "other." *Différance* does not take ownership or depend on belonging in "any sense whatever," even negatively; one can hardly imagine a more strident disapproval or a stronger rejection of the most internal and crucial motif in Heidegger. Rejection may be Derrida's mode of turning from the proper, but for a thinker who has so taken on Heidegger's methods and concerns as his own, this is somewhat questionable; it is a gesture, in the Heideggerian sense, of disowning. And the threat is there—isn't it?—that when you disown the very thing from which you have already gotten everything, you will come to an impasse, an *aporia*. It is not mere fate or some divine retribution of intellectual history that Derrida should catch himself in the trap of ownership; it is rather a consequence of the way he rejects appropriation, *like the struggle with women that ends in bed*. Kafka notes down this analogy, which exposes his jealous, repressed, and typifying ideation around women, after this more general proposition: *one of the most effective seductions of evil is the invitation to struggle*.[36]

Struggles, both explicit and veiled, against Heidegger's *-eigen-* punctuate Derrida's writings until the very last texts. The final seminar on *The Beast and the Sovereign* is still concerned almost on every page with what is said to be "proper to man,"[37] a concern, in 2002, uncannily similar to the question of the "achievement of man, the appropriation of his essence" in "The Ends of Man" lecture from 1968.[38] No matter how and how often he had "deconstructed" the proper, Derrida never put it behind him, for whatever reason. Maybe he thought the anti-appropriative lesson had not yet been learned by his readers and students. Maybe he was not convinced himself that he had managed after thirty-five years to philosophize without properness, property, and propriety "in any sense whatever."

One place where assertions of properness would naturally come into question is around the phenomenon of personal death. The place Derrida comes closest to overcoming the proper is then, we could surmise, in

Aporias. Owning your own death is already a major aporia in Heidegger, of course, and Derrida says as much. The logic developed in Division II of *Being and Time* makes "my" death into my most proper possession through an aporia—since of course death is also the moment in which the self that could own anything dissolves. Nevertheless, Heidegger argues that death is the most proper, and he does so along these lines: no one can substitute for me in my death and I cannot substitute anything for death. It is inescapable, but more than this, and Derrida fastens onto this point, it is also inalienable. It cannot belong to another. One deduces from its nontransferability that death is therefore "mine," although this doesn't necessarily follow—it could be nobody's—and furthermore one infers that death belongs "to me" in the same way that other things belong, but more intensely. Ownership of death is the same kind of ownership but an extreme, indeed a limited version of it. Through this highest belonging I come into ownership of myself. Of note here is the way Heidegger and then Derrida in pursuit of him and their shared fetish take for granted that the sense of "own" and "proper" is *in extremis* irreplaceability, inalienability, and means "none-other-than." In 1968 Derrida writes of the belonging of being to man and man to being in Heidegger as the impossibility that anything alien could come between them: "Man is the proper of being . . . "; "Being is the proper of man . . . "; "Propriety, the co-propriety of Being and man, is proximity as inseparability."[39]

A small step from here leads into the logic of the alter and the alien that *Aporias* criticizes at times and at times supports. It is hard to contest Derrida when he says that there are no *Jenseits* and *Diesseits* that could be once and for all distinguished from one another, and therefore you cannot say that to die (*sterben*) is categorically different from to perish (*verenden*), as Heidegger does. All talk of death, Derrida notes, is thus improper; it is impossible to be "speaking properly" about it. And nevertheless, the opposite of the none-other-than me, the intensified "mine" of death, is for Derrida penetration by others from whom I cannot separate myself. The functional opposite of "proper" for Derrida is "alien," meaning "of another," another's thing, belonging to another. Take for example this passage: "If death, the most proper possibility of *Dasein,* is the possibility of its impossibility, death becomes the most improper possibility and the most ex-propriating, the most inauthenticating one. From the most originary inside of its possibility, the proper *Dasein* becomes from then on contaminated, parasited, and divided by the most improper."[40]

This thing, the most improper, obviously belongs to itself, that is, it is the proper, self-appropriated improper, which belongs to no other; it carries its qualities—non-properness—and guards them for itself with total vigilance. Otherwise it could not contaminate the proper and divide up its members in the way Derrida says it does. Otherwise it could not be as clear and precise a concept as Derrida needs it to be. "My" death is the most improper to me—as it is for Heidegger the "most" proper. Improper here means "proper to another" or to "otherness" in general. Another's death stands in in Derrida for the owned and self-producing death in Heidegger. The death of another, often elided with the death of "the" other, is conceived along the same lines as my death is conceived in Division II. Death does not belong to me but it does belong to someone. "The death of the other thus becomes again 'first,' always first." And: "The death of the other, this death of the other in 'me,' is fundamentally the only death that is named in the syntagm 'my death,' with all the consequences that one can draw from this."[41]

Other, alien, not-I, not mine: hers, his, theirs. If it will not be my death it will be another's, proper to her or to them, or even improper, but still wholly improper, with all the characteristics that belong to impropriety in tact and permanently so; in the last instance even impropriety must be proper to itself. It must have a place and be inviolable. This is to some extent the consequences of working with concepts. Something must be proper at a minimum to a concept, in order that any one concept can be exchanged for another. Still and all, we have not said yet what "the proper" means for Derrida. He is not often as candid about the meaning as about his desire to be rid of it or to put it in its proper place. In discussing Diderot and Seneca on the "mineness" of life, where the two maintain that life is one's own "property" such that an untimely death could be thought of as a robbery, Derrida, borrowing a formulation from Seneca, tells us that "the proper" arises in the act of jealously guarding something. Derrida goes on to remark: "What is therefore in question is to think the very principle of jealousy as the primitive passion for property and as the concern for the proper, for the proper possibility, in question for everyone, of his existence."[42]

And here seems to lie part of the problem. If Derrida wants to be rid of proper talk, it is not enough and potentially contradictory to conceptualize it and propose an alternative concept, alienation, projecting an other who takes possession of death before me. The other's death, even if it occurs in me "first" and takes away the irreplaceability of my death, nevertheless does so jealously. If it is not mine it is the other's: this is how the deconstruction is to be carried out. In order to move beyond property one has to, it seems, clutch it ever the more tightly. And yet, at the same time, talk of jealousy shifts the proper talk out of the conceptual into the phenomenological register, and in this Derrida has discovered something truly irreplaceable. What will be wanted is not so much an alternative concept to "owning," since as we have seen from Aristotle at least conceptual thought is dependent on "owning" to explain itself. What will be wanted is a different mode, a social mode perhaps, that isn't jealous—a communicative mode that doesn't hold onto concepts akin to Derrida's yielding writing style.

No doubt, "belonging-to" had many valences for Kafka and his friends in the late teens; from private property to group inclusion in Zionism or Czech nationalism. Whichever rubric you supported and made yours or whichever you criticized and disavowed, belonging was the watchword on all sides. In 1919, to give one reference from the period, Kafka recommends to his youngest sister Ottla that she read *Die Bodenreform: Grundsätzliches und Geschichtliches zur Erkenntnis und Überwindung der sozialen Not (Land Reform: Fundamental and Historical Aspects of Recognizing and Overcoming Social Need)*, by Adolf Damaschke, a central figure in the German land-reform movement.[43] Damaschke wanted to counteract the sharp spike in the cost of land that was driving up rents and pushing workers out of their homes. The long book argues in brief that land should not be the object of financial speculation, and that it is the prerogative of the state to control the use of land through policy. Two complementary solutions are proposed, that all land be held in common and that rights to any portion of land be determined exclusively by use.[44] And yet the common land would not be completely common, nor the right to use a portion of it completely deeded to the user. History steps in to explain a restriction on rights, and more than history, theocracy. The historical paradigm in question is Moses. "What meaning did the most powerful lawgiver of all times ascribe to the land question?" Damaschke asks. Moses's power was used in order "that the people have enough to eat and live securely in the land."[45] His power did not derive from rights or from needs, but rather from God. "From him alone therefore emanated the most valuable possession of his people."[46] Damaschke makes the relationship more precise in the next sentence: "Only those who belonged to the people of Israel were allowed to possess occupancy [*Grundbesitz*] in the praised land, and also only occupancy [*Besitz*] and no ownership of property [*Eigentum*]. The right to ownership of property God held in reserve for himself."[47] And so even in support of common property and its practical distribution by use, the whole schema derives from a higher "jealous" belonging, on the model of belonging to a nation or people. One cannot have the land by deed or contract, but neither can one ultimately have the land by use, if the use does not correspond to the people's constitution as embodied in the will of their God. Ownership is held in reserve, *vorbehalten*, and withheld from people in the form of "the people." Damaschke quotes *Leviticus* 25:23–24: "But the land must not be sold beyond reclaim, for the land is Mine; you are but strangers resident with Me. Throughout the land that you hold, you must provide for the redemption of the land."[48] Redemption comes as an intervention of a "him" to whom the land belongs. *Es gehört ihm, sein Land, sein Dasein*: or better: *sein*. Whatever freedom or right the people have to fulfill their needs is ceded to a higher possessiveness over which the people have no right or power—except insofar as you can say that, although God owns all, they own the God who owns the land. All is God's, but God is theirs, *their* God.

We would be overstepping the bounds of prudence to suggest that the discourse on being in Athenian philosophy whose open secret is an underlying belonging-to is analogous to the power hierarchy challenged by the German land-reform movement in the early twentieth century, or analogous to its sources in the *Tanakh*. "To the lord your god belong the heavens, even the highest heavens, and the earth and everything in it" (Deut. 10:14). In Deuteronomy belonging takes a similarly transcendent place beside God, before being and beings. The lord of the patriarchs has dominion over the earth through the power of belonging. This has an echo in the patriarchs' way of life. Upon encountering a stranger, the first question to be asked was: "Whom do you belong to, and where are you going, and who owns all these animals in front of you?" (Gen. 32:17). Belonging-to is a diasporic or nomadic necessity, born of fear we might suspect, which is grounded in jealousy—in this instance Jacob's fear of his brother Esau, who refused his brother's messengers sent to fulfill his brotherly jealousy. Instead of ceding anything of what was his, Esau came to meet his brother instead with a band of armed men. The messengers say: "We belong to Jacob." When that fails, Jacob asserts a higher belonging, to God. Jacob becomes God's "servant," which doesn't only mean that he will worship, obey, and serve God but also that these activities make sense to one who imagines he is living in God's household. This particular birth of "Israel" is a reassertion of creation as the primal event of the coincidence of the world with God's household, a belonging-to God that can be translated easily into the internal coherence of the group. Belonging-to God undergoes an inversion and is ultimately claimed as what makes the group, as "theirs." How are the most intractable earthly conflicts settled? By attributing belonging to a higher owner. Does a trace memory of the dire economy amid nomadic herding families on arid, unforgiving soil haunt Greek philosophy, Jewish and Christian theological thought, and the everyday parlance of Europe for three millennia? Most likely not exactly in this way. And yet the jealousy that Derrida identifies as the attitude that supports "belonging" seems hard to overcome and helps explain the tenacity of belonging-to as the secret meaning of being. An atheological reformation would have to encourage, though not necessarily discuss conceptually, an attitude that is not jealous.

6. Language for Other Purposes

The three exemplary beings of *metaphysica specialis*—God, world, and soul—Kafka does not exactly avoid, but he does not present them in their recognizable forms in his treatise. Each appears as something else. God is less than nothing, world is that which threatens us and at the same time the only shelter in which we can take refuge, soul is a confused and instrumental fiction. Making God less than nothing prevents one from calling this negative theology. In any case, when he does include a divinity in his theorems Kafka never worries about its existence. Neither the being of God, gods, or a god, nor the thought of a god as the supreme, most real, or most perfect being is ever at issue. I don't think this is because Kafka takes for granted either divine existence or inexistence, or that he thinks the question is poorly formed. If it is anything, existence is another assertion of belonging-to. World, as we shall see, does have a fallen character, at least in the way Kafka first thematizes it, but this is less a state of the world or its history than a practice arising from the afterlife of a set of legends, the narratives in Genesis, which Kafka, rereading, rewrites. World is at once the totality of threats to any human being or animal, the origin of suffering, and a set of construction projects, begun and continued by human beings or animals—not always by the same constructors or constructions—for the prevention of suffering and postponement of death, with a myriad of narratives, all the offspring of Genesis, as guides and justifications (though justifications are also "constructions"). The world's trap, sprung at strategic moments in these legends, lies in its promise to prevent suffering, where precisely that promise is the cause of the worst kind of suffering. As for the third node of special metaphysics, the soul, it lacks even the kind of intuitive presence that Pascal's "heart" has. *The observer of the soul cannot penetrate into the soul.* Our hopes cannot lie with introspection in matters of faith or in matters of psychology. *Arguably however there is a boundary zone in which he comes into contact with it. Knowledge of this contact is, however, in fact knowledge that even the soul itself does not know about itself. This would be cause for sorrow if there were something besides soul, but there is not.*[49] Soul becomes a continual source of non-knowledge of itself, and, in a move that will become emblematic of the logic of these passages, instead of trying to solve a problem, Kafka leaves it unsolved and observes that the existence of it as a problem is a major motor of human activity.

The three classical objects of metaphysical speculation—God, world, soul—pose especially intractable problems because it is not immediately apparent how one could come to possess them. Knowledge about them is at minimum a claim that we possess knowledge about them. And knowledge comes as a claim to knowledge in a linguistic utterance, a sentence or a name. Returning to "being," we can see that it is no accident that Kafka treats this austere topic through an offhand and trivial-seeming German pun. This linguistic accident, it bears repeating, is the inverse of a linguistic act of possession, or seems to be. German does not possess the insight—the coincidence of *Sein/sein* does not "belong to" German in the way its vocabulary does or its grammar. Nowhere does it say "being is belonging to." And thus German does not "speak being." Rather, it conceals belonging-to and yields it up freely where it doesn't even try to take possession of this insight, this tiny and momentous bit of knowledge. Language, on its mere surface, does no more than hint at an identity of existence (*Dasein*) and possession by a him or an it (*Ihmgehören*) who is absent or indeterminate. This mode, hinting, is in fact the mode in which many of the thoughts give us access to things that do not acquiesce to possession-taking. Indeed, the general inscrutability of the thoughts should not be attributed to their content, as though they presented a wisdom more wise than we can understand (Brod), or to their form, as though they were written in a genre that means more than it seems to say (Gray), or to their communicative structure, as though they emitted an esoteric message for an elite group (many Kafka scholars). The pun becomes, accidentally and in the very fact that it is an accident, a mode for saying without asserting possession. Indeed it eschews these markedly possessive modes, claiming and asserting, and instead it gives a sign, without fulfilling it or owning what is signified by it. For *language can be used for everything outside the sensible world only in the manner of hinting* [andeutungsweise], *but also never approximatingly in the manner of a comparison* [annähernd vergleichsweise], *since, corresponding to the sensible world, it is only about property and its relations.*[50] In the two uses of language spelled out here, one corresponds fully to the account of being as possession we have been constructing. And this use is certainly at home in the history of philosophy. Language insofar as it says being in a strong way "has" or "holds" beings within its domain. How, then, do we conceive of a language to talk about what, in Kafka's terms, we do not or cannot possess? The highest metaphysical objects pose precisely the problem of ownership, and in this way the critical philosophy with its anti-transcendent tendency, can be seen as an admission of the possession-character of being. Critical philosophy fails, however, where it sees experienceable objects as fully possessable and experience as "mine."

Language, in the limited realm of human experience, claims property and specifies its relations; for everything else it "hints." In fact, language is the quintessential medium of possession, of itself, of objects, of the self, of the future and of the past. For one thing, relations of possession are asserted through language in possessive adjectives and pronouns. Language expresses relations of possession. More importantly, Kafka argues, there is a covert claim to possession in every kind of language that isn't hinting. Asserting and claiming always implies that the claimed and the claimer are "ours"—what is is what there is for us, for our culture, nation, epoch, family, linguistic group, and so forth, what Heraclitus called *to koinon*. The thought of the common has an egalitarian flavor, but Kafka does not idealize in this way. The "our" takes the form of "his/its"; the ultimate subject of belonging is a father possessor or an impersonal world of nature; it is religion or science. In this one basic atheological trait—his/its—science and religion are indistinguishable.

Unpossessable things cannot be said, at least not directly. There is no hope for metaphor or simile, no image that language produces that could be said to grasp, take possession of, transfer the right to what lies beyond immediate things. Language can point toward it, *andeuten*, but its pointing implies two things. It implies the apartness of the superproprietary. And this makes some sense. Being is what speech "deals with" (*handelt von*); being and speaking coincide indeed because language is always "dealing in" entities around us, and dealing like this depends on the appropriative action of language. German says this, *handeln von*, to transact something. The subject verb object structure is a possessive structure. Moreover, the thought says that language itself is "used" (*gebraucht*) in the same way that a possession is. Language *handelt von* things and itself; it is the self-disposing possession in which all other possessions are taken up and used. Appropriating itself first and foremost, language says, simply by speaking: these are the things that belong to it, to our world, it claims them and so long as it does, these things cannot be anyone else's and we cannot be other than we are.

The question is whether the word *Andeutung* can be possessed such that this can become a positive element of our transactions. It reminds us of the internal gesture of negative theology. We acknowledge that God exceeds our knowledge through a gesture of resignation; at the same time, we grip onto this gesture with the same force and conviction with which we previously clutched a cross or a bible.

With this claim about language, however, one runs the risk of nullifying the very hope that hinting, insinuating, merely indicating, brings. We want to learn something from Kafka, to take something away from our encounter that we can use again, make our own. It is true, isn't it, that once we say of language that it can only hint at higher things, once we have a vocabulary and a place for hinting in our rhetoric, once we can say "hint" we can trade in hints as though they were any other asset. And yet the argument is not nullified, at least we hope not, by Kafka's assertion of the hinting power (*die Sprache kann . . . nur andeutungsweise . . . gebraucht werden*) of language. For one thing, he goes on to write down many more notes and thoughts, and later he returns to stories and a novel, though perhaps after the treatise in thoughts he writes in a different manner than before. In short this reflection on language does not stop him from writing the treatise or anything else. Perhaps it gives writing a new purpose though. What we have to ascertain is the difference between writing, and the writing in these thoughts, and language that "has," "uses," or "trades." Had Kafka stopped writing, as if the terrible truth about language was that it was stained by an irremediable empiricism and possessiveness, we would have to stop as well. There must be, we can assume, something more to hinting.

You can take or leave a hint. Yet in the fictions hinting is the supreme power and the supreme seduction—in the parables chiefly, but also and most emphatically in *The Castle*. We struggle to find a detail in the novel and in the town that is not also a hint—in these fictions it is almost impossible not to take the hints. But we mustn't surmise from this that there is no choice. A hint is not obligatory. Taking a hint is in some sense stealing, even if it is obvious. That we can only insinuate anything beyond empirical things has, first of all, a negative consequence. We learn that, as in critical philosophy, talking about metaphysical things directly is prohibited. Whenever we speak about a higher world, it ceases to be metaphysical. In each utterance about them the gods are dragged out of their heaven and become possessions like any other. But we can hint. And in proposing this, we are led to believe that it may not in fact be the beyondness of its objects that causes language to fail. This is, after all, the key tenet to a metaphysics of language. Instead, there is a linguistic disposition that locates the cause of its failure in a more powerful elsewhere. To hint: to actively not say what cannot be said. We say that this limit lies within language, and thereby we hint at something beyond what is sayable that does not have limits at all. All possessive language hints at a magical language that would not possess but abandon. And the magical language implies, at the same time, that these highest most difficult to possess things are its special province and indeed its chattel.

What a game he is playing!—with this thought on language the stakes of an atheological treatise in thoughts are raised a level. For theo-politics, it is crucial to be able to identify deceptive ways of speaking about God or other theologoumena. That is, it is important in critiques of religion to replace the divine with another possession that is *more easily possessed*. Historical events were the true signified of the divine. An intellectual capacity for moral judgment, practical reason, is the true source for the power that is, for Kant, ceded to God through prayer.[51] Allegory and prayer are the mistaken linguistic modes through which natural and human phenomena are transferred onto theological ones. They find their place in the two most powerful forms of theological influence, scripture, which for Spinoza is allegorical when it is not providing examples for moral life, and daily life or ritual, which for Kant is supported by prayers to the divine. And prayer and allegory are versions of hinting. Insofar as you pray, you imply the existence of the respondent; allegory says in another form what cannot be said in its own form. So hinting is crucial to theo-politics; indeed, the instruction to read this or that as a hint, as an indirect intention, parasitic on a primary intention, is fundamental to the genre. Theo-politics specializes in converting hints into statements that the original hints do not in fact make.

We are left to wonder whether to hint is a linguistic power opposed to possession, or to hint is in fact a clandestine assertion of possession over the unpossessable, and so in fact stronger than assertion. True, the hint lets its object slip away. It is harder to control implications than denotations; they shift, lead to others, evoke several objects at once. Yet the objects can still be transacted in this way and enter into the economy of possessed things, *even while they remain unpossessable.* Hinting handles these objects despite their resistance to possession. Furthermore, and this is the decisive point, although constative language is a manner of possessing sensible things, insofar as this is done in the open, things, and language, are malleable. They can also be dispossessed; its objects can be cancelled, transmuted, destroyed, erased. Insinuating, hinting language has less room to move, since it claims only the slightest contact with what it insinuates. In a hint the highest and least sensible beings, which cannot be seen directly, make themselves more lasting by being said indirectly. Heaven cannot be spoken of, possessed, given being, so it cannot be refuted, denied, sold off, cancelled; if it can be hinted at this makes it much more likely to endure. *Heaven is mute, is only an echo to those who are mute.*[52] On one hand, heaven does not speak. But this does not matter. We possess a language that corresponds to it: silence. We are an echo of heaven's silence that resounds the more strongly so long as we cannot say anything ourselves. The specific hinting modality of non-speaking harmonizes perfectly with the specific heavenly modality of non-speaking. Little has changed: what is is what is possessed, possession holds being, and the news here: what is most deeply possessed is what is not said directly but only insinuated. What everyone is silent about are in fact global truths. Hinting is also the main linguistic mode of words such as "his." It may be the main mode of meaning, for when we call speaking "direct," we certainly do not mean that it divulges everything. We say that is "his house" in order to find our way to it, but we do not ask in this or in most instances what type of possession "his" implies, or how this possession has been granted "him" by authorities. The greater sphere of meaning and the nexus of implications that lie behind any minor attribution of earthly belonging-to are but hints, and a hint, being tiny, encompasses an exponentially larger field than either the referent or the sense. *The Castle* is a chain of tiny linguistic gestures. Insofar as a hint gestures obliquely at what cannot be corroborated by extralinguistic means, it opens itself to what cannot be corroborated. Perhaps language itself came about in this way, as a kind of interim antidote to the trauma of a nothing. With language and its hinting powers, nothing could become an "all." One could say also that language, as the capacity to hint, is the horizon of the total hinting potential in any act of speaking. Or: hinted at in any act of speech is also language itself. An act of speaking implies language, and in order to say something or think we have said something, we must already have taken the hint that there is language, that language is this or that, that we have it, and at the same time that although it is bigger than all metaphysical things combined, it nonetheless belongs to us.

7. Possession, the Possessed

Possession, the act and the supposed right, appears undisguised in Kafka's novel *Amerika (Der Verschollene)* in the shape of a small soldier's suitcase, although the larger spheres of property and belonging, familial, corporate, national, are no friend to Karl Rossmann, the protagonist. He abandons or is abandoned by everything that could be called "his," his family, his room, his home, his nation, even his adopted nation. He is almost abandoned by the possessive pronoun "his," and would have been, except for the grip his suitcase has on his imagination. We find him, arriving in New York Harbor, obsessed with the suitcase, which in some ways is more central to the novel fragment than he is.[53] The case floats through the novel, from hand to hand, in and out of Karl's dominion, marking the limits of his ability to lose himself. He becomes *der Verschollene,* the one not heard from again, as a function of the case's disappearance but remains enthralled with belonging to the extent that the suitcase keeps coming back. His existence is carried in it, the possession that keeps belongings together. And the value of belongings increases the fewer they are and the deeper Karl enters into the alien land; this is the logic of traveling, and traveling is no more than the opportunity to pack and pack again, to constantly chase and reclaim his own things.[54]

The things in it—pocket bible, letter paper, a photograph of his parents, a putrefying Italian salami—have an internal order that no amount of distance or reshuffling can alter. All the necessities are there.[55] The ship's stoker is familiar with this logic. "Either the suitcase has been stolen, and then there is no help for it and you can cry for it until the end of your days, or the man is still watching it for you."[56] Life means having the suitcase to the end, to give him not only all he needs to live but also the sense that he is, that he exists, insofar as he can at any moment open the lid and have a view of his things.[57] A desire to survey one's possessions at any moment also characterizes the late story "The Burrow." As is perhaps to be expected, the suitcase comes to Karl as an inheritance from "him." Before it was his, it was "his": "As his father handed the suitcase over to him forever, he had asked in jest: how long will you have it?"[58] The question is a joke to the father, but not to the son, whose days are numbered by the slow dispossession of "his" suitcase and of "him." A stranger picks up the lost case on the ship, and it passes into the possession of Karl's uncle, the father's stand-in in America. To send Karl away, his uncle first sends away his suitcase. A friend, to Karl's mind, is one who "carries his suitcase." For the suitcase owner, love is when a woman has her hands in it, until at the end of the affair she slaps it rudely shut. He is vulnerable when it is left open, safe and alone when it is closed. " . . . and now this expensive suitcase was already perhaps actually lost."[59]

Through the case, Karl continues to be possessed by his parents. An event that preoccupies him for half the book—losing their photograph— does not lead to freedom. On the contrary,[60] Rossmann is pursued by his belongings, through which the past continues to levy its claim on him. The situation is this: through possessions he is possessed, first by the parents, then the uncle, women in hotels, friends, and most obviously by employers. Late in the book his "friend" Robinson insists he take a job as servant to a bedridden woman. His only work is to move her household things up and down the stairs. "If I stay here a minute longer, I'll belong to them," Karl moans.[61] In this nexus of possession, a quagmire in which the most private and personal goods become the point of entry into an exclusive bond, Karl has that limited sense of freedom, the freedom to dispose of your things, which is a one-way street into the closed system of rights and obligations within which there is no liberty with respect to the system as a whole.

"Belongings" are simultaneously a reification and an obfuscation of the nexus in which they have come to belong. The things themselves are tiny, trivial-seeming conduits through which a system of rights and obligations takes charge of the one who thinks he is in charge.[62] In Rossmann's case, the family keeps hold of the son. By "belongings" is implied an intellectual and linguistic act through which the relationships between objects become plastic enough to stretch over long distances and times. Yet through this plasticity there enters a higher obligation: you become subservient to the system that grants you these liberties. If anything, this is what Kafka banishes in his protocol for a "possessionless workforce" in 1918.[63] It seems to be a collective with consumption but no possession. *Only the following possessions are allowed: the simplest dress (to be prescribed in detail), things needed for work, books, foodstuffs for personal use. Everything else belongs to the poor.*[64] No suitcases needed, in other words.

Think of belongings as objects of the will: just as my own will triumphs over the belongings, over the wills of the objects, at the same time I submit completely to the tyrannical logic of willing, and if I don't I forfeit everything. Almost the first person in a position to represent this relationship to himself is Joseph K. in *The Trial*, although a representation of the relationship is not, in the end, much help to him. The painter Titorelli tells K. "half as a joke, half in explanation, 'But everything belongs to the court.' 'I didn't realize that before,' said K."[65] The curtness of Titorelli's response hints at the problem: "yes," he says. Titorelli's little "yes" implies that he already knew this fact, that it is in fact generally known. "Even my studio properly belongs to the court chancelleries, the court has however placed it at my disposal."[66] The cost of having anything at your disposal is being perennially at the disposal of the court. The modern European court is analogous to the cosmos of the ancients insofar as it is the entirety of orderliness, a whole of infinitely subtle divisions of rights and liberties that can and cannot be taken, and which can also be taken away, a whole that is named with one name, court, when previously it had been named with another, nature or fate. In place of Rossmann's suitcase, Joseph K.'s legal case holds within it all that pertains to him. By virtue of separating and restricting access, the case takes free details from K.'s life and turns them into contents that are alienable, turns private belongings into, in the last instance, possessions of the court. And like the family, which insinuates itself secretly into Rossmann's freedom through the suitcase, the court reaches secretly into

Joseph K's experience. It is only his "case" that he confronts and never the court, which withdraws each time he approaches, trying to gain an overview of what it has on him. Yet nowhere is the institutional, projecting, deputizing, dividing, and concealing activity of the one highest owner more obvious, and still that is not very obvious, than when the institution itself summons, albeit by mistake or out of its severe lack of self-knowledge, a servant to draw the boundaries of its property. The ironclad logic has its cracks, and these widen in *The Castle*. "The young man excused himself very politely for having woken K., introduced himself as the son of the castle castellan and then said: 'This village belongs to the castle, so anyone who stays or spends the night here is, so to speak [*gewissermaßen*], staying or spending the night at the castle.'"[67] What is this "manner of speaking"? If we read this sentence right, the town belongs to the castle, or this is how some of the townspeople speak about it. Undoubtedly, the question of being as the assertion of belonging-to is addressed again with a new explosive potential in *The Castle*.

In the novel, many of whose motifs were first broached in the *pensées* of 1917–18, the right to make claims about what is—being—is wrenched away from the ontological and given over to the political, which had always governed it anyway. The dimensions of the onto-political are: arrogation of right, deployment of right, scope of authority, and, no less importantly, exclusion for prohibited activity. Outside his *pensées*, Kafka divulges the political-proprietary nature of being three times, first in the form of personal existence, the possession of one's own "life"; next in the form of the court and its anterooms; and finally in the town/castle. Karl Rossmann's personal existence consists in the little familiar world of things that he clutches. Life is the defensive posture against dispossession. Thus when the photograph of his parents disappears, Rossmann is not less but more alive, insofar as he can chase after it. His travels consist then, at least in part, in displacing himself to new parts of this fictitious America so that the family image may come to be his possession and not he its. The second divulging of political being happens in the court, which possesses everything and only lends out the right to others, like Titorelli, whose art shows the true result of this "free disposal" of court property. Disposer disposed, he paints only dependents of the court from whom he might expect little favors. Here the scope of being is obviously legal, and it extends therefore to deeds as well as to their interpretation (see the chapter "In the Cathedral"), but it does not yet extend to the political order or to everyday life. The possession structure of legal existence comes as a surprise to Joseph K., who has to be arrested for it to begin to become apparent to him. This concealment is already no longer in effect in *The Castle*. Not only is the being/possession equivalence all-pervasive, and hinting language along with it, at least two other critical aspects of the equivalence come to the fore. In addition to the now nearly universal scope of possession-being—it covers nearly all human relations (work, love, memory, narration, family, local politics, education, etc.)—the reaction of the system to potential disruptions becomes hysterical. The self-justifying, self-perpetuating logic of belonging becomes the subject of endless allusions and warnings. It is as if the more extensive the possession structure grows, the more vulnerable it becomes to exposure. What is the land surveyor K. except the walking potential to expose and perhaps ruin the reciprocal possession of town and castle, to turn the myth of belonging into an empty secret.

The circuit that turns around itself is just this: "everything belongs to the court," "whoever resides in the town resides in the castle," statements that take possession of the whole. Where the whole is actively and obviously commandeered, it is also the weakest. The irony is that the atheological basis for the circuit is the statement itself, which in each case is made by a figure with only questionable status in the system. Is the son of the castellan authorized to say this? Is the painter not a threat to the court, given what might show up in his paintings? Is Rossmann not, in a similar way, a rogue, unable to fulfill any responsibility? The preservation of the whole takes place nonetheless in the most marginal and unauthorized claims. The right of the family, the court, the castle to possession of its members, courtiers, subjects is asserted most strongly where most in question, in these sorts of claims, by these sorts of figures, and in all three cases, little or no further demonstration of authority is at hand.

8. Against Having

A myth cannot be dispelled without destroying the world that tells it. This is why demythologization is a violent, world-emptying act. And yet destroying myths never destroys mythic thinking, since destruction and all the attendant fantasies of change, power, rebirth, and so forth, are something like the ur-myth of culture itself.

Destruction, the myth that the world can be destroyed, and indeed the myth that there are moments where its destruction is the only and perhaps even the best critical response to the world, springs directly from a conviction in being as having: it is a myth told at the high point of possession frenzy. What "is" not and is not held fast and possessed cannot be destroyed. Those who think it is are using words incorrectly. *Toward avoiding a word error: what is supposed to be actively destroyed has to be held fast by glance and hand beforehand; what crumbles, crumbles, but cannot be destroyed.*[68]

How to begin to deal with other fantasies about loosening "glance and hand" that hold the world fast? Kafka proceeds in three steps to disabuse us of the revolutionary idea that things can be scrapped completely and built anew. First an argument about attitude. Imagining that one can destroy the world coincides with the attitude of God at the moment of creation. *The world can only be seen as good at the position from which it was created, for only there was it said: and see, it was good and only from there can it be judged and destroyed. When I want to come into a right relationship with it, I must do it from there—.*[69] Little more than this is said about the "creation" theologoumenon in Kafka's *pensées*, and yet, coming into the *richtiges Verhältnis, the right relationship,* to the world requires that you stand at the position of the creator. All other positions, this implies, are wrong. And furthermore, at that single point where creation is possible, destruction is also possible, but only at that point. What's more, judgment about the whole can only take place there. World creation and world destruction, as well as moral judgment, according to the opening of Genesis—Kafka's continual reference here—in short, all critical positions with regard to the whole are no longer possible at any subsequent instant. In the middle of the world, nothing can either be destroyed or created, and nothing can be good or evil; everything can only belong or not belong.

The second attack on the myth of destruction comes in the form of laughter at *the old joke: we hold the world and lament that it holds us.*[70] A long-standing tendency is to lament this fact, to lament that we cannot start the world over one way or another, or thoroughly condemn it. On the lament form: it is not totally without reason that Job comes to Brod's mind when he wants to place Kafka on a biblical stage, but lamenter is precisely not the role Kafka wants to occupy.[71] Lament is accusation; it throws the blame for the state of things away from the accuser. If Kafka were Job, the poor nobleman from Uz would have come to see, despite his suffering, that he was the problem, or his lament; and yet his very lamenting kept him from seeing the extent of his possessiveness with respect to his former life. Lamenting the way the world plays with us, the way we are subordinated to it, is a self-deception; in fact we hold it.

The third attack on the held world and the fantasies of becoming god-like that circle around the word "destruction" takes the form of a denial. *Destruction of this world would only be the task if it was, in the first place, evil, that is, contradicting our senses and, in the second place, if we were capable of destroying it. We cannot destroy this world, since we have not constructed it as something independent* [als etwas Selbstständiges aufgebaut], *but have gone astray in it* [uns in sie verirrt], *and still more: this world is our going astray* [Verirrung], *as such it is however itself an indestructible, or rather something that can only be destroyed not through rejection but through carrying it through to its end* [nur durch seine Zu-Ende-führung].[72] No doubt this leading—*führen*—is related to the *zurückführen* to first principles that Kafka identifies in a letter to Felice as his task in this period.[73]

For "holding" dressed up as "being" that wanders the world as if it were "created," there are few remedies. A possessive act dissimulates itself as the essence of everything and dissimulates the dissimulation by throwing the burden for destruction on those who have wandered into it and are without perspective or means or strength to act.

It is fine to hint, but one may also worry that it doesn't lead anywhere or that in the end no one takes the hint; it is fine to joke, but perhaps this does not carry you to the endpoint of the world. The task is to release ourselves from tasks: an oxymoron, unless you read "task" (*Aufgabe*) as the gift laid on us, the gift for giving up (*Aufgeben*). Destruction? "Gib's auf!" (Give it up!) Judgment? "Gib's auf!" The treatise is full of exhortations to give up the kinds of presuppositions that make the world seem "created" and unassailable in the first place. More than exhortations, the treatise can be seen as a set of experiments in giving up these claims to total possession. Two such experiments especially stand out.

In one experiment, a "he" responds to the simple, bald-faced revelation that being is possession. *His response to the contention that he perhaps possesses, but he is not, was only trembling and heart-pounding.*[74] This *he* is given the keys to the world and immediately succumbs to fear and trembling. This is certainly not an appropriating response, this paralytic shaking, this somatization that is accompanied by a Kierkegaardian affect: *Angst*. No doubt it is a kind of release from possession, but it is a dumb one, a negative sign of the hold being still has on *him*. The experimental subject, "he," when he receives the revelation, is lost without the attribution to being of an independent, impersonal essence. When it is put into his hands, when told that he has, holds, grasps but cannot be said to "be," there erupts in him something like the Kierkegaardian reaction to the nothing of the world—trembling (*Zittern*). He cannot take possession but neither can he release himself from the task, and least of all can he imagine another mode of living besides being-having. Direct revelation has the effect of convincing *him* that there is only being, and he can't have it, although some greater being might.

Note that the one who receives this "bad" news is a "he," and so the bad news has already been displaced, not produced by an "I" and not demanded or commanded of a "you" in a maxim. It is a report on an experiment in which the subject is told his world is a deception, an experiment in ideological critique or world opening, the threshold of a phenomenological modification without, once again, the resoluteness or strength to accomplish it. Another way to say this: one cannot take possession or own for oneself the revelation of the possession-character of being.

Let us look for a moment at this type of revelation; it is an Enlightenment genre. Spinoza announces: "faith amounts to nothing more than credulity and prejudices."[75] Kant later declares: "all religions, however, can be divided into *religions of rogation* (of mere cult) and *moral religions*, i.e. the religion of *good life conduct*."[76] We are all too familiar with the Feuerbachian/Heinean/Marxian comparison of religion to a drug. The speech genre in which the theological is bluntly revealed to stem from human motives or to exist for the purpose of human ends finds its critique in Kafka's portrayal of the response: fear and trembling. And to be sure, these exemplary revelations did produce anxiety. Kant's text was banned. Spinoza was subject to a writ of *cherem* and expelled from the Amsterdam Sephardic community for "abominable heresies." The history of thought however has canonized these intellectual acts and interpreted the anxiety they produced as a sign of superstition yet to be overcome. As we have begun to see, these revelations only sent the possession-character of being further underground, where it could spread its roots even wider.

The burying of the "his" or "ours" is expressed also in the pronoun "he," with which Kafka experiments here. The appellation of a "he" is the single necessary condition for the formation of a community, religious or intellectual, which reactively constitutes itself out of a first "he" to whom it ascribes ultimate possession—*es gehört ihm*—and derives all powers to appellate I's and you's from this originary displacement of belonging. The logic is plain but important. Third persons can either be founders or enemies, and of course historically always they are masculine. "He" is a public pronoun, it is used in each case to advertise within the bonds of intimacy the doings of a nonmember or a proto-member, and, most importantly, to project ownership of something—an opinion, an action—away from the group. This may be either the power to create or the power to destroy. When I say "he," I am talking to you and removing him from the powers we accord one another, to speak and to listen, to share secrets, secrets about "him." Founders and enemies are silenced, but in silence they hold the key. The silencing happens within the address of "you" to "you" about "him." And at the same time there occurs an even more surprising projection. Silencing him is a concession that his power is greater than ours.

This is the first experiment, and it is a negative one. It shows the effects of ideology critique. Revealing the profane source of divine things leads nowhere. It produces fear and trembling, since what you thought was being was merely having, and all your justifications for "what is" become null and void, and yet because of this you go on and seek stronger justifications, higher grounds. A second Kafkan experiment starts from the opposite assumption. One says: *there is no having, only being, only being that longs for the last breath, for suffocation.*[77] Take away having and leave a being that, as a consequence, does not have anything, even its breath. Being that is not having is disaffected, impersonal, of concern to no one, rejecting everything and rejected by everyone. This being is simply the longing to exhale the last bit of itself, and inhaling is but a detour through life to death. Yet this experiment is also written in the genre of revelation or ideology critique. It is told as though by someone who knows the truth to someone who falsely understands being as possession. What you have been told is wrong, there is no possession, only being that abandons all possessions, and as a consequence, abandons you.

A semantics of affect and physical symptoms seems to be the degree zero of this logic. Having is based in a bodily metaphor of grasping and holding. Thus a search for other physical metaphors marks these experiments. Yes, physical metaphors for being can be extended, varied, changed, as they can for politics. The body of being can be brought to trembling, paralysis, suffocation—.

And yet both experiments appear to fail. The failures stem, at least in part, from the internal logic of the sentences. Meontology is also ontology; attributing nonbeing to something reifies it and strengthens the powers of being. You are, you are not. What is not is not in the same way that it once was: eternally, unchangingly, a unity, and so forth. This is akin to the problem of the ascetic, who, giving away all worldly things, holds even more tightly onto their absence as the key to the other world. You cannot give up having by holding desperately onto nothing.

Although failures, the experiments point toward another mode of attack. If having and being, although confused, are indeed distinct, and this is Kafka's presumption, and beyond distinct, if the two share no traits whatsoever, whatever being is, it is not holding, not possession, no right can be exercised in its name, what is cannot be claimed by me or by my representatives; "we" do not possess anything simply because we are, we don't even have ourselves. He "is," whoever he is, but he cannot even dispose of his own being. Being then, in a sense we don't yet quite understand, can be a name for what I or you or we cannot claim, keep, or dictate over; it comes from an absolute not-us, which you could call God if in calling it this you did not again claim it or attempt to possess it. It comes, perhaps, from someone else's God.

Knowing this, however, still does little toward accomplishing the task of loosening the possession-character of world. Instead we might sing a little song:

> *I don't know the content*
> *I don't have the key*
> *I don't believe in rumors*
> *all understandable*
> *since I am it myself.*[78]

This ditty that Kafka jotted down on November 24, 1917, is remarkable for its negations: not knowing, not having, not believing. It is also remarkable for its pronouns, I, I, I, I—a progression in self-assertion that ends with the most peculiar and seemingly fruitful assertion, "I am it." The German says, *denn ich bin es selbst*, since I myself am it, an impersonal pronoun that is the target of the knowledge, having, or belief of the I. In the formula for self-reflection—I am I—the contents of "I" would have to be known in advance for it to be a valid assertion. The existence of the subject of knowledge would have to be believed in. The question remains, and becomes even more desperate: maybe, maybe I am I, but what *is* I? One says first of all, puzzlingly, "I am it." I is not not-I ($A \neq {\sim}A$)

and I is not-I (A=~A) are intimately related in Fichte and Hegel. Saying each has the same prerequisite. One has to have known the one and the other in advance in order to have told them apart and subsequently placed them together. This knowledge, of the absolute distinction between nature and subject, is, because of the *reductio* of foreknowledge that constitutes it, arbitrary and nondialectical. In contrast, Kafka does not oppose the "it" to the "I." His "it" makes one thing clear, that this theo-logic will not ground its claims in the certainty of self-knowledge, even if it is knowledge of a self alienated from and constituted in its relation to another.

The bit of doggerel, written on the same day as the thought on trembling and heart-pounding, sings about the usual modes of access to "I"—self-observation (psychology), decipherment of a code (genetics *avant la lettre*), belief (religion)—and of their failure. It celebrates these failures as proof of the true substance of the "I." The relation between the "I" and "it"-self is being, and not knowing—if, that is, being is in fact a relation, which the song suggests it is not.

A song does not have to own what it says; the commitment to its contents is half-hearted, easily retractable in the next verse, the next song. A song or verse is to some extent "about" its inability to make a serious assertion about the world. And at the same time those things that fare poorly in assertions come to life in songs. Not for nothing do we prefer to sing or hear songs about love and death, phenomena about which, when asked to assert anything, we utter clichés, which amounts to being speechless.

Song, now split within itself into poetry, music, and prayer, has kept in all three parts of itself a tendency against ownership. It is a crime to do this to Descartes, I confess, but the sacrilege shows better than mere analysis how Kafka's ditty drains reflection of conviction, assertion of being.

> Ac proinde hæc cognitio,
> *ego cogito, ergo sum,*
> est omnium prima
> et certissima[79]

The weightiest of phrases from Descartes's *Principles of Philosophy* has a delightful music. Sing it and you are singing for this first of all things and this apex of certainty, singing for it, winging of what you, or "I," do not have. The modern departure point for philosophizing predicates my being on my thinking, telling a tale in and of the first person. The guarantee for philosophizing and attributing being to anything remains, from Socrates to Descartes, the attribution of being of the I to itself, through the meaning of "am." What *ergo* says in Descartes's phrase is: *sum* means *cogito*. "I am" means "I think."

Kafka cancels the equivalence of "am" with "know" and "think," and he does so according to the same purported reasoning, through self-experience. He is a realist when it comes to the self in much the same way as he is a realist when it comes to the body. The atheological account of that is: we don't *have* a body, we *have* a growing (*ein Wachstum*).[80]

9. Thing Being

A few of the thoughts and other evidence from Kafka's oeuvre suggest that around this time he had an alternative in mind to being as possession. It involves, not surprisingly, an inversion of having that should be of extreme interest. Belonging-to, if we follow his reasoning, would mean shirking responsibility for the thing had. Once something is possessed, once the right to dispose of it has been presumed, one ceases to take responsibility for it. One can treat it well or poorly, worship it or destroy it, but the claim of belonging involves a suspension of the difference. In English we say that one "takes" responsibility and then "has" the responsibility for something; in German one usually "takes on" or "takes over" responsibility (*Verantwortung übernehmen*) and then one "carries" or "bears" it (*Verantwortung tragen*). Naturally this repeats a rhetoric of personal possession, predicated upon an original self-possession, but whatever leads languages to preserve this possessive way of speaking about responsibility, it says this, but it means in fact the opposite. To have responsibility for a thing is to respond to a claim it makes on you, a right it exercises over the one who purportedly owns it. Responsibility means being taken over by the object.

The context for this Kafkan thought is the history of religious practices. *The first worship of idols was certainly anxiety about things, but along with that also anxiety about the necessity for things, and along with that also anxiety about the responsibility for things.* This anxiety could well explain the advent of monotheism all on its own. The one God would quell the anxiety, assuming total responsibility for the things of the world. And yet, the word one associates with monotheism is rarely responsibility.

No—surely not that word. Power, knowledge, promise, covenant: these are behaviors of the one God toward humanity. Responsibility attains among earthly ones, and yet and even though it is unavoidable, it is too onerous for them. Indeed, *so monstrous did this responsibility appear that one never even dared to impose it on a single superhuman being, because even through the mediation of merely one being, human responsibility would not have been alleviated enough, intercourse with this one being would have been much too stained by human responsibility, and for that reason one gave each thing the responsibility for itself, still more, one also gave these things a commensurate responsibility for the human being.*[81]

Kafka's penchant for thinking about primal religious gestures, indeed about the sources for gods, and thus about motives or complexes that precede any formal theo-logic, was aided by the Swedish Lutheran theologian Nathan Söderblom's 1914 book *Gudstrons uppkomst (The Coming to Be of the Belief in God)*, which Kafka began reading in the summer of 1916 soon after it appeared in German under the title *Das Werden des Gottesglaubens: Untersuchungen über die Anfänge der Religion*. You cannot reduce Kafka's thoughts about divinity to what he found in Söderblom; for one thing, the latter's book is sociological; it is concerned with myths about the arrival of gods only so far as it can show how worshippers derived social power from these myths. Despite Kafka's comment about Söderblom that although he was "archbishop of Uppsala" the book itself was "quite scholarly without personal or religious sympathies," Söderblom nonetheless does tacitly present pagan beliefs and gods as opposed to Christianity. One note from the record of this reading stands out. In some Australian groups, Kafka remarks, "the people themselves in primal times formed their totem animals through the performance of ceremonies. The holy rites thus themselves produced the object toward which they are directed."[82] Here you can see Kafka's interest in the formation of the sacred, the emergence of objects and contexts out of the rites performed. The conclusion he draws from his interpretation of this episode from the Söderblom book is interesting. Whatever beliefs take hold afterward, divinity is not produced by human hands alone or by a superhuman power or theophany; on the contrary, the acting out (*Ausübung*) of rites produces the divine objects, which then become objects.

The anthropological attitude with which Kafka reads Söderblom, however, succumbs to atheo-logic in the treatise. No longer is Kafka under the sway of an anthropological description of practices or the desire to show the social uses of religion; he performs an analysis on the ideas that give shape to the axis of sacred and profane, which poles subsequently define the world. The fundamental concept in the process is not intellectual, however. Driving the production of divinities is not imagination or a frustrated desire for knowledge; instead what drives it is need, the need for things. Needs precede all higher determinations of metaphysics—nature, essence, or god—and they also precede the need for society.

In the thought, Kafka depicts a chain of anxieties that give birth to society in the first place. In no way is the first disposition toward things a claim of possession. Nothing could be farther from the origin of our original relationship to the world of things than "belonging-to." The thought does not give the reason for our early "anxiety about things," but we can hypothesize that, at least in part, this "first anxiety" is soothed by worship, mollified by setting things on a higher plane and as a consequence setting ourselves lower then things. The anxiety may well stem from our proto-parity with things, or else from our desire to put ourselves above them in order to move, use, enjoy, or consume them, when we have no right and often not even the power to do so. Yet even these activities are secondary to the "first anxiety," *a reaction to* the need for things.[83] Out of our dependency on things comes a huge responsibility, charged with fears of every kind of threat against our existence. Since the scope of our being does not end with us but extends into things with which we do not share an essence, since we are unable to live without them, we spend our days coddling and caring for them in order to stem the fear at the prospect of losing ourselves by losing them. In this pre-economical thought lies the origin of the drive to identify being with possession, which, by this logic, is co-originary with animism. If the need for things is constitutive of us, if an alien "they" are in part what "I" am, in an economy of sufficiency we begin not by taking possession but by taking responsibility. Belonging-to is a development of responsibility. In Kafka's image we are hyperbolic creatures with a reach too elliptical for all that we must do and be. Here too is the origin of social being, and a problematic core of the social in an act: a shared and impossible being-responsible for what cannot care or speak for itself. We are so deeply in things' debt, however, that we cannot even claim to take responsibility for them, let alone carry it out. It is in fact things that have responsibility for us, and our way must be the most difficult and anxiety-promoting letting or permitting ourselves be cared for by non-life, by something far out of our control.

Because no mono-god can sufficiently relieve us of the responsibility that exceeds our powers, and from which we desperately need relief—we give each thing the responsibility for itself. We make out of this failure and desperation a world of independent entities. Only after the world has been cut off in this way, falsified and reified, can we claim it as a possession, adding thereby one falsification to another. Our dependency on things, their responsibility for us, we transform, displace, and invert into their dependency on us. Witness the birth of metaphysics out of the denial of dependence. You could say that the highest moment in this inversion is consciousness. The inversion by which things are made independent and then ex post facto appropriated is the basis on which I can imagine something like consciousness as a repository for things, my objects (which I need, which preserve me, which I can't take responsibility for, which I set free and then violently attempt to take and hold.) By this inversion too consciousness comes to be thought of as my primary possession; it becomes "my" consciousness, and my experience thus becomes "mine" when indeed it is the world's or things'.[84]

Things are independent: this is the tenet from which the concept of consciousness—unhappy consciousness—arises, although it is, following Kafka, a rather crude dissimulation of our dependency on things. The independence and autonomy of consciousness, into which things are led like tamed animals into a cage, transfigures and veils the opposite truth, that the unconscious being that we are is ringed around and held in place by things, and *for that reason one gave each thing the responsibility for itself, still more, one also gave these things a commensurate responsibility for the human being.*[85] Kafka means here idols, the result of a process of apotheosis, when things become gods. These special things are transformed into animate beings who take care of us. The anthropomorphic god, which he comes to terms with in other passages, is a late result of this illicit transfer of the power of things to humans and then back again. Things become gods, not now through the sacralizing power of the ceremony, as he had thought while reading Söderblom, not through the ritual mark of difference. Things become gods through an unmarking. For it is originally the case that things have excessive responsibility for human life, and the animistic religion that Kafka imagines here takes our impossible dependency on things and replaces it with their inscrutable power over us. Hunger transforms into submission to a sacred corncob, divine manna, a golden calf. Need, not primarily an effect of power, is sublimated into the power games of worship and submission.

Gods do not have a birth so much as a purpose; and moreover the procedure for recovering that purpose is not through demythologization or the critique of religion. Gods come into being as mirrors of and collecting points for anxiety about the most urgent and most impossible need—the need we always feel to submit or succumb to the world, to yield in the world's yield. It is important that the primary position of human beings with respect to this world should be understood as weakness or the need for care, and not, as it is for Feuerbach, Marx, and many other writers, a type of power.

Responsibility has a different character than possession, although it is not opposed to it. One who possesses something no longer needs to be responsible for it; possession brings the foreign thing so near, into an intimate zone of power where responsibility makes little sense. Quite the contrary—possession is a license for irresponsibility to the point of violence. One apparently trivial product of the use of this license is trash. Trash comes into existence when the possessor exercises her arbitrary will over her belongings, banishing them from the circle of need and demonstrating by this power that they need her more than she needs them.

During the months of intense writing between the end of 1916 and April 1917 when Kafka produced more than a dozen stories, he raised the question of responsibility, although he did not yet formulate it as directly as he would a year later. He wrote Martin Buber that he planned to call his story collection *Verantwortung* (*Accountability* or *Responsibility*); later he decided to call it *Der Landarzt* (*The Country Doctor*); this story collection sketches out the important facts about our often paradoxical experience of responsibility.[86] How does one account for and act toward a group whose principle of being is not belonging? What is the being of beings if each and every mode of belonging is taken away? The stories give us beings that do not have a territory or whose territory is threatened ("Jackals and Arabs," "While Building the Chinese Wall," "The Hunter Gracchus," "The Next Village," "An Old Manuscript"), beings that do not have a future ("The Bucket Rider," "While Building the Chinese Wall"), and beings that for a variety of reasons do not belong to their families or to themselves ("The Bucket Rider," "Jackals and Arabs," "Cares of a Family Man," "Eleven Sons"). They give us a watchman whose job it is to keep the dead from flooding out of the cemetery into the kingdom. In the draft of "The Watcher of the Tomb," an exasperated prince cries: "Don't speak of responsibility," although this line is excised in the published version. How can one be responsible for the dead? The prince of this land has enough trouble being responsible for his own people. The source of this impossibility is biblical. The prince, a new Nimrod, has emptied the state treasury trying to build a successful Tower of Babel, yet it will take more than gold to save his people from death. These stories give us an ancient figure, "The Hunter Gracchus," for whom no one can be responsible. "The thought of wanting to help me is a sickness that must be cured by lying in bed," he says.[87] And the collection ends with a picture of a rural community whose debt to the country doctor "cannot ever be made good."[88] An alternative to possession it may be, but *Verantwortung* presents its own difficulties.

Its difficulties become virtues when its relationship to possession is clarified. Each functions if and only if the other is set out of operation. An owner is she who does not have to answer for her things or her treatment of them. A responsible one has to answer for her behavior toward things, and indeed she can only answer for herself on behalf of those things that are outside her domain of possession, those beings not slaves of her will or deeded her by contract, things that outlive her, do not include her, such as the dead, or for that matter the living.

10. What "Am" Does

"And as long as you say 'one' [*man*] in place of 'I' [*ich*], it is nothing and one can recount this story, but as soon as you admit to yourself that you are it yourself, then you are positively pierced through [*förmlich durchbohrt*] and horrified."[89] So laments Eduard Raban in "Wedding Preparations in the Country," with a wink at the all-important question of the Kafkan pronoun. When a woman on the street looks at Raban, he worries that she has penetrated his secrets. He imagines telling her the story about how he came to look so tired, the trials at the office, the impending trip to the country, the ceaseless drizzle. To do that would require that he present his past under the sign of ownership, emblazoned with an "I." Raban hesitates to use this most common sign. When "one" does this or that or this or that has happened to one, one may refer to a general habit or tendency, what is customary, shared. Heidegger knew not only that we were dispersed in "the one" (*das Man*) but that it was also the easiest designation to use when you wanted to throw attention off yourself. In short, what "one" does is not owned by anyone; it is rather lent to one from elsewhere. Borrowed is the possession marker of the normative.

The distinction between "I" and "one" is neither grammatical nor pragmatic, that is to say social, in the passage from "Wedding Preparations"; it derives from what lies behind the placeholders and their context. Behind "one" is no one in particular and potentially anyone; behind "I" lies a claim to possession and self-possession, and it is this that leads Raban to envision paralysis and horror. The suggestion that appears already in 1906–7 returns with force in the treatise. Raban addresses a second person about the echontological difference between saying "I" and saying "one." Becoming "I" is not just a matter of using a different pronoun; it is also not a matter of a subjective rather than an objective position. Rather, as Raban says, "you" must admit that "you are it itself" and this admission (what is being said is: "I am it because I own it") precedes the telling of a story in the first person: "I" claims the events are yours.

Shame, obligation, and desire for exoneration are affects that accompany you when you assert possession over an experience. Kafka strains against the idea of self as self-possession[90] in the treatise, and the straining is in large part a response to the Brentanian doctrines in which he and his intellectual friends were immersed.[91] To understand what Kafka thought of when he thought of "I" or "self," we need to recall a few arguments from Brentanian descriptive psychology. When he announces in a notebook entry *Never again psychology!* [Zum letztenmal Psychologie!], Kafka refers to these arguments.[92] The exclamation "never again" is the most strongly and stridently expressed assertion in the treatise. When he draws a line through the exclamation, indicating that it should be deleted from the fair copy, he does not however remove the anti-psychological sentiment from the treatise. It recurs over and over across the thoughts, and the effects of the exclamation are felt in almost every individual thought.

The lectures on "Descriptive Psychology" by Kafka's professor Anton Marty adhere closely to Brentano's arguments about the epistemo-psychological self, intentional consciousness.[93] Consciousness consists of three modes of apperception of an object: presentation (*Vorstellung*), judgment (*Urteil*), and what Marty calls taking interest (*Interessenehmen*),[94] which is a general term for two related aspects of willing, liking and disliking. These modes of apperception are also called secondary intentions, because they are apperceived alongside the object. As recorded in the written notes to Marty's lectures, which were probably delivered when Kafka was a student in 1902: "Whenever a psychic phenomenon arises in us, there also arises in and with it, alongside it (Aristotle says ϖαρέργῳ), an immediate, sure perception of this phenomenon, through which it at the same time sees through itself and grasps itself with immediate evidence as presenting itself and also in turn recognizing itself as itself."[95] What is immediately evident apparently needs the most emphatic assertion. There is a pathos in all these reflexive verbs, in the *sich* and *selbst* and *sich selbst*, an uncertainty that the repetitions in this passage try to cover over and also at the same time intensify, despite Marty's insistence on the simplicity and straightforwardness of this truth. Whatever the difficulties in asserting the self-ness of the self, we learn many things about consciousness reading this passage. Firstly, it is, as the passage says, immediately available, and secondly, it is certain and true. "Even an almighty being could not deceive us about it."[96] What descriptive psychology offered was an infallible method and a true image of the self that did away with skepticism about its being and powers.

Kafka's friends Brod and Weltsch take a Martyan position in their 1913 work of descriptive psychology, *Anschauung und Begriff,* a text Kafka read carefully. Here Brod and Weltsch try to bring about a revolution in the sciences by demonstrating that concepts are the self-consciousness of mental representations (*Vorstellungen*). They adhere strictly to the principle *nihil est in intellectu quod non est in sensu*. This comports with the general impetus of descriptive psychology, and yet in the work of older Brentanists, the authors contend, concepts were still being conceived of not as *anschaulich, visible,* but as discursive or even mystical. And so they try to rid thought of the last nonapparent substrate, the non-image by which images and ideas are organized, judgments made, will exercised. Instead of a transcendental structure of thought and a pure sensibility, a two-level mind, they propose that even the relations between images, between subjects and predicates, and between acts and objects are imagistic. The problem they need to solve, they realize, is subsumption into categories. How does a particular image of a dog get recognized as a dog? What accomplishes this, they say, is the process of abstraction, but only insofar as this process is also imagistic. What distinguishes an abstract image, the concept, from a particular image, the object, is not more or less generality. Brod and Weltsch propose a relatively peculiar theory in which the fundamental element of both perception and cognition is a variable ratio of distinct and indistinct elements in an image.[97] The more distinct an image, the less "body" it has, and the more abstract it is. A pure abstraction has very little indistinctness but also very little "flesh" on it. Furthermore, an abstraction builds up through a process of comparison and exclusion of indistinct parts. The resulting skeletal image remains in a storehouse of abstractions against which any new perceptual experience can be compared. In this way concepts are formed strictly out of perceptual material, and therefore remain as "true" as individual psychic objects.

In their book Brod and Weltsch hold Marty and Brentano's basic attitude: although the structure of the psyche is complex, it is nevertheless stable and unified. How a tissue of individual psychic acts, of intentions primary and secondary, might make up a whole was certainly a question that exercised Brentano and his students. Brod and Weltsch take on the challenge by showing the continuity of percept and concept. For them, as for Brentano and Marty, it is in secondary intentionality that the unity, that is to say the self, lies. One apperceives, obliquely, the degree of blur, and by this one recognizes when one is thinking as opposed to sensing. The difference is technical; Brod and Weltsch fully believe what Marty says in the lectures, that every presentation in the psyche is also a "self-presentation, a self-knowledge, and an act of self-interest."[98] Each mode in the threefold character of an intention—*Vorstellung, Urteil, Interessenehmen*—is also a threefold self-reference. There is a self of images, a self of judgment, a self of willing, though these are all ultimately the same self. Brod and Weltsch show that this is true for judgments. The principle, however, is the same. Each time a new psychic act occurs in time, in consciousness's "moments," as Marty calls them, a self is referred to. This is a "multiplex consciousness" (*mehrfaches Bewusstsein*)[99] in two ways: its selfhood is distributed into acts and kinds of acts. And yet it is never anything but this double distribution, a self that owns the temporally apportioned acts and a self that operates the transcendentally apportioned faculties. Marty makes a telling slip when he tries to talk about the higher identity of this doubly distributed soul, calling it at one point "psychic substance" (*die psychische Substanz*), but cautioning that nothing more can be said about this. We can have no experience of the soul substance that precedes the multiplicity of our perceptions, though we assume, he reminds students, there must be one.[100]

If you disagreed with this whole project, you might say *psychology is the description of the mirroring of the earthly world in the heavenly surface.* In three separate thoughts Kafka associates psychology with mirror reading. The operative theopolitical metaphor here is not projection or sublimation, as it is in Feuerbach, Nietzsche, and later Freud; it is rather reflection in the mundane sense of the word. The only difference between the mirror and the scene reflected in it is that, being set above us, it misrepresents itself as independent of us and higher, yet still for us and about us. Kafka now makes a correction. It is *better* to call it *the description of a mirroring, in the way that we, soaked up with world* [Vollgesogene der Erde], *imagine it, since a mirroring does not happen at all, only we see earth, wherever we may turn.*[101] Kafka interests himself here in the medium for the invention of psychology, in the phenomenological presuppositions that precede its practice and principles. In place of the parergic inner gaze that captures the truth of the way we perceive, Kafka sets the image of the psyche looking for itself outside of itself. How is the psyche invented? Through a double displacement: we imagine a mirror, but the image we invent is only possible for those who can only see the earth. All of the elements of the psyche are but tiny distorted likenesses of our experience. Marty imagines psychical science as analogous to physical science. "Descriptive psychology is simultaneously an *anatomy* of the life of the soul."[102] Kafka describes the contours of Marty's wishful imaginary with some finality four months after his first thought of the mirror science and a few weeks after writing: "never again psychology!" *Psychology is the reading of a mirror writing, therefore arduous and productive with regard to the always correct result, but nothing has actually happened.*[103] Psychology is "always correct" (*immer stimmend*) in the sense that Brentano and Marty mean when they refer to the roots of the German *Wahrnehmung*, most often rendered in English as "perception." Perception is always to be taken (*genommen*) as true (*wahr*) in descriptive psychology. Kafka recognizes this as a tautological movement. Psychology says, we see what we see because we see it. Look here in the psyche: here is our life. The absolute nontranscendence of psychological knowledge, then, in order to give it the appearance of a truth higher than an affirmation of appearances, is written in us, higher than us, and backward so that we must look in and upward, and make an effort to decipher it.

More than this, psychology is the mirror writing in which the psyche comes to be reflected back to us as the unifying, continuous source of phenomena, the source for "acts" and "intentions," the simplex ground of the multiplex, and so forth. As such psychology acts as a retarding force on transformation, by referring to an invisible, law-giving standpoint beyond the reach of "mere" perception. Don't, Kafka seems to say, look in the mirror. Descriptive psychology is tautological and theological, reflecting everyday life as it already is onto a higher but inaccessible plane. The meaning of "am," and the self that it calls into being, is fortified and indeed invented through the fantasy of an intention reflected back to itself in distorted form, preserved through the fiction of independence, and yet, through the need to decipher it, also at the same time confirming, with no real evidence—certainly not with immediate evidence—that the intention must come from beyond the one deciphering it. Psychology and theology here may be seen to derive from an act of imagination, whereby a simple phenomenon is made into a secret code.

Kafka continues to think about the delusions under which psychology concocts a self. In a set of premises, he attacks the assumptions underlying its technique. The first premise is: *the observer of the soul cannot penetrate into the soul.* A corollary to this premise is: *of course there is however a stretch on the edge upon which he touches it.* Up to this point Kafka's argument is an imitation, a parody perhaps too, of descriptive psychology's presuppositions. The second premise overturns them: *knowledge of this touching is knowledge that the soul does not know about itself.* Brentano adds back into the philosophy of mind the scholastic and ultimately Aristotelian topos of oblique perception, perception of perception—apperception, which he also calls "noticing" (*Bemerken*). Kafka notes that apperception cannot in fact have apperception as its object. If it did, there would be no need for a science, since all our thoughts would simply be true. The science and its secondary perception, inner truth/perception (*Wahrnehmung*) is added to the soul by artifice or by mere assertion and does not properly belong to it. The self, if there is one, if it is aware of itself, if indeed it is this awareness, lies outside the soul, on an infinitesimally thin edge. At this edge, however, all the self is aware of is that it does not know itself. The conclusion to be drawn is the following: *it* [the soul] *must therefore remain unknown.* A second conclusion, more like a consolation, says: *this would be sad if there were something other than the soul, but there is nothing other* [than it].[104]

It seems that, after all, there is no need for an attack on psychology. No reason to deconstruct what does not exist; one must only remember not to practice it. Ridding our conceptual world of "soul" could make room for other substrates, of course, and other sciences—Eduard Raban's "one" for instance, and perhaps sociology—and this is why Kafka preserves the soul but leaves no access to it. One can say "I am" but this must be an assertion of nonknowledge and at the same time, since there is nothing other than soul, it must put an end to trying to know the whole in whatever form. Kafka enlarges the soul to encompass everything, but takes away the possibility of epistemic practices with regard to it. To be sure—producing motives and conditions for abandoning practices is one of atheology's main gestures. It often does this in place of critique. And yet, when we abandon soul-practices we should not abandon the psyche altogether. Our negative experience of the soul allows us to say and to continually experience our non-possession of ourselves and everything else.

11. Foreign That You Are

"Am" is less a question about knowledge of the self than a question about self-coincidence, a matter of heterology.[105] In the absence of an epistemic path to the soul, what is expressed in "am" (that is, absolutely not "I know myself") is reduced to an assumption, the assumption of an internal mutual familiarity among alien parts. Asserting unity is an attempt to resist the vortex that opens when knowledge of the soul can no longer be grounded in determinate ignorance. The conceit of philosophies based on determinate ignorance is that, although we can only know that we don't know, the soul must nevertheless be familiar, intimate, ours, a whole to which we belong and which in some way is us, our center and the place to which our inner diaspora always returns. A distinctive logic of representation underlies the assertion of the self's unity. Because an object seems to remain the same over time, we feel we can assert a meaningful unity of the self. And yet the warrant for deducing the unified self from the representation of sameness is not given. It is deduced *ex negativo*, in the main because no other logical alternative offers itself. Without ado, Kafka asserts the converse, that *there are in the same human being cognitions that despite complete diversity nevertheless have the same object, such that it can only be deduced* [rückgeschlossen] *that there are diverse subjects in the same human.*[106] From the same datum that motivates Kant and phenomenology to conclude that the subject must be a unity—namely, the unity and continuity of an object—Kafka concludes, with a similar degree of logical necessity I might add, that there is no transcendental unity of experience. Now what he means here may seem murky, and even if his inference does not make sense, the conclusion is invalid, or there is some other problem, the motivation is clear. He attempts to deduce a diversity (*Verschiedenheit*) of subjects from the diversity of cognitions (*Erkenntnisse*) in the same human being (*im gleichen Menschen*), because of the self-sameness of the object.[107] Among the thoughts that address the heterogeneity of the self, this thought presumes an irreducible heterogeneity of cognitions with no inherent order. In the Zettel version of the thought, Kafka changes "can" to "must": *it must be deduced* [rückgeschlossen] *that there are diverse subjects in the same human.* Then he strikes the thought completely. Neither this thought nor Kafka's significant redaction of it should be lightly abandoned, however.

For one thing, it is evident that Kafka is looking for a logical maneuver by which to conclude that consciousness is not a many within a one but manys around or among a many. He calls the intellectual operation "deduction," but the phrase *in total diverseness* [bei völliger Verschiedenheit] *represents* another difficulty. Transcendental psychologies do not permit the diversity of cognitions and the diversity of faculties (or intuitions or categories) to become complete. Complete diversities do not lend themselves to transcendental operations, to deductions, for instance. For Kant and Brentano, and even for Heidegger in *Being and Time*, the self is only ever a partial diversity and the parts belong to a whole which is prior. In contrast, Kafka's is a thought, not unlike Hume's,[108] of a thoroughgoing internal diversity. Here it is necessary to return to Brentano's division of difference into separable difference and distinctional difference. For Brentano, differences within consciousness are of a kind that cannot be separated from it or from each other. Kafka asserts of the self instead something like separable difference. The differences internal to the self are like the differences between things. And yet Kafka wants this to be more than an assertion, and this is where a difficulty arises. How do you "deduce," with the same necessity with which Brentano deduces the unity of consciousness, that different cognitions of the same object proceed from different subjects, and not from one subject only partially, superficially and temporarily, differentiated. How can you deduce this when deduction is a movement from parts to the hidden, transcendent whole? No answer to this question is offered here, but there is a suggestion about why it might not be answerable in the terms of this thought. The suggestion lies in the modal shift that occurs between the notebook entry and the Zettel. Kafka begins with possibility: from multiple cognitions of the same object multiple subjects "can" be deduced. This proposition is not falsifiable, obviously, and so Kafka proceeds to perform an experiment, changing the mode of the assertion to necessity. From multiple cognitions multiple subjects "must" be deduced. "Must" is the sign of a transcendental deduction, and this is where the problem arises. Deduction always transits from a multiple derivative to a unitary origin and from a contingency to a necessity. The necessity of the movement of deduction lies in the unitariness and necessity of the a priori. If there are multiple subjects for multiple cognitions, deduction should not be the right method because necessity ought not be the right modality. To suggest that multiple cognitions can belong to multiple subjects may not be enough to prove that this is the case, although it should be enough to disprove its opposite. If multiple intuitions of a self-same object can be ascribed to multiple subjects, if there is a chance that this is true, then an originary unity cannot be deduced but only asserted. Thus it is never correct to refer to anyone as "I" or "he" or "she," or as a self, or it is just as correct to say that the self is a company and to refer to everyone as "they."

And so we learn that the subject, lacking the necessity to be one, can be many separate subjects. Kafka is interested here in the subject—or subjects—of intuitions, the one—ones—to whom an object is mentally presented. Here he tracks the multiple-subjects of intuitions: *Diversity of intuitions* [Verschiedenheit der Anschauungen] *that one can somehow have of an apple. The intuition of the little boy who must stretch his neck barely to see the apple on the tabletop, and the intuition of the man of the house who takes the apple and gives it freely to his dinner guest.*[109] That the difference in intuitions falls between physically separate beings, a child and a father, is trivial for a theory of multiple subjects, although of course the difference in power relations is critical for Kafkan social theory. Important for us is the fact that the subjects are as separate and incompatible as the intuitions they have of the single apple. The unity of the object leads to the diversity of subjects.

The unity of the object becomes an index, then, of the polyspectivity among a company of subjects; whether this occurs within or between physical beings doesn't matter. One must remember that this is not a psychological theory but an echontological one. In a psychological theory of a multiple subject, Freud's topographical model for instance, the regions of the landscape are ultimately incorporated into one psyche that owns them. One "has" repressions in the same way that one "has" parents.

Kafka's theory could be psychological only at the point where a schizoid psychology goes completely over into social theory, into a social theory that does not tolerate the diminishment of the number of possible intuitions of any single object and thus does not diminish the number of possible psyches.

Polyspectivity among a company of subjects, who, one imagines, themselves might contain or be or be dispersed into a multiplicity—where would this multiplication stop?—this has an understandably negative effect on the medium of space. If the boy could reach for the apple, would he reach out the same distance and find it in the same place as the master of the house? Does the guest receive the apple at the coordinates where it is left by the master?

A general schema of an uncoordinated spatiality grows out of the theory of multiple subjects, and this leads Kafka, perhaps with oblique reference to the theory of special relativity, to the effects of multisubjectivity on time.[110] A well-known parable written down among the thoughts recounts *an everyday occurrence,* which Kafka calls *an everyday heroism. A. has to finalize an important piece of business with B. from the neighboring town H.* This simple task is the most difficult for the self who does not know it is multiple. One character's instant does not coincide with another's, perhaps owing to the fact that the character's instant does not coincide with his own. Time seems to stretch and contract, but this is an effect of the displacement of time points, of multiple simultaneities that make it next to impossible for the A. within A. who has business with B. to meet up with his business partner.[111] The postulate of multiple instants within and between subjects does not nullify traditional temporality; it only complicates it to the nth degree. Kafka pushes this temporal argument to its most extreme stage in a later thought: *A. could neither live united with himself nor leave himself, and therefore he shot himself; he thought in this way he could unite the un-unitable* [das Unvereinbare vereinigen zu können], *riding off into the sunset with himself.*[112] Despite his valiant attempt to bring various A.'s together in death, this one A. cannot derive wholeness from finitude.[113] This seems to be the limit of a certain logic: even in death "A." cannot find the potential for unity. Death gives no possibility; the view of finitude as the source for possibility is an idyll about an ultimate reduction to a single self. Even if I can't find my one self in life, after all is said and done, I alone will die—no one else.

Where multiple intuitions of a single object mean multiple subjects that do not meet even in death, and multiple instants mean that these subjects do not always meet themselves, or if they do it is by chance, the underlying principle of multiplicity differs in character from a principle of unity. These are less concepts or states of being than principles of activity. Unity reduces, multiplicity multiplies itself. In other words, the same dynamism that would allow a transcendental reduction to unity, produces an explosion of multiplicities. This seems to be what happens when the transcendental unity of the self is denied: reduction and deduction become instantly explosion and dispersion.

If this is the case, when you go seeking yourself, you should be seeking another and ever another, where you least expect yourself. One place to do this is in travel literature.[114] *It is too narrow for me in everything I signify, even the eternity that I am is too narrow for me. If for example I read a good book, some sort of travel description, it wakes me up, it gratifies me, it satisfies me.* Kafka names two affects or dispositions associated with the movement toward the foreign: exhaustion (*Müdigkeit*) and refreshment (*Erfrischung*). The former is a result of the experience of a single consciousness thinking that it is eternally itself; the latter is a result of superconscious travel, which in this case corresponds to reading. And yet the assimilative powers of reflective knowledge are almost too strong for these excursions from the self. *From a certain level of knowledge onward, exhaustion, dissatisfaction, narrowness, self-disdain must disappear, namely at the point where I have the power to know as my own essence what as a foreign thing earlier freshened, satisfied, emancipated, elevated me.* Reflective knowledge enters and incorporates foreignness. The feeling of freedom and new life is quashed when knowledge assimilates and homogenizes it. At that point the foreign thing did not only *cease being foreign, but moreover it began to be "I."* Kafka adds a note. *But the foreign that you are is no longer foreign.* The negation of everything foreign by reflective consciousness is as narcissistic and world-denying as Hegel's absolute subject. If consciousness negates everything foreign by assimilating it, there is a contradiction. Echoes of a problem in German idealism can be heard just here. "I am I" is tautological and empty, Fichte discovered; "I am not not I" brings the world into the self, however, in a world-cancelling way. The foreigner that you are is, by means of this negation, no longer foreign, but the negative image of you, an image, once again yours. And this is logically impossible, since, where you justify yourself on the basis of the foreign, you cannot at the same time assimilate it. *Saying this you repudiate the creation of the world and refute yourself.*[115]

One way to avoid this dilemma is to sidestep reflection and its appetite for incorporating and assimilating. At one instant Kafka imagines a tripartite or rather a dual (that is, self-diminishing) atheological formula for avoiding reflection:

> *Threefold:*
> *Looking at oneself as something foreign*
> *Forgetting the look at oneself*
> *Retaining the profit*
> *Or only twofold, since the third encompasses the second.*[116]

12. Two-Sided Faith

Kafka is attracted to faith even though he knows he has to find a way to struggle against it. He is attracted to it because to his mind it does not accede to being but offers in its place a mode of not-being, and his respect for it grows the more it causes him to struggle. Brod, taking his cue from their friend Hugo Bergmann, proposed that love and neigh-borly work could bring about moral change, which he called grace, in this world.[1] To some degree it may have been Brod's certainty that grace could be achieved that impelled Kafka to struggle, not against grace, work, or love, but against certainty in their rewards, where certainty was the profit faith paid to the present. Certainty was an immediate reward; it had to be, since what is to come is constitutively unpredictable (oth-erwise it is in some form already here). In neither case, if the future is unpredictable or if the future is already here, does one need certainty. Only in one case does certainty make sense. Faith was a bulwark against an uncertain future, a construction, a security measure, a Tower of Babel that more often than not failed at what it most desired, a moment's rest from falling. Faith is a minor term in the lexica of Weltsch and Brod, for whom love and freedom were the holy duo that brought *gratia sufficiens et efficax* into the world.[2] But faith is a major term in Kafka's thoughts. Secret justification and engine of grace, faith was present, though con-cealed, in all of Kafka's friends' theological plans and convictions.

Here was a term, a concept, or better, an activity, that did not take for granted the possession character of being.[3] What-is, what-truly-is, is that which we do not possess—or so it proposes. Yet faith is also a carefully timed plan for repossession; this is how Kafka saw it.[4] On one hand, when we have faith we actively own up to the dispossessed character of being; we get comfortable with not-having, with not being what we by rights ought to be or are. And yet, on the other hand, in faith, in the word, in the concept, and especially in the activity, a duplicity operates. Faith has two faces. We place our faith in something, and that something, by a clandestine transfer, places itself into us such that we are empowered to believe. That something Kafka calls "the indestructible"—this is for him the only thing that would be worthy of what we call faith. But where does it reside, the indestructible—in eternity or in us? The answer is obvious. *The human being cannot live without an enduring trust in something indestructible within himself, whereby the indestructible thing as well as the trust can remain enduringly hidden from him.*[5] The nature of faith undergoes a critical operation here. In the everyday, faith looks just like trust, a relatively long-lasting trust, but trust nonetheless. And trust is subjective. As we usually conceive of it, it proceeds from a subject toward an object. Indeed, faith is the subjective side of the relation with God, and yet by rights it should not be possessed *by* the subject of faith; it somehow ought to spring *from* its object—ought it not?[6] How would it be worthy of the highest thing if it did not come from it? And this is perhaps why the enduring trust in the indestructible must remain enduringly hidden. To this Kafka adds a codicil: *one of the possibilities for expressing this remaining-concealed is the faith in a personal god.*[7] In other words, the personal god comes to stand in for and camouflage the subjective and even psychological nature of faith.

Why can one not "trust" openly in this thing that cannot be destroyed? Why is it not cause for public celebration, this inner relation to a permanent core of oneself, this trust? Instead of making us joyful, for Kafka, trust should cause us to blush. In theories of the soul, the indestructible part of man is what is supposed to commune with or participate in the indestructible per se. *The indestructible is one; each individual human being is it and at the same time it is common to all, hence the unparalleled indivisible connection of human beings.*[8] The oddity of faith is elaborated here: the indestructible is within each and somehow also at the same time outside of any single individual. What's more, the word enduring—"enduring trust"—sounds all the weaker for being blatantly temporal and in truth also temporary—as though something that was

"lasting" could ever lead to something "everlasting."⁹ Faith exhibits this
terrible duplicity: it is subjective but claims to be objective or holistic, it is
human but also divine, it is temporary but also eternal.

Faith's doubleness or duplicity was obviously not absent from theological discourse before Kafka. Luther's dictum brings faith's duplicity
back into religious consciousness with a crash. Only faith, faith alone,
but whose faith, from whom to whom, in whom, by whom? Faith must
bring together the most unequal of partners, but it itself must remain
one, unaided, the only one and one only. If one wanted to, one could
trace the duplicity in Luther's word to the differences between Pauline
and Johannine teachings, or between the Dominican and the Franciscan
interpretations of church doctrine. To a great extent in Luther, faith's duplicity expresses itself as a conflict between the heart, the faculty of faith,
and the Word, its instrument, object, cause and effect. Yet the duplicity
is also in the Word, since it is both the transmitter and receiver of faith.
Scripture brings faith to us and also demands faith from us. John records
Jesus enjoining his public to have faith in his Word, but more precisely
to have faith, through his Word, in his Father.¹⁰ Does one have faith in
the word or through it? Paul, in contrast, emphasizes the passions that
fill one with faith: in the main, joy and peace.¹¹ Is faith a passion or is
it . . . something higher? The heart is in the word, and yet the word must
come from elsewhere. And, too, heart and Word—a pair Luther tries
to synthesize—are dissimilar media, often at odds, certainly a doublet
that would have to be overcome to achieve a consistent idea of faith. As
they bring faith near, heart and Word add a new distance. If Luther had
been able to say "faith!" by itself, it would have been a signal that he had
overcome the duality. That he had to add "alone," or "only" does not just
indicate the rejection of the Church as an aide to faith, which is what the
word also implies; "alone" also indicates a worry about the source and
the exclusivity of faith. For if no other force supports it—language or
feeling—the only route to faith is faith itself, through faith to faith, as
the catchphrase at Romans 1:17 tells us, and so it is also internally riven,
self-distancing, and in search of itself from before it is even thematized as
the fundament of church and the salvation of the ecclesia.

This distance, the internal striving between faith and itself, which is
the same as that between the divine gift of faith and the all-too human
use of it, may reflect an ancient distance within Greek *pistis*, between
conviction and persuasion. Religion—Protestantism, certainly, but per-

haps all Abrahamic religions—occupies the distance within faith, filling
it with logic and images, stories and principles, liturgies and practices,
but it does not and cannot annul the distance. Another way to express
this: *whoever believes cannot experience a miracle. By day one does not see
stars.*[12] Religion's major task, one surmises then, is to conceal the internal, anxiety-provoking disunity of faith, an incompleteness and incoherence without which, however, religion would have nothing to do, no
room to move. Were it not necessary to *say* and separately to *feel* that "it
is by grace you have been saved, through faith—and this is not from
yourselves, it is the gift of God," it might be simple enough to have this
faith alone (Eph. 2:8). John's Jesus is very sensitive to this problem: "I am
the resurrection and the life. The one who believes in me will live, even
though they die; and whoever lives by believing in me will never die. Do
you believe this?" (John 11:25–26).

Do you believe this? Christ adds another faith, a third kind, the faith
needed to approach and possess the life-giving faith, which comes second. With this we arrive at the matter of possession. One comes to possess faith through getting and keeping faith in faith. "Si credis, habebis,
si non credis carebis," Luther says: "Glaubst du, so hast du" (If you believe, you have); the corollary being of course, "Glaubst du nicht, so hast
du nicht" (If you don't believe, you don't have).[13] The peculiar marriage
of faith and possession also has precursors, some called upon and others
not called upon by Luther;[14] he both does and does not want to admit
that faith is an ersatz mode of possessing. At one crucial moment John
lets Jesus say that the believer already "has" eternal life, as soon as he
believes (John 5:24). This statement closes down the rift within faith too
quickly, and yet even within this hurried statement there operates the
very persuasion that has to happen before one gets faith. It is perhaps
Paul's greatest gift to have articulated this movement. There is, in the
words of Romans 1:17, a righteousness of God himself that consists solely
in a movement toward faith, "a righteousness from faith unto faith" (*ek
pisteōs eis pistin*) that is revealed in Jesus' good news (Rom. 1:16). In a
manner of speaking, faith moves constantly to take possession of faith,
and this movement toward itself—from persuasion to conviction, word
to heart, faithful to God—betokening an unbridgeable distance, is the
duplicitous means by which the faithful imagine they will earn or have
already earned (unbeknownst to them) eternal life. This is just a manner of speaking, since, insofar as the self-possession of faith has to be

asserted, faith is the very fact we are to be persuaded of. "Do you believe this?" Such an epistemic question should call into question every claim that one "has" faith. Through faith one obtains faith in possession of the most enduring thing, eternal life; the good news is this news, the news about faith, and concealed within it is a negative scripture, the dilemma that to believe the message, notwithstanding Paul's eagerness with regard to the Romans, one would need to have had faith already.[15]

This history of splits and doubles in the idea of faith insinuates itself into Kafka's treatise in thoughts. One way it entered was through Kierkegaard, whose paradoxical presentations of faith Kafka read some of later in the winter of 1918.[16] In a letter to Oskar Baum, he mentions reading *Fear and Trembling* and calls Kierkegaard "a star." To Kafka, who was hugely sensitive both to the ambiguities of images and to his friend Baum's blindness, this must have been an ambiguous image. A star to a blind man would be a missing light, a light for everyone except for the one who needed it, a light to stumble around by, or a point of total indifference. Was it made any brighter when he shared this star of faith with Baum? And let's mention another theological event, also involving his blind friend—when Baum visited Zürau at the beginning of January, Kafka read aloud to him an astounding article by Ernst Troeltsch. On this occasion, Baum and Kafka, each in his own way no doubt, listened to the story of how Luther inaugurated and at the same time inhibited progress in Christian history. Kafka learned then from the scholar-theologian Troeltsch how the Protestant Reformation was most interesting for its inner contradictions.[17] With profound ambivalence, Troeltsch publicly celebrated the quadricentennial of Luther's Ninety-five Theses, while Kafka was privately preparing his three hundred or so thoughts, many of which celebrated the inner contradictions of the same theologoumena. The Kafkan atheological reformation takes this from the Lutheran reformation as Troeltsch understood it: a reformation is more interesting for the contradictions it preserves and transmits than for those it resolves.[18]

Luther's Reformation did not so much overcome medieval prejudices as send them underground. Erasmus, Luther's great antagonist (and German idealist *avant la lettre*, or so says Troeltsch) placed his hopes for reform in human reason and the freedom that comes from autonomy,[19] whereas Luther's Reformation carried forward the restrictive institutions of salvation, secreted within the reformed confession and glossed over by the word "reform." Modernity is a continuation of the Middle Ages in slightly altered form. Institutions like the monk's ethic were transferred to the routines of everyday life. The new obedience was a self-subjugation to faith, and the new Church was scripture. Far from being rid of the Church, "the institution of salvation contracted itself in the miracle of scripture and grew back out of it."[20] No less miraculous, no less institutionalized, no less powerful and present, no less demanding of obedience, and yet much more clandestine and so perhaps more effective because harder to resist, the very absence of freedom that marked the ascetic lifestyle and the Church's doctrinal and professional hierarchy liberated itself once and for all from any limits in Luther's claim to have overcome it. Unfreedom intensified itself in the "freedom" of a Christian. In the loose hands of the old Church the route to grace had still been negotiable, proper conduct was various and revisable, there was a difference between the cleric and the layperson, the institution and the congregation. When freedom became not just attainable but assured through faith and scripture, *norma doctrinae* and *medium gratiae,*[21] unfreedom disseminated. Modernity was a farce in which the most intensive submission masqueraded as the purest liberty.

In carrying the Middle Ages into the middle of the modern, Luther also carried forward a healthy confusion, what Troeltsch calls "the conscious paradox of his faith."[22] This overt acknowledgement may have secretly pleased Kafka. All Luther's concepts, at least the early ones, were double, and some were ambiguous to the point of madness; a few were even self-contradictory, until in his later writing he became possessed with establishing a doctrinal legacy and because of this his concepts became "flattened." Troeltsch gives an example of one such early paradox: the certainty of grace comes only when one sins continually; this is the perverse ratio of Lutheran salvation.[23]

The new miracle and the new church is grace; and faith is at once the foundation of the institution and the access to the miracle. Because he conserves the miracle, internalizes it, leaves it unexplainable, and makes us unfree with respect to it and only free "through" it, Luther is "an endlessly conservative revolutionary."[24] Because this unexplainable moment is within us and we are totally beholden to it, the paradox of faith is endlessly troubling. Salvation, mediated by faith, is "in the world and yet not of the world."[25] Indeed, faith has become the unique this/other worldly contradiction, the site, we could say, of the ontic-ontological difference. So great is this paradox that other theologoumena no longer even really count. Miracle before miracle, grace before grace, "the authentic miracle is faith" writes Troeltsch:[26] because it cannot be, it is. It has what it is and it is what it lacks, faith: the self-seeking given. Only in not finding itself does it preserve the miracle that it is. *Whoever believes, cannot experience a miracle. By day one does not see stars.*[27] Kafka wrote this on November 21 or 22, 1917, more than a month before he read Troeltsch to Baum. This fact is no miracle. Kafka develops faith out of the unmiraculous, an arena populated by fakes, frauds, impostors, and other darknesses against which a light point can be surprising. In one sense, then, these are the real miracles, the endarkening conditions for the twinkling of a star. That is to say that in Kafka's thought, faith dwells farthest from the divine, among the infidels. As Max Brod is fond of mentioning derisively in his treatise, *Heidentum, Christentum, Judentum*, Luther wrote to Melanchthon, "be a sinner and sin boldly," for there is no grace without plentiful sin of which to repent.[28] This is the part of Luther's personal religious experience, the experience of a continual impossibility, that he transmits into the new confession. For this reason Troeltsch calls Protestantism a "transitional construct" (*Übergangsgebilde*),[29] which now—in 1917/18—has to be overcome, and this for the theologian means finally resolving the central Lutheran conflict. Luther transformed the ancient *complexio oppositorum* into a *coincidentia oppositorum*, the most important step toward simplification (*Vereinfachung*) and summary (*Zusammenfassung*) that would need one more stroke to remove these oppositions for good.[30]

In the article Kafka encountered a typology of opposition that must have reminded him of his own. He also became familiar with the historian's image of a sudden *Verinnerlichung* of European experience, an internalization of theological structures that is also said to be the advent of the modern subject and psyche. He could also hear echoes of another interior, the hidden recess of history, not the salvation history that would have been the outer shield of Protestant theology, which Nietzsche is often remembered for denouncing, but the troubled and troubling, conflictual and self-concealing origin of these doublets and duplicities in scripture.[31] He may have found to his surprise in January, reading Troeltsch on Luther to Baum, confirmation for some of his thoughts from November and December and courage, even a reason to continue. The revolutionary tone of the article was unmistakable. Troeltsch lauds Luther for preserving "the salt of renewal" for European intellectual life, even if "admittedly in its restless movement [this life, its conflict] must be resolved always anew."[32]

Troeltsch wants to exchange salvation history for the quintessentially modern history of continual conflict and resolution. Yet there is a different way to see this history. You can argue that, if stars are not visible by day, if miracles are not for the faithful, they have strictly nothing to do with faith. Where there are miracles, there is no faith. Miracles, if they are truly miracles, are atheological: they do not need faith and indeed may destroy it.[33] Where there is faith, there is no miracle, and if faith becomes the miracle, it only in fact exists in the most rigorous abstention from belief. An extreme mode of *apistis* that is not doubt drives atheology. Kierkegaard certainly does not go this far. The leap leaps over this strict inversion; the leap goes too far in order to arrive at faith; how far would Kierkegaard have had to go to think faith as there where it is not needed and needed only where it is not achievable?

13. Faith and World

The worry that faith is hubristic, that it is actually incommensurate with its object, produces the discourse on faith, inside and outside scripture. To be worthy of its object, faith—as a carefully timed plan for the repossession of fundamental goods—must be able to hold in its memory God the Father, the next life, the miracle of the passion and death, Abraham's sacrifice, and so forth and at the same time not make them so present that it obviates the need for itself. It must give it all up, to be sure, but in a remembering and thus a possessive way, and, in exchange, it cannot allow you to believe that giving up is all there is to faith. Faith gives up possession but never gives up the principle of possession and the image of what it desires to possess. Faith has, in the meantime, images and principles. In light of this, it is not necessarily wrong to say, as Felix Weltsch does, that "it [faith] is the thing that defines everything. It gives religious experience its meaning and sense, it creates truth and existence, indeed it also creates God."[34] And yet, Weltsch also gives a very negative description of this theologoumenon. Faith appears as a deception, as in Feuerbach; it projects, inverts, and consequently conceals the real processes behind it. It seems at first that Weltsch simply sees the critique of religion in positive terms: for example, whereas Feuerbach sees faith as an act of projection, Weltsch sees it as an act of creation. As we have seen, he describes the precise mechanism by which faith creates. "Faith overcomes itself when it creates. For as soon as something is actually believed, it no longer says: it is, because it is believed, but rather: it is believed, because it is."[35] This kind of inversion is common to critiques of religion, but here there is an added dimension: an acknowledgement of faith's power to modify the way fundamental things appear. The critical gesture is to say: faith is not faith in something that preexists it; it creates its object and through its phenomenal powers makes it appear to precede what created it. Weltsch says this, using the German idealist vocabulary that he favors, often also following his chosen model, who is none other than Troeltsch. Creation, positing, faith—the philosophy of reason and the theology of creation undergo a great reconciliation in Weltsch's book *Gnade und Freiheit*.[36] On some counts he reminds us of Kant. Faith takes a subjective and relative judgment, "I believe," and presents it as an objective and absolute, "it is."[37] Faith wants to posit being (*er will konstatieren*). It doesn't want to seem to create, it wants to seem to confirm what is (*Vorhandenes feststellen*). "It says A is B and not: I make A into B."[38] This is the point at which Kafka parts company with his friend. To be sure, this is a powerful description of faith's ontological mechanism. Perhaps Kafka adopted this structure from the texts by Weltsch that he read before that winter (*Gnade und Freiheit* he read in manuscript and later corrected the proofs). On November 12, 1917, Weltsch writes Kafka about the difficulties he is having developing his ethics project, which turned into this book. On November 21 or 22, Kafka severs faith from its power. It cannot position itself after its creation and make us believe in a preexisting world, since *one does not see stars*.[39] Outside its peculiar deficiencies, outside an almost total context of faithlessness, disbelief, confusion, and suffering, faith cannot affirm anything. On November 31 or December 1, he went a step further. *Faith means: emancipating the indestructible* [das Unzerstörbare] *within oneself or better: emancipating oneself or better: being indestructible or better: being.*[40] Being is what faith means, despite its dalliance with nonbeing. Faith substitutes for being where being could not by right or by power fulfill its promise to provide us with possession. As merely a promise, faith is in fact the better fulfillment. It gives us being without any right or power over it. It gives us the highest being and the meaning of being, which otherwise eludes our possessive gestures. The indestructible within us is what being wants and faith has. Faith means, *bedeutet*, being; and this act, *bedeuten*, is not quite the same thing as Weltsch's description of faith's creative power.

The friends' projects run parallel for a while but soon deviate. Weltsch's faith, in its groundlessness and positing power, is a propae- deutic to the highest freedom, which is the freedom to create. Here he departs from Luther along Troeltschian lines. Protestantism erases every moment of freedom with its doctrine of grace.[41] The antidote to this is to free up freedom, by means of faith to be sure, but in order to become this means faith must be reconceived as a free decision, an act of will raised to an act of creation, where "A is B" is not a judgment but a posit. It must be noted that the two, act of will and act of creation, differ only in scope for Weltsch. An act of will is the overcoming of an obstacle, an act of creation is the free positing of a world. Weltsch's reading of Schelling here is contaminated by a certain reading of Nietzsche: "there are free decisions of the will by human beings of such penetrating power that in them nature is recreated, reborn."[42]

The book promotes faith as the sense (*Sinn*) and power (*Kraft*) of life. On the first page Weltsch quotes post-conversion Tolstoy: "without faith man cannot live." Kafka modifies this sentiment to: "without enduring trust in the indestructible in himself and an enduring concealment of this from himself, man cannot live." Two changes are remarkable in the Kafkan modification: faith has not only religious or theological objects. It is attracted to the indestructible in any form, and as the sine qua non of living, it is first and foremost attracted to something like the self—the very self that could enact a "free decision of the will."[43] Secondly, it must remain concealed. Weltsch's faith precedes god, is equivalent to a pure act of mind. The power of Kafkan faith seems to be derived from its concealment. The whole complex operation has to be hidden away, and this is the source of faith's effectiveness. By concealing its dependency on an indestructible that precedes it, faith presents itself as the only way to the miraculous, transcendent, divine, by feeling or by absurdity, by step or by leap.

The difference between Weltsch and Kafka on the meaning and value of faith is perhaps also due to a difference in the meaning of world. Weltsch puts the great power of faith into human hands, where it becomes something like a faculty, in keeping with the philosophical vocabulary he admires. Kafka agrees that faith is necessary for life in the world, but he disagrees, let us say, on the value of the faithful life. Weltsch celebrates it. "Faith lends [*verleiht*] the finite existence of human beings a sense of infinity—a sense that will not be destroyed through suf-

fering, through lacks, through death."[44] The Schleiermacherian mood of
this is unmistakable. Weltsch has faith take possession of the infinite as
the meaning of existence. And if it cannot claim to be *of* or *from* the infinite, that is, if it cannot bring about actual infinitude, it can "lend" the
world an infinite meaning. Weltsch does not change the negative aspect
of faith: world cannot possess the infinite, and faith is an expression of
this nonpossession. It can, however, have the infinite on long-term lease.
Here Weltsch alters the modality of faith slightly. Instead of a promise
of future possession, one possesses all of being, the infinite, though with
two caveats. Possession is revocable, that is temporary, and possession is
indirect: one does not have being but only a "sense" of it. That the indestructible appears here is not a surprise, although it is quite diminished—
what one has is an indestructible sense.

Kafka, more than anyone I have come across, more than Weltsch certainly, yields to faith. Call it a struggle, a battle, *ein Kampf*: he loses,
although by giving in to its decisive characteristic, faith's duplicity, he
thereby lets it take its proper place. It turns out that those who believe
most resist faith most; they want it to become the principle of the world,
when in fact it is the principle of the world's incoherence. And so they
conceal its peculiar problem and conceal the concealment from themselves. Faith is not the same as having, as Luther thinks it is; it is not the
same as being, as Weltsch thinks it is. It is rather a distancing gesture by
which the great force of illusion is called into action. It is the expert teller
of tall tales. Faith produces a false distance between the believer and the
believed and then offers to bridge it, but at a high cost. The cost is the
disappearance of the whole operation.

Kafka supposed that so-called secular theory held onto an enduring
trust in something indestructible within the self; it held onto as well the
concealed self-concealment of the whole complex. Exposing the duplicity
of faith, he shows at the same time how it pervades all spheres equally.
The faith complex ignores the distinction between sacred and secular.
Whatever is called life is life by dint of faith. The most general motivation for this all-pervasive belief in faith he at other times called consolation (*Trost*), a "life affect" more necessary for living than any act or
concept, more necessary certainly than epistemic belief, although this
can also serve as a means to consolation.

To begin the process of yielding this belief, yielding to it and through
that yielding it up, one begins with the world, not an idealized world,

not one that is nursed along by its sense, its *Sinn*, but this world. Much emphasis is placed on the demonstrative "this" in the thoughts. But what is "world"? We cannot know it in total or in general, only in some of its traits, of which some are more and some less definitive, and one trait is the most definitive. *The decisive characteristic of this world is its transitoriness* [Vergänglichkeit]. *In this sense, centuries have nothing on the momentary moment* [haben dem augenblicklichen Augenblick nichts voraus]. *The continuity of transitoriness can therefore offer no consolation* [Trost]; *that new life blooms out of the ruins demonstrates less the endurance of life than the endurance of death. If I want to battle against this world now I must battle it in its decisive characteristic, thus in its transitoriness. Can I do that in this life and indeed in actuality, not only through hope and faith?*

You thus want to battle the world but with weapons that are more actual than hope and faith. There probably are such weapons, but they are only knowable and usable under certain conditions [Voraussetzungen]. *First I want to see if you have these conditions.*[45]

The minor mistake of those who believe in faith, Kafka might say, is that what they think exalts actually diminishes. Yes, faith drags God out of heaven and makes him dance to a human tune. Beyond this something much nearer, a major mistake—reason is not faith's antipode; that is reserved for "world." Faith is a specific manner of fleeing the world. In this way "life" and "world" are opposed throughout the thoughts.[46] Life means looking away from the world toward a higher purpose, by means of a faith that lifts one's gaze. And here Kafka raises an objection. In the attitude of faith one does not struggle against the world, one flees it, leaves it to itself; in effect the world conquers the faithful precisely to the extent that they believe in something other than it. When one decides to flee from it, the world has in effect already won.

Important Kafkan categories emerge in the reflection on the world's "decisive characteristic": conditionality, the decisive factor (*das Entscheidende*), antipathy to hope and faith, the "this" of the world and the kinds of battles (*Kämpfe*) one can wage against it, weapons (*Waffen*) appropriate for such battles, consolation (*Trost*), transitoriness (*Vergänglichkeit*), the continuity of death, and so forth. Yet we mustn't forget that in this thought a polylogue takes form: "I do this," to which someone responds, "you want this." The thought comes to no conclusion; it does not issue an injunction to do this or that. It is, rather, the event of a wish or a hope, and at the same time a caution. I want to battle the world. You must first say what the world is and then you can find the weapons to subdue it, or at least to resist it.

We immediately understand that this battle is not against faith and certainly not against believers. A speaker proposes that the world is the target of his struggle: this is the position of one who has faith. The speaker then asks what would actually be needed to overcome it. And the answer is not faith. We don't yet know what about the world provokes one to struggle against it, but we hear that the struggle commonly employs hope and faith as weapons. The world, as Kafka understands it here, is pure actuality; it is what is the case. What faith and hope are supposed to provide, a thought of the reversal of everything that is the case in the medium of progressive time, is thus useless against the world. Nothing possible has an effect on the actual world, and the world is always actual. How can we understand this? Birth, growth, development, "life" thought of as a lifetime with stages along the way, cosmic movement, history, revolution, and change per se all imply that actuality is to come—all of these are weapons of faith, akin to hope. One hears an echo of Marx here, although Kafka seems not to have read him: a call to transmute the critique of weapons into weapons that critique. Kafka begins, in this call and response, the call for an actual battle against the possible, and for that he has to find a way to cancel or suspend hope or faith. Assuming you can become able even to imagine such conditions, I want to battle the world without an image of a future, without a promise, without redemption or change, without past, paradise, origin, and thus without a present either.

First, you will have to imagine a world without possibility, and this means without becoming. Kafka chooses to do this by proposing a world without the flow of time. The problem is a deep one: how to imagine a world in which actuality is not a transitory stage between possibilities. Kafka's answer is to leave no time for transition, no room—between or across moments—for actualization. No moments. His thought is not of eternal repetition but of paralysis. The world is barren; it does not know birth. The lively life of life is death. One comes to the world to die swiftly and properly and once and for all. Hope has no hold, but this can be said better in reverse. Hope had always hidden the world's decisive characteristic. The psychological side of faith, hope allowed the world to appear as not-transitory, as duration. Instead of a continuity of duration, Kafka proposes a continuity of transitoriness. The only promise a constant, and instant, passing makes is to dash every hope, even a hope some have placed in the instant itself. On the continuum of dashed hopes, which here stands in place of our concept of time, the instant cannot be an *Übergang*,[47] a way across, but only an *Untergang*, a downfall or demise, which is not, however, to be confused with descent. Zarathustra's *Untergang*, the pantomime of a descent from the heights of reflection to the nadir of communication, is not the issue here. One way to yield to faith is to give it its power without holding anything back. Faith lends the world its continuity of duration, and buries the continuity of dashed hopes. Don't despair! When hopes are dashed continually there is no time for hope. A strange kind of happiness becomes possible when hope is abandoned in the smashing of time. It is actual happiness, dependent on no hope for a better one. *Theoretically there is a perfect* [vollkommene] *possibility of happiness: to believe in the indestructible within oneself and not strive toward it.*[48] This thought, however, predicts a theoretical happiness. A practical happiness would of course be the opposite of what could be articulated theoretically in a *pensée*, pure actuality. In sum, duration is the medium of world flight, hope its guiding feeling, possibility its modality. And yet, from the perspective of thinking, actual happiness might look exactly like despair, like hopelessness. In the shackles of this dialectic, there is a single effect, a "perfect possibility," which as soon as it becomes possible becomes actual. This is one of the conditions for battling the world in its decisive characteristic—a weapon of high sophistication. A possible that is so possible it is immediately actual would return one directly to "this" world. And here is the single option: sever faith from striving. That is to say: eradicate time as a medium of possession and turn possibility into fiction.[49]

"Transitoriness" has to be distinguished from the Kierkegaardian term that was in the air and in the Kierkegaardian texts Kafka was reading that fall and winter, the instant, *der Augenblick, Øieblikket*. It is not enough to theorize "the instant," or even to exist in it, to capture what Kafka means by "Vergänglichkeit." The instant, although it doesn't have duration, still has that other trait of traditional time, direction, and thus it is not transitory but transitional, and that is why it can be analogous to a leap. In it the impossible becomes possible. Nothing is said here of the actual. The knight of faith takes a leap.[50] Yes, Kafka replies, the leap leaps over the actual. It has nothing to do with the world and so does not actually resign or renounce anything; the world grows stronger in it; the world is all the more justified when you flee from it—because it is the one thing you cannot flee; when you leap it, the world claims you fully for it. From the perspective of possibility, the leap leaps out of the world. From the perspective of actuality, it is the more strongly trapped. Why? Because no matter how short the instant is it still has duration, enough to get a foothold, enough to renounce or to pretend to renounce, enough ground in this world to use it as a springboard for leaping. Otherwise Abraham would not have been fool enough to attack his son, bundle him up, lug him up the mountain, and give him the gift of a trauma that never ends. Heaven has already come to earth. And so there is no resignation, no "giving up" because time is still expected to pass and to give it all back. Even those who worry about the future are less pretentious than this. *Whoever only cares for the future is less precautionary than whoever cares for the moment, because the latter doesn't care at all for the moment, only for its duration.*[51]

Kierkegaard's leap stays with Kafka, but in a strong sense he was already over it. The leap requires a foothold beyond the single individual, a foothold in duration, for its launch. "He who loves God in faith reflects upon God."[52] Conversely, a continuum of transitoriness whose units are momentary moments offers no place to stand, no time for reflection. What is needed, instead of a knight of infinite resignation, whose mood is despair and whose walk is nonetheless "light and bold,"[53] is *to grasp the happiness/luck* [Glück] *that the ground on which you stand can be no bigger than the two feet that cover it.*[54]

An ontological principle of parsimony might be formulated with this as one of its expressions.[55] Feet yes, but no foothold: there is no broader basis for my being than the narrow place I take up. Nothing has a reason to be what it is or how it is beyond its slim perch, and this says something in addition about the principle of sufficient reason, as well as about principles per se, which always go beyond, are broader, more solid, dependable, more explanatory, sufficient, than things alone.

There is little precarious, risky, or existential about a leap. If you can do it, you are already on solid ground. What was formerly assured by mystical union, natural reason, scripture, Church sacrament, and so forth, is now assured by the leap. And this very grounding of the leap, its surety and fixity, implies a world firm enough and elevated enough to provide a jumping-off point. "The dialectic of faith is the finest and the most extraordinary of all; it has an elevation of which I can certainly form a conception, but no more than that. I can make the mighty trampoline leap whereby I cross over into infinity . . . "[56] Thus Kierkegaard. In defiance, Kafka: *the true way goes over* [geht über] *a rope that is not stretched up high but right over the ground. It seems more intended to make you stumble than to be walked on.*[57] In both H. C. Ketels's 1909 German translation of *Fear and Trembling* and *Repetition* (*Furcht und Zittern; Die Wiederholung*), which Kafka most likely read, and in Kafka's notebooks, the verb is *übergehen*.[58] Kierkegaard postulates a way to go over, *übergehen*, into infinity, while Kafka shows that the false height makes you stumble.[59] No doubt a confrontation between Nietzsche and Kierkegaard occurs in this line, between Zarathustra in his "Prologue"[60] and the knight of faith. Rather than stretched precariously over an abyss, this tightrope is so well grounded it lies on the ground and has just enough elevation to fool you into trying to walk on it. *In the battle between you and the world, take the side of the world* [sekundiere der Welt].[61]

14. Faith and Life

We have yet to encounter a negation of faith that does not breed a new, stronger and often more clandestine faith, either in an alternative to faith (such as despair, power, or the leap), or in the power that the negation of faith itself gives us. Kafkan atheology loves to expose forms of the bizarre equation: whatever claims to weaken faith makes it stronger. At the height of this activity atheology reveals that life itself is equivalent to faith.

"No one can say we lack faith. Alone the simple fact of our life can in no way have its faith-value used up." "There is a faith-value here? But no one can not-live." "Precisely in this "no one can not" hides the lunatic strength of faith; in this negation it gets its contour."[62] Two voices debate about faith. In truth it is no debate, because the first voice has laid a trap into which the second cannot help but fall. An argument is made by some in the "secular age" that a renewal of faith is necessary. But such a renewal is superfluous, because we do not lack faith. Life is pure faith, endless faith, or so the first voice proposes. The second insists that this is impossible, since in the secular view, life is all we have, and so we do not and indeed we cannot have faith in it. We have life, it is all there is and there is no alternative. We are not dispossessed of life, so why would we need faith in it? To the first voice, this insistence is sufficient proof that life is the object of the strongest faith—strong, enduring, self-concealing. When all else fails, after the death of god, the death of the soul, and the dissipation of world, the only *metaphysicum* left, it seems, is life. Whatever it might mean—life remains even when the other ideas have been sidelined or deconstructed. In the sentence, *the human being cannot live without an enduring trust in something indestructible*, the phrase "cannot live" indicates a similar iron sentiment.[63] When all

objects of faith are discredited or out of fashion, life, which underpins them anyway, appears and faith shows its "lunatic strength." The more thorough faith's negation, the more madly tenacious its hold.

If the treatise is obsessed with a single image, it is the image of the two trees in Eden. *Tree of life—master of life.*[64] Kafka recalls again and again that even after the Adamic transgression, the tree of life is still proscribed, and with the fall it becomes our master in all things. Two meanings of "life" are in operation here. The image of the tree dominates our experience of this lowly life. Another life, eternal life, is the object of faith. The proscribed tree gives a gift to faith: the two "lives" and the distance between them that it needs to operate. *We are reciprocally separated from God: the fall separates us from him, the tree of life separates him from us.*[65] This double-sided separation is the proper milieu of faith, we understand, but still: the thought empha-sizes the ends of the equation: fall and eternal life. What comes between them is not mentioned. Eternal life separates God from us; this life is that in Him which we desire and cannot have. In this way the tree casts its long shadow back over life. For only by perceiving our separation from it do we come to believe that our lot here is poorer. Through the perceived separa-tion, we learn that we are limited to the other tree and finite moral knowl-edge; through the perceived separation we learn that this life is toilsome, brutish, and finite. While we are standing facing this tree, it also faces us. We read on its face its special glory and its glory also shows us what we do not have. In its shadow and only in its shadow can this life be judged dis-possession, and thus we read in the tree of life the subordination of this life and make it our master. Faith in this life is faith that we are subordinated.[66]

Moral states of subordination, subjection, deferral, imperfect judgment, institutions such as law and politics, bodily processes that even when func-tioning well lead to decay and malfunction, not to mention wealth, com-munication of wisdom, social practices, and so on—everything we associate with the limited potentials of this life—are secondary objects of the same faith whose primary gesture is to reach toward the moment of their over-coming. The secular and the atheistic, the profane and all other things that we manage to think and do insofar as we think alternatives are only possible in another kind of life—these are all in fact themselves objects of faith, and, Kafka insists, this is the fiercest and most ineradicable kind of faith. It is, in this inversion, belief in this life—the belief that life is insufficient—that makes the higher faith and higher life necessary in the first place. "Life" in that event is the primary object of faith, faith that there is something like this-life that we could distinguish from not-this-life.

Two more voices speak. This time the topic is "justification," *Rechtferti-gung*. Voice A asks, *What does justification consist in for you?* Voice B replies in the negative, *I have none.* A is incredulous: *and you can live.* Voice B then explains why *Rechtfertigung* is unnecessary, and the explanation goes a long way toward clarifying the relationship between this life and faith, and it also gives a glimpse of an alternative. B. says: *For the very reason that I couldn't live with any justification at all. How could I justify the multiplicity* [Vielheit] *of my acts and the circumstances of my life.*[67] The logic here is complex, yet it is still Edenic. What is justification? It is an attitude that holds that life is or was good, on the basis of this or that reason. In order to give a reason that life was good, life would have had to be one thing with a single character. To justify life means to abrogate its multiplicity and thus not to live; there-fore, life is not justifiable and whatever can be justified is not life.

Life is not life, Kafka will go on to argue more generally, while trying to counteract this Edenic logic, if it is lived in view of anything outside it, whether that thing is the object of faith or the source for justification. Our task, then, will be to distinguish this lack of an outside from negative theolo-gies and atheisms. Like Kafka, we do not want to perpetuate the dialectical view that this life is one, that it is what it is and nothing else. For in this view the only hope for change comes from something outside, whether be-yond the end of time, after the revolution, or from something deeper inside, within its nature or its law. The truth is wholly outside it, the truth is wholly inside it—negative theology and atheism—both accounts lead to the same attitude: faith in one absolute meaning of this life. Transcendent and imma-nent theories are dialectical in this way. If the multiplicity of life cannot be overcome, however, then, while life certainly does have only an inside, the critical difference is that this inside does not hold one single truth. *Life means* [Leben heißt] *being in the middle of life.* If this sentence seems too much like the articulation of an immanent truth, Kafka goes on to propose that even this truth has to be seen from the middle of life. *To see life with the very same gaze with which I created it.*[68] We now have two alternatives to the "lunatic" faith in the absoluteness of this life (absolutely fallen, absolutely all there is). You can see this life as an unsynthesizable multiplicity, or you can see it as having only a middle and no ends, with the corollary that in any moment, since it has no beginning and no end, it has de facto been created by you. A third alternative suggests itself as well. How can you be sure that you have not secured your place in life through an illicit trip beyond it? How can you say "middle" without negatively indicating an origin or an end that would be "higher" that this life? How can you unseat the tree of life from its position as master? In February the third alternative suggests itself. *Two tasks of the beginning of life: to constrict your circle ever more severely and to check over and over again if you are not hiding somewhere outside your circle.*[69] Perhaps you can suspend faith in this life, if you accomplish two difficult tasks. You can restrict what you consider to be your life to the smallest possible scope. Yet you must also remain constantly vigilant that none of your activities within this scope have secretly communicated with anything outside it. This seems a high price to pay for ridding life of the "this," of the lunatic faith that it is not a matter of faith, but it is as of yet the only way Kafka thinks of. He imagines making the scope of this life so narrow that eternity doesn't notice it.

15. The Progress Idea

Solutions to perceived problems affecting Jews in Central Europe in the teens of the last century ranged from plans to leave Europe, en masse or family by family, to designs for renewed Judaisms in diaspora. The general feeling on all fronts however was that things needed to change and quickly. What the Jews should do in order to better their situation was a topic of constant and very public discussion, and Kafka was neither deaf to the urgent and conflictual clamor nor immune to the specific arguments being made. He read and heard much more about the matter than we can possibly reconstruct. A prominent position in these discussions was held by Martin Buber, who delivered a renowned series of lectures in Prague, at least one of which Kafka likely attended. In the "Three Speeches on Judaism," Buber rejected suggestions for "continuation and improvement" (*Fortsetzung und Verbesserung*) as weak and instead called for the immediate "reversal and conversion" (*Umkehr und Umwandlung*) of Judaism, which meant it had to pass through "a crisis and a shaking-up and a becoming new from its root all the way to the branches of its existence."[70] One thing that Kafka and Buber share, although it may be the only thing, is an aversion to the idea of progress. "Whoever is no longer able to demand the impossible can only achieve the all-too possible," Buber announces, decrying the diminishment of hope among contemporary European Jews. "One may only hope to become the exponent of a small 'progress'. . . ."[71] Kafka was looking for a way to liberate the entire "human and animal communities" of course, not the Jews in particular, but discussions of the Jews offered paradigms to which he could refer and from which he could deviate.

The tree of life may have been unreachable, but the Jews could have their own glorious existential tree—not grown over a long period, ring by ring, but born at full height and "new from its root." Buber's vocabulary hides few of its assumptions: the new tree that was supposed to spring to life in a blow would alter Judaism's political situation, but prior to this the Jews would have to revolutionize their sense of time. Jews were in a privileged position to develop a more radical temporality, he claimed, both for themselves and as an example to non-Jewish Europe, because their sense of time was already better developed than their sense of space. Territory still eluded them, but history had become their home. And yet this meant too that their sense of time was one of slow movement, tree-like growth. The psychological correlative of "Jewish" slow time was hope (*Hoffnung*), which was indeed "the authentically positive and constructive element" of Judaism throughout its history, even if Buber argued that it now needed to shift from hope for change to actual change.[72] Buber adds a messianic corollary to what he sees as Jews' settling for slow progress. The messiah is to come, but the idea of an absolute future has already arrived, and for this reason "messianism is Judaism's most deeply original idea."[73] The future is the source of renewal no doubt, and yet the future is already carried by Jews in the form of the messianic idea, which travels with them from their most ancient past. Renewal is not a question of time at all, it turns out. In keeping with his own Kierkegaardianism, Buber celebrates the true Jew, the one in permanent contact with her eternal substance, the one who communes with the unchanging absolute within her. The opposite figure is the *Trotzjude* who defiantly affirms her Jewishness as a reaction to being designated "Jew" by anti-Semites.[74] This is the reason for Buber's choice of the word "renewal" rather than transformation, revolution, resistance, or any other more historical term where difference outweighs identity. Through historical exigencies the Jews became temporal, yet the renewal of Judaism implies that time be shown to be illusion. This is not a contradiction, since everything Judaistic has both a relative and an absolute meaning. Time is its relative meaning, essence its absolute meaning, the former semblance, the latter truth. Until the absolute is attained, relative Jews (relative to other peoples, religions, to their own history, to God) battle against absolute Jews, in a dirty fight that takes "the form of an intellectual battle [*eines Geisteskampfes*]."[75] Each Jewish intellect is the scene of a fight between history and essence, and Buber in his "Three Speeches" presents a program to liberate each Jew from the retarding force of one on behalf of the other.

There is an intellectual equivocation here of course, which runs through Buber's three lectures like a red thread. Jews are only temporarily temporal, as the distinction between relative and absolute implies. Buber

has in mind, we are compelled to admit, a higher movement, a course
in which time itself undergoes a becoming: from false time to eternity.
Another time, true time, allows for the transition between relative and
absolute Judaism, between history and eternity. And this is precisely the
kind of intellectual trick and back door progressism that Kafka staunchly
refuses.

Early in the writing of the treatise, on October 20, 1917, Kafka records
a thought. We know that the weapons for battling this world have to be
"more actual" than faith and hope. Buber certainly agrees. Hope belongs
to gradual time, and faith is directly related to this, although how is another matter. What is clear to Buber is that "already in the most ancient
times in the middle of Jewish religiosity there stood not faith but the
act."[76] Acts change the world; faith and hope allow the world to continue
as it is until another day, holding onto time even where they promise
renewal, and they do this most significantly by presupposing a higher
temporal continuum in which this world is contiguous with another.
Kafka looks around for better weapons, one of which appears at first to
be, like Buber's, an "act," though a peculiar one. Kafka calls it "letting
fall" (*fallen lassen*). *The decisive moment* [Der entscheidende Augenblick]
of human development is when we let our concept of time fall everlastingly
[immerwährend]. *This is why revolutionary intellectual movements that declare everything previous null and void are right, since nothing has yet happened.*[77] Letting fall is Kafka's answer to the fantastical and contradictory
exhortation made by Buber: Jews should not hope that in time their circumstances will change, yet they will need at least some time in order to
shift out of hope and into true Jewish life. Kafka sets before our imaginations a special kind of moment, a moment until which nothing has been
decisive, and a special kind of act, one that doesn't do anything positive.
Formally speaking, the decisive moment is the first and only moment,
since it alone distinguishes itself from the time series, whose moments
are indistinguishable from one another. Here then is a profoundly anti-
temporal thought: the only event worthy of the name "Augenblick" is
the moment that marks the event in which time as we understand it
ceases to operate. Instead of the intellectual battle between temporal and
atemporal Judaisms, Kafka gives us a battle against the kind of intellect that limits itself to these two possibilities. The distance between his
"moment" and Buber's is vast. Is "the soul of Judaism [*Judentum*] ready
for the moment of liberation [*den Augenblick der Befreiung*]"?[78] Buber

describes a process of urgent development toward freedom, in which Jews become aware of their double self, the historical self and the coming future self. His rhetoric of drives and striving, progressive synthesis and growth, shared work toward a goal and activation [*Aktivierung*] in "the great process of Judaism" betray a belief in messianic progress from one to the other.[79] Buber urges Jews not to abandon progress but to speed it up. They should transition from physical to metaphysical time.

Just because time is not real, it does not follow that it therefore has to be ideal. Lending time the reality of spirit in place of the reality of the world shifts the locus but not the structure of progressive time. Kafka's pivotal thought tells us that time is neither real nor ideal but a concept, a *mere* concept we might add, and furthermore it is "our concept." Time is not the stuff of spirit, but a cognitive tool. Where faith is an attitude of the heart and hope an attitude of the psyche, time is an instrument used by cognition for particular purposes. Time is human, to be sure, but not exactly in the way Kant imagined. As a form of intuition and as the inner sense, time is still too necessary and too naturalized. Time *qua* concept is, conversely, neither naturally part of our cognitive structure nor is it necessary for our kind of experience. Instead, it is a habitual association, an instrument for understanding, and furthermore, it is one of our belongings. It is important that Kafka designates time a concept, but it is equally important that he says it belongs to us—it is "our" concept and indeed it may be the most carefully guarded possession we have. We possess it and in turn we are possessed by it; we cling to time when hope is our affect, faith our ontological position, and either radical change or slow improvement our desire. Both radical change and slow improvement, it should be said, presuppose a time through which—quickly or slowly—the good is attainable. Time is thus a pivotal moral concept, the one that allows us to recognize the defects of this moment in the light of a future moment.

Kafka does not think "improvement" should be a desire held by humans or for that matter by animals, though not because time is too slow. The idea of a medium in which the good can be secured comes under fire from all sides in the treatise.[80] In a parallel thought he refers to the time concept as "progress," and thereby clarifies its relationship to faith. *Faith in progress does not mean faith that progress has already happened. That would not be faith.*[81] Progress, a more precise expression of "our concept of time," is not a concept like other concepts. It is not a mental picture or a definition of time that makes our experience intelligible for us; progress is therefore more than a mere concept. It also involves a wish: that time turn out to be as it was conceptualized, a means for attaining the good. It is easiest to see this in contrast to the temporality of the understanding. The understanding can understand only things that have already happened; it allows judgment only of things that already belong to our experience. Progress, in contrast, is said of a future experience; it is an idea, and its faculty is consequently not understanding but faith.

We must gain a clear image of the circle that appears in this thought. Faith implies a movement toward the good or a movement of the good toward us, and the good and its movement implies faith in that movement. A look at the intentional structure of faith will help us see the nature of this circle. Faith has an in-what, a for-the-sake-of-which, a whether, and a by-means-of-what. The in-what of faith is the heart or some interior region of great power; its for-the-sake-of-which is the better life or the good or redemption; its whether is our certainty about future possession; and its by-means-of-which is progress (time) on one hand, and faith itself on the other hand. This last intentional vector is the more worrisome of them. The fact that there are two means for achieving faith's objective, progressive time and faith itself, is a sign that something is not right in the logic. To help us understand, we can observe how faith's structure differs from hope's: hope does not have a whether and it implies no means for fulfillment. It is only logical that hope has no opinion about whether it will attain its object; indeed it is totally indifferent to this. In addition to indifference about its fulfillment, hope also does not imply a means of attainment. How a hope will be fulfilled is left for another to say or attempt. In order to achieve what it wants, faith, conversely, provides its own means. If you have faith, the rhetoric goes, you will attain what you desire—given time and the potential for progress. Faith is both knowledge and act, and includes the certainty in eventual success (progress) and the means for attaining it (time). In this way, faith is internally divided into two modalities: *faith in* the existence and being of the divine and *faith that* we will arrive at it. And one could add a third division, whose modality is not at all clear: faith in faith. Yet the self-reference of faith here differs from the self-reference that Weltsch and Nancy venerate. Their circle of faith is creative. For Weltsch, faith freely posits its object and then it returns and treats it as given. The circle Kafka notices is a decreative circle. Faith in a means, progress, that will deliver faith its object, shows an empty spot in faith, a moment of fear that this attitude is not in full possession either of its own power or of the course of the future.

This circle is apparent in the idea of progress, the concept of time, and the attitude of faith—each assumes itself and projects itself as a means to become itself. And yet, although the idea, the concept, and the attitude are problematic in this way, in practice, things may be quite different. In 1920, around the time Kafka returned to the thoughts to add a few new ones, a fragment addresses a pragmatic consequence of sincere belief in the progress idea. "The most essential thing in the whole undertaking is the thought [*der Gedanke*] of building a tower that reaches into heaven. Next to this thought everything else is negligible. Once it is grasped in its greatness, the thought can never again disappear; as long as there are human beings, there will also be the strong wish to build the tower to its completion. In this regard therefore no one needs to worry about the future; on the contrary, humanity's knowledge increases, the art of building has made progress and will make further progress; a job for which we now need a year, in a hundred years perhaps takes only half a year and is better besides, more durable."[82]

The "strong wish" to build outweighs building itself, the passage reveals, and therefore the community does everything it can not to rush the project. The strong wish corresponds to faith in progress. If this faith were lost—it would be a catastrophe much greater than waiting another few years for the messiah to come. The loss of the progress idea would mean rebuilding humanity on another model. And furthermore, there is a structural reason that losing progress is unfavorable. When the building is finished, progress will perforce be abolished. What will humanity be like or do then? The story is told that, if things are truly going to be better in the future, one should not bother, with present imperfect methods, to hurry the future along. And so everyone takes their time—they take time, make time, but also through their sloth they produce a new dark age in which progress slackens gradually into total lassitude. In delaying completion and preserving the underlying, persisting, consoling wish for progress, they preserve the idea of progress but also abrogate its effects. An attack on progress may not be necessary if a purer and more complete faith in progress allows humanity to deviate from its path incessantly in the conviction that all it does belongs to the plan.

16. Letting Fall and Yielding

In part, the pivotal thought on time is still too Buber-ish, too messianic. And so the phrase *when we let our concept of time fall* gets edited out in the fair copy of the thoughts. This deletion makes sense: how can the act of abandoning time happen at a point in time? Abandoning time knows no when. If it happens within time it inaugurates a new series, which becomes an extension of the original series, and so on. Furthermore, what brings time to an end cannot be an act, if acting involves a duration in which the act would be carried out and a future in which it would have an effect. Still, "letting fall" implies an event that is not willed, not a "doing" but a "letting"; and it is also Kafka's attempt to articulate an event that is not a process and has no effects, a true end of time. Yet he abandons this formulation. According to Buber's own logic, the Jews are precisely not the ones to suspend time. Oriented toward an absolute future, Jews tend, according to Buber, toward acts in time—even if he urges them to speed up. Buber's Jews are more defined by their motor skills than their perception, their art is more gestural than formal, their religion is ritualistic—even the law is primarily centered around acts. The essence of Judaism is the act.[83] Law is the basic modality of Judaism only because acts precede and follow laws; laws regulate acts and only make sense in a milieu full of them. The Hasidim come to be model Jews for Buber because, according to him, they perform Judaism's essential nature. The fate of the world is in the hands of the ones who act,[84] and the signal act of the Jews is "to prepare" (*bereiten*) for the arrival of the absolute and the end of time.[85] When the messiah comes, acts will be unnecessary. But this leaves the modality of the messianic "when" impossible and unexplained. It can't be an act, since it stands beyond all human acts, and it must be an act, in order that the messiah be a Jewish messiah. Moreover, in Buber's argument it is hard to tell whether time underlies acts, or acts underlie time. No matter for Kafka, for whom, in the logic of his thoughts about time, any reference to "when" has to be abandoned, and along with it sequentiality, atomic time units, messianic coming, paradoxes of time, and acts, acts that support and extend the structure of time. If there is an end to time it is neither an act nor a consequence. To avoid the contradiction in the first version, after editing, the thought comes to read: *the decisive moment of human development is everlasting.*[86] This sentence is no longer a program, a protocol for how to let time fall. Time can only ever already have been abandoned.

From one perspective Kafka has merely switched paradoxes. Paradoxes, let us say, have expectations, which they foil, and they have revelations, which they offer. The revelation of the paradox has shifted, even if the expectations against which it operates are quite close to those of the original. "Letting" is not yielding. It looks like yielding, but if to yield is considered an act that originates in an actor, it has not yielded enough. Time may yield and be yielded, but it cannot be acted within or upon without initiating time once again. The first paradox is pernicious; it is based on one confusion and promotes more. In the second paradox, the end of time requires no appointment. It is not an end, therefore, but a new kind of perpetuity. All we have to do, once we accept this argument, is decide how to remove the concept of time that falsely labels what is happening now, if, that is, "now" can be emptied of its temporal meaning.

Kafka abandons the phrase "letting fall" in the final version; that other fall, *der Sündenfall*, the "Fall of Man," echoes through the thoughts, and "falling" is obviously tainted by the appurtenances of the fall legend and the meaning of moral time. So the fall will also have to fall. That is one weapon in his attack on faith and hope and time, yet all the weapons, all the strategies in the battle will require an elaborate and somewhat esoteric campaign to redefine timelessness and to describe procedures for bringing it about. He will have to imagine a kind of being without time that "letting fall" was supposed to produce when instead it produced more time. What is left, a productive paradox, makes it at a minimum impossible to imagine a now as a moment in a continuum. The formulation also poses a task to thinkers of humanity and its development. *The decisive moment of human development is everlasting. For that reason revolutionary intellectual movements are right when they declare everything earlier null and void, for nothing has happened yet.*[87] We cannot say that humanity is in crisis about its meaning or direction, since that would imply a pre-existing theory of what humanity is and means, which when it does not come to pass causes a crisis, such that the meaning of "human" becomes open for decision. We are asked to adopt a more troubling attitude. Nothing before this very moment has been decisive. And this one, and this. In this formulation, the last deeply edited version of this thought in the fair copy—*the decisive moment . . . is everlasting*—we are not, however, I think, asked to envision a moment that is infinitely divisible, an infinity within any unit of time, as, in a Leibnizian vein, Jorge Luis Borges proposes.[88] Zenonian paradoxes do not apply here, specifically because the mathematical metaphor with which time has most often been described and theorized is abandoned. What is a decisive moment? It is a happening, a pure origin or a pure end. It is always both. Kafka asks us to adopt an attitude toward time in which time is continually beginning and ending, and so happenings occur in it freely and are not to be compared with the past. Even what is happening now has to be ceded to the "not yet" of perpetual decisiveness. In one respect, this doesn't sound all that different from Aristotle's limit point, *to nun*. The Aristotelian now is ecstatic, beyond itself, always hyperbolically into the next moment, even at the instant that this moment has begun. The salient difference lies between a now conceived as a limit between durations and a decisive moment that is in principle unlimited. Kafka loves the effect a decisive moment has on the past, the way it refutes anything that looks like a development, a series, or a duration. *From a certain point on there is no turning back. This point is to be reached.*[89] The decisive moment cancels the past qua past. And this happens when the past brings us to a point at which the past is emptied of influence, when the past releases us from its claims. And then: this release is perpetual, he asserts. No turning back, one says this if the past has determined us so thoroughly that we can't escape what it has prepared for us. There is no turning back also means, however, that the past has done what it set out to do and no longer has value, if we cannot access it or relive it, if it is over and has no more influence on us or on our present. At the point of no return the past yields its possession of us and we cease to belong to it. Kafka imagines here a confluence of absolute determinism and absolute freedom.

And still, how we bring about, let happen, or stumble upon timelessness has not been clearly established. One traditional way to escape time is to transit into eternity. *This development does not exist, a development that would exhaust me with its absurdity (an absurdity that is only very indirectly due to me). The transient world is not sufficient for A's anticipatory concern about the future* [Vorsorglichkeit]*, and for this reason he decides to emigrate, with the world, into eternity. Be it the entrance, be it the exit door: it is too narrow—he cannot get his furniture cart through. He casts blame for this on the weakness of his commanding voice. It is the bane of his existence.*[90] An Abraham packs up to emigrate out of the shtetl to a better place. This Abraham is not to be confused with the historical figure or the biblical progenitor of the generations. He is Kierkegaard's knight of faith, quite obviously, as well as a function in a Kafkan proof that demonstrates the incommensurability of time and eternity. Kierkegaard's Abraham has become a variable in a Kafkan equation. He has too much furniture, the allegory goes, to fit through the narrow pass; whenever we envision eternity we have always hauled too many temporal accessories with us. One of these is power. The mistaken idea that leads A to this foolish endeavor is the thought that he can command the door to open by the strength of his voice. He surely doesn't recognize his weakness as an asset and has not heard the other revelation about the truly decisive moment when his furniture disappears.

In mid-December 1917, Kafka postulates the principle of the mutual exclusion of time and eternity that causes A's travails. *An over there* [Jenseits] *cannot follow an over here* [Diesseits], *since the over there is eternal, and so it cannot stand in a temporal relation with the over here.*[91] If time is not a medium for passage into eternity, it is the obstacle to it, insofar as it is thought of on the metaphor of motion.[92] Rest is not removed enough from the motion metaphor to enable this passage either; rest is internal to motion, to time, as is, for that matter, interruption. No interruption of time can alter its march. Insofar as the interruption is "of" time, it remains in its thrall. As if picking up the conversation from this very thought, Kafka writes on February 9, 1918, a companion and converse to this principle. *Eternity is not however temporality at a standstill* [das Stillstehn der Zeitlichkeit].[93] A thought about rest and its dialectical relationship to motion logically follows one about time and eternity; to wit, rest is the punctuation without which movement is inconceivable and cannot proceed, and so a temporal discontinuum is not a weapon against time or a viable way into eternity. Moreover a suspension of time is too formalistic. Time in the atheological reformation has its moral character exposed. Time is a means of achieving the good, and thus it is not to be conceived of on geometrical, arithmetical, or physical analogies. A break in time would correspond to a suspension of evil, and it is easy to see why this is not sufficient to allow a passage into eternity. One begins to feel as if this very thing we are left with, time itself, is precisely that which is eternal, albeit in a different way. It comes from nowhere and it leads nowhere, and nothing can be done to abrogate or interrupt it, since, indeed, it has no purpose or direction. What's more, it has no moral opposite; Kafka is invested in this procedure: to demonstrate the contradictions of every possible passage to eternity, including the understanding by which the good is reached through effort, which is the moral meaning of time. And yet even the quasi-Edenic thought that through effort one can make an exit from this world is contradictory. Insofar as we have gained the idea of effort without effort, it is less like a climb and more like a slide into eternity. *Someone was astonished how easily he traveled the path of eternity; that is, he careened along it downhill.*[94] Where the landscape tilts toward eternity already, where we have faith in something within us that is already eternal, just their effort or activity, and time as their medium, must be false notions.

17. A Twofold Truth

What of the relationship of faith to truth? Kafka writes that truth is double. *There is for us a twofold truth. . . .*[95] It is not immediately certain whether we ought to take this assertion as a gesture toward the common way in which truth has been considered double. The doubleness of truth in the Pauline understanding of faith terminates in the major question of our times, or one of them, to wit: whether there is room for two truths in the world, in democracy, in capitalism, in education. Can a truth of the heart and a truth of the mind, truth of faith, truth of knowledge, of Jesus and Aristotle, coexist? Within European philosophy, this now traditional alethic doublet with its plentitude of inner tensions led to a well-known plan to integrate faith and knowledge and have one truth at last. To come up with a form of reason that would be palatable to faith was the medieval formulation of the plan. To come up with a form of faith that was palatable to reason was the Enlightenment formulation. Obviously the schema was never as straightforward as I have presented it. And yet in an important sense Kafka, who is not interested in the technicalities in the history of thought, sees intellectual positions and conceptual systems as valuable where they become primitive and vital "precepts," accessible enough and abbreviated enough to operate in everyday narratives and decisions. In this light Kant's paradoxical formulation of a reason that makes room for faith, and the hope or plan for reunification that he registered in a letter to Stäudlin, are but highly technical versions of concepts that are also at work in the general opinions and activities of Europeans. Despite the abstractness of the formulation, Kant gives us an important view of the problems in the more colloquial double view of truth.

Kant wrote to Stäudlin that he had found a synthesis of faith and knowledge: "With the enclosed work, *Religion within the Limits* [of Reason Alone], I have tried to complete the third part of my plan. In this book I have proceeded conscientiously and with genuine respect for the Christian religion but also with a befitting candor, concealing nothing but rather presenting openly the way in which I believe that a possible union of Christianity with the purest practical reason is possible."[96] In the now famous monograph that he mentions, Kant integrates a restricted notion of religion into his theory of practical reason. Within the restricted religion—a religion restricted by and contained within reason—faith has an even more diminished role to play than religion does. Many things are more important than faith in a religion of reason, chief among them the distinction between good and evil, or between true evil and diminished or empirical evil. To incorporate into your moral maxim the ability to deviate from it is radical evil, an evil that strikes at the root of morality. This "evil" is not a judgment of the content of an act but rather names a formal contradiction, a permission to deviate from duty at the root of duty. Radical evil has little to do with faith, although during the discussion of it faith surfaces suddenly. In moral religion "only faith in the practical idea in our reason has moral worth."[97] Faith is judged by its moral worth, that much is apparent, though not for its special access to moral truths, the good, and so on. The practical idea in our reason referred to by Kant here is the idea of freedom, what allows us to set our own maxims in the first place.[98] Moral freedom is the freedom to posit and follow maxims, and faith is a subjective conviction strong enough to hold the idea of freedom even though it does not admit the certainty and deducibility of objective knowledge. There is an ambiguity here, a rather intractable one, that very soon will be exploited by Hegel. At one and the same time faith is subordinated to moral reason, to duty, and, in a stunning reversal of the Pauline trajectory, also to law—faith is for the purpose of supporting law-following—and yet faith is also raised above these as the route to the "truth" of freedom, that is, as the subjective condition for the possibility of setting a maxim at all.

Like Kant, although in all probability in ignorance of his discussions of faith in either the critical or the postcritical writings, Kafka is less interested in doctrinal faith or confessional faiths than he is in faith as a fundamental human capacity that is thought to lie at the root of higher activities such as morality. Where Kant sees faith as the capacity to hold the idea of freedom in absence of any experience of it, however, Kafka sees faith as itself an idea, a fundamental precept that gives rise to a world in which experience and freedom are separated and can be later reunified through human effort.

Truth is double for Kant, let's say, in this way: some are truths of experience and some are truths of ideas. The former are accessible through knowledge in a theoretical disposition, the latter through faith in a practical disposition, or in the kind of theoretical disposition that belongs to practical things—it is hard to say. Ideas, it will be recalled from the discussion in the "Transcendental Dialectic," refer to the whole of experience that is, however, not experienceable and so not knowable objectively, and they are useful for regulative but not for constative purposes.[99] Kant's version of the doublet is different, we can see, from other versions in the Pauline vein where knowledge is temporal and faith atemporal, or knowledge is a fact of the intellect and faith a fact of the heart. The two truths enter critical, transcendental philosophy and are transformed. Yet the doubleness of truth survives, and an aspect of the Pauline trajectory also lives on in Kant: the two truths have different relative worths. The distinction between Kant's two truths, and between the members of all of the doublets in this trajectory as far as I can see, is one of value. Kant may go back and forth about their relative worths, but worth is still the measure. On one hand the truth that reason seeks is higher and more valuable, because it gives us certainty in our knowledge and morality in our actions. Faith is then relegated to a minor role in the subjective functioning of practical reason. Its value is then overtly low. On the other hand, faith is so strong a subjective capacity that it finds its way into the fundament of practical philosophy as the guarantee of its success; by dint of faith the idea of freedom will be active in us and we will in fact and in practice obligate ourselves to follow the maxims we have given ourselves. Its value is thus covertly high.

Kafka is close to Hegel in one respect: he thinks that knowledge is dependent on faith, that without faith, moral knowledge may seem absurd or may be impossible to actualize. He posits, like Hegel, another faith higher than the distinction between faith and knowledge. Hegel's view, in the booklet *Faith and Knowledge* in which he reviews the differences between Kant, Jacobi, and Fichte on the truth-doublet, is that without a larger sphere in which practical and theoretical reason are unified, their relative places in human life will not make any sense. For what purpose do we act morally or know objects, at what time one and not the other? In short, Hegel takes issue with the Kantian doubleness of truth and the equivocation about faith, implying that the ambivalence must be overcome and the doublet must be unified, and, remarkably, it happens through faith. At the very least, if we want to claim that the doublet itself is "true," it has to have a grounds for its truth. Let us quote a key passage from the booklet:

> For where faith as such is bound up with an awareness of itself and negates formal, finite knowledge [there the question arises] whether a faith that has this reflective attitude to finite knowledge is truly able to raise itself above subjectivity and finitude, since no rational knowledge is supposed to be achievable. This is the negative and conscious shape in which faith occurs in Kant, Jacobi and Fichte. In true faith [however] the whole sphere of finitude, of being something-on-[one's]-own-account, the sphere of sensibility sinks into nothing before the thinking and intuiting of the eternal. The thinking here becomes one with the intuiting, and all the midges of subjectivity are burned to death in this consuming fire, and the very consciousness of this surrender and nullification is nullified.[100]

Talking of "true faith," Hegel envisions a fire that burns up all the little dualisms of philosophy, the agreement of knowledge with experience, the mechanisms of moral law-giving, in a conflagration from whose ashes there rises a supercharged faith, an objective faith that embraces both of Kant's truths. Faith is an objective relation to the supersensual, the absolute, and is equivalent to an intuition of the whole that has a seat in no single faculty. Within a few years this intuition will be associated instead with the historical movement of spirit.

Something of the grandeur of Hegel's vision is at work in Kafka's thought of truth. There was no need to read the liege lord of German idealism, however, since the kernel of the vision is held in the Genesis narrative. In this way, Kafka's thought is, as Hegel's is in intention only, historical. The two truths behind the movement of time correspond to the two trees, and the Garden legend, or one of its aspects, is the narrative that attempts to show their inner relation. At first sight, through the tree of knowledge and the tree of life is *presented* (as Kafka writes, *dargestellt wird*) an unbridgeable division. Even God treats them as absolutely divided. The bifurcation of truth in the Pauline trajectory is expressed in the two trees, through which in turn are presented, on the one hand, truths of mind, experience, objects of knowledge, and, on the other hand, truths of the heart, the unexperienceable, being, life. We should also remark that each tree clearly has its own temporal index, the one—time, the other—eternity. It is this latter aspect of the absolute division that allows Kafka to show not that the trees share a common root, but that with a shift of perspective there is only one tree. Unlike for Hegel, however, this tree is not the union (*Aufhebung*) of the two into one another but the cancellation and eradication of one.

There is for us a twofold truth, as it is presented by means of the tree of knowledge and the tree of life. The truth of the active person and the truth of the resting person. In the first, good divides itself from evil. The second is nothing other than the good itself; it knows neither from good nor from evil. The first truth is really given to us, the second in the manner of a presentiment. That is the melancholy view. The joyful view is that the first truth belongs to the instant [Augenblick], *the second belongs to eternity, and for this reason the first truth is extinguished in the light of the second.*[101] There can be little doubt from this thought that one of the trees in the Garden is of greater interest, and of greater use for Kafka's atheological project. The tree of life lets off an extinguishing light. The truth presented in this tree consists in the snuffing out of other truths. How, then, his challenge seems to be, can he let this extraordinary kind of light be seen, along with its benefits. This kind of light has an effect similar to the effect of atheological timelessness. Instead of sublating time into itself (as the ceaseless judgment of temporal deeds, which is the activity of the first tree) atheological timelessness cancels time and its correlates—faith, effort, suffering. The tree of life works on these three as well. Instead of intensifying them and essentially making them permanent as the tree of knowledge does, the other tree weakens them until they turn into their contraries—faithlessness, indolence, and bliss. There is no need to wait for these qualities of course; they were already in the Garden. This is the "truth" of the one and only tree. The two trees do not correspond, for Kafka, to the temporal and the eternal, such that the question is how you climb one in order to leap over to the other. The very doubleness that the trees at first seem to represent, the doublets time-eternity and knowledge-goodness—these belong only to the first tree. You might say that this tree has a double trunk, and gives the illusion of a second tree.

This tree produces fruit, is fruitful. The other is fruitless. Why, we might ask, given its barrenness, is the second tree blocked off? Who would be tempted by a tree with no fruit? The answer: no one. The first tree seductively offers us its yield, the other is too yielding to be allowed to stand without protection, and without a colorful story about its prohibition. As atheological timelessness extinguishes time, the tree of life extinguishes knowledge and its seductions. This is why in Genesis it doesn't bear fruit and the snake is uninterested in it. Moreover, the snake does not have to seduce Eve to knowledge. Knowledge is the seduction, according to this small parable, seducing you into thinking that through knowledge you can attain eternal life, when in point of fact eternal life cannot be attained. It is not a possession or a possible possession but rather a way of abandoning possessiveness. The little parable, like a logical deduction, has several stages or premises.

Point one: "us"—in the inclusive sense of anyone for whom faith is a point of orientation—the twofold truth is "for us." This is crucial because it suggests another attitude might be possible, if we can learn how not to accept these truths or this fold in truth, or if we can become other than the we for whom it seems to have been meant. Hegel accepted the doublet faith and knowledge and tried to overcome it to the advantage of faith; Kafka takes us through a set of maneuvers at the end of which neither has much meaning.

Point two: our truth is double. *Zweierlei* is the German word, which suggests one thing received in two ways. Truth, for us, is double-mannered, ambiguous at times and also at times deceptive, saying one thing while meaning another. If we take this to mean that facts are divisible into truths and lies, however, we are missing the point. Here there are two independent manners of truth corresponding to two attitudes or models of behavior, neither of which is in itself mendacious.

Point three: the trees in the Garden present the bilateral truth for us.[102] As noted, it will turn out to be extremely important that truth is presented (*dargestellt wird*) in something like an image. The atheological reformation will have to change its ground, later, to take this fact about truth, its presentedness, its image-character, into account. Kafka's work will become a battle between presentations. Here the battle is staged as a competition between the two trees—soon though, later that winter, it will become a battle against images. Presentation will be shown to belong, in effect, to the first side of truth, to the first tree with its promise of a move beyond images.

The inner overlaps between the two truths have to be considered, but before we can do that a perspectival oddity should be made visible, if it can be. Only from the perspective of knowledge is truth bifurcated. "For us" truth is double, which is to say that this parable has been written for those of us under the sway of the first tree. We are allowed to guess, however, although we have no way to understand what it would look like or be like to encounter it, that there is another option, where truth looks undivided. Genesis says after all: "And the Lord God said, 'Now that the man has become like one of us, knowing good and bad, what if he should stretch out his hand and take also from the tree of life and eat, and live forever!' So the Lord God banished him from the garden of Eden . . . "(Gen. 3:22–3). Secularity begins here and is associated from that moment on with finitude, and knowledge—our consolation, substitute for, and route to life. The perspectival fantasy is: from the position of the first tree one only has to stretch out one's hand in order to reach the second.

Point four: there are two subjects of truth, two protagonists in this drama, but this is not equivalent to the double truth of the Pauline trajectory, darkened vision here, clear and bright vision once we have crossed over into true life. There are two different kinds of protagonist, each with a different view of truth: one an agonist, the other unindustrious, unconcerned even, asleep under some tree. The tree of knowledge incites and leads to action, the tree of life does not incite, that is, it does not tempt us into activity.[103] This is the perspectival oddity: the tree of life presents no truth; it doesn't present at all. Either it is a figment of the active person for whom truth is double, or else it has no image. In reality the second tree might be any of the other trees in the Garden, which serve no doctrinal purpose, only lend shade and give non-deleterious fruit for eating.

Point five: being active, *tätig*, means believing the good is distant and has to be achieved. For Kafka then there is an alternative to morality, not a beyond so much as a beneath good and evil, where a figure can be imagined, like Dostoyevsky's Myshkin perhaps, who doesn't distinguish between the two moral poles, for whom there are not two trees, but only a single pleasant canopy wherever he strolls. In short, ceasing to make distinctions, being an idiot in Dostoyevsky's sense, is not true but it is good, although you shouldn't call it this because good without an opposite cannot be anything other than a confused idea. The Garden legend is a treacherous story, it seems, so treacherous that every time it is repeated it emblazons its premises and their monstrous

complications on our thoughts and wills. Eve and Adam may have sung
a song about this treachery:

> *What alas is prepared here for us*
> *bed and camp under trees*
> *green dark, dry leaves*
> *little sun, damp scent*
> *what alas is prepared here for us*
>
> *To where does longing drive us*
> *To do this? To lose this?*
> *Senseless we drink the ashes*
> *And choke our father*
> *To where does longing drive us?*[104]

The Garden can be taken as a horror story in which idyllic symbols of rest
are ominous enticements to longing, change, suffering, and death. The
bower is a decoy; the domestic hollow formed by the trees is camouflage
and at the same time the means and medium of seduction to the disaster
that lies beyond it.

> *To where does longing drive us*
> *Out of the house it drives away*[105]

This is the truth of the Garden story, the truth of the image of two trees:
the Garden story is told by the snake. The first tree does not lead, through
the medium of moral time, the time of toil and the search for the good,
to the tree of life, although the image of two trees seduces us to think
that it does. In Kafka's song the trees that promise shelter become an
amplifier for God's voice. God, because he speaks through the trees as
their rustling, comes through as a puzzle, a rune to be solved. In this way
language, which could be quite beautiful, is equivalent to a sickness.

> *What seemed patient to you, rustled*
> *through the treetop*
> *and the Lord of the Garden spoke*
> *in his runes I seek*
> *to study change's spectacle*
> *word and boil*[106]

18. The Garden Antinomy

Time is the obstacle but it cannot be overcome willfully or let fall, or simply disbelieved, since the disposition that produces time—faith—is the temporal disposition par excellence. There remains a possibility: to attack time where it emerges, not in physics or metaphysics, but in the disposition of faith. Having dealt with the concept of time, Kafka will now turn to the paradigmatic object of faith, which happens also to be the origin of time, the paradise topos. *If that which in paradise is supposed to have been destroyed was destroyable or destructible, then it was not decisive; if it was not destroyable/destructible however, then we live in a false belief.*[107]

Here we find the first truly historical event in Genesis, the condition of possibility for calling anything a historical event, the situation, the "Stand" that inaugurates time. The loss of the situation is coincident with the onset of biblical genetic history, though in this thought the loss of paradise is denied its usual effects. No matter which of the two versions given here turns out to be the case, and one of them has to be, *tertium non datur*, the expulsion from paradise cannot have occurred and human time cannot have begun, whether time is thought of as beginning in an original fullness that could be regained on behalf of a lucky present or in an original emptiness against which the meaningful, ever-building series would unfold itself in the progressively improving activities of a self-observing *Volk*.

Let us break the argument down into its elements. The alternatives given are, respectively: with the expulsion of the first humans and the snake—(we mustn't forget the snake; its plight will be as important to Kafka as that of the humans)—paradise (a) was destroyed and (b) could not have been destroyed.

Beginning with alternative (a): at the expulsion of Adam, Eve, and the snake, *paradise was destroyed.* If this is the case, that which in paradise was destroyed would always in essence have been susceptible to destruction; worse, insofar as it was from the beginning exposed to destruction, its beginning, the beginning before "in the beginning," before the Genesis narrative begins, insofar as it came from non-genesis and must already have been capable of becoming less than it was, created precisely in order to degenerate into that lessness, already less than a beginning in willing to become what it was not—insofar as it was a priori defectively paradisal, paradise never could have been the eternal bastion it has been represented to be. If we could describe one, a Kafkan theology would start not from the fall or from finitude, but from a tendency away from grand claims. A not grand paradise might mean that the paradisal qualities had been illusory and therefore our current understanding of human nature and purpose—not to mention their medium of actualization, time—to the extent that our understanding relies on belief in a perfect beginning, despite our obvious alienation from it (and indeed by reference to the obviousness of this account), is wrong. In fact we are not alienated: paradise could not produce a fall, and thus it is not we who are defective but our purported alienation, our supposed condemnation to time. And anyway, belief in the Fall is driven by a fateful nostalgia, a wish to reverse the expulsion, to retract it (*rückgängig machen*) and return to paradise.[108] Kafka reminds us in these passages that alienation and the "Fall of Man" (*Sündenfall*) first and foremost express this wish.

A different, less wishful reading discovers that when the Garden was destroyed paradise was shown never to have existed. Let us also keep in mind the dual valance of "zerstörbar" in German: it may be subjective or objective. It may mean "destroyable," liable to be desolated by an act undertaken by someone, or "destructible," liable to be wrecked by a flaw innate in the object, and, without clarification, it may mean some combination of the two. Since in being destructible/destroyable it never would have existed in the first place, its destruction is trivial, deceptive even. Paradise that is destructible/destroyable is in the beginning, before the beginning, already destroyed as an idea, and thus the name misleads us. The only thing taken away from man in the expulsion then is the fiction that it had been paradise, and so the word "destruction" applies to it only as a metaphor or a dream, a credence or a credulity, due to a wicked innocence that protects those who have faith in this illusion (with the violence necessary to maintain it). Far from being guilty, fallen man moves in a disastrous naïveté, born out of blindness to the implications of the story on which the belief in her own culpability is based.[109] If anything, the mistaken reading of the Garden episode as a tale of the end of grace and the inauguration of history is, for Kafka, the first sin.[110]

Given how controversial the implications of this version of paradise are, Kafka has to present an alternative. Thus (b): at the expulsion of Adam, Eve, and the snake, *the Garden could not be destroyed*. According to this proposition, the Garden was in reality indestructible . . . was therefore in fact paradise, and we—all those who believe this, and to Kafka everyone living does—we live in a false belief. Kafka does not say in this fragment precisely what the belief is, nor does he name the kind of falsity to which it is subject, but we can guess. Since by definition paradise cannot be diminished, corrupted, or damaged, let alone destroyed, it must, as Kafka puts it in another passage and in pursuit of a different argument, be a "state" (*Stand*). Elsewhere, referring not to the Garden but to its mirror image and in some legends the preface to its re-establishment, the Last Judgment, he calls it "martial law" (*Standrecht*), a groundless and open-ended rule imposed on life through executive force. In this version of paradise, (b), as with the former, (a), the Garden was never paradise, at least not the Garden portrayed in Genesis, whose loss prompts the chain of events leading to the cycle of building and destruction that culminates in and is to some extent supplanted by Mosaic law. The Garden, to the extent that it was divine, was not an origin for time or humanity. *We were made to live in paradise; paradise was designated to serve us. Our designation has been changed. That this also happened with the designation of paradise is not said.*[111] According to this thought, the change in the human condition has little to do with paradise. To emphasize this fact from the other side: *Only human beings were cursed, not the Garden of Eden.*[112] And although it is clear that either there was a Garden or there was a fall but by no means both, there is not yet cause to celebrate. For in either case—whether paradise is found to be destructible/destroyable and so in effect was never paradisal, or if it never could have been destroyed and thus remains a permanent condition, existing somewhere somehow—its effectiveness as an origin is cancelled, since what emerges and continues from it cannot have commenced in it. This thought presents something like an antinomy, though unlike Kantian antinomies each version of paradise, each term of the antinomy—a or b—is perfectly ambiguous on its own. The assertion made by the entire thought, then, is that at the beginning of the Book of Genesis no definitive view of an originary genesis can be had.

It would be a useful exercise to compare this thought with other self-contradictory or antinomian theologoumena. It could be brought to bear, for example, on the frequent comparison between Kafka's writing and the varied and complex systems and practices grouped under the name Gnosticism. His insight here goes against at least one strand common to many things called Gnostic. Kafka does not support dualism, radical or mitigated; how could he, since, lacking a true Fall (since even if man falls, it cannot be from paradise), there are not two worlds. It would also have to be distinguished from Kierkegaard's knights of faith and infinite resignation, about which Kafka began to read in February, as well as from Theodor Adorno's thesis, derived, or so he claimed, from Kafka's fictions, on "inverse theology."[113] Max Brod thought this little antinomian passage on paradise proved that Kafka was the modern Job;[114] yet Kafka hardly challenges theodicy and he certainly doesn't accept divine rule again in the end; nor does he turn personal suffering into clarity about God's inscrutable justice and infinite power. Here he makes no complaint about the arbitrariness of divine justice—this is not a complaint, it is an antinomy. What's more, instead of bemoaning his personal suffering, Kafka commits a rather pious act: he reads scripture. A year prior to writing his treatise, he had noted in his diary: "Only the Old Testament sees—say nothing about this yet."[115] In his diaries and notebooks from this period the majority of bible references are to Genesis. A year or so later, when he begins to note down the thoughts, he seems to break his self-admonition to keep quiet, although he speaks to no one and says next to nothing, while nonetheless cataloguing what Genesis sees.

In contrast to almost anyone writing at his moment and in his milieu, Kafka proposes that paradise may well still be around. *In its main part the expulsion from paradise is an extra-temporal eternal incident* [ein außerzeitlicher ewiger Vorgang]: *the expulsion is therefore indeed final, life in the world inescapable; but the eternity of the incident, or from a temporal perspective the eternal recurrence of the incident, makes it nonetheless possible not only that we could remain in paradise lastingly, but also that we in fact are lastingly there, regardless whether we know it here or not.*[116] The antinomy unfolds further. That *the Garden could not be destroyed* means that, insofar as the expulsion belongs to the Garden, it keeps happening. Since it emanates from paradise, the transition out of eternity—the expulsion—is itself eternal, and the conclusion to be drawn is that it could therefore never be completed, the expelled never completely, that is to say never actually, expelled.

Is this what the "Old Testament sees," or part of it? Is this part of the atheological vision that Kafka wills himself to reserve for later? There could hardly be a worse time than the end of the war to assert that paradise existed here and now. It would not be hard to imagine a host of reasons for a German-speaking Jew in Prague to keep silent about this. And Kafka did keep silent, in a way. Soon the curtain rises on a series of explanations for his silence on scripture and on Judaism as a whole—self-hating Kafkas, assimilationists, anti-Zionists, atheists. Yet the facts about his interest in Jewishness and commitment to Jewish causes are clear. He moved in Prague circles steeped in the cultural Zionism of Ahad Ha'am, Martin Buber, and Micha bin Gorion (Berdyczewski); he had a passion for the Yiddish Theater, read "den kleinen Grätz" (one of the foundational texts in the *Science of Judaism*, whose general historical thesis, if we understand Kafka's reading of Genesis, he rejects), Pinés's Yiddish literary history, and Fromer's *Organismus des Judentums*, among other Judaica; he supported with a passion such social projects as the Jewish People's Home in Berlin (founded in 1916), and participated directly, with Max Brod, in the foundation of the Jewish elementary school in Prague, not to mention his virtually uninterrupted study of Hebrew from 1917 on. But which of these affinities or projects explains his interest in the *Tanakh*, or as he calls it, the "Old Testament"? And which of them addresses the strange manner in which he finally breaks his self-imposed prohibition and begins to say what Kafka sees that the "Old Testament" sees?

Beyond these historical and personal reasons, it may be that something in the revelation itself induces Kafka to hold back. For indeed what is revealed in his reading is anything but clear and distinct—the vision is neither easy to discern nor easy to accept. At this time Kafka works out a mode of reading traditional theologoumena and of writing about traditionally theological concerns that allows images of transcendence to become foggy. In a word, he makes scripture harder to read and theological truths yet harder to accept. The difficult atheological news might be stated like this: one can be in paradise, but not seek it. Kafka's recommendation is essentially linguistic. Insofar as the word "paradise" is a cipher for the seeking attitude, two options remain: to stop saying it—but this could be a kind of seeking in disguise, seeking for another, truer word, roughly equivalent to secularization—or to say the word against itself, to use it without meaning it or to show where it fails to name what it claims to name.

Watch where you step: a snake winds through these passages, and several others can be found coiled up in Kafka's *Nachlass*. Revelation is spoken with a forked tongue. *The mediation of the snake was required: evil can seduce the human being, but not become one*[117]—a thought Kafka later crosses out. A non-divine yet superhuman element with an intrinsically plastic form intercedes early in the thoughts. The snake's figure—or lack thereof—and its slippery mode of speaking—for Kafka not only seducing us but confusing us by telling two different truths at once and representing this as the one truth—expresses Kafka's insight about paradise. If we are honest, Genesis is made up of the snake's words. As knowledge, the stories are as tantalizing as ripe fruit. And the snake's own doublespeak is the focus of several of these thoughts. Mediating for evil,[118] the creature seduces toward the kind of seeking activity of which the Garden's occupants had hitherto been innocent. As its words begin to point beyond paradise, the snake also seduces toward a particular view of language, as carrying contents beyond itself. Such doublespeak introduces a trace of historical time into paradise. The fact of language, already—its seductive powers, its power to produce an image of what lies beyond it, to promise, and promising to insist that its promise will still make sense at a later date—is at home in the Garden, once the snake speaks. In notes Kafka took during his reading of Genesis in 1916, he associates these aspects directly: "the two trees / the groundless prohibition / the punishment of all (snake woman man)."[119] That all three should be punished is puzzling. Why should God expel the snake? Two reasons come to mind. Punishing the snake conceals what Kafka calls "the ungrounded prohibition" (*das unbegründete Verbot*).[120] The prohibition against eating of the first tree only has a ground if grounds and consequences are already available—if paradisal creatures can already judge for themselves, and if language is already a matter of predicting a future consequence. Paradise, however, has to mean the absence of judgment, and so the prohibition is in fact ungrounded. The snake is punished in order to draw attention away from the already fallen or non-paradisal nature of the Garden. Not Adam, the snake—the snake is one of us, the first human—so much so that *after the expulsion from paradise, Adam's first house pet was the snake.*[121]

The value of deception in theology is almost thoroughly negative, but as thoroughly negative it also has a positive function. Augustine sums up this sentiment as it fits with one strand of Christian doctrine: there are but better and worse lies; the world is in essence deceptive. Only one lie must be avoided at all costs, the lie in service of faith. Such a lie may be useful, and it may even do good, but precisely for this reason it is the most immoral. This lie is not simply deceptive, but destroys the grounds for deciding between deception and its contrary, since it introduces de-

ception into the chain of revelation.[122] This is similar to what Kafka calls
"false belief." False objects of belief—false Gods or untrue doctrines—
are trivial in comparison to this kind of falsity. One notable exception to
this tradition is Kierkegaard, who inverts Augustine's order of mendacity
and makes deception into a tool of revelation and a basis for faith. He is
also an exception in another way: he is one of the extremely few theologians on whose arguments Kafka comments directly; and he is certainly
the only one with whom Kafka opens a theological debate. He does this
in several thoughts and in letters to Max Brod over that winter.

Brod, in a characteristically insistent way, urges Kafka to read Kierkegaard, because of an affinity he sees between their theological perspectives. In contrast to Brod's unreserved reverence for Kierkegaard, Kafka
responds from Zürau, where he has capitulated and read *Fear and Trembling*, with somewhat cautious praise. Brod poses this question: if Kierkegaard overcame his theological problem by adopting pseudonyms,
could he not have saved the trouble and refused to publish books at all?
Does publishing not betray the highest things in a way that silence, a
silence more true than the ironic pseudonym "Johannes de Silentio" indicates, could remedy? The aesthetic books are pseudonymous, Kafka
writes back in the first of his two letters on the subject, "and in fact
pseudonymous almost to the core."[123] Publication does not contradict
their theological aims, however, because as publications the books are
thoroughly ambiguous; though published, there is little about them that
is public.

Taken alone, however, the pseudonymous books can, "despite being
confessional, count very well as confusing letters of the seducer, written
behind clouds."[124] A confusing text attributed to a false name intensifies the confusion to a productive point. "Kierkegaard's method," Kafka
notes in a parenthesis, is "to yell so as not to be heard, and to yell falsely,
on the chance that one might be heard."[125]

From these letters it becomes apparent that Kafka's critique of revelation is written in the margins of another radical attempt to rethink
its limitations and potential. Yet they also show how Kierkegaard was
chastised by Kafka. The seductive writer of letters was undercut by a
prudish letter writer, the yelling falsifier was muted by a much quieter
one, and Brod, sometime theologian, was listening in. *Veröffentlichung*
(publication) of Kierkegaard's books is no threat to *Offenbarung* (revelation), precisely because the contemporary "external image" (*Außenbild*)

of the religious relation has in Kierkegaard's time "no significance" (*keine Bedeutung*), and boisterously publicizing a deceptive text in a time of general deceptiveness constitutes a perfectly reasonable response.[126] Indeed, a false authority telling falsehoods in a false time is vastly different from a true authority—a god say, or a government—that lies. The former is structurally true, and this comports with Kierkegaard's position vis-à-vis his highest objective, the seduction toward faith in a truer truth. By lying, the Copenhagen Cretan proves truth to be of a higher order. Kafka summarizes the Kierkegaardian aesthetic procedure in this formula: "Now, the religious relation wants admittedly to reveal itself, it cannot however in this world, and for this reason the striving human being has to set himself against the world, in order to save the divine in himself, or, what is the same thing, the divine sets him against the world in order to save itself."[127]

Revelation is seen in just this way in the treatise. False because its truth is not of this world, revelation triumphs in the end because, in order to be restituted, it persuades human beings to sacrifice themselves for the sake of concealing its falsity. Notable in Kafka's formula here is the verb *offenbaren*, found almost nowhere else in Kafka's writing. The center of Kierkegaard's doctrine, what Kafka calls "the religious relation," demands to be revealed, and his falsifying aesthetics carry out the will to *Offenbarung*, despite the costs.

With regard to the actual costs of Kierkegaard's deceptiveness: to quote once more from the letter, Kafka advises Brod that it is safer to leave Kierkegaard behind, to go "one wingbeat farther."[128] The Dane offers a rhetorical phantasmagoria that cannot be taken for doctrinal truth, thereby drawing readers away from the aesthetic toward straight doctrine.[129] He proposes, in other words, that beyond this beautiful illusion lies truth. If one wonders what the snake sounded like, one only has to read Kierkegaard. "So," Kafka concludes the discussion with Brod, "the world has to be raped by you as by Kierkegaard, now more by you, now more by him, but those are differences merely from the perspective of the raped world."[130] "Rape" underscores a worry that Kafka expresses often in his stories: that violence is needed to maintain the fiction that the world is false. For, it is not the snake's lie that is damaging; indeed, the temptation to transgress God's prohibition is negligible. What is evil is what the creature implies about the advantages of eating the fruit, that it will turn his colleagues into gods.

The creature's promise cannot be fulfilled. Knowledge of good and evil does not make Adam and Eve "like divine beings" (Gen. 3:5). *They did not become like God; instead they received a capacity that has remained indispensable to them, to become like God.*[131] Belief in this promise drives them continually to seek the means for transformation.

In the first draft of Zettel no. 86, there is a parenthetical remark, and although Kafka excises it in the final draft, he does so most likely for the reason he often cuts a passage, because it reveals too much. For us the remark, half-hidden and then removed entirely, gives insight into Kafka's answer to Kierkegaardian "revelation through falsehood." In the Garden thoughts, Kafka recalls that falsification is in full force in the title "Fall of Man" (*Sündenfall*), which gives the appearance that one could and even should spend one's days climbing back up.[132] This is the temptation and the proto-falsity. In response, Kafka writes: *(With its advice the snake did only half its work; what it brought about it must now try to falsify as well, therefore in the authentic sense bite itself in the tail).*[133] Having once falsified, the seducer should now turn the fact of falsehood and the paradisal dreams of its removal fully into fictions. These would be lies to the second power, fictions that actively prevent belief in a higher, purer origin, a mode of speaking that does not point negatively to truth. To thoroughly finish the snake's work, which God interrupted and theology misconstrued—this is one way to view the task Kafka sets himself at this point.

19. The Messianic Share

We turn now to an exceptional use of language: statements about messiahs and principles of messianic arrivals.[134] These statements and principles reach out to a meaning or event that they have no right to state or to make principles about. The problem is fairly intractable. For one thing, it cannot be solved by simply negating statements about messiahs. In the statement or principle, "no messiah will arrive" or "there is no messiah": to what does "no" refer? This too is a kind of messianic doctrine, there will be no messiah. Insofar as the statement has meaning—that is, insofar as it can be understood and its sense preserved until it should prove true, it will have predicted a messianic arrival, albeit the arrival of nothing like a messiah. When we say "there is no messiah," messianism will have been secretly at work. What becomes interesting in this case is the intransigence of messianism where it is denied. What is the source of this special persistence? One obvious place to look is the syntagm that forms the basis of both statements. If we could show that the syntagm, "there is," operated as a species of prediction or, dare I say, as prophesy, we could know that it was the source of the problem. It is true: the existential marker "there" in English encourages us to think of ourselves as awaiting the fulfillment of our speech in a state of affairs that is fundamentally different from it, a being or situation whose existence we assert but with which our assertion does not coincide, even if that being or situation appears present while speaking. It is assumed that the existential marker "there" derives from the locative "there" but does the existential marker sever all semantic ties with the locative in order to become "existential"? One could also ask why English does not derive the existential marker from "here." The decision or inheritance may in fact say something about existential claims in this language. This "there is," the syntagm of existence, insofar as it has been conceived of as pointing toward something beyond it, may be messianic in this way: it awaits confirmation in the arrival over there of the truth status of the statement.

The assertion "there is no messiah" does not cease to announce an arrival, to predict a location elsewhere, to project certainty about a coming thing. And the thing awaited arrives first in language, in advance of its true self. Arriving in advance of its truth, the statement is neither that which creates nor even that which discovers the arriving thing. Instead, it is a mimetic instrument that draws its authority from the deferred arrival. A minor and deficient arrival before the major and full arrival, the pre-arrival in language nevertheless, despite its deficiency (it is not yet the thing), has effects proper to it. For one thing, in both syntagmas "there is" / "there is no," time is projected as the medium both of arriving things and of things that definitively do not arrive. "There is a messiah," like its negative counterpart, implies that time "is there" to support the state of affairs and the theory of language it silently announces.

Awaiting something, awaiting nothing: both maintain, on the basis of the concept of arrival, a sense that the period until the arrival is consistent with itself. Both "there is" and "there is no," first and foremost, in the order of implication, assume a continuum linking language and event. This is not to say that atheism and monotheism are the same in every respect, nor that this rather coarse manner of asserting a belief or a fact—there is X, God exists, and so forth—is their only recourse. It does seem, however, at a minimum, where they rely on principles, that atheism and monotheism share an inability to rid themselves of a structural messianism, an internal belief that a moment will arrive to confirm their truths, finish their sentences, and prove time to be ultimately what "there is."

There are many reasons to want to deny elements of the messianic complex—historical reasons, natural-scientific reasons, moral reasons, and religious reasons too. And yet the negation of a messiah's existence leaves untouched, or so it seems, a messianism that is more deeply concealed. Negating a messiah does not release us from the grip of the messianism internal to the principle form and its temporal assumptions. A messiah lives on to the very extent that, although the existence of the messiah may be challenged, our concept of time remains, strengthened even by the frontal attack. No messiah is the messiah of anti-messianism. And so, to sum up, the syntagm "there is (no)" contains an idea of a messiah, projects into the future a messianic figure (messiah/no messiah), and presupposes time as the bondsman on whose credit both the idea and the figure produce and maintain their shape and meaning. If the arrival of a messiah cannot be cancelled and a messiah idea cannot be destroyed by negating it, the whole complex begins to take on a tyrannical character.

A messiah who did not arrive would be hard to recognize. A messiah who might still be coming or might have already come or whose coming did not take the form of an arrival and whose "way" did not take the form of time would not return in the way all messiahs, even negative ones, do—to satisfy the terms of a contract drawn up and signed in the deepest history, a contract on the meaning of time.

Statements about messiahs assure us that we live in the middle of the contractual period, under the rule of "our concept of time," and not at either end. Messianic subjects can be relatively sure their responsibility for the order of things is minimal, living under a law whose revered legislators are dead and whose all-powerful judge has not yet opened the final trial.[135] No-messiah and messiah constitute time in this way, as deferral of judgment. And messianic statements and principles participate in or enact again each time this deferral. This is why messiahs must arrive or be about to arrive and cannot just come or be "to come." Arrival is their mode of appearance, where arrival means at a precise destination. That they are meant for us and us for them is the reciprocal guarantee that our actions in the meantime have meaning, that they are both means to that end and also merely the mean between distant extremes, while we wait for all we suspect is the case to be confirmed. The connection between irresponsibility and meaning will have to be investigated elsewhere. At the center of this reasoning, however, lies a discrepancy. When historical messiahs did arrive, after believers had sold their belongings and dressed themselves for a new life, disappointment almost always followed. The messiah then proves to be not the true messiah or goes away again to return at the *right* right time. For beings accustomed to meantime,[136] to making do with meaning (and not possessing) and a level of irresponsibility with regard to fundamental decisions, her/his departure must also be a relief. Disappointment in the failure of actual messiahs to deliver on promises may reflect a desire that the messiah not arrive. But this does not diminish the central part the concept of arrival plays in messianisms. Even where believers postpone arrival in order to preserve "our concept of time," the concept of the messianic arrival still operates.

Meantime—time that uniformly metes out its contents and reduces extremes to means—is hinted at in the thought: *the decisive instant* [Der entscheidende Augenblick] *of human development arrives when* [wenn] *we let our concept of time fall away everlastingly.*[137] If the decisive instant, whatever its contents may look like, arrives only when time will have been "let fall," then the time concept is that which produces an unwillingness to decide. The indecisive meantime, as Kafka notes here, is not a property of a metaphysical entity "time," but rather the effect of the concept. One is accustomed to thinking: as soon as the decisive moment arrives, things will change. Change is thought to be accomplished in time, at the "right time." Kafka's premise is that a truly decisive instant has no place in measured time and cannot be reached in it. No appointment can be made for it, no motion toward it can be imagined, no arrival posited. Again, it is not a physical or metaphysical substrate "time" that Kafka attacks here—in contrast to Kierkegaard—but the grim force with which the concept holds us. When, this same winter, Kafka refers obliquely again to "our time concept," it is to teach us just how far meantime is itself the sentence already executed on us by postponing final judgment. *Only our concept of time allows us to name it the Last Judgment, in fact, it is martial law.*[138]

Two of the thoughts Kafka wrote in notebooks in the fall of 1917 mention messiahs, and these thoughts navigate between the perils of messianism and the perils of messianic anti-messianism, to abrogate "meantime" and imagine a medium in which things could actually happen. The thoughts tell us, or try to, how to rid ourselves of messianism without it returning secretly in another form. The solution is not to negate it, but to support it more strongly, albeit in a different way. The thoughts also give a clue how to accomplish the paradoxical suggestion that we "let" our time concept "fall" everlastingly. Both passages begin with the syntagm: *the messiah will come*, a version of a messianic statement or principle. "The messiah will come" is an analogue of the syntagm "there is a/ no messiah," but it also reveals the hidden assumption in the existential syntagm. In *the messiah will come* the existence of the messiah is asserted as true, and at the same time the disjunction between statement and fulfillment is legible in the verb's future tense.

The messiah will come when . . . Both messiah passages, written down several days apart, begin with this clause, and with this clause they also depart from one another. The difference resides not only in the fact that the first relies on the German word *bis* and the second on *wenn* to communicate temporal claims, although this may also be important. But it is as though, after Kafka wrote the first passage, something in it bothered or embarrassed him, and he had to all but retract it, or the important part of it, in the second. The first thought begins with the line: *The messiah will come as soon as* [bis] *the most unrestrained individualism of faith is possible, no one annihilates this possibility, no one tolerates its annihilation, and so the graves open up.*[139] A theological-political treatise that began with this assertion might go on to argue, in an extreme interpretation of Luther, that the *sola* in *sola fides* is what matters, that the route to God can never be walked by a group, that the only purpose of a collective of faith, then, is to give solace to individuals, to commiserate, perhaps, on the difficulty of the solitary journey of each of its members.[140] Yet, a community of faith can be founded upon the most radically individual relationship to God without in the least impinging on the commonality of the contents and institutions of that belief. Ideas of God, believer, scripture, ritual, faith, and most of all of "individual" must be shared, normative even, in order for a practitioner to even be conceivable as an individual. What Kafka calls for here, in contrast, is a radical individuality of idea and institution, based on a multiplicity of modalities and objects of belief. An echo of Kierkegaard can also be heard in the line, along with a critique of his "single individual."[141]

Even those who share belief in the same object—assuming this could be ascertained—will, *as soon as* [*bis*, in Kafka's manner of using the word][142] *the messiah comes,* by the force of this requirement, not believe in the same way. "To believe" will not mean the same thing for all or maybe for any of them. *The messiah will come as soon as:* a variation on the statement "there is a messiah," with this addition: the prediction, the appointment, the waiting, and the time as meantime that are suspended in this decisive moment become explicit. *The messiah will come as soon as the most unrestrained individualism of belief is possible.* This, the opening sentence in the first messiah thought, although it expresses a predictive messianicity, at the same time promotes a loosening of theological restrictions, calling for, at the most extreme point, complete indifference with regard to the content and form of faith. Messianic conditions are imposed here, to be sure. The messiah will not come just anytime or to just anyone. So indifferent must the faithful as a group become toward the form and content of faith, however, that even the dead, who have no reason any longer for faith in anything, can be included in the new definition. In effect the line argues that for the messiah to come, faith has to be so emptied of determinations that it can include the absolutely faithless as full and equal participants in its rewards. This messiah comes on the condition that faith be subtracted from the messianic equation. As such, the parochialism of the messiah—our belief that she will arrive for us and us alone, has to be revised. In short, the messiah can be thought of as arriving only insofar as it, she, or he also arrives for those for whom she, he, or it, was not promised, for an indiscriminate collective whose rainbow of faiths and meanings of faith would seem to predict, as a result, infinitely varied messiahs.

Before one takes Kafka at his word and begins to derive consequences from this prediction, however, one should take into account the second passage, written six days later. It imposes a heavy restriction that cuts into the plurality of faith and non-faith that the first statement seems to assert. However far it may go beyond what Peter said at Solomon's Portico (Acts 3:17–18), Kafka will revise the *apokatastasis pantōn* he supported on November 31.

The messiah will only come when he is no longer needed.[143] The opening of the second messiah thought signals a shift in Kafka's thinking about how to think about messiahs. Between November 31 and December 5th or thereabouts, a different messiah arrives. It may well be that the first in-

sight into a new messianicity disappointed Kafka, these messiahs of a diaspora of faiths, and so the second consists in a correction or an improvement upon it. It is most probably the case also that in his final judgment,
neither passage was satisfactory, since he copied neither into the fair copy.

The second passage is the more famous of the two. *The messiah will
come only when* [wenn] *he is no longer needed, he will come only after his
arrival, he will not come on the last day, but* [only/first, *erst*][144] *on the very
last.* One type of faith is subtracted in the second statement from the
infinite spectrum of faiths and messiahs evoked in the first statement.
Any faith that reflects a human need is not messianic. According to this
Feuerbach-style principle, a messiah cannot resurrect the dead, at least
insofar as the dead want to be alive or we want them to be; she cannot al-
leviate suffering, cannot restore the monarch to the throne or the people
to their geography. She cannot even prove to all believers that their belief
has been justified, to fulfill the final and most primordial need underlying any act of faith. This would be, by fulfilling their belief, to prove that
it was the right kind of belief with the right object, and, more important,
that faith had been the right disposition or faculty in the first place. Faith
is first and foremost an unfounded, one might also say faithless, decision for faith. In this light, the two thoughts with their two principles of
messiahs appear to contradict one another. The first messiah will have
fulfilled everyone's need, everyone's faith, plus of course fulfilling the
faith in faith. The price for this fulfillment is that faith and its messiah
have to become irrevocably plural. The second messiah will have fulfilled
no one's need, and so not everyone's faith, but only unnecessary, dare we
say superfluous, faiths. Moreover, it will certainly not have confirmed the
underlying faith in faith, which fulfills faith's own secret need.[145]

Perhaps this is a good juncture at which to interject a doubt, a minimal
gesture of a lack of faith in Kafka's procedures here. We might ask how
any statement of principle—*the messiah will come when*—could expect to
govern a messiah, if he/she is the one who upon his/her arrival suspends
the law that has been in effect in the meantime, even when she/he does
so by fulfilling it perfectly, as Maimonides, for one, held. Isn't this mode
of language, the principle, a reflection of our need for certainty, authority, and permanence in the meantime, while we await true certainty, authority, and permanence? A lot speaks against messianic principles. They
substitute for the true authority but they also diminish it. A messiah
who was subject to a law, any law, but also and especially to a law of

messianicity that says a messiah is a messiah under this or that condition would be as unmessianic as anyone who lived in the meantime. Moreover, a messiah subject to a principle would in effect be forever awaiting her-, him-, or itself. In order to remain the messiah, *the messiah will come when*—to borrow Kafka's legalistic formulation—the messiah will come when and only when the principle of her or his or its arrival has been abrogated, when principles and "the law" no longer apply.

It is highly peculiar that Kafka would write—or, as he says, not at all write—in this way, in categorical statements of fact or principles written with the calm stroke of certainty and a light of clarity that could never be mistaken for hesitation or cloudiness. This is not the Kafka of the parables, or so it seems. Nothing in the tone or form indicates that these passages pose problems of interpretation. The first passage deduces an absolute diversity of belief. The second passage infers the superfluity of the messiah's arrival with respect to human need, and proclaims it as though it applied to everyone in all instances.[146]

A principle is a sentence that ranks before other sentences and other truths and authorizes some or all of them. It would seem, then, that the two are highly compatible, principles and messiahs: both arrive "before" everything else, before themselves even. To write down a principle, like evoking the messiah, is to take dictation from a prior or even an a priori truth. And yet, the enunciation of a principle is not its fulfillment, just as the evocation of a messiah is not her or his arrival. Sentences about arrivals, even if they repeat predictions made first in the deepest past, do not bring about arrivals; instead, they detain the messiah in an indeterminate place. In effect, then, principles belong to the meantime.

What we mean when we say messianism, *was Messianismus heißt*, can only be determined at a later date—and so we wait, in some sense without knowing whether waiting is the right activity or whether what we are doing is in fact waiting. This may be a clue to reading the second part of Kafka's reflection on time. *The decisive instant of human development arrives when we let our concept of time drop away everlastingly* goes on in the following way: *That is why revolutionary intellectual movements are right when they declare everything before them null and void, since nothing has happened yet.*[147] Nothing has happened before the messiah: this negation applies also to the speaking of messianic principles.

When, on or around December 5, 1917, he writes that the messiah *will come only* [erst] *after his arrival*, we could make the provisional hypothesis that Kafka betrays the promise of principles, leaving the messiah to determine, only after appearing, the shape of the messianism that could have preceded him or her. She comes a-messianically, which is to say, without either announcement or audience, and thus without an arrival, something like an "unmessianic messiah" (*not* a messianicity without a messiah) who rejects all formal guarantees of the futurity of the future.[148] From the perspective of this messiah, the formal itself is a restriction on the future, and so, in contrast, a messiah of contents—whose uncontainable elements "stick out" of whatever form or law, just as the elements of the thing called Odradek in Kafka's story "The Cares of a Family Man" ("Die Sorge des Hausvaters") do—rejects even the hope for absolute alterity. Rosenzweig insisted "Truth is not law [*Gesetz*] for the world but content [*Gehalt*]."[149] The difference the messiah brings may or may not be absolute, since the event comes after the desire has petered out—that is after its "arrival" for us at a scheduled appointment—after itself, beyond the constraints of any prediction or principle, including the constraints of "our concept of time." Still, one question is forced upon us by the final syntagm of this messiah remark: what is the difference between the last day and the very last day? Could the answer not be: no difference at all or better, no specifiable difference or nothing specifiable as a difference? If it were not specifiable, then the desire for a difference, the wish to be able to specify the instant of the messianic arrival, would be exposed as phantasmatic. To give up time as meantime means to give up the ability to say that the messiah has arrived even after she has come. For when could you know that one day or another was not just a quotidian last day, like a Saturday or February 28, 1918, but was indeed the last of all possible days? You could know only on the day after, when you ascertained that no further day had followed it. This is the joke. A messiah that comes after her/his/its arrival disregards the temporal conceits of language, the messianism inherent to principles; his/her/its amessianic messianicity denies time as meantime, as a means to—even to an open or absolutely heterogeneous future. In this context the meaning of "after" cannot be temporal. "After" should indicate what does not appear as temporal.[150]

20. Kierkegaard Codicil

While his friend Felix Weltsch occupied himself "with Augustine, Pelagius, Luther and now also with Maimonides," at a moment when for Weltsch "the ethical" that he had been thinking through for some time was "flowing slowly over into religion,"[151] on November 14, 1917, Kafka had a visitation from an otherworldly being. Not to be coy: it was a mouse. Weltsch thinks about faith in Kierkegaardian categories, Kafka lies awake nights listening to rustling and scratching.[152] In the midst of his rural idyll, near as he could be to farms and to the wild, he met a creature he could not abide but which abided in the middle of the domestic scene. The mouse would not withdraw. The plague of mice (*die Mäuseplage*) seemed to surge from "the darkness behind the coal box" in a corner of his room.[153] That darkness seems to hold one pole of Kafka's theological development. The creatures' otherworldliness consists partly in their monstrous capacity to work, day in night out, without rest. They are an epitome of postlapsarian humanity, a human God of infinite toil and suffering. *On the seventh day He rested; then we filled the earth.*[154] The "frightening mute noisy people [*Volk*]" takes over where God falters. God must rest; a mouse is "an untiring being."[155] Kafka has a special ear for this monstrous brand of eternity, endless stamina—it is precisely what he, in his illness, is losing. His hearing refines itself each day until he can sense the miraculous work as it proceeds "claw by claw."[156] Recounting the *musophony* to his theopolitical interlocutors, Weltsch and Brod, in more detail than any other part of his experience in Zürau, Kafka opens a discussion on a theological buzz phrase of the time. Perhaps neither friend recognized it as theological. The "night of the mice" is what precipitates Kafka's fear and trembling. As he says the day before in a letter to Brod, referring to a contemporary book by Hans Blüher containing a psychoanalytic reading of his "Metamorphosis," psychoanalysis "satisfies you astonishingly in the first moment, but shortly after one has the same old hunger again."[157] It is true especially in this case, the psychoanalytically "easy to explain"[158] fear of mice is hardly satisfactory. Mice produce effects without revealing themselves; this is the tenor of the mouse revelation: a voiceless voice that communicates nothing but belies a monstrous stamina, a potentially eternal creativity or destructiveness, or as the case may be, a gnawing in such a manner that nothing is ever created or annihilated . . . *what crumbles crumbles but cannot be destroyed.*[159] The mice nibble at the edges of the walls, widening cracks that are already there, enhancing the walls' porousness "like an oppressed proletarian people that belongs to the night."[160] Neither destroying nor creating—avoiding, that is, the two extremes of paradisal religion—not viewable directly, but only hearable or overhearable, the mice are "not fantasies" (Kafka himself writes this); divinities of a humble order: Kafka writes about them often in the coming years. There is no little irony in the mouse episode and in the length at which he describes it to Brod and Weltsch. There is also irony in a remark: because of the mouse plague, Kafka only gets "a couple of moments [*Augenblicke*]" with the author he is currently reading, "(now Kierkegaard)."[161] "Mouse fear and trembling" (*Mäusefurcht und Zittern*)[162] is the comic prologue to a serious disagreement with many of the then infamous Kierkegaardian theologoumena, which he read when he could, between rodent interruptions.

As with the mice, with Kierkegaard he could not simply have a disagreement, though for different reasons. This does not seem to worry Kafka, since he has thought through many of the Kierkegaardian theologoumena before without having read much of him. Indeed, when he read several books that winter—aesthetic works: *Fear and Trembling* and *Repetition*, as well as polemical-didactic works: *The Moment*, and sometime later we think also the "upbuilding" *Stages on Life's Way*—Kafka had already surmounted many of the faux barricades Kierkegaard pretended to erect before faith. Kafka had already been Kierkegaard. The notebooks and letters from that winter show his almost retrospective first engagement with *Fear and Trembling*; his remarks echo from a great distance, nostalgic almost for a moment in which he might once have believed in writing like this.

That Kafka no longer follows a negative path to transcendence is evident in several of his thoughts on Kierkegaard in letters and in the treatise. He focuses on two questions, the question of communication and the question of knowledge. In short, he sees how dependent Kierkegaard is on transmitting knowledge through the stories he presents. One must come to know the situation as paradoxical in order to conclude that faith is what Abraham has and what any believer must come to have. And this depends on a procedure with several steps. Knowledge of the divine must be denied, the denial must be communicated, the paradox of acting without knowledge must be cognized as a paradox, and this paradoxical knowledge must be interpreted as universal.

When Johannes de Silentio says, at the conclusion of *Furcht und Zittern*, "the highest passion in a human being is faith,"[163] he is not discounting the other passions he has discussed—Abraham's anxiety about the sacrifice, Abraham's joy when he is truly within the paradox, his love for God that does not supplant but intensifies his love for his son, and so forth. Each of these passions is a step in the path Kierkegaard paves from a Christianity lost in its history toward the new truth. The steps move through the negative to the positive. Within decrepit Christianity one fears what exceeds representation and explanation; fear turns to puzzlement as the paradox approaches the threshold of the ethical; and then within the religious, where the paradox—this specific mode of non-knowledge—is undone, puzzlement turns to joy. What kind of passion, then, is faith itself, faith alone?[164] The other passions, fear and joy are markers on the way to truth, first negatively, then by a dialectical movement, catapulting into the positive. As long as one is on the path toward faith, passions are, let's say, "feelable," representable, recognizable. You know when you're having them and you know what they mean. About faith however you must be silent. Since we have no access to God through the intellect, and we thus (according to Kierkegaard) cannot make assertions about him, we instead make an assertion about his non-assertability by remaining silent. To Johannes de Silentio at least, who should know something about it (depending what the "de" means or does), the silence of Abraham signifies only one thing, that he acts out of faith and faith alone. This silence of withholding speech is louder than actual speech. Again, Kafka on Kierkegaardian sigetics: "(screaming so as not to be heard and screaming falsities on the chance that he might nevertheless be heard)."[165] Unmistakable in Kafka's description of this style is the author behind the layers of subterfuge, whose message—I have nothing to say—is transmitted perfectly by the style.

Readers do not and cannot know what Abraham thinks or experiences. He is always ahead of us on the path or above us on the *scala paradisi*. As we look up toward where he stands, we are led to believe that at Abraham's stage it is not a matter of knowledge. After all, this cannot be a book for the education of future Abrahams. This Abraham can neither think nor, truth be told, feel; his consciousness would have to be as pure and empty as the sky above Mount Moriah. Such an empty-headed figure appears in the treatise under the code name "A": *A's intellectual poverty and the low mobility of this poverty is an advantage; it makes concentration easier for him or rather it is already concentration, whereby he of course loses the advantage that lies in the exertion of the power of concentration.*[166] The absurdity of the situation as Kierkegaard sees it becomes quickly transparent to Kafka—the situation is not absurd, it is silly. This is all a matter of knowledge: claim to know, claim to not know; either all knowledge claims are impossible or there is no faith. Faith can only be present, according to Kierkegaard's rigorous criteria, where one cannot assert faith, and yet the nonassertion of faith is itself an assertion, and in this nonassertion you lose whatever advantage you might have had by actually and openly asserting it. Abraham's intellectual poverty is, therefore, not in and for itself; it is for the purpose of receiving the paradox, and thus it is not only not poor, it is in fact a specifically intellectual stupidity, not feigned—like Socrates's—but nonetheless performed for the sake of intellectual gain.

There is another species of silence—at least one more (who could limit them?). Kafka begins to introduce this species as an antidote to Kierkegaard's sigetics, where the *lack of communication* speaks volumes. Kafka establishes a difference between a transcendental silence and a hermeneutic hush. *The incommunicability of the paradox exists perhaps, but it does not express itself as such, since Abraham himself does not understand it. Now he doesn't need to understand it or should not understand it, therefore also not interpret it for himself, he is of course allowed to seek to interpret it for others.*[167] The situation is indeed laughable. In Kafka's version, it is not Abraham who is silent, but the paradox, and yet Abraham understands what he is supposed to do, that this is a paradox, that this is what a paradox is and is for, to present to others. And so, thinking he has authority from the silent paradox, thinking he knows what he cannot know, thinking even that it is a matter of knowledge, he falls silent and his silence teaches everyone about what they must know and do in the face of the highest things. In this way Abraham's silence falls into the long tradition of transcending silences, alongside Aristotle's *thauma* and Kant's dynamical sublime. Only an a priori conviction that this was a paradox and not, say, a simple error, that this was *the* mountain, this *the* son, this voice *the* voice of *the* God, only a full complement of knowledge could assure anyone that this silence was the in-breaking of divine speech in a world constitutively unable to transmit it. Understandably, Kafka is tentative about attributing existence to the paradox of faith. Perhaps because he is not engaged in a life-and-death struggle with German idealism, and surely because he is not trying to reform radically a religion while saving its basic principles—rather, he wants to keep the faith . . . with faith's ambiguous foundations—what he is equipped to do is to show how the interpretation of Abraham does an injustice to Abraham's experience, and, at the same time, how faith once again betrays the ambiguity of its foundations.

At twilight, Abraham's silence is no longer the fully meaningful sign of his true encounter with the paradox; and so the paradox is not paradoxical . . . enough . . . for faith. Even if resolutions elude us, paradoxes are nevertheless formally intelligible. A deformed paradox, a seeming paradox that deceives you about its paradoxicality, or, more toward what Kafka wants to suggest, a dispersal into a number of interpretations, some of which might be or seem "paradoxical"—these are figures Kafka had been experimenting with for several years, developing his version of a multi-value logic. In line with these experiments, we do not need to turn to God for the most unintelligible things: the smallest things of the world are unintelligible enough. Kierkegaard's "world" denies anything that cannot be known through universals. His allegories convert single individuals into ideas—"the single individual" is the highest and most deceptive of these universals. A tragic hero sacrifices herself for a universal, erasing her own aberrances for the sake of the norm, no matter what suffering it causes her personally. And yet the personal is already not personal. Kierkegaard converts Athenian tragedy into a type, the hero's plight into a lesson for mankind across history. Abraham sacrificing Isaac, Kierkegaard insists, is not Agamemnon sacrificing Iphigenia.[168] And yet Agamemnon is not universal tragic man; he is one mythical proto-Hellenic king. It is Abraham who must sacrifice the contingent, arbitrary, historical, and linguistic singularity of his desert experience to religion and to the whole future, not Agamemnon. Kierkegaard writes fairy tales; idiosyncrasies are marshaled in support of the total quest, and everyone settles down afterward into the same lukewarm fate. This is why anecdotes go on virtually endlessly in his books. They can exemplify, but they cannot teach. It is also why the didactic writings are unattractive. Outside the aesthetic presentation the doctrines deflate and the ideas seem commonplace. It is, as Kafka notices, more Kierkegaard's shouting than his doctrine that catches our attention.

Beyond Agamemnon's differences from Abraham, Kierkegaard has missed another idiosyncratic moment in the Hellenic myth, a moment in which the idiosyncratic per se afflicts any universal. Agamemnon's idiosyncrasy is guaranteed by the tendency of universals to be less than they claim. *The universal too in this sense is not unambiguous, which expresses itself in the Iphigenia story in the fact that the oracle is never unambiguous.*[169] In order to champion the single individual Kierkegaard has to idealize the universal; only then does it make sense to write allegorically in the Kierkegaardian style. And yet on two fronts Kierkegaard betrays the knight he champions. First, by placing the single individual "higher" than the norm, he becomes a beacon, an example, a lesson, in short a victor "over" the norm, which is thus reified. To do this he initiates a dialectic that fortifies the universal past any bounds of reality. If the norm is not itself "high," but low, debased, confused, partly incommunicable, and always in part not fully communicated, if it is not a "norm" but rather a wayward law on the books, who could become an exception to it? The singular, if such a concept could be thought, would, without a flawless universal, be unparadigmatic to the point at which its way of not being a paradigm would also be singular. This means however that it could just as easily give the appearance of following the norm to the letter.

Kafka prefers the logic of Babel to other more redemptive logics. The most unintelligible, the most absurd thing is what is multiply intelligible, where following a principle means different things in different instances and in the same instance, and meaningful speech is in many ways indistinguishable from babble. The mice unsettle Kafka. He cannot occupy his room and his bed; he cannot assert his own position, since the mice can appear anywhere at any instant. To live in this environment one has to become, like the cat, multiply attentive, but this is not all. The cat horrifies Kafka almost more than the mice do. While the cat fights the mice, trying to reduce their hordes, Kafka stops sleeping. Caught between fear and trembling, trembling at an unpredictable multiplicity, fear at a Kierkegaardian cat of faith who eats up the unpredictable—Kafka abandons the room.

There is a difference, however, between Kierkegaard's position, his "authorship," and his texts. Kafka writes Brod that Kierkegaard's oeuvre as a whole refutes his position; indeed it is not in his position that Kierkegaard can become an example, but in never settling on one. In this Kierkegaard is beyond even himself. Brod, who is at times more a book factory than an author, worries aloud to Kafka whether Kierkegaard publishing his books contradicts his basic position against communication. On the contrary, Kafka says, the sum total of the books are not communications and not not communications; taken together they are simply "compromising."[170] "They are not unambiguous and even when later he develops himself into a kind of unambiguousness, this is also just part of his chaos of intellect, mourning, and faith." Even his unambiguousness is ambiguous, when taken along with his earlier writings. Who is to say that the "upbuilding" texts will be taken as the solution to the pseudony-mous ones? Who is to say that "Kierkegaard" is less pseudonymous than his avatars? Since his texts are "pseudonymous almost to the very kernel," the true authority cannot be extricated from their internal chaos of anec-dote and fantasy. The multifarious oeuvre is the grounds by which what-ever is said by "Kierkegaard" can be subsequently called into question. In this way the Dane redeems himself from his own dogmas and where he does not—as in the case of Regina Olsen, whom Kafka recognizes as the primary victim of the books, which make up an elaborate torture scheme—history itself redeems him. The more he writes, the more am-biguous his message becomes; and the more he tortures Regina with his universal substitute for her and a consolation for himself—faith—the freer she becomes. With their repetition and intensification, florescence and self-contradiction, his constant attacks release her from culpability. She becomes, Kafka writes, despite and because of Kierkegaard's entire oeuvre, "almost as guiltless as a little lamb."[171]

Kierkegaard's religious position, on the other hand, is marked by a "seductive clarity" that leads to a horrifying consequence. Kafka does not usually mince words, but this is a particularly strong expression. The result of Kierkegaard's arguments is the rape of the world. The noth-ing where the object of religion is so indeterminate that the world must be violated—*vergewaltigt*—in order to give religion's object, negatively, a modicum of meaning. What he takes issue with here is the conversion of "nothing" into an "anti-world." Kafka makes the violence and horror of this position clear when he quotes in the letter to Brod from an an-thology of Kierkegaard's autobiographical writings that he had read four years earlier:

> And the following passage is not from the Talmud: "as soon as a human being comes who brings something primitive with him, so that he doesn't therefore say: one must take the world as it is (the sign that one, as a min-now, freely passes through), but who says: however the world is, I stay by an origin [*Ursprünglichkeit*], which I would not think to change according to the state of the world: in the same instant that this word is heard, a transfor-mation happens in his whole existence.[172]

In this quote there are three elements: the world as it is, as a prison; the world as that which can be overcome by faith, by standing by an origin;

and the minnow who freely passes through. Kafka supports the minnow. On February 26, Kafka takes a few direct notes from *Fear and Trembling*, one of which is the word "meaning" (*Bedeutung*).[173] The rape of the world takes place on behalf of this meaning, which tends toward reducing a multiplicity to a unity and a vagueness to a clarity. The act committed on behalf of meaning is a kind of quest, where meaning means a single, unified, unapparent, objective, true, goal toward which one must move. This is the source for Kierkegaard's continued use of the word "movement"—the movement of resignation, the movement of faith, the movement of repetition. He argues strenuously against "mediation" as a mystical remnant in Hegelianism and the unacknowledged weakness of the dialectic, and yet Kierkegaard clings to "movement," since it is obvious (to him) that we must not remain where we are.

> For the relationship to the divine withdraws itself first and foremost for Kierkegaard from *every foreign judgment*, perhaps so very much that even Jesus could not judge how far one of his followers has advanced. This seems for Kierkegaard in some way a question for the final judgment, therefore unanswerable—insofar as an answer would still be needed after the end of this world. *For this reason the present exterior image* [Außenbild] *of the religious relationship has no meaning.* Now, the religious relationship wants under all circumstances to reveal itself, but it cannot in this world, and therefore the striving human being must position himself against the world, in order to save the divine in it, or—what is the same thing—the divine positions him against the world in order to save itself. Thus the world must be raped . . . [174] [emphasis added]

A special sort of integrity and resistance must characterize the world, if it can become cause and recipient of so much hostility. The world does not simply roll over. The gist of Kierkegaard's argument is just this, for Kafka. The resilience and integrity of the world is the originating point for all the hostility toward it; it can be the origin of this attitude and many others, because it refuses to become meaningful. Unlike eternity, the world is a nothing that freely gives of itself. God wants desperately to reveal himself; he gives himself, creates, commands, sends floods and sons. The world is content to remain clothed, to hide, to disguise, and not to reveal even whether it is essentially different from its disguise. It resists and must be forced. God could safely stay one among the world's multifarious nothing, if, that is, he did not try to become the only meaning.

God is absolute, the world dissolute. With its special sort of integrity that God doesn't have, the world bests God. This is why the world does not have to dissimulate itself. God is absolute but lets himself be dissimulated, offered freely in parables, allegories, implying that he will permit some to approach him and not others. The dissolute world, fully and loosely dissolved into itself, includes God and everything and is truly unapproachable in itself. All statements about the divine in truth fortify the fact of the world; this is the other side of the dialectic that "moves" away from the world. It produces a countermovement back into the world, and the world itself, according to Kafka, is the countermovement between itself and its mythical outside.

There are thus two moments of Kierkegaardian religiosity for Kafka. The first is acceptable and corresponds to experience taken in good faith, but also to history and in part to truth. The relationship to the divine withdraws itself from every foreign judgment. God is only present to himself, in himself, and thus he is absolute, as Kierkegaard often writes of him. Yet this is no usual form of monotheism, with a withdrawn God. Here it is the relationship that withdraws; it is not the withdrawal of an object to which I am related, but the withdrawal of the relationship, without affecting the object at all. Kafka insists on the total withdrawal of the relationship. For Kierkegaard the relationship withdraws only partially, eluding the aesthetic observer, the aesthetic communicator, the ethical subject, and even Abraham in the most obvious, legible, and tangible way, that is, in the form of a paradox. *Bedeutung* ("meaning"), Kafka jots down while reading *Fear and Trembling:* the stubborn point of dogma in Kierkegaard's otherwise brilliant kenosis of knowledge. Religion is something, no doubt, to Kafka; it is the name for an image that offers no meaning, where God is a guarantee that we cannot interpret the image and should not try. Kafka cannot dispense with God, for this would bring the divine back in an even more virulent way. Religion, it turns out, is the best narrative or practice for keeping the image of human grounds and purpose, nature and future empty of meaning. If we look at an image of something, we may say it is of God; if we look at an image of nothing, we may also say it is of God. This is the religious significance of the Jewish prohibition on images. An image that is murky or confused, however, which may or may not be of anything, or may be just a stain, a passing cloud, a *palineidos* of two or more images, this we can speak about at length without arriving at faith. Insofar as the Kierkegaardian religious experiments suggest this further "wingbeat," this other nothing, they are important to Kafka.

The second moment of Kierkegaardian religiosity important to Kafka is treacherous. If the withdrawal of meaning can be given meaning, if it is the withdrawal of meaning as a reaction to some human fault, for some divine purpose, in view of a future return, and so on, then meaning has not actually withdrawn. And thus in the end, Kafka's discovery of a Kierkegaard he had, unbeknownst to him, absorbed and surpassed, may be seen as a dispute over scripture, where Kierkegaard prefers "knights" of faith such as Abraham and Job, who serve as witnesses to the fake withdrawal, and Kafka prefers the Babel story, in which a community is put asunder and speaks among itself nonetheless; or else he prefers the expulsion from paradise, the self-inconsistent myth about our removal from God. Where *the relationship to the divine* has withdrawn, all biblical stories are equally plausible, and so, since he founds human history on ambiguity, Kafka is the more "religious,"[175] and Kierkegaard, since he founds it on meaning, is the more "philosophical."

§   Excursus: For a Kafkan Logic

21. Two *Logoi*

At least two logics are at work across the polylogue of thoughts, a logic of sense and a logic of speech. Although these headings are not exhaustive, the principles that could come under them promote the general aim of the thoughts: to return Europe's central theologoumena to their originary confusions. We know that the value of confused principles for Kafka is the opposite of what it was for Kant, to whom confusion meant "indifference" and motivated the intellectual and historical need for critique. Kafka's method has to be distinguished absolutely from critique, as well as from the theory of history that underlies it. Wherever Kant attempts to subtract confusion from principles, and where the confusions are found to be irreducible—the antinomies are a ready example, though to interpret them as antinomies is already to subtract confusion—this irreducibility becomes grounds for excluding them lock, stock, and barrel from philosophy. In contrast, Kafka attempts to reduce distinctions to confusions, which are shown in turn to be the cornerstones of our cares and commitments, philosophy included (which he calls psychology, after the Brentanian typus). In this way Kafka avoids even the slightest possibility of a *reductio ad infinitum* of principles, given that only finite, unequivocal principles need further principles to justify them. If there are no single, distinct originary principles, there can be no problem of ground. Confusions cannot be judged either sufficient or insufficient. Now, when "sufficiency" is translated into theological language it is called justification. Whereas a principle or law is either sufficient or not

147

to ground a knowledge procedure, a theologoumenon either justifies a moral activity or it doesn't. A confused theologoumenon will not justify, since the routine of these justifications and rectifications is to lead us back to one source, one reason, one judge, one good, and so on. A judgment arrests a confusion. And so confused theological principles—atheological principles—will not judge; this also means that, in a typical Kafkan inversion, confused theologoumena also ludicrously need no justification themselves. Indeed confused principles, wherever they cannot be made clear and distinct, may be the only things in any and all worlds that, in refusing the question of justification, are truly autonomous, though also of course their use is not at all apparent.

The move to confused principles is carried out in the treatise by means of one kind of logic, the logic of sense. There is also a separate order of what some would call—for want of a better phrase—the logic of "address." The "personal pronouns" that appear and shift within and between calls and responses in the thoughts are the variables with which the polylogue presents its calculus of position, attitude, tradition, receptivity, expectation, response, and refutation. In the polylogue, *ich, er, wir, du,* and *sie* do not stand in for nouns or proper names—and so the formal grammatical term "pronoun" doesn't properly apply. They are general in their reference, and yet they are specific and precise in their positioning. The two typical ways of understanding pronouns, the linguistic way, as anaphora (standing for a noun), and the referential way, as deixis (pointing to a thing), do not adequately describe the function of these words where they appear here. Each of these little words gives a place for a plural but finite cline of forces and relations, both linguistic and nonlinguistic. Let us take some examples to illustrate the difference. The German word *er* ("he/it") attributes power over speaker and listener to another, to one who stands outside the intimate duo, thereby freeing the pair to "live" unfettered in the world. Literature is the place where the *er* cline is explored. So it is with Sancho Panza in Kafka's comic tale "The Truth About Sancho Panza" ("Die Wahrheit über Sancho Pansa"). When he says *er,* the word detaches him from responsibility, sending the agent and actor, Don Quijote, the locus of responsibility, out into the world so that *you* and *I* may be free. In another thought, uttering *er* inaugurates a parabolic situation, where, without privileged access to the consciousness of the one involved, *you* and *I* are faced with an enigma—he does this, he does that—which has to be interpreted and yet cannot be interpreted with certainty or finality. This is, we might say, the logical value of what Walter Benjamin first described as the gestural element in Kafka's fiction (and, lest we forget, also in his drawings). Gestures happen to, from, and at a "he" or "she." *Er/sie* are points of opacity, and because we have no special access to their motivations or goals, a scaffolding of interpretation and power must be built around them through the other positions, *ich* and *du, wir, Sie.* If we generalize this reasoning, *er* is the puppet of an authority outside him, an "it" that becomes the locus of responsibility outside "us" and a focus of moralizing for "you." Perhaps this is what Blanchot meant by the authoritative silence behind the *il* in French; behind and across the "it," a hidden conversation goes on, a communication between the perceived authority, the author, who has a special license to narrate the world from outside it, and the reader or listener, who, in the end, accepts the authority relayed through the medium of the third. For Blanchot in the novel and especially in Kafka's novels "he/she/it" is a by-product of a higher level conversation between I and you. This can also be read in reverse. For the reader is the one who most desperately needs to place an authority somewhere in order to trust in the narrative, and so when "it/he/she" is said, we hear a pronouncement made by a hidden authority, a distant and ultimate *il* discoursing continuously in the background.[1] Blanchot tells us that the difference with Kafka is that the distance between the narrator and the author, which is usually stabilizing, is carried into the center of the fiction such that the communication is "shaken" (Blanchot's word).

In the treatise, each cline has its own territory, making these words or positions less anaphors than juncture points; that is, they are the limits and the forcibly spaced out points for the taking place of complex social transactions. Furthermore, each juncture—*wir, sie, ich, du, er, sie,* and so on—contains and refers to each of the others in a distinct pattern from a unique perspective. As we have seen, the narrative juncture *er* is the point at which the listener's desire to place authority in an author crosses with the simultaneous wish to occult the fact that the reader, on little authority besides her or his own, has done the placing. Each of these clines or junctures—he, she, you, I, it—displays a different intermingling of wishes, attribution of authority, origin and directions of linguistic force, mood, and mode, and each particular intermingling of effects cannot be read in the pronoun alone but is ensconced in the context. Their surroundings structure them as much as they structure their surroundings.

The junctures or clines are not independent variables but are reciprocally determined by and determining of the intention of the sentences in which they are found. No set of rules, no grammar can isolate and regularize them. Each cline participates in a scene and a setting that colors its meaning and is colored in turn by it. And a cline comes with a history, as does every thought in the polylogue. Indeed, in the treatise the ultimate horizon of the setting is always in some way or other tradition, whether the tradition or traditions that precede the treatise in thoughts or the ones established within it by operations of iteration. For this reason, when moral matters are spoken about through a *du* ("thou/you"), we have to understand this juncture of relations and this cline toward possible meanings not only with reference to its scene, but also against the tradition of how these kinds of sayings have traditionally been made.[2] Every *du* has a horizon of expectation set by its ancient and ongoing place in commandments, prayer, summonses, and so forth. The "second-person standpoint," recently codified by Stephen Darwall, is also, as he says, the cornerstone of secular moral theory, at least since Kant.[3] This is largely because it is the index of commands, the mode of linguistic force by which a maxim is imposed. With only this short introduction, you can see how moral theory depends on the cline "you." It also depends on the interpretation of "you" as a "second person," in a scene of communication that has similarities with a *theophony*, a human being hearing and hearkening to the voice of God. Moral speech is always the imitation of a total authority speaking to an unauthorized servant, and "you" derives its force from this absolute unequal relationship, at least in moral matters. Even when, as Darwall points out, I am speaking to myself in the categorical imperative, "me" is not simply an object-form of myself, as it would be were I to perform some non-moral action on myself. I may dress myself or pinch myself, but in a moral self-relation I am always effectively if not actually addressing myself as "you," that is, submitting to myself. The categorical imperative is "second-personal."[4]

Let us accept that moral theory at least since Kant has a strong "second-personal" tendency, and let us recall also the theological tradition that precedes it, a theophony in which a mortal ear receives divine commandments. Kafka's thoughts themselves are often addressed to a "you," a *du*, especially when traditionally moral matters are at stake. In the thoughts Kafka produces a plethora of commandment-like scenarios. For that reason, after describing the logic of sense, it must be asked precisely how, in the speech logic of the polylogue, Kafka might employ the traditional functions of pronouns and their implied positionings, and then at key moments betray them.

22. The Logic of Sense

ERROR

Wherever an institution is conceived of as a complete whole in the fictions, letters, and diary entries, the bureaucrats, agents, attorneys, as well as those who seem to be in charge of the institution are subject to sudden and unexpected deviations. Officials make errors often, even the highest ones. Yet only because whatever institution is rumored to be perfectly consistent can the "errors" count as erroneous. An error is measured against a rectilinear hall, an idealized procedure, a perfect protocol, a conclusive trial, a unified judiciary, and the people, language, reasoning, and actions subject to these idealizations are repeatedly haunted by the possibility of mishaps. At the same time, the constant threat of errors points out what could be called the intrinsic errors (*Grundfehler*)[5] of Kafka's world. First of all, the logic by which the world operates is as strict as the most stringent mathematical proof. Against this strictness all deviations become errors. No mystery here; the court, the castle, Amerika, China, the burrow, all these regions are supposed to be spatially sinuous and gaplessly consequent in their logical operations. Yet an oddity in this gaplessness rankles us. There is never any chance for sedition or resistance against the world and its seamless operation, and reform is not on the horizon. "Errors" are also the only alternative to perfection. They are moments of play in the algorithm, usually quite trivial ones (*Kleinigkeiten*), but this does not diminish their significance. Despite their triviality, they cause a lot of worry and speculation.

> In such a large authority as the count's, it sometimes happens that one department will arrange this matter, another that, and neither hears about it from the other. A higher supervisory department [*die übergeordnete Kontrolle*] checks everything, and very closely too, but of its nature such supervision comes too late, and so a little confusion can still arise. To be sure, that is only in the tiniest of minor details [*nur winzigste Kleinigkeiten*], such as your own case, and to the best of my knowledge no mistake of the kind has ever been made in matters of real importance, but the minor ones [*die Kleinigkeiten*] often give trouble enough.[6]

For personages in *The Castle* it is de rigueur to speak in generalities like this. Officials are the worst of all. The little errors that the town superintendent exposes here are lent an air of predictability by the generalizing way of talking. "There are always little things . . . "—*Kleinigkeiten.* The deviations and conflicts that happen to arise between various divisions in the administration, say, and the way they are talked about, as here by the town intendant (*Vorsteher*) imply another logic. Coordinating a big administration where internal divisions of responsibility are necessary and at the same time threatening, not only produces but requires little errors. They become necessary in order that the supervisory command can arrive to put things right, and the image of the whole ultimately arises out of these repeated acts of supervision of tiny mishaps. The errors are produced by the conceit of a whole that they in turn produce; through the constant intervention of authorities arises the illusion of a system.

Institutions are not the only things subject to error. People are as well. Kafka only ever calls two people "error free" (*fehlerlos/fehlerfrei*), but even this designation is telling. Barnabas in *The Castle* is free of error. The poet Franz Werfel (Kafka's counterpart, "little Franz") is too. This may be because they are deeply naïve rather than because their logic is flawless, however.

Let us try to imagine a literary text, or, rather, without getting ahead of ourselves, let us imagine a "piece of writing" as a set of premises derived from an axiom—a rule for their combination—that leads to the production of a valid conclusion from the good combination of premises. We can imagine the ideal behind this, the ideal of consistency, movement, and the lending of truth. There are minor mistakes in Goethe's *Iphigenie*,[7] Kafka notes in his diary, though this is perhaps less easy to understand than the mistakes he finds in Max Brod's plodding 1915 novel *Jüdinnen* (Jewesses),[8] compared by Kafka with a formula or procedure for "seeking and finding a solution to the Jewish question."[9] If this is the logical procedure of Brod's novel, Kafka notes in 1911, it contains at least three mistakes. First, anyone even remotely concerned with the problem and its possible solutions is merely peripheral to the story. Second, the group of Jews about whom the story turns lacks non-Jewish spectators who draw them into the open, advance on them, and shock them into confusion, doubt, and envy. Finally, one character, a Jewish youth who gets the best of everything and is hardly tainted by the ills of being Jewish, could be dispensed with.

Kafka corrects the errors in Brod's literary political formula, but, unsurprisingly, he saves the most cutting schoolmaster's strikeouts for his own writing. When he reads it aloud to friends, he discovers "ineradicable errors" (*unverwischbare Fehler*) in his story "In the Penal Colony" ("In der Strafkolonie").[10] When he returns to finish "The Village Schoolteacher" ("Der Dorfschullehrer") in 1914, he laments that it already has "two incurable errors in it" (*zwei unheilbare Fehler in sich*).[11] These are not merely the "scribal errors" (*Schreibfehler*) that preoccupy him from an early stage.[12] And they are not the other kind of mistakes in language usage, about which he obsesses continually. He is often preoccupied with his and his friends' Prague German.[13] The two types of errors, linguistic and logical, share an archetype. From behind the perfect, errorless story and the perfect, errorless High German utterance there scowls the terrible school exercise. Either the student enters the warm comfort of the group or else she is exposed as an alien and a fraud. Error is thus not only a mark of the failure of a logical operation; it is also, from childhood in its real occurrence in the classroom, the most traumatic cause of social exclusion.[14] In this sense, "error free" does not necessarily mean that Barnabas and Werfel are innocent or perfect, but rather that they do not stand out and thus for a while at least can avoid shame.

When Kafka talks about his stories as if he had been given a problem set and had stayed up all night trying to solve them, it is hard to imagine what standard, what protocol he is following, and who the authority behind it might be. This is not the way we imagine the artist at work, and especially not the "modernist" author.

So we have three questions to answer, or so it seems: What is the set of problems that Kafka sets out to solve? What procedure and what rules does he intend to follow? Why does he see his project as demanding consistency and nevertheless tending to produce errors? And further questions suggest themselves. Who is the authority imposing the particular problem set for Kafka's writing, what are the standards for validity of the procedure, and who evaluates the truth of its results?

As a possible answer to these questions, let us quote a passage that Kafka repeats three times. He writes it once in his diary, as a draft toward a final letter to Felice. Once he copies it into a letter to Felice, in fact, the penultimate letter he sends her. And once he copies it from there into a letter to Brod.

Toward a letter to F, maybe the last (1 Oct)
    When I test myself against my final goal, it turns out that I do not really strive to become a good person and to correspond to a highest court,

but, quite the contrary, to gain an overview of the entire human and animal community, to know their fundamental proclivities, wishes, and ethical ideals, to reduce them to simple precepts [Vorschriften] and to develop
myself as quickly as possible in their direction, so that I would become thoroughly pleasing to everyone and indeed (here comes the leap) so pleasing
that, at last, without losing the universal love, I, as the only sinner who is
not roasted, could be allowed to bring out into the open all my immanent
spites and meannesses. In summary, it depends for me only on the court of
humanity [here he adds, in the letter to Felice, "and of animality"] and, besides, I want to defraud it, though admittedly without cheating.[15]

The procedure he announces here for arriving at simples by means of
complexes he calls reduction or leading back (*Zurückführen*), though we
should guard against the obvious confusion with Husserlian bracketing
or its later methodological formalization in the various reductions. It is
clear from this passage that the treatise in thoughts either is or is very
close to the actual carrying out of this *Zurückführung*. It is also clear that
the aim of Kafka's "reduction" is neither epistemological nor phenomenological; he does not set out to bracket a "natural" disposition, or to transit through semblance to essence. It does not lead to consciousness, but
rather to a set of commitments, taken not as the structure of a being, but
rather as precepts habitually followed, *Vorschriften*. This is not the way
things really are, then, but what has been pre-scribed. It is implied that
behaviors and attitudes, cultural forms and ideals all derive from these
precepts. We learn that a relationship that could be called derivation, descent, entailment, influence, tradition, or some such dynamism links the
originary precepts with a huge variety of attitudes and commitments.

In the letter to Brod, Kafka also calls this plan: "a blinding piece of
self-knowledge."[16] This is how Kafka envisions his life task: as potentially shameful; he also calls it with no little irony his "epitaph." Needless
to say, in light of these remarks, unlike Husserl, Kafka is not setting
the foundation for a science that anyone else could practice. He plans,
through this "leading back," in the ultimate gesture, to sacrifice himself
by exposing his own intrinsic "errors," all the internal basenesses (*Gemeinheiten*) that make him a representative of the human and animal
communities. An important wordplay is at work here the we shouldn't
ignore: the community, *Gemeinschaft* has something in common with
the errors of its greatest student, with his *Gemeinheiten*. He plans to turn
these errors from sins into idiosyncrasies, and to show the community

that it in fact is based on them. His "ultimate goal" ("Endziel") is to identify these precepts, develop in their direction, and expose his base-nesses, and yet reaching the goal will mean ceasing to act as though his life were judged by "a highest court" ("einem höchsten Gericht"). He does not plan to eradicate his errors, only to celebrate them in their proper medium. A final, authoritative court of good and evil is not the proper judge of social errors. These are not judged at all in fact, but are exposed in the milieu of shame. Kafka writes Felice of the human court in which such things are adjudicated, "and this I will moreover defraud [*betrügen*], though without cheating [*Betrug*]."[17] Why is this fraud but not cheating? Because the human court always makes reference to a higher court, just as positive law makes reference to natural law, earthly authority to a highest authority. Kafka's fraud is precisely not to accept this principle of the human court. It is not cheating because the tran-scendence of law and judgment is a deception. Thus when he exposes his errors to the community, he teaches them through his shame that the community, *Gemeinschaft*, is a community of basenesses, a *Gemein-heitenschaft*, with no access to ideals. Their sins *qua* errors do them good and should not be eradicated.

NEGATION

The fascination with error reminds us that Kafka believes his and others' literary works ought to serve a demand for internal consistency. What the consistency of a story or novel might consist in is a topic for another occasion. The treatise in thoughts, however, serves a slightly dif-ferent demand. The central logical operation of the thoughts, in a logic whose objective is to slow rather than to promote the movement of truth across premises, is negation. And yet, negation cannot be only a logical operation, unless you want it to become positive. Not A is equivalent to positing the opposite of A; indeed negation in propositional logic is a form of positing. In order to avoid becoming instantly positive, the nega-tive too must be subjected to negativity. It must not become immediately productive of an entity, a placeholder, a premise; it must be slowed and if possible stopped, such that it remains negative. *Doing the negative is still enjoined on us, the positive is already given.*[18] This is first of all an observa-tion about a kind of logic, even before being an opinion about a historical moment or the plight of Jews in Central Europe or workers under indus-trial capital, although it likely has to do with these as well. The thought is not a maxim exactly; it is a descriptive entry in a guidebook to practical reason. Kafka describes a way of dealing with two non-equivalent logical dispositions, the positive and the negative. A positive statement is always tautological—even if it is "synthetic"—because its attitude toward its object is as something given. To say something positive, to posit or assert of something that it is what it is, even in a synthetic judgment, is in effect to say nothing. The negative, in contrast, is a "doing," *ein "Tun,"* which steps beyond the given. It is enjoined on us as something to be done, the negative; up to now it has not given itself fully, has stopped before it reached its end, so that it can return once again to do what has not been given.

Around the time Kafka returns to edit the thoughts in 1920, in another series of passages sometimes known as the *er* fragments, he jots down the following remark: "The power to negate [*die Kraft zum Verneinen*], this most natural expression of the forever changing, renewing, dying-off coming-alive human warrior-organism, we possess always, but not the courage, since after all life is negation, and so negation is affirmation."[19] One could easily confuse this sentiment—*all life is negation*—with sociological dogmas about the speed of change, the instability of modern life, the loss of tradition. One could also think this was an existential statement about temporal beings. And yet, listen to the work of negation in the passage itself. Kafka sets out the problem as precisely as possible. Negation is an expression of our life and death, an expression of the struggle between the two that is the being of the human organism. In short, it is an expression. So first of all, neither death nor life is negative with respect to some otherwise whole and positive being. It is not that either life or death is nothing, a nihil. That is to say, negation is not something that affects us, so not physiological or psychological—not an organ or a gene, a need or an attachment, a drive or a personality trait. Negation is two things in the passage, an expression and a "power." It is an expression of the self-differing being, the self-negating being, the being in battle with itself. One is, or as Kafka writes "possesses," negation as the most basic power, and yet the one thing that one cannot negate is this type of negation that springs from the essence of the human being, *Kampf.* Here Kafka introduces a distinction between negations. For if life is struggle, and if negation springs from this struggle, then this kind of negation, Kafka notes, is simply what life is, "after all," and so *Kampf* is not negative but positive, not a negation but an affirmation. In this thought, the *volta* comes just here, where negation, not to mention also "life" or whatever it will subsequently be called, flips into affirmation. Negation is affirmation insofar as struggle is the essence of life. In negating, one struggles . . . yet again. In the treatise Kafka sought to resist this inevitability. But he had to do this obviously without struggling, and so a different negation was needed. There is a logical issue at stake here as well. Negation depends on a prior affirmation. This is how it has been conceptualized in propositional logic since Aristotle.[20] This is why a double negation in logic is equivalent to an affirmation.

Between the 1920 thought of negation and the 1917 thought of the negative a conceptual tendency emerges—Kafka wants us to believe that negativity needs to be rethought, redoubled, redeployed. Its great powers have been cut down and turned into their opposite. One might say, the negative needs to become something else, needs in some as yet unthought way to negate itself.

To negate the negative cannot mean to do to itself exactly what negativity had been doing all along.[21] Negating negation, for Kafka, is not a matter of self-referential inversion into an affirmation, nihilistic repetition, or dialectics. Kafka's negation is supposed to deny itself its customary habits, block off its habitual routes and disrupt its routines, become less or more than it was; and on the way it has to be given different names. The aim, we mustn't forget, is to release the "doing" of the negative from any posit, to treat it as not yet given. One way to do this is to think of negation itself as unfinished, as not perfectly negating, as not fully what it is or does; for, it is logical to think that as soon as the negative accomplishes its task it becomes something given, and ceases to count as negativity.

Even in Hegel where the negative is dynamic and really precedes affirmation, affirmation still always precedes negation ideally. Affirmation is the goal and end of negation and determines its activities a priori, even if what is affirmed is a composite of the negated and the new. Dialectical change is different from the simple alternation alluded to by Kafka in the 1920 fragment but it is still a combination of dying-off and coming-alive, and so it has affinities with the dialectic. Hegel says it succinctly: "the negation of negation is something positive."[22] And although we are only at the simplest moment in the dialectic, in the thrall of mere existence, nevertheless as double negation becomes further defined—it is certainly interesting that once it "becomes" mediation, the negative operator never itself needs to be negated again, as if something had to stay primitive, stunted, underdeveloped, undialectical, in order for the dialectic to proceed—the conversion of negative into positive repeats again and again. In truth, even in the dialectic of "mere existence," in the most limited concept of the negative: negation is a movement beyond negativity.

We should never forget that the negation of negation continues to operate within all positivities, concrete and abstract, singular and universal—Hegel reminds us; the day always has the night within it. Kafka is not referring to Hegel and probably not to dialectics, and nonetheless a critique of dialectics takes place in the 1920 fragment. In sum, it says there is nothing negative in dialectical negation. Insofar as it is consistently negative, historical dialectics is equivalent to affirmation, to stating "what is" or "what has been given." This can be read in the modality of statements about negativity. In an affirmative judgment such as "the *mediation* that the negation of negation is"[23] the power of the negative is already diminished. Wherever the "source" of history, spirit, and the concept is negation, there is little negation—wherever, that is, negation is judged by its results. Yet negation "itself," Kafka wants to point out, cannot be posited. It is the most contradictory, let's say, or the least defined. "It is" the undetermined per se, and yet we cannot say even this without determining it, that is, without betraying its injunction.

What does it mean when Kafka writes to Max Brod in 1919 about his new correspondent, Milena Jesenská, using an altogether different double or perhaps a triple negative? Milena, he writes, is "not-Jewess and not not-Jewess, in particular not not-Jewess, not German, not not-German"?[24] The logical operation in this locution, hard as it is to sum up in a word, has by the time of this letter become one of the central Kafkan modes of negation, and at least in part it satisfies the demand that the negative be "a doing" and never finished, remaining "enjoined on us." Let us call this indefinite negation. Whatever Milena might have meant to Kafka personally at this moment, for a moment she became a variable in a logic experiment that had already been in the works for several years. Her position in Vienna, where she lived with a husband she couldn't live with and yet took responsibility for, was untenable by any standards, and this was what Kafka tried to express to Brod, the character of a life not affirmable. Milena spoke and wrote Czech before other languages and she came from a non-Jewish family, and yet she also wrote German and was fascinated with Jews and Jewishness, and maybe she exhibited a few traits

Kafka associated with being a "Jewess." None of this is surprising for a citizen of Austro-Hungary on the eve of its dissolution. Yet Kafka writes the syntagm as an identity statement, communicating something beyond hybridity of heritage, cultural affinity, or linguistic habits.[25]

"Not and not-not" is an attempt to negate without thereby also positing. It sketches out an arena of tendencies and associations without asserting belonging. And most of all, it restrains itself from evoking a prior or for that matter an ultimate affirmation. In a sense we know less about Milena from this statement than we assumed we did before. We do learn by it, however, that several determinate negations do not apply to her, the most common and the most urgent either-ors of the day and the region—German/Jew or German/Czech or Jew/Czech—and so in fact Milena will have been de-determined by a mode of negation that refuses to fully determine itself, by including within itself both a not and a not-not. This is a form of inclusive negation by which whatever it was in *Deutschtum* and *Judentum* that allowed the social and political lexicon reciprocally to determine the one by the other and vice versa would falter. Inclusive negation, in this situation, means that the determinates are not negated for the sake of other, more precise ones; Milena is included in the category "Jew" and in the category "Czech" but the way in which she is included is indeterminate, its meaning still "enjoined" upon us.

A comparison with Kant may be fruitful here. We know that in notes and sketches as well as in the lectures on logic,[26] but most famously in the *Critique of Pure Reason*,[27] Kant distinguishes between a negative judgment, in which the copula is negated, and what he calls, observing a distinction in sentence logic made by Wolff and other predecessors going back to Boethius, an "infinite judgment,"[28] where the predicate term is negated. Not-x is the form of the infinite judgment. Kant calls it infinite because it does not give a finite determination, but instead by negating a single finite determination it opens the subject to an infinity of possible determinations that, except for not being x, are not further specified. Just because Schopenhauer condemns infinite judgments as "a hair-splitting farce" (*eine spitzfindige Posse*), as Albert Menne reminds us,[29] does not mean we should be so quick to dismiss them; indeed, Schopenhauer's dismissal may give us cause to linger over this strange, hybrid judgment, which has at times been assimilated to affirmation although it has a negative form, and at times to negative judgments although it does not judge, at least not in the usual way. What can be said about these judgments oddly within and also beyond affirmation and negation is that in them determination does not achieve the intended end of marking out the boundaries of the object in question. Kant calls the release from determination that this sort of judgment gives rise to an "unrestricted scope" (*unbeschränkter Umfang*). His example is "the soul is not-mortal" (*nichtsterblich*).[30] Taking away the single determination diminishes the scope of possible determinations quantitatively not at all, although qualitatively it can no longer be counted among the types of things that are "x." The soul example is telling, because unlike judgments that affirm an infinitely large set of alternatives—for example, "the fruit is not red" or "the number is not 1"—"the soul is not-mortal" conventionally assumes only a single alternative: "immortal."

This is presumably why Kant includes "infinite" judgments under quality as opposed to quantity, as almost all his predecessors did. The resulting determination is quantitatively unbounded in possibilities; though qualitatively it may say a single crucial thing, such as "souls never die," in an infinite judgment no limitation diminishes further possible determinations. This is related to the sense Kant has that an infinite judgment doesn't "do" anything. He says it "leaves all content unaffected."[31]

However he may diminish the threat of infinite determinations, one thing is clear: the issue is determination. Beatrice Longuenesse shows that infinite judgment is a type of limitation, and that limitation is a conceptual operation of the understanding that substitutes and obviates the need for an *ens realissimum* as the ground or standard for experience. Instead of God, we have a sphere of all possible predicates. "The category of limitation thus becomes pivotal for the other two categories of quality. Indeed, it is the category of quality. For, by its means, all positive determinations (realities) of any object as appearance are thought as delimited against the background of all the determinations that do not belong to it (negations), all of which, however, belong to the common infinite sphere of the concept 'given in the forms of space and time.'"[32] A thing gets its place in the world not from a comparison to God, as a creature or an emanation say, but instead from its delimitation against all the things it is not. To be sure, its "place" can only be known in this manner negatively (x is not [infinite] not-x), but the negation under which it falls limits it to a set of positive possibilities.

Stopping at this preparatory step, Kant goes on to insist, Longuenesse tells us, that a total set of positive determinations making up "reality" would have to be thinkable in order for even this sort of negative-positive determining operation to function. More than this horizon of determinability, an actual determination of every object would have to apply, whether we knew it, could know it, or not. The section "The Transcendental Ideal" gives the details. Suffice it for us to focus on one crucial detail: Kant imposes a "principle of thoroughgoing determination" (*Grundsatz der durchgängigen Bestimmung*).[33] This principle states that for a thing to be a thing, not only does one out of all the possible determinations have to determine it, but also contradictory determinations cannot and have to be excluded. The principle of non-contradiction depends on the principle of thoroughgoing determination. No need to ask whether Kant considered the other kind of contradictory proposal that an object could be both not-x and not not-x, that a third possibility beyond negative and positive might apply. Infinite judgment is an epistemological measure taken in a world whose thoroughgoing determinacy is posited a priori and the description of this determinacy is: *tertium non datur*. An "all" of possibilities is necessary for anything to be determined, but this all itself is not just a mere possibility; it is a set of fully determined entities. The "all" is variously talked about as a principle, as a "transcendental presupposition,"[34] as required for cognizing a thing, as a concept that cannot, however, be exhibited *in concreto*, and finally as an "ideal of pure reason."[35]

To sum up, there are two parts of Kant's principle of thoroughgoing determinacy.

1. "The proposition Everything existing is thoroughly determined signifies not only that of every given pair of opposed predicates, but also of every pair of possible predicates, one of them must always apply to it."[36]

2. "All true negations are then nothing but limits, which they could not be called unless they were grounded in the unlimited (the All)."[37] ["The unlimited" not being the same as the "undelimited," of course—PN.]

At first glance we might feel unsure how these premises could be consistent with one another, and yet they are not at all in tension. This is because the "all" is thought of as a quantitatively unlimited set of determinations, such that any possibility is a possible thing, that is to say a latently actual determination. Predicates, even possible ones, are for applying, just as judgments are for determining. Leaving the more obvious situation of contradiction aside, how you *know* which of two possible (noncontradictory) predicates should apply (*zukommen*) is unimportant. What is set out here is a deduction of the principle that one of them must always apply, and this results in the confirmation of a fully determinable world. We see now in Kantian terms how the positive is given and the negative is already positing. This is what Kant means by a "true negation."

Now we also begin to see, on the one hand, how strange it is in this history of negativity for indeterminacy to hold such a privileged position for Kafka, and, on the other hand, how Kafka's convictions about the world are fundamentally different than Kant's. The thought keeps returning. Things cannot be determinately negated because they are constitutively indeterminate, and so the kind of real negation one might call "destruction" is a category error, a logical or ideal negative used for a real situation: *what crumbles crumbles, it cannot however be destroyed.*[38]

Kant identifies a need for a logical and ontological ground for a nature that is a totality of positivities, within which negation functions only as determination (*Bestimmung*), through limitation on possible series. Kafka denies the need for this ground, suggesting that the very idea is pernicious and brings about, on the one side, the illusion that it hopes to avoid, the false idea that one is negating when one is determining objects; on the other side, it brings about suffering, a sense that one cannot bear the thoroughly determined world and must therefore escape to freedom from determination, or perish trying.

Indefinite negation differs from infinite judgment in several ways. In the first place, it does more than negate a predicate. It also negates the negation, without cancelling its effect. Contra Kant, there are negations that are not limits, even if they are logical and ontological negations. Paradise for instance, by Kafka's reasoning, is no less not-paradise than it is not not-paradise. In Kant's vision, the intuition that corresponds to the concept of limitation is space. This is why the negation of a predicate, while producing an indeterminate judgment, points toward a sphere of determinacy, the sphere of objects in absolute space. Everything in space is determined, except for space itself, although space is just another name for the infinite possibility for further determinations. Even if we keep to this spatial medium of non-compenetrables—what in Kafka would be, rather, one very specific kind of intuition, call it architectural or the milieu of "construction"—Kafka's indefinite negation would not look like the drawing of a specific limit within a sphere in which the only possible expression of negativity was delimitation.

"Not and not-not" has strong affinities with the "a" in atheology, which itself is not not theology, that is, not atheism, and still it is other than theology, not the logos of god. Indefinite negation bespeaks a paradisal situation, one precisely not human and not divine, although it may not be a paradise to which anyone would want to return. In the treatise, indefinite negation is the gift paradise gives to history. Here paradise shows its atheological provenance. *If that which in paradise was supposed to have been destroyed was destructible/destroyable, then it was not decisive; if it was indestructible, we live in a false belief.*[39] This thought is both an example of Kafka's indefinite negation and an explanation of its origin. The Garden, being not-paradisal and not not-paradisal, destructible and indestructible at once, gives rise to all the indeterminacy that follows. One can say the same of Adam as Kafka says about paradise, as Kierkegaard does at one point:[40] if he had been corruptible, he was not innocent; if he was innocent, there could have been no corruption. Yet instead of preserving a first, perfect Adam, in whom one has faith, and a second, derivative Adam, who lives in history, Kafka imagines them combined. Paradise both can and cannot be itself; one might say that it is truly itself if the effect it produces in us is neither disappointment nor hope. Such is the negativity of "Genesis" for Kafka—it keeps asking us to rethink its actuality, on the suspicion that it might be impossible.

In a late chapter of *The Castle,* the official named Bürgel tells us that castle secretaries are only helpful when you catch them off duty, and, furthermore, that at that precise moment their help is not valid. Since Bürgel himself is a castle secretary, K. must determine whether this general rule was stated in his official capacity or not. In this way truth is impeded by logic, not facilitated by it, and not because the logic is invalid, or because a self-referential paradox cannot be overcome; truth is impeded because the logic is specifically a logic of what stands outside it, and this is not possible, or at least not conceivable. Beings are also impeded by ontologic: there are many examples of creatures who seem to come under indeterminate negation—Odradek in Kafka's story "The Cares of a Family Man" comes to mind, as does the CatLamb in

"A Crossbreed." Josef K. lives the indeterminacy in *The Trial* and yet he cannot name it; if he could he would say that he is not guilty and not-not guilty. The side-room, the corridor, the closet, the multiplicity of doors—in their circumparambulation these non-places describe the low likelihood that he will receive an acquittal, a *Freispruch*. What can it mean for something to not not apply (and not apply)? An alternative to the law of contradiction lurks here, as does a challenge to the common notion of change. The two of course are linked. Something that cannot logically be different in the same aspect at the same time can only suggest a time in which self-identical states are successively left behind, such that aspects do not conflict, but instead alter. Logic and "our concept of time" are in league together. Aristotle thinks this is true not only of natural entities that develop, but also of intellectual faculties that learn. One only knows *after* one does not know, never before, and one is never ignorant and knowing at the same time. Kafka takes issue with the inner contract between logic and time. In a dictum from the era of the latest editing of the treatise in thoughts, in 1920, he writes: "I am able to swim like other people, I only have a better memory than they do, I have not forgotten my former not-being-able-to swim. Since I haven't forgotten this, however, being able to swim doesn't help me at all and after all then I am not able to swim."[41] This image teaches that the core of any ability is an inability that precedes it and makes it possible, that a self depends on a negation of a former self, on an ability to be not oneself: this is what "being able to" means. Here however, the inability, although it precedes the ability, cannot be pushed back comfortably into the past. The inability precedes the ability at each instant at the same time in the same respect such that it can be said also to follow the ability. The inability to swim is within the ability, it accompanies each stroke, such that swimming is less the actualization of a potential than the accessing of a primary impotence. This logic is demonstrated perfectly with the example of swimming. Water: in equal parts it buoys you up and drags you down into its depths. Because the swimmer can only swim to the extent that he is not sinking, swimming is not a power, a potency, an activity, a possibility, a positivity. Rather, to swim is to drown again and again, and one's resistance to drowning is drawn from the profundity under it. Anyone who has tried to swim in a puddle can verify this.

23. The Logic of Speech

THE DOMINANT CLINE

Let us start with a surprising statement about the second logic, the logic of speech. The *du* form is promoted in the grammar of the poly-logue: *You are the task. No student far and wide.*[42] This appeal, this imposition, this improper, intimate, unauthorized communication—about the absence of a third person to receive the schoolteacher's lesson: what linguistic force works in and through this peculiar appeal? It says that no one else is around when teaching is happening; not even in point of fact an "I." Teaching will have happened in and to a "you." Refer only to you, it says. There are other pronouns and other kinds of addresses in the treatise, to be sure. Yet we hear in this thought a rule for all teaching: there shall be no other than you. A maxim says, stereotypically: do not foist responsibility onto another, you are subject and object of this judgment, you are the ideal unit of ethical material to be shaped, you are the substance of change. It says: only you. Let us not assimilate this too quickly to an "other": other is not "you." Other is a third person, he, she, it—over there, coming, alien.

Our hypothesis that there is only "you" in the polylogue, with the corollary that the other pronouns or junctures or clines are subordinated to "you," is confusing at best, paradoxical if you look harder, and perhaps at bottom impossible, certainly by the standards of sociolinguistics, for which the *socius* is a coordinated, functional plurality of third persons ordered by relations of authority and power, in other words of distance and exteriority, which ultimately attach to a self, seen, for the purposes of scientific study, as a self-substance. How could there be only "you"? One benefit: were there no "she," society would not need to be explained, since explanation is a method for accessing alien, impersonal substances. Persons are the most impersonal. Yet how can we constitute ourselves as a group if we do not begin from persons? What is a group if not some multiple of "she" units? Where there is no group, there is just a single po-sition, or this is the fear—fear of solipsism, or, on the other hand, totali-tarianism. And what about the speaker? Must he, must Franz Kafka or whoever speaks in these missives, not be or have been an "I" in order to initiate the address? No, the speaker is "you" as well. Before we discover how to think about this strange structure in which each pole is you or "a" you, we should note that, if it is true that "you" is the fundamental or indeed the only real position across the thoughts, then we would have to dispense with most of the aspects that linguists attribute to pronouns and persons.[43] The inclusivity and exclusivity exhibited in "we" and "they" ("we" on its own can either be inclusive or exclusive of the speaker, inclusive or exclusive of third personal others)[44] would not be operative, nor would the narrative mode or mood, and the distancing, objectifying, semanticizing gesture at work when you say "he" or "she." When *you* say "he" or "she"—here begins the real difference. Each pronoun or speech position, every juncture or cline at which a constellation of power and distance, appearance and disappearance, force, resistance, and submission collects and distributes itself originates in the most intimate *du*. "You" is the grammatical-personal presence of care as speech. Whatever is attributed to an alien thing is first of concern to a "you." Whatever the grouping principle, "you" has to accept it. We can show how this is so in the polylogue, with a few arguments.

First, to distinguish our argument from narratological considerations, let us take a thought written at the end of February, one of the last thoughts to occur to Kafka that winter. *"But then he returned to his work as if nothing had happened." That is a remark familiar to us from an amorphous wealth of old stories, even though it might actually appear in none of them.*[45] If we provisionally set aside the content of this remark and the commentary appended to it, although it is an important question whether it refers to God, interrupted during creation, or, as is more likely, to Kierkegaard's Abraham, a figure with whom Kafka was occupied over these weeks—; if we set these questions about content aside and focus on the genre, as Kafka himself does, hearing the quoted sentence, you take "he" as emblematic of "old stories" (*alte Erzählungen*), or so the speaker claims.[46] Something about the sentence leads us to place it in an amorphous tradition at an indeterminate time and place, such that the "old" story to which it belongs stands beyond the span of events we consider "ours," although it can be recounted. Although it can be recounted the narration never brings it any nearer. "He" is a marker of distance, meaning in effect "not you." Much can be said about the magic of distance that seems to emanate from old stories in Kafka's fictions. The other set of *pensées* written in 1920 almost without exception shift their basic pronoun from *du* to *er*, and the force of the pronoun also changes. *Er* is much closer to *du* in those passages anyway. Some of the magic of that "he" derives from its ability to leap over intermediary epochs, leaping over history altogether. This is an important Kafkan insight, a central motif and operation for which Benjamin invented a category. Kafkan beings often belong to "the unforgotten." The deep obligation our world has to forgotten things, and the surprise they produce when they address us, lead us to designate them with the third person alien. Nothing is closer to consciousness in Kafka's stories than the unforgotten *er*, an ancient creature emerging from the mists. A distant impersonal event becomes intimate and urgent, the forgotten becomes unforgotten; but this only means that "she" comes to "you," becomes a "you." The comfortable distance is abrogated and the third person bows before the second. There is no such thing as an old story: you are the task, no student, and so on.

When "he" is spoken out of a fund of old stories, when you hear tradition speaking in its impersonal, distant voice saying "this concerned them (not us, and potentially us, again)," this too—each time again it speaks intimately and with a particular kind of force to "you." Indeed "he" is always said by a you to a you. Karl Bühler called the overarching semantic category "appeal" (*Ansprechen*), opposing it to "expression" (*Ausdruck*) and "representation" (*Darstellung*). These correlate roughly to the force of grammatical second person, first person, and third person, respectively.[47] What is remarkable, and Bühler does not say this directly, is that every representation ("she") and expression ("I") has to be an appeal to a you that hears or overhears it, now or at a later date. All these events of language as events are implicitly intended for a you, and perhaps also for one beyond "you" to whom you may be speaking, a you who is not intended, a second person secondary to the intimate and immediate speech act in its presentness. We can hear a silent searching second person within *you are the only task*. It says "this is for you" and the question is: for whom? Yet this can only be answered ex post facto.

Who addresses you? Who says "you"? It would be only natural to imagine an "I" making these appeals, waiting for a response, appealing or commanding, with its own motives and agency.[48] It is as absurd to think of an "appeal" in Bühler's terms without an "I" as it is to think of speech without a speaker. Whether *The Trial* narrates the story under the guise of an I or a he, we nevertheless pick up in the background, as Blanchot witnessed for us, well beyond the narrator even, an ultimate person whispering above all the narrative chatter directly to the reader.

In the fictions, more often than not, you can comfortably assert that they are not for you, not about you, but told by a third person about some further third person. Disavowing involvement is part of the moral structure of the modern novel and I believe Kafka plays on the tendency toward disavowal when he famously changes the pronouns in *The Castle* from I to he, and when he writes the second set of thoughts whose protagonists are all *er,* the mode of address of one displacing responsibility onto another. In the polylogue, however, the "I" that could by rights take responsibility for these thoughts is already "you." The relationship is asymmetrical: there can be no first person without a second person, no subject without a co-ject, even if the second person is part of a self address, even if you were speaking to, about, and for yourself. A shift in Kafka's more personal writing may underlie this emphasis in his *pensées.* Around the time of the *Blutsturz* and just after, a cluster of dialogues fills the diary, and, where rather innocently for the previous seven years Kafka had most often addressed journal entries with the declarative or expressive *ich,* he now begins to adorn the entries with *du,* and he also starts to make demands on himself in a different way.

On September 15, 1917, one of the last diary entries before a long hiatus says: "You have, as far as the possibility exists at all, a possibility to make a beginning. Don't squander it."[49] The *du* address is closely associated with the imperative mood. It is also closely associated with the idea of address itself. But before we can discuss the subject and predicate of a sentence, or the speaker and receiver of a communicative act, we need to consider two proto-linguistic gestures. The hail and the petition. The invitation to receive a command flies out before the command, a pre- or proto-address is issued, a first risky, open-ended quasi-speech gesture makes a plea for the receptivity for further speech. "You," even if it is said silently is a "hail" that can be associated with the divine address of the first humans in the Tanakh. Kafka quotes the framework or bare structure of divine address that underlies the prohibition and punishment that will come true in the fall: *When . . . you must die.*[50] Commandments are given with a prior hail, a *du!* that initiates the address. As often happens in the *Tanakh,* in Kafka's thoughts the proto-address, the "hail" comes from nowhere and is addressed to no one in particular. Every "you" in the treatise, before being part of a command or an appeal or an address to an addressee is first of all a summons to no one in particular to become the receiver of an address. "You!" is not a communicative act. Nothing is communicated in it. It is also not a speech act. Nothing is "done" with words. The hail is the originary opening to the possibility of a linguistic event and it makes the receiver receptive for the first time, or else it doesn't. It is highly precarious. Whether spoken out or left implicit in a verb conjugation, "you" is said first in order to make way for speech that may or may not happen. Through a hail, receptivity is bidden before anyone has even become receptive. We must not immediately confuse it with a call or summons or a request for a response; these gestures are already too directed, too solicitous, too act-like, too determinate in their context and motivations. They involve a prior recognition, one that itself would have been made possible previously by a "you" and a raising of the head, a pricking up of the ears, or the opposite, resistance and deafness, or distraction. In the hail there is not yet any recognition, only a making ready for an interaction without a single assurance that anyone will respond or know how to. "You" hails blindly, daring a correspondence, proposing an encounter, proposing too the possibility of speech, and in so proposing already being the most general speech and encounter, spoken to no one of nothing.

We wouldn't want to call this a dialogic self, or for that matter an uncanny self. It is not a double I or half of an I-thou; it is you and you alone—all alone except for you. Awkward as it may sound and feel, we continue to say only "you." One of its characteristics is that each time it is said "you" deflects attention from the source to the receiver. It is the pure deference of "you," "no you," "no you." Such a picture of deferential receptivity can only become understandable if we hear, each time, the "you" turned back on its speaker, so that the speaker is seen not from her own perspective but already from "yours." In the shadow of "you," we could almost claim, there is no "own" perspective,[51] and so we step beyond perspectivism, since even in Nietzsche's dispersed reflections on it, perspective, while certainly a way to pluralize the understanding of the world, still preserves a multiplicity of first-person-like positions, single conduits through which sense data is in each unique case uniquely schematized. His is after all a philosophy of the will, while in Kafka's . . . the second person is yielded to and has already yielded to "you."

A hail makes room for a polylogue, a series of seconds, each second to the other and to itself, with no number higher than two (never a plural you; no "you all") and no number lower than two, no single individual. A hail positions respondents as yielding, as having already yielded their self and their primacy; it constitutes them as needful of something only "you" can give, an ear, a seconding. In a dialogue, when you say "I," you are first and foremost offering yourself as a "you" to someone else.

It doesn't matter whether "you" prefaces an imperative, an accusation, or a defeated cry. "You have destroyed everything without having really possessed any of it. How will you ever put it back together?"[52] In each case "you" hails and then petitions, though from before it yields. The hail, the petition, and the imperative are all opportunities to submit, to become a you. For one thing, the one who issues the hail or petition or command borrows the power of speech from the one who is spoken to. In this way I really does derive from you, as itself secondary and, truth be told, in a kind of deception. "I" is "you" with a false name. *Proof of a real previous life. I have seen you before, the miracle of pre-time and at the end of times.*[53] "I" does not see "you" without already having been seen by you. Dialogues written into the diary in August intensify our suspicions that this second-personal dependency may be basic. One dialogue takes the form of a case study for a game of address. Interlocutors are labeled, for the purposes of the experiment, A and B. Of all things they could discuss, A and B first discuss the nature of petition, here presented as seeking *Rat,* counsel.

Around August 4, A and B have this exchange:

A: I want to ask you for counsel [Rat].
B: Why me exactly?
A: I trust you.
B: Why?
A: I have often seen you in society.
    And in our circles it always comes down to counsel. About that we are united. Whatever kind of society it is, whether one play-acts together or drinks tea or quotes great minds or wants to help the poor it always comes down to counsel. So much the worse for an uncounseled people! And more than it seems, since those who give counsel at such gatherings give counsel not only with the voice but with their hearts they want counsel for themselves. They always have their Doppelgänger among those seeking counsel and they zone in especially on him. In front of everyone, however, he leaves unsatisfied, disgusted, and draws the counsel-giver along in pursuit of him, to other gatherings and the same game.
B: It's like that?
A: Sure. You know it too. But it's also no merit, the whole world knows it and their petition [*ihre Bitte*] is all the more urgent.[54]

In this experimental encounter petitions for counsel are shown to be the foundation of society. The group in question has an air of narcissism, it's true; everyone says: hey you, tell me something about me. The desperate pursuit of counsel is circular, however, and by accident it gives insight into the petition-structure of the thoughts. You cannot say anything until you have been hailed, petitioned, and re-petitioned. Speech is a development out of "you": you can never say "you" unless you have already been addressed. Asked for and given in intimate consultation between seconds, counsel is the language game that cannot persist outside of a relation with a second person.[55]

Society, as is clear in what A tells B above, arises as a consequence of hailing and petitioning. The object of the petition, counsel, is but a formalization of the act of petition. Counsel is not separable from the petitioner and petitioned in their reciprocal *duzen*. Unlike truth or wisdom, the power of counsel lies in its structure of address. It is not something communicated to a group about a third person, but intimately, privately, deferentially, debasing the giver of counsel in the service of the other you. This *socius* needs to be rigorously distinguished from that based on the mutual recognition of I's, where I stands for "individual" in a Hegelian register. That is, there is no *ich* in this *wir*. In Hegel's *Phenomenology* at least, recognition cancels and absorbs the secondness of the second person. Yet there is a strongly marked place in the dialectic for a second person. The mediator or the mediation, the middle or the means—the second position—must always be passed through on the way to the third. A Hegelian "we" then ignores the "you" and even leaps over first-person positions to a third kind, an impersonal mega-individual with one norm and one name, the state.

Kafka's purpose in these thoughts, each of them a social scenario in miniature, is similar to the Nietzsche-inspired saying that he paraphrases, *in order to make you into what you are.*[56] What you are—what "you" is: the being of the second person is secondness, which is not derivative of firstness. Furthermore, *Du* marks out a field of deference and responsibility altogether different from the nation-state. Its linguistic modes are imperative, demand, incitement, appeal, hail, petition. The ethical standing of the "you" that receives these modes Kafka equates with permanent responsibility, not, however, as something superadded to the "you," not that you "have" responsibility, *but that you are this responsibility itself.*[57]

SECONDNESS

Grasp the sort of language-thing "you" is and you will also want to know what this communicative position and mode of speech and social organizing principle does to truth. Bakhtin's correction to dialogism is instructive here: a dialogue is not made up of two distinct and individually unified voices or positions. The secondness or subordinality of the second person extends into the dialogue itself and contaminates the other position. No contribution to a dialogue is complete or fulfilled on its own. There is no first speaker. Rather every utterance is completed by the receiver; its completion, and so the fulfillment of its truth, lies not in itself but in the response. This might make you think that the second is first, the weak will inherit the earth, but in Bakhtin's logic, the second only becomes itself in the response *that follows it*, and so on ad infinitum.[58] An incomplete utterance is not completed by a response but is rather cut off by it and cut into by it, once again each time reformulating, redirecting, ignoring, partially receiving, making it less than itself, and forcing it to yield. More than cut off, interrupted, the first statement has its sense given to it ex post facto by the rejoinder, following a principle similar to what Bakhtin calls *exotopy*.[59] "Unsatisfying" Kafka often says, and maybe the two are similar. Truth lies with the second utterance, with you and then with you. Because the truth of any utterance follows it, and because the second, which holds the truth of the first, is also awaiting its truth in its second, because any statement is already seconded before it is able to stand up and act as a principle, the meaning of truth itself is affected. *There is only a twofold: truth and lie. Truth is indivisible, therefore it cannot know itself. That which can know the truth must then be a lie.*[60] By lie he means the second of the twofold. But we must not confuse secondness with belatedness, with a temporal coming-after. In this world there is no serial time; secondness is not an ordinal rank or a relation but a quality, a way of being in dispossession of firstness and thirdness. Moreover, as we have seen, in this form of conversation *du* always precedes *ich*, so to speak. Likewise, secondness precedes firstness in this logic, but this is also to say that as a quality, a mode of truth, it is a mode lower than "the" truth, and so secondness is not primary—it always yields its position. In terms of truth and lie, lie seconding the truth, Kafka effects a revision: truth is merely the null point of lying and has no positive content. Sancho Panza makes a life out of this form of truth that runs ahead of him until all that is left behind is a rumor, and this is enough to keep the stories alive. According to a short interpretation of the *Quijote* that Kafka writes in October, Quijote's lackey manages to separate his devil from himself and become his second. Everything he lives, learns, knows, understands, he does at second hand, by serving, putting himself lower than his master to the point of allowing himself to be defecated on, never piercing illusions or adopting them as his own, always suspicious—living in the "sub." The truth of his life is indeed fiction, although it is not *his* fiction. *Sancho Panza, a free man, maybe out of a certain feeling of responsibility, yet imperturbable* [gleichmütig], *followed Quijote on his forays, and from them he had a grand and useful entertainment to the end of his days.*[61]

Let us call this facet of truth in the treatise "secondness," and speculate that it follows like Sancho Panza, *gleichmütig*, imperturbable. We shouldn't confuse this with secondariness, which is the sign of a value judgment that is anything but *gleichmütig* and regrets a perceived deficiency in a world that prefers firsts. Instead of as assertion, one way to understand this mode of truth is as "submission."[62] In December, Kafka formulates this as a general command. *In the struggle between you and the world, second* [sekundiere] *the world.*[63] You are told that the world is stronger, and if you choose to fight it you will surely lose. The proper response to this bit of anti-revolutionary wisdom is to stand by, to let the world fight while you look on. The more ready you are to stand by, the more likely it is that you are not taken as an adversary and can sit it out. The picaresque term *Sekundieren* commands you not to become the world's opponent; following it, you do not provoke it. The truth corollary of this stance is the following: *You refute in a certain sense the presentness of this world.*[64] The world to which one is subordinated, by which one is pushed to the side, the world that one does confront as an object has no truth in an objective sense. You refute it; "you" refutes it, in a certain sense. The world one seconds, with respect to whose activities one secedes, is not *vorhanden*, and its truth lies not in what is present before you. That the truth would stand before me is arrogance. Secondness is related to the moral comportment of *humility* which *gives everyone, even the lonely despairing person, the strongest relation to fellow human beings* [zu Mitmenschen] *and indeed immediately, though only with full and lasting humility. It can do this because it is the true language of prayer, simultaneously petition and firm connection. The relation to fellow human beings is the relation of prayer, the relation to the self is a relation of striving; the strength for striving is drawn from prayer.*[65] Truth is a prayer for truth; it does not wait, there is truth now, here, but it has the quality of belonging not to you but to "you"; that is, it is in the yielding. Truth occurs in the mode of a petition to a second, even if that second is yourself. As with Sancho Panza, there is truth, but it is not for "him."

Revelation comes secondhand. We cannot forget this prime example of atheological secondness; not only did God reveal himself repeatedly and to different people, but revelation seconded itself in echoes, indirections—"Then the Lord said to Moses . . . "—, inscription, reported speech—"Say therefore to the Israelites"—, injunction to make the whole people into second persons (this prefaces the whole of the mosaic revelation as told by Aaron, the second brother, at Exod. 4:28), riddles and shibboleths ("I am who I am"), miracles, the "presence of the lord," a vision glimpsed in passing by, as well as more mediated modes, such as signs, "great sights" (Exod. 3:3), and prophecies. All these forms share a characteristic structure. Revelation is passed to a second for a second. Someone besides the source will announce it, and they will do so for themselves but it will count in fact for an indirect recipient, some unintended position; one may perhaps die, as Moses did, before the benefit of the revelation can be realized, yet there is always a second. In scenes of theo-phany/-phony in the *Torah*, voices and images, messages and morals are in key moments received from surrogates or understudies.[66]

PART II

Death and the Will

§   The Problem of Our Art

24. Death Knowledge

In addition to historical messianism that gives shape to communities, peoples, or traditions, there is also a messianism of the single lifetime, whose moment of suspension and transmutation, the advent of the final and most complete possession of someone's being, arrives with their own personal death—possessed, that is, as that which cannot be owned but is anyway by proxy in word and image. In the case of personal death, the theic and atheic views are the same; with death comes finality, the only finality in life, excepting perhaps truth. First and foremost, we would like to isolate a small but significant difference between philosophies of finitude and Kafka's understanding of death. What gives possibility back to "leveled," factical existence for Heidegger in *Being and Time* is a recognition that the end cannot be held at a comfortable distance. The end is not pending but impending. The difference between this *schema mortalis* and Kafka's can be condensed into a brief formula, which we can then explain more thoroughly. In the existential thinking of finitude, the end is always in each moment about to come. The end is possible, permanently possible; certain and yet indeterminate as to its "when," it is pure possibility. In these texts by Kafka, the end is already here, is actual, if you will; in any case, possibility will not be the modality on which he pins his hopes. Even in a thinking that has, as Heidegger told his students about his own, the appearance of the most rigorous atheism, a messiah is still that which arrives; death is messianic. The good news is that the moment of arrival cannot be held at a distance. It is the most near, and this small shift permits the major shift in the concept of time from dynamic to ecstatic. The reason for the large shift is the following: if the messianic end of my life can be any moment, time can obviously not be lived as steps on a path from birth to death. One lives dying and every act is provisional, since any act can be the final act. Despite being unpredictable as to its when, the end is still as certain and because of this combination it is transformative.

Heidegger's messianism of the end preserves the absolute value of death for the system "existence."[1] It is definitive, setting the *finis*, and even though the limit cannot be definitively placed in time and Heidegger asks that we carry the limit and its indefinite "when" near us instead of off at a distance, it is, despite its indefiniteness no less definitive. The final limit is the total definition of *Dasein*, giving existence the required wholeness (*Ganzheit*). Heidegger asks, in effect, for a pervasive, permanent messianism, escapable in no moment. Freedom is, somewhat counterintuitively, acceptance of the certain-uncertain messianic limit ready to cut us off at any moment.

If you don't know what a limit is, death is not unrepresentable, it is meaningless. The storied "unrepresentability" of death implies, in its most fundamental gesture, the same inescapability, a localized and unchanging place and status for a generative limit, a sacred, untouchable site. It may be in fact that its unrepresentability preserves its status as the most final and certain and useful non-thing in our vocabulary. After all, death could play the role, in a rigorously atheistic universe, of the last transcendence. If death is representable—we have to admit that despite the prohibitions on images, divine and clerical, it is *represented* all the time—if it is representable, then it is liable to judgment, critique, revision, and even derision or scorn. Death uses its purported unrepresentability to preserve its power over life.

Kafka puts the problem of personal death in the following way. Turning to Genesis 3:3, he writes: *"When . . . , you must die" means: this knowledge is both at once: a step on the stairs to eternal life and the obstacle to it.*[2] This depicts the fall before the Fall, the threat of death that becomes a piece of knowledge. A student of the snake, Kafka knows that death comes to us not as itself but first in the form of knowledge. Further, to obey God's interdiction is itself already equivalent to eating the apple; if one follows it, one already knows. God's interdiction begins to look like a desperate act, a crime even, or a terrible deception. The interdiction is the seduction that later is blamed on Eve and the snake. Yet they are the heroes of the story because together they expose God's ruse for what it is. The apple is a symbol of how full and ripe the contradiction of paradise was before it burst into narrative, time, toil, and there grew from it legends of death and promises of overcoming.

Paradise is conditioned by death and knowledge; and not even death, just knowledge—for it is paradise within the limits of knowledge alone that conditions our actions, not mortality per se, which has not yet come to anyone. *"When . . . , you must die" means: this knowledge is both at once: a rung on the ladder to eternal life and the obstacle to it.*[3] How is the knowledge of the consequences of an action a rung on the ladder to eternity? Because if you obey it, the maxim goes, you will live forever. How is it an obstacle to eternity? Because, in obeying it, you have already bitten the apple. That is, you have accepted knowledge in place of silly, holy innocence. With this in mind we begin to understand how finitude does not and cannot save us. Its concept hurls us back into the paradisal contradiction. If one could conceive of a limit that was not simultaneously knowledge of the limit . . .

. . . on the other hand, if it were not made into knowledge, negative or positive, death could not exercise its power; it could neither enslave us in toil nor free us for "our" existence.

At stake in Kafka's "presentation" of death in and around his atheological-political treatise is the crucial difference between what cannot be represented, seen, known (itself never a pure negation but instead always the representation of a negation, a vision of an absence, knowledge of ignorance, and so forth) and what is not even unrepresentable. And so he interprets God's interdiction: *"When . . . , you must die" means: knowledge is both at once a rung on the ladder to eternal life and the obstacle to it.* And then he elaborates: *If you will want to arrive at eternal life according to the knowledge you have gained—and you will not be able to do otherwise than want to, since knowledge is this will—you will thus have to destroy yourself, the obstacle, in order to build this stairway, that is the destruction.* And he concludes therefore from this reasoning that *the expulsion from paradise was thence not an act but a happening,* in the verbal sense, an infinitive—an event (*ein Geschehen*)—not a deed (*keine Tat*).[4]

The expulsion happens and continues to happen every time we exercise the knowledge form. The Nietzschean character of this insight is hard to miss: the will to knowledge is a highly diminished will. As happens elsewhere in Kafka, the text or thinker mentioned least in his diaries and letters may be the most significant for his thinking. This is true of Plato, but it is more true of Nietzsche, who is almost never mentioned.[5] Knowledge is will to knowledge, as this thought tells us explicitly, and in this way knowledge has its own lively life of striving, struggling, of setting goals and setting out in search of them, of intimating permanence and imitating God. Knowledge, in other words, is act (*Tat*). Death—word, image, thought—is the ultimate object of and example for all knowledge because it is what eludes all striving and produces permanent struggle. Death offers knowledge's ideal of certainty, clarity, unambiguousness, distinctness, singularity. Those criteria that Heidegger himself lists for death—it is nonrelational, certain, and unsurpassable [*unbezüglich, gewiß, unüberholbar*]—show, in short, except for the indeterminacy of its "when," that death is the perfect object for knowledge. In fact the indeterminacy of its "when" allows death to take on, in *Being and Time* and certainly for many of the book's readers, the aura of a timeless truth.

What Kafka sees, if we can put it this way, is that these things are much too temporal in a conventional fashion, that is to say, hopeful; and they are too aesthetic, they have a kind of old-fashioned Cartesian ring to them, where beauty, in this case characterized as clarity and distinctness (it is unsurpassable [*unüberholbar*] and cannot be confused with anything else), is truth. Death is the ideal of knowledge, where knowledge is that which presents and represents perfection, unity, certainty, and singularity, but as a representation is in fact not the thing itself but a will to the ideal, and as a will, it belongs to living, let us say, and not at all to the death it seeks to represent. Therefore, in this logic, knowledge appears as the path, but the path is the obstacle, and so you destroy yourself, but only because you know that destruction of knowledge is then the better path, but that too is knowledge. The circle is truly vicious. The only good in this circle is the following inkling: because paradise is this circle, paradise is already outside itself. No one had to produce an expulsion through an act, God's or Eve's or the snake's. The expulsion happens and keeps happening with and as paradise.

25. Death Image

In the thought of finitude presented in Genesis 3, there are three data. *Datum primum*: finitude is knowledge of finitude. The Genesis myth shows us how knowledge is both the cause of and the consolation prize for expulsion from the Garden. Kafka is astonished that humanity, with this story in hand, would make the sin into the reward. And yet, it is also true that, the only thing that "happens" in Genesis is that knowledge goes from being implicitly the stuff of Adamic humanity to being explicitly its stuff. You will have death but you will also and only have knowledge of death; and you will not have any other kind of knowledge until you first know the fact of your death, the highest and most perfect fact for knowledge, the model object in all the ways described above. The model above all of permanence in a fallen world, death lends its temporal signature to knowledge as certainty.

The *datum secundum* seems to contradict the *primum datum*, but in fact it does not. The second point is: knowledge overcomes finitude. What Genesis says is: when you learn how to know explicitly, when you openly prefer knowledge to, say, pleasure, experience, strolling around, you become mortal, finite, and knowledge becomes the only possible overcoming of death. A succinct but perhaps overly condensed way to sum this up takes the form of a conundrum: the knowledge that makes you mortal is knowledge of the fact of mortality. This should not, however, be confused with a subjective idealism that says death is a projection of the idea of death, all in our minds, a product of human fantasy. Quite the contrary, this would be to reify knowledge. Kafka does demonstrate here, I believe in a way not seen elsewhere, that the idea of death is fully within the concept of knowledge, as its ideal, say, in a fallen or dare we say also an atheistic world. His argument would not be the idealist's argument that the mind is real but death is not, but that they are equally fictitious and in need of rewriting. This also implies, of course, another reading of the death sentence, one toward which Kafka often inclines in these thoughts. If one can somehow rid oneself of knowledge, replace the knowledge idea with another idea, one could come closer to eternal life, although, it goes without saying that one can also never know it.

Datum tertium: knowledge of finitude will one day overcome both knowledge and finitude—such is the hope. The hope internal to knowledge is a hope for something other than knowledge. It is the hope of "religions" and in some sense the promise of the Garden story, in a different way but with the same vehemence and conviction that one finds in existential philosophies. But the situation in Genesis is more complicated than the hope would have us believe. There is more than one meaning of death around the tree of knowledge, and in fact there are two interpretations, and they conflict. *According to God, the instantaneous result of eating from the tree of knowledge is death; according to the snake (at any rate one could understand the snake this way), it is becoming like God. Both are incorrect in a similar way. Human beings did not die, but became mortal; they were not like God, but received a capacity, which was subsequently felt to be indispensable, to become like Him. Both are correct in a similar way. Human beings did not die, just the paradisal human being; they did not turn into God, but into god-like knowledge.*[6] By the logic here, "life" is the product of this interpretive conflict. "Life" can be understood as the error and the insight shared by God and snake. Facing a contradictory image of death, life gains a destiny and its dynamism.

These two images, of God's promise and death's punishment, give "life" its contours, motivate actions, and justify decisions. Trouble is, the images are in conflict and the shapes, motivations, and justifications they give are often in conflict as well. The three givens, three data about finitude in Genesis are then (1) finitude and knowledge are born together, (2) knowledge overcomes finitude, and (3) knowledge of finitude overcomes itself to become eternal life. Clearly, the last cannot really count as knowledge; rather, it is the point at which knowledge and knowing go over into something else. Such a point sounds mystical but it isn't, or if it is, it is the mysticism of a logic carried to its inherent end. One could say: we are condemned to collect knowledge instead of living eternally, and the knowledge that we are not living eternally, the knowledge of our own finite condition—self-knowledge, one might call it, or knowledge that we are knowers—is then the highest, the most permanent knowledge, which overcomes itself and achieves immortality. It is a self-fulfilling prophecy. Eternal life is replaced by eternal knowledge of a finite self. This is the sort of commitment that is carried over from Descartes to Heidegger, a commitment to certainty as substitute for dumb eternity. True—certainty is transplanted from soul substance to finitude, from *esse* to *existere*, and it is preserved in the absolute assurance that death, not mind, is the unshakable basis (*fundamentum inconcussum*) for existence. But dumb eternity is never mentioned, never wanted—a bane to existence and to thought. With a possessive understanding of death "the phenomenally sufficient ground for an originary interpretation of the meaning of being of Dasein is secured."[7] Death gives access to understanding in the Heideggerian sense of the term. Kafka found a similar interpretation of finitude that falls in *Fear and Trembling*. There he read the famous line: "the movement of faith must continuously be made by virtue of the absurd, but only we must note in such a way that one does not lose one's finitude, but obtains it fully and completely."[8] A vocabulary of fullness and completeness, of securing and holding, of certainty and singularity, all of this in a superlative mode—the ownmost, completely—surrounds the talk of finitude, along with talk of "obtaining," "owning," "sufficiency," "completion," and something "secured."

One has to pay attention to the proximity between impossibility, that which supposedly makes existence possible, and necessity. "Death is a possibility of being, which Dasein itself always has to take over." At one point, certainly, death is "a" possibility among others, and this comports well with the image of Dasein that has been shown us, the being that "is" its possibilities. Yet he goes on: indeed "with death, Dasein's ownmost possibility for being is imminent." Heidegger's German stages a scene here, breaks out into an image. The verb *bevorstehen* means to be imminent, impending, and so its temporal meaning is legible; but it also makes surreptitious use of the image of a figure standing before something. "With death Dasein itself stands before itself in its *ownmost* potential for being."[9] He comes close here to representing death as a figure toward which an existent leans. We should notice once again the superlative "ownmost." Does a possibility remain "possible" if it is grasped so completely and fully? Here Heidegger begins to use the adjective *unüberholbar* (unsurpassable) when talking about death.[10] That death can't be "surpassed," "outstripped," or gotten over continues the gesture of representing death as an ideal. It also increases the sense that an imperative is being given, a sine qua non articulated, a necessity marked, and this sense increases in a crescendo until Heidegger concludes that "death must be conceptualized as the ownmost, unrelatable, unsurpassable, certain possibility."[11] If we can count on it so strictly and without exception, does death not surrender some of its potential? Death without exception: this is what we are to be convinced of, a fixed place, a wall and at the same time a portal, and a necessity that time and again, without fail and paradoxically, produces possibility.

26. *Schein zum Tode*

In place of a steady font of possibilities, Kafka sees something else issuing from death, whose character is not the most possible, the most purely possible, but more like bottomless illusion.[12] Death is aesthetic, not ontological. In the treatise, Kafka turns away from relatively fixed alternatives such as finitude/infinitude and atheism/theism, and he does so on the basis of an outside from which these alternatives seem to derive.

If dividing up Kafka's lifework were our aim, we might call this his "aesthetic turn," but "aesthetic" is surely not the best word. The turn to semblance may arise, one might suppose, from an unholy synthesis of Brentanian psychology, particularly the form it took in the thinking of his friends, Anton Marty's acolytes, Brod and Weltsch, and the Nietzschean problems with inescapable Schopenhauerian overtones that occupied him. We also can't ignore the obvious deformities introduced into these aesthetic theories by a non-philosopher whose understanding of the issues was highly idiosyncratic, and more than this, by one who professed a devotion to "literature" above all else.

And still the aesthetic—sensibility, image, light and its relations with truth—plays an important and somewhat technical role in Kafka's hollowing out of European theologoumena.[13] A minor motif of the polylogue on theological and political origins and their ambiguities might be labeled "Against Finitude." And while infinitude, living on past, over, and through a transcendent frame, is no alternative, finitude itself is supported by a whole mythology. Kafka refuses this secular myth, effectively stopping the baroque "dance of death" that had pranced on for three hundred years. This effect is not just a by-product of his fiction, or even a result of a personal opinion or faith. Kafka recognizes it as a task of extreme importance, and he develops a set of strategies for removing finitude without returning to its traditional alternatives.

What is, he asks, the being of death, the nature of this idea, the idea of a limit—and perhaps the nature of all limits? We receive an answer in a lesson about death and semblance that is also a reading of the *Tanakh*. Let us quote it in full:

> Anyone who has once seemed to be dead [had a near-death experience, been *scheintot*] can recount horrible things, but how things are after death he cannot say, he has really never been nearer to death than anyone else, in principle he only "experienced" something extraordinary [*etwas Besonderes*] and the ordinary, his habitual life, has become more precious to him because of it. It is similar for someone who has experienced something "extraordinary." Moses for example on Mount Sinai certainly experienced something "extraordinary," but instead of yielding [*sich ergeben*, giving over to, submitting,

giving up one's pretenses and pretexts, hopes, expectations, abandoning one-self, the self] to this extraordinary thing like someone seeming dead [*wie ein Scheintoter*] who doesn't report back and stays prone in the coffin, he took flight down the mountain and naturally had important things to recount and loved the people to whom he had taken flight even more than before and then sacrificed his life for them, one can perhaps say, in thanks. From both, however, from the seeming-dead one who has returned and the Moses who has returned one can learn a lot, and yet one cannot find out [*erfahren*] the decisive thing [*das Entscheidende*] from them, because they themselves have not experienced [*erfahren*] it. And if they had experienced it, they would never have come back again. Yet we also don't want to experience it at all. This can be easily verified. Occasionally, for example, we could wish to expe-rience the experience of the seemingly dead or the experience of Moses, with the guarantee of return "with free passage," even to the point of wishing to die, but we would never in our thoughts want to be in the coffin alive with-out possibility of return or to remain on Mount Sinai.

(This doesn't really have anything to do with anxiety towards death [*Todesangst*]).[14]

This text, half rigorous deduction, half fable, is much more than a depo-tentialization of the first leader of the Jewish community, although it is this as well, and it is more than a counterrevelation, in which it is shown that origin of the law is no origin, and so, as he writes elsewhere in the treatise, "we live in false belief." This is a literary-critical reduction of the death idea to semblance. Clearly, the death idea at issue is the idea of per-sonal death, of one's own death, not the death of others. Kafka's reduction shows that there is no real contact with one's finitude, and not for lack of existential power, or because of a convenient seduction by distractions, but purely for logical reasons. God has had Moses set bounds around the mountain to keep the people out (Exod. 19:23). He is allowed all the way in, across the boundary. The decisive thing, *das Entscheidende*, is the other limit, the point or line that the fence around the mountain dissimulates, the one that marks the significant difference, the sine qua non of theol-ogy, transcendence, the other fence that is not a fence and of which the mountain is a weak symbol (and thus Moses and Aaron must protect it, fence it off, sanctify it, so that no one discovers it is only a mountain, and a low one at that). We learn here—in a tale whose purpose is teach-ing—not only that Moses does not experience the decisive thing, but in effect, that he could have no way of finding it, since its place and its character cannot be experienced. Moses does not experience the unexperienceable in all its negativity; he simply does not have an experience, and the renewed love with which he approaches humanity again proves that he never for an instant left humanity.

What Kafka envisions here, in his return to the literal situation atop Sinai, is the ruthless and objectless semblant character of the ultimate limit. He could not know of course that *Angst* would become a decade later precisely the mood that lets death appear for itself. That Kafka was no stranger to anxiety is well known. He suffered "general anxiety" at life. When he rejects *Todesangst* he does not at all reject intense, permeating, crippling *Angst* but he does reject it as the last possible ground of appearance for death. Whether it is the theological limit or the atheistic one, the original point of contact between God and humanity or the coffin-trap beyond which there is nothing, the event refuses itself to Moses. The place of this nonoccurrence can be pinpointed exactly. The place where no limit can be specified, where a simple clearing or bush comes to seem like a presence, can be described precisely. *Our salvation is death, but not this one.*[15] This thought is one source for Kafka's realism. When he depicts the point of the nonoccurrence of the limit, this simple displacement where entire regimes of "seeming," of *Schein*, take hold, the semblance begins to fade or lose its power as a link in the real. Kafka's realism involves pointing out primary fictions, and the most primary, if we can say this, is the death fiction. All other semblances emanate from the myth that one has been near the limit, has made contact. As the single moment of the real in secular, realist, capitalist fantasy life, death is the first of and model for all the elaborately composed images that in some way refer back to the primal illusion. Seeming-toward-death, *Schein zum Tode* is relentless and does not let up even in dying. Death-bed scenes are all semblances. *The death-bed lament is actually a lament that nothing has here in the true sense died, and still we have to keep on being satisfied with this dying, we still play the game again and again.*[16] Dying *in the true sense* is presented in the lesson about Moses and his fantasies. Death's truth is that it teaches no lesson, from which the only lesson we can draw is: death as it must be, in order for us to lament as we do, is never for us, and it cannot be used to motivate a people, found a religion, write commandments.[17] Enoch may be a counter-Moses. Kafka copied this passage into his diary in 1916: "And while he led a divine life, God took him away and [he] was not seen again" (Gen. 5:24).[18] There is no such thing as dying. Already in 1914 a diary entry has it: "unfortunately it is no death, just the eternal ordeal of dying."[19] Yet dying without limit, dying that cannot truly make reference to death also cannot be what it claims to be. We play the game of death again and again, and so we stave off this fact, which, for Kafka, is the only fact that could possibly transform us, the fact that there is no such thing as death. Kafka is not very hopeful that even this point will change much, in any case. The semblance at work in semblant death has powers as great or greater than real death would, if it existed. *The most horrible aspect of death: a semblant end causes a real pain.*[20] One cannot help tracing a line from this insight to Kafka's experience of his own illness, but let us hold off doing this, at least for now, until the order of this thinking becomes more legible.

Death is always near-death, with all its rituals and culture, and semblant-death, a set of images, *Scheintod*. In its shadow, life becomes a semblance of being-toward the seeming end. Semblance brings death into the sphere of aesthetics, indeed into its very center, as the simplest, most unconceptualized image without any content. Death is pure image. A host of images gather around the pure image, and indeed the whole sensible world may revolve around it. The purity of the death-image can be loaned out to art or politics, storytelling or even to dreaming, but in a certain regime of meaning where personal death is the highest and most certain phenomenon, it never relinquishes its position as the purest image.

According to Kafka there are two kinds of sensible material, two types of image: evil and good. *It is not really the sensual world that is semblance, but its evil that admittedly constructs* [bildet] *the sensual world for our eyes.*[21] He calls the "being for our eyes" of the sensual world: *an emanation* [Ausstrahlung] *of human consciousness in certain crossover-points* [Übergangsstellen]. Evil sensible material[22] is an emanation of consciousness, a projection, if you will, and so this is a brand of idealism. But the idealism only holds, let us say, at particular crossover-points, that is, at points of transcendence. There is no word in Kafka, late or early, as suspect as *Übergang*. The word here, *Übergangsstelle*, names a limit position guarded with weapons where the only distinction between the landscape over here and the landscape over there, is, indeed, the crossing-point. In light of this reasoning, death is evil, perhaps the primordially evil semblance. The main attribute of evil, across the whole range of the thoughts, is its association with seduction (*Verführung*) to a crossing-point.[23]

This evil is seduction toward a reality beyond semblance. A Platonic analogue is perhaps helpful here. Evil seduces you toward a reality beyond semblance; that is, evil is evil because it makes a claim to be an appearance of something else. Kafkan good has a Platonic analogue as well. Good is that which does not look beyond itself; it is technically *aussichtslos*, without a future. *You complain about the stillness and silence* [die Stille], *about the hopelessness* [Aussichtslosigkeit] *of the stillness and silence, the wall around the good.*[24] Unlike the wall around the Garden, which lets on to other places, walls them out and threatens expulsion to them in some future, the good has a wall that protects it absolutely; its wall is a prohibition on looking beyond. To say that this is Platonic is only half true. The good is set apart, in its separate space, and yet there is no door through which even an ethicist could enter. When we find phenomena that look out on no future, we can say these are good. Death, insofar as it is imagined in any way as a doorway, is evil, cancellation of the good. The prerequisites for a phenomenon to be good are stringent, and here they have no Platonic analogue. *Evil knows from good, but good doesn't know from evil.*[25] We shall have found the good when we find a figure, a thing, a phenomenon that cannot distinguish between itself and evil. And one final criterion. In response, clearly, to his auto-mandate to think a thought that does not console, it occurs to Kafka that he has been describing a phenomenon that does not substitute one object for another. *The good is in a certain sense without consolation* is a thought that comes at the end of November.[26]

Zarathustra also has a snake. And though Nietzsche's name is virtually absent in the Kafkan corpus, none comes more easily to mind when one reads the treatise in thoughts. Kafka read *Zarathustra* aloud to a girl he met in 1900 when he was seventeen and on vacation with his parents, and he defended Nietzsche publicly against Max Brod's attacks in 1902. Nietzsche was in the air, in the journals, in the mouths of his philosophically minded friends after the turn of the century. And Zarathustra's shadow continues to fall on Kafka when he thinks about good and evil, illusion, and the myth of a truer world that winter. "Once Zarathustra too cast his delusion beyond humans, like all hinterworldly."[27] Soon, however, the thinker-teacher learns not to cast beyond anything; he accepts this impossible lesson, and tries to teach his followers, man and beast, how not to look for an "elsewhere." All movement toward the beyond takes a "death leap." "Weariness that wants its ultimate with one great leap, with a death leap; a poor unknowing weariness that no longer even wants to will: that created all gods and hinterworlds." Thus far Kafka follows Zarathustra, but he stops short of self-overcoming. The hinterworldly is intransigent and cannot be overcome. Kafka has been bitten early by the terrible duplicity of Nietzsche's famous exclamation in *Twilight of the Idols*: "The true world is gone: which world is left? The illusory one, perhaps? . . . But no! *we got rid of the illusory world along with the true one!* (Noon; moment of shortest shadow; end of longest error; high point of humanity; INCIPIT ZARATHUSTRA.)" If there are not two worlds, Nietzsche realizes late in the day, then there is no one world.

Nietzsche's challenge, in *Zarathustra* and later in a starker form in *Twilight*, is to rethink the Zarathustran position such that a world without this fundamental opposition between truth and illusion becomes possible. Kafka is less concerned with bringing metaphysics to an end than he is with making the way across, the *Übergang*, seem ludicrous. Nietzsche's way, however, his method if you will, is precisely this, to transcend, to overcome the distinction, to get beyond it—however ironic the "beyond" may be.[28] In effect, Nietzsche makes the *Übergang* central to his solution. We might say that the *Übermensch* dwells in the *Übergang*, and this is the key to the will to power's success. Because of overcoming the universe can be viewed as "becoming." Becoming streams out of the river of overcoming, out of "the unexhausted begetting will of life." "That I must be struggle and becoming and purpose and the contradiction of purposes—alas, whoever guesses my will guesses also on what crooked paths it must walk!"[29] The crooks in the path are *Übergangsstellen* and so what Nietzsche has done is rid himself of a true world by pluralizing transcendence. Transcendence is "life itself," which is full of crossover points. What's more, there is as much necessity in multiple points of transcendence as there was in the one true world. "And this secret life itself spoke to me: "Behold," it said, "I am that which must always overcome itself."[30] And although this is not a philosophy of existence (it is not a "will to existence"), there is as much, or more, dependence on death in it. The will to power intensifies being-toward-death ("a tossing of dice unto death") and all this finitude has the purpose of overcoming good and evil, opposition, and truth itself.

Each time the will overcomes itself it transits through death. What needs to be invented is a technique or a procedure for diminishing death, for puncturing its power without tapping into the greater metathanatotic power that uses death to overcome. There are then essential differences between noon—light without shadows, *appearance* of a sourceless light, things that show themselves only from themselves (Heidegger)—and twilight—in which there is no other world but there are also in an important sense no phenomena, because there are no shadows at all. At twilight phenomena are not pure but indistinct, and this makes it ludicrous to assert either truth or illusion. Things are not themselves at twilight, although you would not say they become otherwise. If there were a motto of *The Castle* it would be: "this happens at twilight." In the failing light "the castle's outline began to dissolve." More than this, as K. looks upward toward the castle, twilight produces a singular uncertainty. He cannot tell whether he is looking at the castle or whether the castle is looking at him. It doesn't matter, since in the *Dämmerung* "the glances of the observers could not hold on to him and slid off."[31] Twilight does not allow vision to take hold; it suspends the attentive gaze.[32]

Made into a technique, *Dämmerung* would have the effect of obscuring anything that could be called an "image," including the most intensely imagistic image, that of death.[33] *Death hangs before us like an image of the Alexanderschlacht [Kafka is referring, one imagines, to Albrecht Altdorfer's 1529 painting* The Battle of Alexander at Issus*] on the wall of the schoolroom. Everything depends on whether we can through our own acts darken or totally extinguish the image.*[34] We ought to recognize that the image work that is being proposed here is not the same as conceptual work.[35] We are not asked to think differently or adjust our theic commitments. What is worked on in this image is the image mode, by means of image-altering techniques, without reference to anything that might draw our attention away from the images. It is a darkened image, rather than an extinguished one, but an extinguished one does not proclaim the transcendence of its object either; on the contrary, it makes no claims about the object, but only dims the view, in order to diminish our faith in the medium. Make no mistake: this is not iconoclasm. In a pivotal thought, Kafka remarks that the fall from paradise cannot be reversed, it can only be beclouded, muddied up, *getrübt*. It is left to understand what the words Kafka uses, *trüben* (becloud, muddy up), *verdunkeln* (darken), and *auslöschen* (extinguish), contribute to his aesthetic theory; specifically, we should ask what they add to the Nietzschean dilemma of semblance—the insight that when the true world is destroyed, the illusory world is destroyed along with it. In brief, iconoclasm does not work. What on earth are we to do, if exchanging one image for another or one class of images for another class changes nothing, what are we to do if—for that matter—exchanging no images for images also changes nothing?

Kafka proposes a modification that transforms images without destroying them. He needs a way to modify them that does not lead you to believe that a better image would better serve the purpose. In this case, an image of nothing or a prohibition on images is unsatisfactory. We continue to recognize an image of the divine in the blackness or the injunction. And so he needs a way to modify images that prohibits one from concluding (a) that the modified image represents the absence of what it once represented or sought to represent, (b) that the original image has been destroyed for a higher purpose, or (c) that the modification itself signifies a new kind of truth. *Verdunkeln*, darken, and *auslöschen*, extinguish, express their essence in *trüben*, becloud, which accomplishes (a) a modification that does not cancel the image so that it can be replaced by another; (b) an effect that ought to have no higher meaning or truth (it is tantamount to saying: it got dirty, it oxidized, it faded, nothing more); (c) despite offering no consolation, one can no longer look at the image in the same way; and (d) one still looks at the image, even though it no longer exercises the attraction of truth. Despite the modification, it is still an image, and so it can give the satisfaction we take in images *qua* images. Schoolchildren understand this modification intuitively, when, captive in their seats, heads turned up toward the picture on the wall, they daydream. Freedom is not in leaving school; rather, it consists in not receiving the image as a lesson about an object. The lesson of *trüben* is that it enhances, rather than weakening, the image character of the image. Things in themselves of course cannot be muddied, and so they are, in being strong, unmodifiable, useless for Kafka. What can be muddied can only be an image, and the stronger it is *qua* image, the more it can be muddied. The second lesson of *trüben* is that, as noted, it weakens the "consolational" aspect of the image. Even if one falls back on the idea that images refer beyond themselves, one cannot make out what precisely the image is of. The image remains vivid while the object is obscured. The third lesson of *trüben* is that it offers no alternative. This must be what Kafka means by "extinguish" (*auslöschen*), which couldn't name an ontological activity. It means to rescind or dissolve the surface without exposing, unveiling, or unconcealing any fundamental being or nonbeing. Nothing is deconcealed except perhaps the medium itself and its susceptibility to modification. A fourth lesson we could take from the muddied image, although this is as yet not so obvious, is that it is *good*. For it has had its seductive force taken away. The good, it turns out, is disconsolate, offers no way out. For all those who imagine death in terms of the clash of great armies, along the lines of Altdorfer's *Battle of Alexander at Issus*, where dying is a sacrifice for the living, for all those who dream of this birth of Western imperialism out of the death of the East, for those who place a hero in their image, one who, like Alexander, is victorious over death (at the expense of so many others), and for all those artists, like Altdorfer, who build their reputations on the glorification of death and on this mode of "historical" image-making, Kafka has a simple answer. Do not make any more art and do not make anti-art; muddy what is there.[36]

27. The Illuminated Corpse

An artist who could accomplish this would be in possession of special powers. After all, she would be different from all other artists and non-artists, living and dead. She would neither make images nor break them, only diminish their attraction. The ability to muddy images without making new ones would make this artist one figure in the world not susceptible to images. She would operate in a strong sense outside the limitations of the world. Social ideals would not appeal to her. Even death, image of images, would not catch her in its wily snares. In one way of thinking, this artist overcomes herself, overcomes art, even overcomes death, by means of what Nietzsche in a late note called the "primordial artistic force." No doubt a species of the will to power. And yet what if this too were an image? What if the artist too had to be muddied up, darkened, drained of art's idealizations and the call to become and overcome? What if the new law had to be applied to art itself, and the "victorious energy of the artist," "a surplus and overflow of flourishing corporeality into the world of images and wishes,"[37] were in fact the most seductive image of all and hardest to extinguish? How would one begin to drain this last tenacious, sacred image—the artist—of its promise?

There is a special case of death, the death that happens to a writer, or rather the death out of which a writer wholly consists while living. Kafka describes aspects of this special case of death in a letter to Max Brod. Enough has been written about Kafka and *Schriftstellersein*, "being-a-writer," to satisfy all writers everywhere. His writerly being is treated often and best by Maurice Blanchot, who, in his lifelong investigation into the values of writing, first as a fiction writer and later as a devotee of the ordeal of writing about writing, kept returning to Kafka as exemplum, prototype, enigma, and, what concerns us here, as a rich fund of thoughts on the "primordial artistic force" that writing possesses through its special relationship to death. Death and writing, Blanchot's great twin themes, he positions very near to Kafka in "The Last Word," a chapter of his book on friendship, *L'amitié,* which explores the limits of *Freundsein.* An exemplary limit crosses the friendship between Kafka and Max Brod. Nothing is truer than that these two saw writing differently. Blanchot concentrates his analysis on Kafka's letters, the richest and most candid of which, on the topic of death and writing, is addressed of course to Brod. Blanchot has the unparalleled insight that Kafka's letters to Brod differ from his letters to almost everyone else, in that he never debases himself before Brod, never deprecates himself.[38] The letters are proud volleys in a real struggle, in which Kafka never loosens his grip on his weapons, and the letter on death and writing is no exception.

Overall, Kafka's letters provide Blanchot with "a better sense of the curve of this rare existence," a phrase that perfectly expresses the attitude of collectors of such rarities, for whose cabinet of wonders Kafka is the rarest and most coveted treasure. Blanchot is captivated by this one letter, which in some important ways transcends his curiosity about Kafka the rarity and Kafka the writer. In this letter Kafka does indeed describe in complex and sometimes highly ambiguous terms some of what would come to captivate Blanchot and others. Kafka talks about how writing emerges from "the dark experience in which he finds himself," as Blanchot calls it, referring to Kafka's encounter with his illness and the specter of his own death. Blanchot has a surprising take on the illness. He calls it "his spiritual fight,"[39] and he is right: it is a fight against a medical, psychological, or existential understanding of the illness, in short against any commonplace view of it as treatable, regrettable, or burdensome, and so also against Brod's efforts to treat his friend like a patient, which Kafka resisted with all his scant strength. This is why Blanchot fixates on this one letter. It is as strategic an advance in Kafka's battle with Brod as it is a singular maneuver in his "spiritual fight," which is not against Max, and which entails a very different account of his own impending death and of death in general. Although it can be taken as a paean to the rarity of writerly being and of Kafka's troubled life, the letter also transcends the peculiar enabling relationship between personal death and writing, going on to say something harrowing and almost unrepeatable about death itself. The discussion revolves around a rather tenuous distinction between writerly death and actual death.

This letter of July 5, 1922, mailed during the writing of *The Castle* (a manuscript Kafka abandoned—or it abandoned him—in August or early September), begins by describing the writer's life as fundamentally anti-life, as against the conventions and conventional aspirations of Kafka's social milieu. This is one kind of death. Blanchot fastens on this kind, which is derived no doubt from Kafka's complaint about his own situation, and Blanchot raises it to a general feature of writers, but more precisely of "writing" as a sort of transcendental activity: "To write is to put oneself outside life, it is to take pleasure in one's death through an imposture that will become a frightening reality."[40] To support this claim, Blanchot comments on some lines from the letter of July 5, which appear in his text in single quotation marks, as though they were the writer's soliloquy about himself: "'My whole life long I have been dead and now I will actually die. My life was sweeter than the lives of others, my death will be that much more horrible. The writer in me will naturally die immediately, since such a figure has no ground [*Boden*], has no existence [*Bestand*], is not even made of dust; is only in the most amazing earthly life a little bit possible, is only a construction made by the craving for pleasure. This is the writer [*Schriftsteller*]. Yet I myself cannot live on [*weiterleben*], since I have never lived, I have remained loam, I haven't used the sparks to make fire, but only to illuminate my corpse.'"[41]

It is important to note that in Kafka's letter, this analysis of the thanatozoic writer is quoted. The analysis is described as "the thought" (*die Überlegung*), not necessarily the experience, of an exemplary writer. The "thought" quoted in the letter is a development of "what the naïve person often wishes [*wünscht*] for himself."[42] To wit, the naïve person wishes to experience his own funeral in order to see who shows up and how sad they are, that is, in order to assess the meaningful impact of her life. The writer who makes this wish into her life, "such a writer," dies before she lives, so that in her remove from life she can watch for her impact continually and mourn the fact that, in this strange case, because she has died before she has lived, there is no life and so very little impact and nothing to mourn or bury.

Caught in a net of guilt between his friends Brod and Oskar Baum, Kafka sends writing to one and then to the other—letters, telegrams, postcards—to one instead of the other, in place of going in person. He had been supposed to visit Baum in the Thuringian resort town of Georgenthal, but cancelled at the last minute, after Baum had already rented him a room there. He cancels because of a "general fear" derived from a "fear of travelling," which was in fact "a fear of being noticed by the gods," and ultimately, it seems, from the order of expression, at bottom a "fear of death." His explanations and excuses for cancelling his trip form the context, yes, but also the impetus for the thoughts about death that follow. The letter to Brod of July 5 gathers up a variety of problematic types of "death": the living social death of the writer; the special death of a writer when she gets together with another writer (there cannot be more than one; if there are, they cease to be writers); and "actual death." Out of these threads a complex argument is woven.

It is the last type or moment we are interested in, both because it informs the others—it is that to which they are compared and from which they draw their meanings—and because it illuminates—to cite this special word that Kafka uses with respect to the writer's corpse—the critique of finitude in the 1917–18 treatise in thoughts. Let us move through the special case of the writer, then, toward the wholly unspecial case of mere or actual death.

Reflections on fear of travel, being noticed by the gods, other writers, and death precede and inaugurate reflections on writerly death and "actual" death. Once the theme is introduced, Kafka's experience recedes and a reflection of another type takes its place. He opens an investigation into the commonly shared wish and the special thought of the writer respecting their own deaths and finds a horror. Although Blanchot doesn't say so, a sort of victory in the "spiritual fight" with Brod over the meaning of his illness happens in the last, long set of clauses, when he uncovers this other end, the mere end.

On the first death, the writer's death: exactly how is the writer already dead whilst living? In the preceding lines Kafka refers to the nuclear family he could never build, his failures at love, business, his deep solitude that is necessary and regrettable at the same time. This is indeed how Blanchot understands this writerly "death": as exile from the normal commitments that characterized adult male life between the wars in Central Europe. Blanchot sees something "more obscure" in the writer's death to be sure, a darker darkness than the anti- or asocial. With his great talents Blanchot describes this darkness clearly without taking away from the obscurity one whit: "increasingly he [Kafka] will associate words and the use of words with the approach of a spectral unreality, greedy for living things and capable of exhausting any truth."[43] In the phrase "exhausting any truth," Blanchot hits on a formula for the procedure of the Kafkan *pensées*.

In essence the capacity Blanchot attributes to the writer to exhaust *any* truth is equivalent to Nietzsche's "victorious energy of the artist" and "surplus and overflow of flourishing corporeality into the world of images and wishes."[44] Neither can be confused with vitalism—in Nietzsche's case because it is not the "vital spark" that overflows, but a fusion of body and image and wish, an aesthetic-voluntarist amalgam; and even more pronouncedly in Blanchot's case, since it is death that overflows into the world to extinguish sparks. Blanchot's thanatism and Nietzsche's aesthetic-voluntarism, as different as their sources and outcomes may be, express themselves in an excess of capacity, the issuance of sparks. The spark that powered art came from life, for Nietzsche, from the struggle of wills; Blanchot's spark came from death. For Blanchot all truths are exhausted except that of writing and death; since death is inexhaustible, writing's power is as well. Evidence for his belief in an infinite thanatotic reservoir is that "the strange nature of posthumous publications is to be inexhaustible."[45]

"But how is it with writer-being itself?" (*Aber wie ist es mit dem Schriftstellersein selbst?*), Kafka asks rhetorically, performing a dance for Brod. He proceeds to demonstrate a dialectic. The sweetness of writer-being correlates with and compensates perfectly for the bitterness of not being a husband, wife, parent, landowner. "Going down to the dark powers" is reimbursed by the sunlight of vanity, the darker and deeper you go down, the bigger the ego payback; the sweet pleasure owes its origin to continual service to the devil (*Teufelsdienst*). And this devil wreaks revenge by consuming the possibilities for simple enjoyment of romance, parenthood, possessions. Kafka asks Brod to observe "on what frail ground or rather altogether nonexistent ground I live, over a darkness from which the dark power emerges when it wills and, heedless of my stammering, destroys my life. Writing sustains me, but is it not more accurate to say that it sustains this kind of life?"[46]

We can follow the Blanchotian logic in Kafka's description of writing this far. The meaning of the writer's death is a blow in the struggle between the two friends that began in the fall of 1917 very soon after Kafka's terrifying diagnosis. The 1922 letter is of a piece with the letters of 1917, and they reflect the same defensive move that led Kafka to conceal from his friend the writing of his treatise in thoughts. His death is not his alone, nor is it properly an end to life. As a writer he is already dead and so what Brod wants to preserve for him—health, prosperity, and social standing—are precisely what he has never had.

It is a myth, is it not, one that attracts critics to writers and motivates writers to write: the unholy power to descend nightly to the underworld and survive, at great cost to one's physical well-being but with even greater reward for one's writerly being. It interests Blanchot that Kafka on his deathbed can no longer communicate in any other way than writing. "As if death, with the humor that is particular to it, had thus sought to warn him that it was preparing to change him entirely into a writer"—that is into "something that does not exist."[47] The writer may not exist, but she lives her nonexistence the way other people live their lives. In death, she converts completely into writing, and writing, like death, is that which survives and never dies. Kafka calls this parasitism on death service to the devil. There is no death here, only servitude to an idea, a type of life. These lines bear repeating:

> My life was sweeter than other peoples' and my death will be more terrible by the same degree. Of course the writer in me will die right away, since such a figure has no base, no substance, is less than dust. He is only barely possible in the broil of earthly life, is only a construct of sensuality. That is your writer for you. But I myself cannot go on living because I have not lived, I have remained clay, I have not blown the spark into fire, but only used it to light up my corpse [*zur Illuminierung meines Leichnams*].[48]

The death of a writer is only a more obvious case of the way anyone thinks about death. It too is the display of an image. Life feeds happily off the image of death. It is just that: what is true for everyone once in a while is true for writers all the time. We imagine our own deaths now and again, when we want to see the "whole" of our existence—as Heidegger puts it. It is for us an epiphanic, momentary—*augenblickliche* —step back from our involvements toward the totality that they will become only after the end. The writer takes this step back continually, for the entire course of her life. And yet—and yet. Kafka is a special case of the special case of the writer's death: he is a different kind of writer.

Unlike Balzac, let's say, or even his beloved Dostoyevsky, Kafka has descended into the darkness for "the unshackling of spirits" and "dubious embraces,"[49] not on behalf of writerly powers. Instead of illuminating his world, lighting up human relations or psychology or the European social milieu from which as a writer he felt exiled, Kafka leaves these dark and instead illuminates his own corpse.

What kind of light does the illuminated corpse shed? It sheds light on our question, whether the artist who darkens images shouldn't by rights also have her image darkened. The image of the artist as the one who commands infernal image-making and image-breaking powers will also have to have its truth "exhausted," as Blanchot so beautifully terms it. What kind of light does the illuminated corpse shed? Not a black light of demonic powers. When the corpse of the writer, the living corpse that through necromancy and special potencies over the living dies—Kafka imagines the total blotting out of the secular writer-savior.

It is striking, is it not, this further return to Genesis, to the creation story? In this telling of the creation myth the holy spark misses its target and instead of breathing life into the creature, it stops short and illuminates the clay *qua* clay. The writer is like the clay: "insubstantial as he is" Kafka comments. "It will be a strange burial: the writer, insubstantial as he is, consigning the old corpse, the longtime corpse, to the grave. I am enough of a writer to appreciate the scene with all my senses, or—and it is the same thing—to want to describe it with total self-forgetfulness— not alertness, but self-forgetfulness is the writer's first prerequisite. But there will be no more of such describing." The writer herself is an image, "a construct of sensuality," or better said, of hedonism, *eine Konstruktion der Genußsucht*,[50] as a consequence of having separated herself from the other pleasures of the world in the first place. The writer and her writing both derive from the basest sort of idolatry and image-making.

28. Nietzsche's Doubt

Finitude and its heroic protagonist death are set pieces in a this-worldly theodrama in which the artist, among other protagonists, including the philosopher, takes on a sacred mantel it is thought "this world" still cannot do without. In shrinking the other world to a minor appendage, death itself has been elevated as the unsurpassable limit, like an atheist god presiding over "life," with the artist and philosopher standing by to protect and serve it. Kafka recognizes the following danger: we can perhaps rid ourselves of the image of death that holds so much power in life and further obscures the fundamental weakness of the yield; yet when we darken death's image, we must remember that this may easily be mistaken for a special capacity to overcome death. And so we must also diminish the apparent necromancy of the artist as well, and thereby the mystical trust in art. Without the artist, however, a further problem arises. After the darkening of death, residues remain that still require the attention of an artist or some figure versed in the tricks and seductions of images. The most critical of these residues is the idea of truth. Kafka treats truth as a matter of faith, on the one hand,[51] and as a matter of images, on the other. Let us look into the latter, the relationship of truth to the image.

Accept for a moment a caricature of Plato, one perpetuated by Nietzsche and picked up by Kafka. The idea of truth implies that there are two worlds, a world of truth and a world of semblance. This idea of truth is a caricature of Plato for several reasons, first and foremost because the two-world "theory" is taken as a truth of his system rather than as a teaching tool, a useful analogy, or a problem to be discussed. And we know for Plato that teaching by means of analogies or "myths" in problematic ways brought the question of semblance right back into the center to plague the assertion of a true world. It is never wrong to see Plato as a literary artist or literary critic, whose self-imposed task was to distinguish between valid and invalid modes of appearance. Indeed in classical philosophy and philology, he is often seen as doing this, although his "literary" concerns are often considered separate and distinct from his "philosophical" concerns. At the very least an adequate account of their interference or even identity has not yet been written. This problem aside, the caricature—"there are two worlds, a world of truth and a world of semblance or illusion"—constructs an argument from a myth about philosophy drawn from a training program in part based in Plato's reaction to the turbulent politics of Athens that he experienced and participated in during his late youth and early adulthood. Nevertheless, this caricature is important. It corresponds to the way both Nietzsche and Kafka believe ideas work on us. Through historical processes ideas become simplified schemata by which we interpret the world, or in Nietzsche's view, schemata through which we abdicate from willing a new interpretation, a new world.

Kafka works with a simplified "two-world" view of truth, as Nietzsche does in some of his later published texts and unpublished notes, as well as in key early texts of the 1870s.[52] Kafka also took seriously what Nietzsche very late called the "history of an error." The error was a false solution to a problem, or maybe the problem itself was originally false, it is hard to say. Nietzsche originally saw the two-world theory of truth as a problem, the solution to which was to do away with the true world, the thing-in-itself, the realm of archetypal Platonic ideas located "above the sky" (*huperouranios topos*). Aiming for a decade or more at an unmetaphysical theory of truth, he found this pursuit in the end to have been misguided or perhaps impossible.[53] In contrast, Kafka finds a way, or so it seems, to avoid Nietzsche's Platonic dilemma.[54] Happily he can preserve the two-world schema without at the same time as a consequence accusing those who live in the semblant world of nihilism. And he does this without becoming a relativist or a hermeneutical pluralist. There is one single, simple, unchangeable truth; it happens, however, that truth's effect is to rebuff all requests for access to it. Truth is the rebuff, no more; it is certainly not any of what it has been imagined to be or do or to offer us. As a continual repulsion, the true world gives life to semblance without becoming the metaphysical or eschatological solution to the problem of semblance.

Kafka's aesthetic turn responds in spirit to an ambiguity in Nietzsche's dicta about true and illusory worlds. Working on the same Platonic metaphors (world, sun, sunlight, darkness), Kafka's aesthetic turn—if that's how we want to think of the focus in these thoughts on illumination, the appearance of truth, and images, albeit with the plan to dim, cancel, or muddy them—is a movement toward a general theory of *Schein* that swallows up even the artist, master of semblances.

These pronouncements, this time of day, this truth effect, this very specific effect of light are not the heroic end of *Zarathustra*'s argument but the point from which it begins. The high point of humanity is not the arrival of the over-man, the *Übermensch* who has "gotten over" himself and humanity. The "history of an error" does not end in truth. When it is discovered that the true world drags the illusory one into oblivion with it, the error doesn't so much disappear as freeze in place. When the true world seems to be taken care of once and for all, the riddle of the two worlds is most active. Noon: the sun overhead. One envisions the brightest light, clearest vision without a tincture of darkness; one feels this as a moment of rest from the constant seduction to look away toward the other world. To Nietzsche in 1888 it meant: the moment of the shortest shadow. No light source is suggested, no sun, no truth. No shadow persecutes us, causing us to doubt what we see. Shadows are the clue in this world that we live in illusion and that that illusion has been produced by a source shining from elsewhere. And then comes Nietzsche's doubt: without shadows, without a negative signpost to something better, purer, more stable, more real, can there be anything at all?

You can't take a step in *Zarathustra* without encountering a shadow, and the same is already true much earlier. "You will know that I love shadow as much as I love light. For there to be beauty of face, clarity of speech, benevolence and firmness of character, shadow is as needful as light," says the Wanderer to his shadow in *Human All-Too Human*.[55] Something has changed in *Zarathustra* though, and the whole complex of light and shadow will be denied its constitutive role in aesthetics, logic, and morals (the beauty, clarity, and benevolence given by the shadow to the Wanderer). Yet along with shadows, in *Zarathustra*, the light is lost. Such is the wisdom a couple of years later. At noon there is no shadow so there is also properly no light, no way to tell the direction of the sun or the status of what is seen. In *Twilight of the Idols* he recognizes this, when noon is exchanged for dusk. Here is a poetic story: the progress of Nietzsche toward the late realization of his error transits through the dawn of the anti-transcendental critique of morals in *Morgenröthe*, stops stock still in the high noon of *Zarathustra* and the highpoint of humanity when the gods have been subtracted, and ends in twilight, when instead of a single sun casting shadows, there is a very troublesome double light source.

Nietzsche is still in doubt with regard to truth. This is the evening of the idols, but it is not clear what should replace them. Throughout the book he champions cheerfulness and full daylight, and yet this moment of doubt can't be discounted. In *Twilight* he can both say: "Heraclitus will always be right in thinking that being is an empty fiction. The 'apparent' world is the only world: the 'true world' is just a lie added on to it . . . ,"[56] and a few pages later " . . . But no! we got rid of the illusory world along with the true one!"[57] The two ellipses, one leading from an assertion, the other leading to its contrary, tell a woefully ambiguous story.

Kafka is sensitive to this ambiguity. Nietzsche in *Twilight* tells us that Europe in its history has presided over a continual diminishment of the truth idea. First in the Platonic moment the wise and good man could attain truth directly. Then in the Christian moment it was "unattainable for now" but promised for the future. With Kant truth was dismissed as "unattained" and "unpromisable," "the very thought of it a consolation." With positivism the true world had become so attenuated it was thought to hold no sway over this world. With the Nietzsche of *Zarathustra* and of lightness and Greek cheerfulness (*Heiterkeit*), at "breakfast" time for the spirit, the true world is no longer needed either as a hope or as a logical foil; a groundless dance of illusions is celebrated. And then comes the doubt: we do not know what to call a world in which, since there is no ground, there are also no phenomena; since there are no limits, there is no experience; since there is no darkness, there is no light; no silence; no language; no negativity; no positivity; no truth; no illusions.[58]

As if responding directly to this dilemma, Kafka hears a thought. *In a world of lies lying will never be expelled from the world, not even by its opposite, only by a world of truth.*[59] In this phrase the "two-world" theory is obviously at play. At first it seems as if Kafka is saying the same thing as Nietzsche, and yet in fact he rejects Nietzschean doubt and invents a solution that would lead to none of the bravado of artist, philosopher, *Übermensch*, cheerfulness, sun, or will to power.

Let us accept one further caricature: Nietzsche inverts Platonism. This type of assertion can only compound the simplification and decontextualization that Nietzsche himself sometimes perpetrated on Plato. To wit, his understanding of "image" and "truth" owe much more to Schopenhauer and early post-Kantian thought than to Platonic theater, and a whole other landscape and vocabulary would have to be adduced to explain the differences. Nietzsche is in fact modifying Schopenhauer much more than inverting Plato, and yet the caricature is instructive for our reading of Kafka. Nietzsche inverts Platonism, or so the critique goes;[60] he makes illusion the new truth and truth the new illusion. Both caricatures are instructive because they imply, not simply a dualism that can be inverted but a doublet with deep inner ties, two worlds with multiple and complex passages between them.[61] This is just to say: truth is the truth distinguished from illusion and illusion is the illusion of truth. The two worlds are fully convertible from the beginning, indicating one another with the kind of necessity reserved for the most absolute truths. The epistemology of "resemblance" that Plato pursues in the middle period works would have to rely on such a convertibility; the concept of "resemblance" requires it. A beautiful thing "resembles" the beautiful in itself; *idea* gives the look to a being and a being looks like its *idea*.[62]

In his thought of a world of truth and lies, Kafka returns to the Platonic caricature, admitting as Nietzsche does that the true world cannot be abolished. At the same time he implies, rather than their convertibility, the *mutual exclusivity* of the two worlds, thereby severing the tie that binds the Nietzschean and the Platonic caricature, cutting the inner identity of truth and illusion. Only a wholly true world will be true. This true world is so thoroughly true that it cannot be said to be the opposite of a lie. "Not-lie" does not equal "truth" and so truth and lies are not convertible. A consequence of this severance is the following: anything within this world of lies that looks like an indication of truth is only a bad kind of lie. *There is only a twofold: truth and lie. Truth is indivisible, therefore it cannot know itself. That which can know the truth must then be a lie.*[63]

Both worlds are there but there is no convertibility, no ways or passages between them—and knowledge is certainly not a possible passage. Other thoughts reinforce this conviction, and they openly and explicitly refer to the underlying theologoumenon. *The crows maintain: one single crow could destroy heaven. That is beyond doubt, but proves nothing against heaven, since heaven means: the impossibility of crows.*[64]

We have to ask two questions at this point; they are crows' questions, doubtless, but nevertheless: (1) What does the world of truth look like and what effect does it have if there is no way to access it (and how does this change the character of lies and lying), and (2) what political exigencies drove the production of these caricatures and Kafka's equally cartoonish responses to them?

As complex as the political context for the production of Plato's *Republic* was,[65] Plato too shows a tendency, at times, toward the slogan or the caricature. Socrates' arguments in this dialogue and others move toward simplistic formulations—this is in fact the purported point of "dialectic" as method—just as the philosopher-king is supposed to be *philotheamonas*, desirous of viewing the one true world.[66] That is to say, the idea that the truth is "over there" or "above" is a very important, regulative idea in the dialogue. Let us say that this tendency toward caricature or reduction of complex reasoning to a slogan or idea is already a response to the political context out of which the book was written. In one way

and one way only the *Republic* is an elaborate movement through coun-
terarguments to persuade Plato's contemporaries that "truth is not in
opinion." In response to the perceived failures of radical democracy; in
response to the obvious excesses of tyranny, in which Plato at one point
was a participant; in response to the by then clichéd antipathy of the polis
to philosophers; in response to its openness to sophists and the rhetorical notion of truth; in response to the alternative model of Spartan order;
in response to oligarchy, democracy, tyranny—Plato said: "Look over
there."[67] Many of the "middle" and "late" dialogues attest to an injunction to transit through illusion to the truth (the "middle" to its possibility, the "late" to its potential impossibility). Nietzsche in contrast enjoins
a move out of the truth, after Christianity and in the midst of nihilistic
Europe, a trip back to the vivacity of illusions. Another way to say this is
that Plato needs an external truth that can be willed into existence, into
possession. *Methexis*, the participation or partaking in ideas of semblances,
is the route to possession of that other world.[68] One could see this presupposition as at work in the very shape of Platonic philosophizing, as
much as it may escape its own shape in many places. The presupposition
is that truth is possessable through a certain kind of work with illusions.
Nietzsche in contrast, under the same assumption, does his work on
"truth," forcing a turn of the gaze back toward what had been blotted out,
not so much toward multiplicity or ambiguity but toward the body and its
appetites. And he does this in a debunking, critical kind of writing.

In this way two radically different political exigencies call into being
the same two-world theory of truth (with crucial inner passages between
the worlds) in order to be able to move from one world to another and
abandon the one perceived to be the problem. Kafka's political situation
may be different from either of the situations mentioned, or it may contain elements from both mixed to a dizzying degree—it doesn't much
matter, because his view of the purpose of philosophy, or in this case
"thoughts," is very different to theirs. A thought, his thought—*In a world
of lies lying will never be expelled from the world, not even by its opposite,
only by a world of truth*[69]—is not for the purpose of moving to the alternative world to the one we're in, be it pure illusion or pure truth. The
thought aims to show that there is no way across in the first place and to
produce with this thought a different political possibility separate from
the will to change, escape, or transit to the contrary. The political context may be the same or different, but the exigency of the relationship

between politics and thought is different, according to Kafka. Thought, however radically it differs in its concept between Plato and Nietzsche, is seen by both as a solution, as a way to make images of an alternative, to move away from the current state of affairs, a directive to look over here or over there.

The political value of truth is obviously different for Kafka. He does not want to emphasize either the thisness of the world as a materialism or biologism, and he doesn't want to emphasize the otherness of the otherworld as an antidote to opinion. Both attitudes are drawn from the same confused theologoumenon. For theo-philosophy the two, thisness and thatness, are an antinomy, but Kafka does not accept the principle of the excluded middle. We live, he might say, without access to either world, but the atheological fantasy that they are both there and equally inaccessible allows us to imagine a point at which we could leave off from incessant philosophizing. This is true as well if we live in the world of lies without access to the other world. We know we don't live in truth, and yet we cannot judge any particular image to be a lie. Plato wills a true world so that we can lift up our eyes from mixed to pure things. Nietzsche wills a world of illusions to break down the nihilism of Europe and refocus the eyes on the rainbow of powers in and over "this" world. Kafkan politics also has to do with truth, but it does not make use of the will, individual or collective. Truth rejects willing. Truth yields and we yield to it without possessing it either as the one and unchanging or the many and changing. You may think of this as a kind of truth-formalism; on one side, there is pure, formal truth, yet it has nothing to do with experience. You may also think of this as an idealism, more Kantian than post-Kantian. There is truth but not a way to it for us. "Life" does not admit of judgment.

29. The Problem with Our Art

Art is left for us to worry about, art—or whatever we call the medium that can communicate the inaccessibility of truth. How can it avoid the Platonic criticism or the Nietzschean faith, that through the power of image-work truth is indicated, even if it is the truth of no truth? This worry is alleviated by ascribing to art a negative value with respect to truth. A negative value is not, however, the same as negative signs within an artwork of a truth elsewhere or a truth nowhere. This distinction should be clarified. When art participates as a negative means and medium of a theo-episteme, art itself is value-ful, powerful, capable of things knowledge and will cannot accomplish. Where it surpasses the limits of cognition and will, art demonstrates unparalleled endowments and efficacy. Plato is very clear on the threatening power of poetry in books 2 and 3 of the *Republic*, and of painting in book 10. Art's intimacy with truth will have to be severed, if Kafka wants to depotentiate it. The problem with our art is its supposed proximity to truth, and yet those who claim that art is closer to truth than, say, science or everyday experience are woefully misguided. *Our art is a being blinded by the truth. The light on the yielding grimace* [das Licht auf dem zurückweichenden Fratzengesicht] *is true, nothing else.*[70] Here is a statement on the truth in art. "Nothing else" is a typical Kafkan negation that diminishes without determining. What we can call "true" is the frailty of art vis-à-vis the truth. Its frailty is what it represents for us through its visible pain and disgust.

A surprising ability is permitted art here, even in its weakness. Art registers at a minimum its withdrawal from truth. Although it has no access, either through representing truth or dialectically through failing to, art has the surprising ability to be and to show the lack of access. What's more, art is the selfsame lack of access to truth that one finds in everyday life, although the everyday cannot represent its cut-off condition to itself, insofar as the everyday still makes reference to eternity or truth in order to express itself in contrast as mundane, leveled down, empty, temporal, and so forth. True art is the everyday severed from its negative transcendental reference, and this, we should add, is the absolutely hardest artifice to achieve.

Art steps into the two-world truth theory at a strange place and with a strained expression. It cannot do what Kierkegaard did with his "aesthetic works," that is, make an infinite representation of the nonrepresentability of truth. If this can be done, truth is indeed representable, albeit in a tortured manner. It cannot do what Nietzsche was already sketching out in the early 1870s, that is, represent illusion *qua* illusion as the new meaning of truth. "Art treats illusion as illusion; therefore it does not wish to deceive; it is true."[71] That is, art that produces either a false representation of truth or a true representation of falsehood never achieves the hardest artifice, to not represent. The illuminated grimace comes as close to showing us the negative value of un-art as is possible in an image. Un-art—some thoughts in the treatise handle this genre, thoughts closely related to the thoughts on truth. Nearer the end of Kafka's life, full-fledged case studies in un-artistic practice appear. First, there is a hunger artist whose ideal artwork consists in slowly diminishing the art and the artist to nothing. In another story, a dog calls "artist" those little "air dogs" who are not tied down by gravity but magically hover above the rest and are always surprisingly well coiffed. Art is how you "elevate" what has a perfectly mundane explanation—that, for instance, the "air dogs" ride in human arms. Finally, the culmination of the nearly impossible and rather terrifying art of no art: a mouse artist grows famous for squeaking in the manner in which everyone squeaks. "We all squeak like that but no one would think of describing that as art," the mouse narrator says.[72] With no special talent, Josefine the "singer" augments the everyday communication of the mouse-people in none of the ways artists do, not by condensing or interpreting, intensifying or ordering, framing or mythifying it. In a portrait of a community where art does not play the cult role of gathering the community around a sacred art object, the squeaking, says the mouse narrator, "is the authentic art of our people or rather actually no art at all, just a characteristic expression in life [*Lebensäußerung*]."[73] "A Hunger Artist," "Researches of a Dog," and "Josefine the Singer, or the Mouse-People" give un-art its special artist, designated milieu, and political situation. In the treatise, however, it only has an abstract description. In working with the light metaphor for truth, Kafka raises the possibility, just as he does about the corpse of the writer a few years later, of an illumination that draws our attention to an absolute refusal to light up, a great "no" to the question of truth or meaning. Rather than an expression of an internal state, the grimace is an instinctive reaction to emerging too quickly into the light. Here is a face without a thread of reason, a discapacity without any higher capacity in another sphere to supplement it. Recapitulated in this image is the moment of mutual blindness in the *Republic*'s cave allegory when the truth seeker returns to the darkness and the cave-dweller looks toward the light. Both are blinded by what by nature they can no longer see, both faces are twisted—the one in an intense attempt to squint through the darkness, the other in an intense attempt to see into the light.[74] Instead of registering a rebuffed desire to see clearly, Kafka's grimace marks the potential this overwhelming, absolute "no" to vision gives the figure who encounters it. Art can retreat, back off. Truth is not for art, but art by means of its unwillingness to get burned shows us our options.

Although the following thought seems aletheically more promising, it nevertheless opens another set of concerns about art's truth-potential. This thought tells us less about truth's absoluteness than about art's intentions with respect to it. *Art flies around truth, but with the decided intention not to get burned. Its capacity consists in finding a place* [einen Ort] *in the dark emptiness where, without the place having been knowable in advance, the light's ray* [der Strahl] *can be firmly caught.*[75] One thing we must accept, if we want to follow Kafka on this space flight, is the conclusion that without art there is no hope of catching even a ray of truth. One could take this as epistemologically positive. Art does indeed receive truth. It is transmitted, albeit as a ray, and as such the truth that art receives is separated from natural truth by a great distance and altered in character. The truth does not lie however wholly or even partially in the character of its reception, as an artistic a priori. Instead, art hews wholly to the character of the emanation. In the manner of its emanation, natural truth transforms from whole, independent, unchanging, and so forth and it forces art to receive selectively, partially, in full abandonment to contingency and luck, capturing a sliver of truth in a specific place whose location cannot be foreknown. It is not art's limitation but truth's. Were truth to give itself wholly, art could possibly receive it. And so truth has to limit itself almost to the point of unrecognizability. There is nothing art or artists can do to improve the situation.

If we want to receive the benefits of what is "true" in art for Kafka, we ought to think through two things. First, art's receding in the face of truth is what is true about it, its pained grimace and yielding withdrawal are the atheological facts we have access to, and this not thanks to art but thanks to the meaning of truth. Truth is wholly true; it does not depart from itself. To this Kafka adds an astral scenario in which light rays are received by chance and luck. Chance is the mode of art. This is apparently because, as truth's light travels, it undergoes a double shift. First, it departs from the sun as a small and dare we say random share of the total light, random at least from the perspective of the artwork that happens to catch it. Second, it appears in any one place and time in one way, and in another another. And that is, we can say, the truth in art about truth's light—to some degree art is about truth's own intractable limits. Let us not confuse the character of those limits with the limits of subjective knowledge, however. Truth departs from itself, divides into shards, the shards become dependent on darkness for their illumination, the whole truth expresses itself and its departure in a multiplicity of contingencies, and art can have a share in their light, but only if at the same time it shows the empty space in which it happened to be caught. The sun does not shine for humans, quite contrary to the way Zarathustra flatters the mighty orb.[76] Here truth is an effect of atheological *strahlen* and *fangen*, not of *scheinen* and *Überfluss*.

30. The Return of the Snake

Kafka worries incessantly about sensibility as the source for knowledge. Unlike a knowledge skeptic, however, his concern is not with the senses' potential for falsity. He worries instead that falsity is a negative reference to truth, a formal indicator that, alongside its bare experience, signals a truth lying elsewhere, stimulating us thereby to strive and struggle, and leaving us to suffer, while we engage in quests and questioning, all of which is in his terms "evil." Skepticism, insofar as its particular yielding is a seduction to know better, is the very faculty of "evil." Worse implies better, and better is not an approximation of or approach to the good in this framework, but rather a detraction from it. Somewhat like Kant, Kafka believes that there are indeed two sources of knowledge, and his concern extends especially to the first source, which, following tradition, he calls "truth." To the standard modern philosophical categories, skeptic, dogmatist, and transcendentalist, we need to add a fourth: artist or fiction writer, whose relationship to truth, knowledge, and the senses has its own procedure, although it may employ terms that look similar: truth, light, semblance, sensibility, and knowledge.

The division of experience into the sensible and the true is what, for Kafka, makes knowledge into a quest and the sensual world into sin. We must understand, however, that the world is not sinful because it is not yet knowledge; Kafka's turn on this screw is to argue that the world is sinful because it feigns to lead out of itself. Sin is not falling for seduction. Sin is seducibility.[77] Sensible experience is open, its appearances and value are patent and obvious, and it is equally patent and obvious what humanity is supposed to do with it. Sensibility is supposed to take us to truth and it does this in the very suggestion of its immediacy and openness. *Sin always comes openly and is immediately available to the senses. It* [sin] *walks on its* [own] *roots and doesn't have to be torn out.*[78] Once again the account in Genesis is authoritative. Sin is a plant with mobile roots, another name for the commitment to knowledge. *What the sin* [original sin] *causes and what it knows are one.*[79] We recall in detail the scene from Genesis: the first humans break God's prohibition and opt for knowledge. Breaking the prohibition is called their sin; however, this way of reading the scene ignores the fact that the foreknowledge of what a prohibition is makes them sinners before sin. Sin is a moral event not because there was guilt at a crime, but because there was always knowledge. *Sinful is the state we find ourselves in, independent of guilt.*[80] In the Garden, sensibility and morality overlap. Sensibility means acts and consequences, pursuits and outcomes, *scientia,* if you will, but also industry and industriousness. Morality, it turns out, can only operate under these twin aesthetic and alethic conditions, that is, in a world in which truth and sensibility are each independently as stable and unchanging as the other, though divided, with the corollary that access to truth is always through sensibility, even if that means doubting sense data. With the Fall, humanity does not become God, but merely acquires an infinite potential for divinity, *only god-like knowing.*[81] As we have seen, this leads to a deep experiential duplicity: sensibility is both the way to eternity and the main obstacle to it.[82]

The fiction writer as image-worker enters this dilemma with a different intent. A skeptic reifies the division into truth and semblance by her very procedure—doubt. Sensibility is doubtful, but this can only be shown against a strong concept of truth, even if the skeptic claims no direct access to it. In this light, a dogmatist is but an intensified skeptic. She has the same disdain for sensibility, but uses it differently. Instead of making doubt of the senses into evidence for a higher truth, the dogmatist discounts sensibility altogether. And so, the skeptic suspends the true world by showing that the sensible is too uncertain to lead us there, while the dogmatist suspends the sensible world by showing that the true world is wholly independent of it. A transcendentalist trades doubts for limits, to be sure, and the difference shouldn't be underestimated. She preserves a balance of truth and semblance in a partial synthesis that depends on the distinctness of the limit. The artist or fiction writer, in contradistinction, does not so much act the monist to philosophy's dualisms, or pursue a higher division on the basis of which she can discover an ultimate synthesis, even a disjunctive one, like the one Schelling pursued. In lieu of a classic dualist for whom each member is kept separate, so that one can guarantee the identity of the other, the fiction writer asks herself the question, then, if we can say this much, how can I move the world, move the two worlds, from duality to duplicity?

The thoughts on the death-image hint at a procedure. In so-called secular European society, in the age of science and technology, of industry, and in Kafka's intellectual circles, death would be the most obvious and also the most intransigent point of transcendence. In each of these spheres, death is a transcendental image, if you will, and its image then is a special type of image. If death can be shown to be a mirage, that is, a semblance without a truth to distinguish it as semblance, then the last passage out of this life, whether to something or to nothing, can be closed. If this closure can be accomplished, we are left with an interminable life whose shifts and origins, images and quests are never definitive; they are without any definite limits, but not, as a result, infinite. Death becomes in this thought wholly unapproachable, and any image of an approach, any word that says it means more than what is shown is the semblance of a reference. This is why death, although it is not a passage out of this world, does offer a passage out of dualism, if only to a deeper more entrenched multiplicity.

Death and art have a share in producing this healthy sickness. Let us say that death is a natural dissemblance, while art is an artificial one. Or let us say that death, like the reproduction of *The Battle of Alexander at Issus* on the wall of the schoolroom, is a highly embroidered, long-cherished, historically settled work of art, whose age and relative fixity, not to mention the prestige of its genre and the accepted powers of its muse, make it the most resistant to darkening, the hardest to extinguish and so the perfect object for a paradigmatic darkening. Once it is freed of its supposed truth, the enormous powers of image-making formerly belonging to death might be freed as well for other nontranscendental purposes.

In some sense, once again, Genesis tells this story. In the same moment that death as finitude was loosed on humanity, something like art appeared. Art, in the sense that Kafka means it, has an atheological provenance equal to that of mortality. In fact, art arrives before death, before the Fall, and thus it alone might deserve to be called paradisal. In its incipient form, art arrives with the snake, but Kafka insists that only a return to the Garden and a new deception can bring art to its full potential.

So many tries at turning semblance against truth! There may be as many ways to do it as there are semblances to do it with. This is the richness of art, which, in its plurality, is bigger than truth, which purports to be only as big as a single star.

This is where the snake slithers in. It comes in full-fledged ambiguity, flickering its forked tongue, speaking an unholy mixture of truth and lies, one and then the other or both at once about the same thing in the same respect. The greatest possible misinterpretation of the snake's speech would be to take it as pure deception, as a big lie opposed to God's big truth. As Kafka points out, God himself either lies or exaggerates in Genesis 2:17 when he condemns Adam to immediate death. In fact, it will not be an execution, but a slow demise; rather than a penalty, death is a "natural" end of life, a far-off eventuality. And let us not forget Eve's interpretation and the way this has colored the snake's reception to this day. "The snake deceived me," she tells the Lord of the Garden (Gen. 3:13).[83] She was led to believe this no doubt by the configuration of things. The verb in question, *hashiyaniy*, from the root *nasha'*, later becomes a standard word for the prophets to describe deceived peoples,[84] and at times it forms part of an entreaty to a people not to be led astray by the illusions put before them by their king or god.[85] In most cases this kind of "deception" is a matter of taking false words to be true, of misrepresenting the facts, saying one thing when the situation is patently different, or so the prophets would have us believe. The word *nasha'* is a crucial part of the prophet's seduction toward another truth. It enacts a messianic operation: through the accusation of deception, the far-off truth twinkles. An accusation of deception can work as evidence *ex negativo* despite all appearances to the contrary. Eve's explanation, deception, is the beginning of this operation—not her supposed seduction—but the snake's work, that is of a different order.

In 1920, when Kafka was returning to the thoughts and beginning to write a new set, we find this among his notes: "Ihr sollt Euch kein Bild—."[86] "You shall not—an image for yourselves." The verb in this biblical citation is left to the reader's memory. *Machen.* Making images was Kafka's stock in trade,[87] and one can say that many of these thoughts are themselves images or conjure them up. Something about the ambivalent value or consequences of image-making catches his eye in these years. Jews are not supposed to make graven images, and all Kafka can do is make more of them. Proof that he is not a Jew or not a good Jew—perhaps. Something else, something in the nature of images, let's say, is signaled already in the ancient prohibition. On the one hand, images are powerful and threaten to displace, conceal, and stand in for God. On the other hand, they have, as it were, nothing behind them; images carry no index of their truth or falsity along with them. By 1920, Kafka can jot this down: "Nothing, *only image*, nothing more, total oblivion [*nur Bild, nichts anderes, völlige Vergessenheit*]."[88] An image is a special version of oblivion, evoking nothing other than itself, a startling intensification of the forgetting of the world.

In a famous essay from 1945, André Bazin exposes the photographic image to an ontological analysis.[89] Two modalities responding to two needs that were unified in painting become separated in photography: the need to preserve life beyond the fleeting moment and the need to symbolize a higher experience than the everyday. In painting these needs, obviously related, result in its twin modes, realism and symbolism, the story of whose conflicts can be written as a history of style. In photography, the symbolic function drops away, because of the bad fame of technology no doubt, but technology is only a means to express and fulfill the "resemblance complex" of the "masses."[90] The need to preserve everyday life has become paramount in the photograph. With this a new relation to death comes about, in which the image's primary function is to be the "object itself," freed from time and space.[91] In effect, the photographic image is the higher experience formerly presented by painting in its symbolic, that is negative, aspect. Photographs are positives. They allow objects, people, individual moments to outlive themselves and circumvent their demise. Moreover, despite being reproductions, despite being "taken" from the world, photographs are in fact its sources and models. The family photo album in an intensified and original way is the family. Two problems arise for Bazin with this shift in the ontological value of the image. First, photography is not cinema. A photograph, in order to give eternal life to an object, has to kill it, by draining it of motion. Second, there is the inexplicable fact that the surrealists loved photography, and this was obviously not only for its theological access to the object in itself. Bazin is fascinated by surrealists' fascination with photographic images. He wonders why the deepest fantasists with the closest affinity to what is both unreal and more than real, for invisible connections, for what is disorderly and what looks nothing like what it seems, would take this new sort of image as the basis for their style. Bazin attributes this to an ontological insight on the surrealists' part. A photograph produces "an image that is a reality of nature, namely a hallucination that is also a fact,"[92] that is, a dream.

But, on reflection, Bazin's argument vacillates between two different accounts of the relationship of photographic images to death, or perhaps even three. One of the accounts is based on Bazin's own symbolic commitment. Images mummify life, embalming the object in order to save it. He hints that this limitation is overcome by cinema, which in addition to the object also preserves its movement. But locomotion is not the only type of change. Despite the grip this association has on us, tainted as it is with an ancient identification, by Aristotle first and foremost, of locomotion as the model for all change, there are other types of change, and other modes of difference that are not confusable with motion. Bazin is committed to a techno-ontological theory of images in which once the image is made, whether moving or still, it never changes, never departs from itself. This is what he means by ontology. The image adds permanence because, as compared with life, the image is permanent and does not itself move. Only with this concept of image can the image hold the true being of the object. Photography, images, art—provide a continuous, permanent record, and viewers are subject to them as they were to idols. The photographic image gives eternal life by overcoming the temporariness of its object. The photographic image takes life as the fleeting experience of life; it mummifies. And the photographic image itself is a frozen deity holding both sides in its morbid embrace.

There is much to suggest that Kafka's model for the "image" was the photographic image.[93] The darkened portraits of castle officials that hang around the tavern are undoubtedly photos. K. takes one of these down in order to hang up the letter from Klamm, as though replacing the faded image of a person's head and face with an utterly ambiguous text were an improvement. In contrast, when the landlady pulls from under her pillow a photograph of the messenger who first brought her a message from Klamm, it is as though the image were easier to understand than the message. And yet it is not easy, at least for K., who sees in the image a young man lying down and stretching. The landlady shows him that the man in fact is leaping in the air over a tightrope on which he has been walking.

Kafka's reference to the picture of Alexander's battle against Darius refers to Altdorfer's famous painting, but the techniques he devises for working with it are photographic. Images are blurred, darkened, or extinguished as though the exposure or focus could be disturbed or a projector could be turned off. Bazin writes, "No matter how fuzzy, distorted, or discolored, no matter how lacking in documentary value the image might be, it shares, by virtue of the very process of its becoming, the being of the model of which it is the reproduction: it *is* the model."[94] That is to say, our belief in the process, the myth of the technical and temporal conditions for making an image, but also—although Bazin doesn't say this—the dependence of the photographic idea on a wholly unexamined mysticism of the real moment, which we might add is and always was inaccessible *except negatively through the photograph*—Bazin admits as much, but then in admitting he does not take the logical step and dismiss photographs as worse than illusions—this is what gives the photograph its ontological status, its eternal life, its priority over experience. Kafka takes the opposite view, the view we might say of some other photographers, André Kertész to name one, Chris Marker to name another, who recognize that the basis for the attribution of reality is not the truth of the technological process, which after all is only "truer" in comparison with its rival, painting, and thus is not real but historical. Thus the truth in photography lies in the style of the image, which corresponds to some clichés about existence, that is, its fleetingness, its graininess, its de-idealizing tendency, where dirt and decay were made the earmarks of the real. The unposed and the unpainted, the unexpected and the between-activity, half work, half repose, caught in the act as it were corresponds to a pre-interpretation. This is of course far from the technical truth, especially in early photographs. All the concoction that went on before the shutter snapped, the dissimulation, representation, symbolization even in the face itself, on its own, with its sculpted features, its set, its expressions, painted with its history, was reduced, with this myth of photographic reality, to something natural. Faces are overwritten with convention, concoction, fantasy; if photographic portraits only documented them, they could not help but document that, primarily. Add the documentary style to the dissimulation of life, and you have a wondrous overlay of dissemblance. If we contrast this with its rival, painting, what the slow application of pigment to a surface did was allow the images already at work in reality to appear as images. Witness the term that had to be used continually to assure people that something stood behind them, "mimesis." That is to say, the process of painting, conceding no or very little natural correspondence with natural processes of appearance (the conviction that things in nature just appear, artlessly), allowed a kind of affinity between painting and nature to be recognized. After all, painting arose on earth, not in the mind of God, and so reality would have to have about it something painterly, something susceptible to an alien medium, something applied, decided on, outlined, colored, colored over, and reworked. This is part of the ontology of painting. In its aura nature looks painted.

If photographs are the model for Kafka's thinking about images, it is precisely because they pretend to add reality to their objects. In them truth returns in as untouchable a form as in myth. Photographs pretend to be the model of what we ought to see or what we would see if our perceptions weren't limited, and this deception is the fatal one. Let not our phantasms be taken from us, only release the myth that we can avoid them. Kafka sees an opportunity in this type of image, in images with a high reality index, to demonstrate the illusory and, what's more, dangerous character of the real. Real images are the images whose hinterlights can be extinguished. Photographs can be darkened; behind each photograph there is, one could say, a skotograph that can be brought to the surface. Photographs can be misprocessed, de-developed so that their evil emerges.

First, death has to become a skotograph; this central image has to be darkened, as we've seen. The impetus to darken the death image was undoubtedly first of all personal. Here is a diary entry from September 1917:

> So far you have taken advantage of this possibility, the possibility to make a beginning. Don't squander it. You will not be able to avoid the filth that bilges out of you, if you want to penetrate. Do not wallow in that. If the lung wound is only an emblem [*ein Sinnbild*, morphologically, a "sense image," commonly rendered as "symbol"], as you allege, an emblem of a wound, whose inflammation refers to Felice and her deep righteousness, if this is so, then the medical recommendations (light air sun rest) are also emblems. Take hold of this emblem.[95]

The *Sinnbild* in question is unmistakably an emblem, mark of an absent authority, an indication of a supersensible belonging, but it is also relevant that Kafka here shuns the term that appears over and over in his work for these types of signifying relations, *Zeichen*—for example, the way K. awaits *ein Zeichen* from the *Schloss*.[96] In the aftermath of his first severe attack of tuberculosis, Kafka admonishes himself to receive the evidence of the disease not as a sign. To illustrate the peculiarity of this word and this admonition, imagine the word the doctors would have used: *Symptom*. Kafka refuses to call the blood that sputtered out of him a symptom; he refuses the semiotic regimen invested in by medical science and by his friends. To this perspective also belongs his refusal of the semiotic regime of psychology. In no sense is this a self-diagnosis of his somatization of guilt. True, Felice's righteousness inflames his lungs. A transferal is at work, though not a transference, a taking responsibility, corporeally, for an injustice he committed. "(Verkörperlichung der Symbole! [Embodiment of symbols!])," he writes Brod in March 1918.[97] He tells Brod he always felt a lack of "lung power" to breathe in the incredible multiplicity of the world. Embodiment of symbols does not mean the same thing as symbols for the body, that is, "symptoms." Here his body has become the screen for representations of a social and political order. He is celebrating, throughout this fall, the transferal of a physiological metaphysics of health and sickness, life and death, into a field of sense images of a different order. He will not die of the disease; the representation of an incapacity will keep him from living, which to him means mixing with the world's multiplicity; if it is a thorough mixture, one simply cannot breathe. He will try to resist seduction by alternative cures and fantasies of nutrition for which he has fallen before; instead, he plans to take action against images. As images, these four emblems— "light, air, sun, rest"—have vastly different meanings than they have for the doctors. Light, we have seen, is blinding, duplicitous, opening the world of immediate sense experience and at the same time seducing one toward a source, "the old sun," as Nietzsche calls it.[98] Rest is a constant theme in the thoughts. Air emblematizes the potential for a person to take the world as multiplicity into herself, the potential that Kafka begins to recognize when it is taken from him.

How firmly the self-commandment to "take hold of this sense image" became a part of his new beginning that fall. He began then to take death and life as images, and to indicate the ancient commitments at stake in them.

The snake enters the scene a little later on, when Kafka begins to track down the provenance of "our art" and images, that is, our dependence on and faith in fundamental visions. The biblical prohibition is one obvious marker of this dependence and this faith. The prohibition is a control on the distribution of images, not at all a diminishment of their credibility—quite the contrary. Witness Genesis, the deployment of sense images in progressively restrictive and ever more dangerous ways. Characteristically, Kafka sees the truth in the fear of idolatry; idols all too soon become gods. And so he turns to the moment in which an image first took hold, the turning point at which the myth of a transition from the real to the image arose. It is this image, the image of an origin for images, that is the work of the snake.

It happens in paradise, as you would expect, though the effects soon grow and become the world. In one fantasy from August 1917, Kafka begins to narrate a scene in which a giant snake has her path continually smoothed out by a gang of workers, who crush all the rocks in front of her so that she can slither effortlessly past.[99] It is the workers who produce the dust, *Staub*, to which the snake has been condemned. Through their toil they keep producing her fallen medium while expressing regret that, now that she has become their life's master, she must still bear the name of snake (*Schlange*). In a real sense she has become their god, but also their child and their ward—*Adam's first house pet.*[100] The creature, which claims its rightful place in the house of man, introduced images as such into the garden. This becomes its reputation and it is this reputation that Kafka will attack. With the snake the illusion that images can be illusory takes hold. "He deceived me," Eve tells the Lord of the Garden. As Kafka points out, the snake was right: these humans would not immediately die. He was also correct in saying that they would gain knowledge. What the creature did not say, perhaps because it did not know, was that knowledge is structurally equal to striving, and so the new difference between humanity and God would be, as God points out, toil, work, struggle, and suffering, all in the name of what will not in the end provide rest but only decrepitude. Adam and Eve had rest, sun, light, air. They were sufficiently mixed with the manifold, unafraid of sensual experience. Didn't the Lord of the Garden contribute to the deception, by making the fruit of this tree "a delight to the eyes" (Gen. 3:6.)? This post-paradisal instance already inside the Garden, hung as it was tantalizingly just out of reach, is the first image, to which all poor later creatures in a sense respond. The sense that there is something better accompanies it and is proof that the Fall was in the Garden from its creation; it is an image that gives post-lapsarian Adam the wrong idea. *He would want to reverse the knowledge of good and evil. Even the designation "fall" dates back to this anxiety. (The snake only half-completed its job with its counsel, now it has to seek also to falsify what it put into effect, that is authentically bite itself in the tail.)*[101]

We now know a few things. The fundamental theologoumena of modernity are at base images, and it is none other than the snake that must take responsibility for responding to the call to take hold of this image (*fasse dieses Sinnbild an*) and uproot it with special implements. It is the snake's work, the altering of images. This creature crept up to humanity and gave it the idea that knowledge was good. One last image is needed, if we can imagine it. The snake and its deception will have to be reduced to an image; it will have to go to work on itself, falsifying in turn the promise of knowledge, as well as the plight of sin and the fact of history. One did not think it possible: Ouroboros can be turned around once more. In "On the Vision and the Riddle," in his vision Zarathustra cries out to the figure with the snake lodged in his throat: "bite off the head! Bite down!"[102] But this is not Kafka's response. The other alternative is to let the ophidian curl around itself for eternity: "it wants itself, it bites into itself, the ring's will wrestles in it."[103] But this is also not Kafka's response. Instead, he decides to take up snake-work, to betray this proto-deception, to produce out of a virtuous circle a vicious circle that continually betrays itself; as a snake in the era of knowledge, he knows he will have to seduce us away from seduction by promising us a reward, though in the end not delivering it. In so doing he hopes to render the snake's bite harmless, pleasant even.

§   The Yield: On Forgoing Power

Neither an *Übermensch* nor a knight of faith can enter Kafka's equivocal paradise. Neither the one nor the other can perform the act or make the movement that is neither act nor movement. So leave aside the leap and the will to will. Do not overcome Christianity or Europe. Do not step beyond the last man or the knight of resignation to become the one after the last. Drop the infinite movement that arrives at eternity. And then . . .

. . . across the treatise in thoughts two struggles come into focus; they are less than struggles, really, although they do demonstrate inconsistencies in the Kierkegaardian and Nietzschean positions. Through and across these thoughts, Kafka is sharpening a weapon, its point aimed at the heart of the German idealism living on in the critiques performed by Kierkegaard and then, with absolute respect for the enormous differences between them, in other ways also by Nietzsche.

The evidence for his dismissal of Kierkegaard that winter is abundant; the evidence for his continued engagement with Nietzsche is less apparent but also less superficial. Nietzsche is the warp across which his thoughts are woven. You never glimpse his pained visage directly, but Nietzsche sounds within and in peculiar dissonance with Kafkan formulations.

31. The Way and the Wall

Don't hesitate, give in! If there is a kernel of Kafka's practical thinking, this is it; yet the maxim is harder to understand than immediately apparent, and even harder to follow. The architecture in his stories leads readers to believe, indeed it most often leads the protagonists themselves to believe (and by sympathy readers), that solutions to the dilemmas in which they find themselves are infinite, that is, that the only answer to an immediately unsolvable problem and seeming constraint on action is total freedom. This is undoubtedly the supposed fact that once made Kafka too easily absorbable into a canon of existentialism.[1] Freedom of action on the basis of the absurdity of circumstances, freedom of interpretation on the basis of a not immediately apparent meaning for behavior—freedom seems to be what some readers gain from the lack of obvious grounds for action by protagonists or interpretation by readers of the fictions. It is odd, however, how the very large number of obstacles to understanding and the deeply fettered movement of thought, of readers as well as protagonists, come to signify, out of frustration perhaps, or denial, their opposite—total liberty. Let us call this the Kafka reaction; it is not wrong, though it is, we might say, impatient.

It is as though, confronted with so many walls, a reader, as happens often to Kafka's agonists, is stimulated to overcome them so thoroughly in her imagination that the obstacle appears to disappear, although it has hemmed her in completely. Deleuze and Guattari's re-imagining of Kafka's world is a prime example of the "Kafka reaction" in its revulsion toward walls, closed doors, blank faces, signs not to be taken, roads that turn back on themselves or lead nowhere. "The castle has multiple entrances," "the hotel in *Amerika* has innumerable main doors," "we will enter, then, by any point whatsoever." The denial of obstacles is so strong that even obstacles are made into pathways. "No entrance is more privileged even if it seems an impasse."[2] Guattari and Deleuze reinterpret Kafka as an emancipatory psychoanalyst, more emancipatory than Freud ever dared to suggest one could be, a clinician who sidesteps old blockages of desire and opens up new paths, escape routes, modalities of becoming, a total garden of totally forking paths. Freedom, in this view, is conceived of as the overcoming of all restrictions, as constraintlessness. This was in part also Borges's reaction to Kafka when he crowned him genius of the labyrinth.[3] You can imagine a labyrinth, however, as an infinity of ways or as an infinity of walls. Infinite blockages do not add up to infinite freedom; each is no more than the same again; they add up to one thing. *There is a goal, but no way; what we call "way" is hesitation.*[4] This thought must not be understood to favor "hesitation" when in fact "hesitation" is the negative term used to condemn "way." Reading Kafka's writings after the treatise, one is confronted by a remorseless theory of ends without means, that is to say, of obstacles without ways, and so not obstacles at all but tableaux, stopping places, points of view on the misguided metaphor of the path. This is in no way the same as a theory of means without ends. The concept of freedom that issues from the latter is conventional and, except for very few cases, apolitical. The concept of freedom that issues from the former—if there is one—is counterintuitive no doubt, but if it can be practiced, it holds great potential for politicization in the sense in which Walter Benjamin used the term.

Kafka's atheopolitics is not a theological apolitics. To see the political details we need to move from a theory of being without becoming, stations without ways, to some account of action—and this too without will and without movement. We traverse an eccentric Kafkan ontology once again, toward an eccentric Kafkan moral theory. We have learned that the action that corresponds to ends without means is not equivalent to movement. If it is true in this sort of world that *what we call "way" is hesitation*, this means that the values of means and ends are reversed. Striving, making progress, following a method, advancing, approaching, pursuing, knowing, and all the myriad of metaphors that liken living to directed locomotion, become, in this reversal, resistance to arriving. The way is the obstacle. To what? To having already arrived.

There is no becoming in Kafka: let us state this outright. Plenty of textual evidence supports this thesis. First of all, no human ever becomes an animal in the fictions; animals are as they are when we find them. Even the ape in "Report to an Academy," who we are told has been captured, taken from his land of origin, and who eventually and quite rapidly evolved, even this recent human, cannot fully reconstruct the path that led into captivity; in any case it is a late retrospective narrative of explanation. The human straightjacket in which he is already pinned when the story begins may as well have always been his. This is the ontological counsel of the oeuvre, late and early: cast becoming aside. The stories: "The Trees," "A Country Doctor," "A Crossbreed," "An Old Manuscript," "A Hunger Artist"—not to mention the novels, are named after things that already are what and how they will be. The only exception to this rule seems to be "The Metamorphosis," and yet contrary to the implication of the word, no transformation happens in the narrative. Gregor Samsa is from the first word a vermin; furthermore, he already was one, and as the curtain goes up on his plight, if he becomes anything he has simply become what he was.

Becoming is the snake's first promise, the first deception. The name of this evil creature, once it is invited into the human household, once it becomes a part of the family, is "capacity" (*Fähigkeit*), whose nearest relatives are potentiality and becoming. The evil of striving derives from this bit of lapsarian hope: that we can become what we are not. The whole complex of words and concepts that carries this slippery core of paradise down to us from Greek sources—*dunamis, dunaton, potentia*, possibility, power, capacity, faculty . . . and lest we forget, "will"—preserves and promotes the idea that there is in us an indestructible source for becoming, that we are "becoming-creatures" by nature. Possibility, will, and the will to power are in this respect the same. They hold onto a precious kernel of paradisal dissatisfaction, of evil. From a Kafkan perspective, this is the explanation for both the apparently permanent pairing of being and becoming and for the tension between them. Being already involves becoming insofar as there is an ideal or essence toward which any creature or thing moves in order to be what it is. Aristotelian-inspired philosophizing, including contemporary natural science, derives from a fundamental dissatisfaction with the way things are, one name for which is "appearance." From this we can draw two conclusions. Kafka will modify the tradition running from, on one hand, Genesis and Aristotle's natural and meta-natural theories to Zionism, and on the other hand from Nietzsche to the Nietzscheans. Since being is bound up with becoming from the beginning, in order to imagine being without becoming, which is something like the task he sets himself in the treatise, he will have to modify the idea of being beyond recognition.

One way to release us from becoming is to change our relationship to images, which function as spurs to action, as excuses for transformation, that is, as motives for hesitating or waiting or postponing the arrival that has already happened. Images are, as Maimonides says of images of messianic things, only images. This is their disappointment and their power.

One way to modify being is to contradict our entrenched habits of thought concerning becoming. Images are instrumental in the functioning of all the terms for becoming—possibility, power, becoming, will. And so, if we impinge on the faith in images, if we make certain key images, and the idea of image in general, unusable as ideals, goals, or wishes, we affect being from the front end backward, as it were. We cut off its future, which never was more than the image of a destination anyway. It is this kind of future that Kafka attends to in October, when he copies his programmatic plan from his diary into letters to Felice and then to Brod. His ultimate goal (*Endziel*) is to reduce human and animal communities to "their fundamental preferences, wishes, and moral ideals."[5]

From the manner in which possession is temporalized as faith, we can see that the first attempt to get at the problem with being leads Kafka in the direction of the will. Possession is a capacity. It has to be enacted, proven, projected on the world, demanded, won, willed.[6] Possession is what you gain, not what you are. And so, in revealing our concept of being as an image of possession and assertion of belonging, Kafka also lets out the big secret: in this family of concepts, there is no being, only acting, where acting is behavior with a view toward becoming something other than what you are. Time is therefore the indispensable means for becoming-obtaining, the way, and also therefore the wall. The way is hesitation. Time is the obstacle.

How can you think being that is not tainted by becoming? How can you think faith without time? As one might imagine, Kafka at first proceeds negatively. One figure that perpetuates this ontology is the intuition of the infinitely large, a primary commitment that gives you the sense that motion is possible. It is the intuition of space, to be sure, but it is also prior to this a hazy, half-imagistic, half-mathematical pledge about the order of things, which, it must also be said, has a crucial corollary in a moral affect. Hope is a pledge that one more step is always possible, a mathematical affect to be expressed as $n+1$. The infinitely large is thus the pattern that underlies both autonomy and progress. The feeling that one can set one's goals and act in such a way as to achieve them—corresponding to the Kantian question: what may we hope?—recurs to this originary intuition about liberty as a lack of restrictions, the grounding idea for which is the infinitely large. Deleuze and Guattari see this pattern as the key to Kafka's novels, "novels that Kafka himself stops, since they are interminable and essentially un-limited, infinite,"[7] where the architecture of structures within them is "an infinite and ungraspable hierarchy." Even Kafka's letters have this quality: "the infinite flux of letters."[8] The names for infinite striving are, for Deleuze/Guattari: law, trial, castle. These are sites of an "immanent power,"[9] and "an infinite virtual movement" identified with an unlimited "process." That they emphasize movement and types of movement over the destination or goal is unimportant. The model is the same. That they trade transcendence for an "unlimited field of immanence" is also immaterial.[10] For this is just the point, the contrary of transcendence is not immanence, which is simply its interiorization as becoming. To decide for this internal immanence, becoming, is to intensify dissatisfaction to a point of total suffering. Everything must always become, move on; nothing is ever enough for immanence. The procedure that Deleuze and Guattari prefer is paradisal, to use their word, to its very heart. The opposite of transcendence is not immanence but being that knows no hope, no becoming, with a corresponding affect, humility, whose mathematical sign would be n-1.

32. No More Than

To begin working against the infinity idea that underpins hope and theories of moral action, Kafka must not promise to replace it with anything, or not with anything much. First, he takes a negative approach: *the idea of an infinite expanse and plentitude of the cosmos is the result of a mixture, driven to the extreme, of arduous creation and free self-reflection.*[11] Here we see through the ironic phrases "arduous creation" (*mühevolle Schöpfung*) and "free self-reflection" (*freie Selbstbesinnung*). Humanity is the source of this idea. If it creates, humanity creates out of toil, effort, *Mühe*, not out of omnipotence or *ex nihilo*. It cannot have the infinite creativity of God, only the finite creativity allotted to a finite power, called in its least aggrandized form merely "effort." Human action is creative but not free. Conversely, consciousness is free but not creative. Kafka approaches the Kantian critical dualism here. And so the idea of an infinitely ample milieu is contradictory from the start. Infinity is purgatorial for human beings. We can, in reflection, when it is pushed to its extreme, have the idea of an infinite field for action, and yet this idea corresponds to extreme toil, and this itself is a deception, since no one can produce infinitely, not even all of humanity for all of time. The combination of free reflection and limited action can also be seen as comic, and Kafka often sees it this way. Frantic activity accompanies freely spinning thoughts; this comedy plays in stories like "While Building the Chinese Wall" and "The Burrow."

Humanity toils away let's say for a long, long but still finite time, and before any toil it imagines a stage on which its effort can be endless. Two images of the infinite clash here: imagination knows no final limit, is expansive, and work/effort must happen each time yet again, is repetitive. Yet the expansive infinity of the intellectual sphere too is "an idea," a *Vorstellung*, and thus it is by necessity contaminated by its own idea-character. In truth there is but a finite idea, the idea of the infinitely large.[12] The infinite is not the form of intuition of space and time—one could argue that both intuitions are grounded in the idea of additive infinity for Kant. No—the grounding for the intuition of infinity is a representation, not a form, or at least Kafka thinks this. The infinity idea is an impossible attempt to push our activity and our imagination beyond their limits. It is a mundane name for transcendence, an arithmetical idea, probably poorly understood, in which the promise of paradise returns. That is to say the infinitely large is evil.

Even the infinity of the natural world is the product of striving. Aristotle's insight that infinity is intimately linked to possibility already indicates as much. The infinite is not itself but strives continually to become it. A commitment to infinity makes it possible to have hope in the face of personal failure or blockage, when you think of your own action as an ongoing task. This too is semblance. *That our task is exactly as big as our lifetime gives it a semblance of infinity.*[13] We can only laugh at those who propose humanity as either an infinite project (Kant) or as workers with infinite potential (capitalism, Marx). "Our task," whatever it is we propose to accomplish by means of toil, whatever excuse you pick to justify and prolong the work, the final and whole product to which our individual efforts will ultimately belong cannot exceed our lifetimes.

Another thought occurred just before the thought about semblant infinity, on the very same day, January 19. *No drop overflows and there is no more room for a single drop.*[14] The thoughts of parsimonious being and semblant infinity may imply one another. The exact fit of our task with our life that gives the semblance of infinity is given here an image. In the image lies the abstract principle. In Heidegger, in any case, the end is overcome at every instant when it is converted into possibility. In place of infinite progress on a line, one gets infinite possibilities for meaningful action at any single instant of existence, or so Heidegger argues. In Kafka's thought of the frugality of being, far from an endless source of possibility, our lifetime allows not one drop extra. The principle of parsimony expressed here in fact extends to three areas: to being as a whole, the cosmos; to a human lifetime; and to individual entities in their milieus. A container whose liquid contents fill out almost to the limit, without, however, a single drop going over into the next container represents Kafka's precarious attempt to imagine a world that gives the appearance of endlessness, offering constant temptations to progress, transcendence, transformation, escape, and yet does not actually extend one iota beyond itself, materially or spiritually. A life that does not extend beyond life, a cosmos just short of the cosmos, or a being barely itself—being is utterly and senselessly parsimonious with its goods and this means that no being includes its own limit. Such a shortfall gives any being the appearance of endlessness, on the one hand, and on the other hand, it makes it plausible to say that any being is unlimited without thus being infinite.[15]

What is an extended thing that does not extend even to the end of itself?[16] One model is an extended thing without any extension, a drop. The barrel is made up of drops, to be sure, and they do not touch each other. The drop points toward the ideal model of this unextended, non-self-touching thing, the point. *From a certain point there is no turning back. This point is to be reached.*[17] Retreating from the infinitely large and its messianic pretensions, we arrive finally at the point. The figure is undoubtedly not without its own difficulties. If it truly does not touch its edges, however, we cannot think of it as making up a continuum or as a destination "to be reached." This sort of point is not a limit, not the endpoint of a line, the corner of a plane, or the vertex of a solid.

If there is a Kafkan ontology, and granted it is not always obvious that there is, if there is something like a theory of being here and in the stories, it is one that shuns the idea of abundance, of excess, and perhaps therefore also the idea of relation, interaction, and certainly it eschews the idea of movement on an infinite and infinitely divisible plane. This may be a variety of nominalism, although it is a peculiar one if it is, an ontological and not an epistemological variety. Each thing to itself, no larger than its limits, not reaching its own limits and so having imperfect coextension with itself repulses universals through a quality that may most resemble defectiveness. It thus becomes a question, under the law of internal self-diminishment of beings with respect to themselves, not only whether anything like universals, but also something like an individual, could establish themselves. Can there be knowledge, universal or nominal, of what is less than what it is supposed to be? Note that this is not a theory of the limits of knowledge, but of the inability of objects to be themselves. Like the central nominalists of scholasticism, Kafka rejects universals, since he believes that superfluity and abundance do not exist; yet he also rejects particulars, objects, individuals as well. Before they reach their defining limit, beings yield.

Doubtless Kafka's yield is in part a response to *Fear and Trembling*, in which "resignation" is a stage in the training program for salvation. Yet resignation is not ontological parsimony; to wit, it can be infinite. Abraham makes a movement of infinite resignation under his plight and thereby borrows an infinity for himself that is, for all intents and purposes, the mirror image of an all-powerful God. The knight of infinity has a gait "as steady as a postman's."[18] The only difference between the knight of resignation and the knight of faith is that the latter has a different gait. Yet leaping is steady too. Abandonment of the idea of infinite resignation in the leap also abandons the yield. The argument runs like this: the knight wants salvation but knows he cannot get it, for he is a mere mortal. If he can be convinced of the total impossibility of achieving it, but only if this conviction is total, he can give up completely, but he has to give it up in every moment, infinitely. At some point, this pseudo-yield, the vacuum where his greatest will was, is filled with faith, and leaps. Resignation, an "infinite movement," is a prerequisite and an autonomous action of an I who can by an act of will resign from will and action. In the terms of our Kafkan ontology, let us say that this being, who looks for all the world like the most humble, the least powerful being, the least able to respond to God's call, has made himself large and powerful precisely through resignation, thought of as a power or capacity. The knight of faith no longer resigns, but leaps on the basis of the absurd, and yet leaping is not for him impossible.

If we want to imagine a being who resigns from even leaping, we can think again of one thing that does this systematically and essentially: a point with no extension. Kafka evokes infinity again, but now completely under the sign of the point. *Two possibilities: making oneself infinitely small or being it. The first is fulfillment, therefore inactivity, the second beginning, therefore act.*[19] Note the inversion again: the end is the act, the means is inaction.[20] The way, that is, is hesitation. "Fulfillment" is anathema to a point. Without the need for technical mathematical understanding, Kafka rejects the logic of the infinitely large that hides in one quasi-secular notion of transcendence, the idea of a route along which directional, coherent movement can happen, and in its place he sets the infinitesimal,[21] where action can no longer be equivalent to movement.

In addition to rejecting the infinitely large, Kafka simultaneously rejects an often unspoken tenet of political Zionism, the admonition to Jews to overcome their smallness.[22] To become large is the common imperative. To give one example out of very many, in December 1917, in the preface to its publication of the Balfour Declaration, the *Jüdische Rundschau* urged Jews "not to be smaller than the time demands [*nicht kleiner zu sein als die Zeit es verlangt*]."[23]

Smaller than the time demands, this is what Kafka enjoins "you" to be but not to become. Be the minimum demanded of you by the times.[24] The problem with this formulation is that the maxim cannot be given as an injunction and the size cannot be compared to what exceeds it. Anything that is big enough to be compared is too big; a point has no size. It would be the smallest "something" that nevertheless has no extension and so cannot logically be itself. Kafka seems to return here to Berkeley's slighting of infinitesimals as "ghosts of departed quantities."[25] Ironic, then, that he presents this counterpoint to us as a choice, and as a choice between two possibilities. For beings schooled in judgment, for paradisal beings condemned to a choice between good and evil, it would seem that just here we would be tempted to gamble. Both are open to us, being and becoming, Kafka seems to say, and each may be judged as to its fitness for our purposes. Again, in his systematic asystemic way, Kafka calls upon the understanding of "good" that comes into view across the polylogue. Good, it turns out, is perfectly describable in terms of the infinitely small. This means that the choice here is illusory. There are no possibilities; the world is actual. Possibility is evil, that is, it leads away from the world. Possibility makes the world an effect of striving to become what it is not. There is thus no number, no "two." What Berkeley knew was that no usual arithmetical operation could give quantity back to an infinitesimal, which remained as small when multiplied as when divided, and did not cause any increase in whatever it might be added to. The fiction of a choice is there in Kafka's dictum, if you will, to be refused. Only if you hear the irony and refuse the choice can you be what you are, a point, that is, not only smaller than anything else, but smaller than yourself. From the perspective of the long trajectory beginning in Genesis, and for that matter in Aristotle's philosophy of nature and ethics, in moral thinking or in movement-oriented telic-cosmic theories of coming-to-be, in genetical histories, then, "making oneself" infinitely small, taking this less-than-a-point as the object of effort, is not an act at all.

"The yield" is the name I pinned on the act in-a-new-sense of being what you are, of going on less than being, without possibility or becoming. You can see in it, as I have tried to demonstrate, an argument against Kierkegaard, for whom a rhetoric of "movements," from lower to higher, leads up to and through the immigration into heaven. There is no knight of the infinitesimal, nothing near so heroic. The dregs of idealism will be drained from Kierkegaard's critiques of idealism, as they will from Nietzscheanism and Nietzsche's own late philosophy of the will.[26] It is a matter of learning to decline power, even if that means giving up the whole world that corresponded to it. Both the knight's leap and the overman's overcoming have to be revised in light of the yield. It is thus interesting that Kafka begins to make this revision under the aegis of a Nietzschean dictum: become what you are.

33. What You Are

It is easier to forgo power when talking about things than when talking about persons, human beings, existents, believers, possessors, or whatever you want to call them. This may be because the being of a person cannot be understood apart from power; it lives, its nature is a coming to be, and not only in the mode of biological "growth" or psychological or social "development." The "ought" of moral activities and relations is a sign of its essential becoming, overcoming, and exercise of its capacities as well. Whatever it is that you ought to be, through whatever toil or power you are supposed to achieve it, you will have to become, your primary activity will be becoming. "Ought" is an invitation to becoming; more than an invitation, it is a demand or command that carries the force, a linguistic force to be sure but for that no less potent, to open a horizon on what is not. And insofar as the "ought" of morality is always directed toward a "you," this not-being is a special possession of the second person. It is part of the concept of "you" that an ought can be directed to it, and what is presupposed to belong to a "you" is this special not-being.

In order to say what you are, first you have to say what "you" is. "You" is the being who can receive the command to overcome and to become. And you is also the instrument of this becoming—the matter and the means. This innocent word, innocent when it is singled out, mentioned, but when it is used—is there a way to say "you" without this use and abuse? without the minimum of violation that is the demand to use power? without the disrespect and invasion of a demand to become what you are not? What a second person "is"—the description has to include the fact of its subordination to, its coming behind or beneath, after or beside some other force or power. But it also has to include the fact that this force is there to direct it to use its own power, to direct it to become. You do this, you do that. And first: you become what is implied in "you." The best expression of this power relation and this implied "ought," for Kafka, is to be found in an unexpected place, at the core of the Nietzschean doctrine of overcoming—a special version of becoming, no doubt, but a version nonetheless—in a phrase that accompanied Nietzsche, quite literally speaking, out of classical philology, through the Greeks, into a renewal of Germanity and beyond the Germans and indeed beyond Europe. "You" was the material and the instrument and the goal of this renewal.

The "you" was beginning and middle and end of the process of renewal that Nietzsche envisioned would be inaugurated with the phrase "Become what you are." This is the formula for Nietzsche's version of "self-reliance," we might say, and so it should by rights have more to do with the self and the "I," as the maxim that corresponds to his ferociously anti-collective view of sociality. Yet it is also one important sign of Nietzsche's understanding of the basic becoming nature of human being. Becoming is overcoming. And yet, a conflict inheres in the phrase, no less because it is addressed to "you." Who speaks here? Is this Nietzsche? Is this your conscience? But the conflict is older than the conscience. Nietzsche inherits the conflict from the very Greeks through whom, by resurrecting them authentically, he hoped to overcome the Germans. "Become what you are," a quotation, at one key moment in his oeuvre an epigraph, at another time a motto, at yet another a subtitle: the phrase is always also in its rhetorical force an injunction, a command. As a command it contains within it an ought and an invitation to become. Yet it also contains a pleonasm. The form itself, the speech act, injunction, implies becoming. The command someone to "become" certainly makes this structure explicit, but it also complicates the structure by commanding you to "become!" The command "become" is double: the form says—become the one who follows orders, be prepared to become what I order you to become—and the content says—become, be more than you are, abandon what you were (yield), be what you are not (the yield from yielding). The phrase is a pleonasm; furthermore, "you" is implied in every command, every injunction: why assert it so forcefully here? Let us indicate then, in sum, that the formula "you become" is a cipher for the "ought" per se. It articulates the unvarnished intention behind all moral commands and maxims; it is a self-referential imitation or mobilization of moral language. Obviously the difference in Nietzsche's version is the oxymoronic seeming addendum: "what you are." Why should that which already is have to be achieved by means of power, that is by negation, the negation, evidently, of itself?

Compared to the injunction "Become what you are," for instance, the vastly different phrase "Be what you are" says little or nothing. It is nearly if not totally tautological. It might be the crux of nihilism. Be what you are says, do nothing. In contrast "Be what you become" would be the keyword of morality as it has traditionally been known, the linguistic instrument of the most demanding and personal "ought." You ought not to be what you merely are, first and foremost, and beyond that you must inhabit this becoming and yet still become no more than what was enjoined upon you, the telos, so that once you have become this, you will stay that way: be what you (will have) become. "Become what you are," in contradistinction, is surely a meta-moral statement. It catapults you beyond good and evil. But in what way precisely? Doubtless it performs an inversion of "ought." It is likely ironic too, this "you ought to ought." It might be thought that, however ironic, through this inversion Nietzsche succeeds in ridding himself of the conflicts within the phrase, but that is not the case. One conflict can already be heard in full bravado in line 72 of Pindar's Second Pythian Ode, which Nietzsche comes back to throughout his trajectory.[27] There the imperative is in the aorist optative middle: *genoi hoios essi mathōn*: "become the sort of man you are, having learned what you are." We should note here that the poet's involvement in the question of becoming is implied in the last part of the line. This involvement is lacking in Nietzsche's formulations, or appears to be. The addressee in the poem becomes what he is "having learned what he is" from the poet in this poem. The way the injunction and the ideal conflict, then, is quite conspicuous in Pindar's ode. The poetic singer records the heroism of Hieron the Charioteer, which the athlete alone does not or cannot recognize. He must be taught what he is. What "you" are comes to you secondarily, in the case of an athlete, through a song of praise. Live up to what is said about you—sings the poet—be appropriate to your *kleos*, for your sake if not for the sake of the poet's reputation. Pindar most probably wrote the ode well after the sporting festival, perhaps years later as an old man. And so, all at once here in the Greek version, a worry that a fact—the heroism of the athlete—might become a fiction—the athlete is no longer himself—and therefore the fact would need to be rescued and restored to its full truth—by the poet's song—which is the only persisting being of the fact—the athlete's greatness—which as a result is no longer in him but rather in the song. Reciprocal dependency, each of them nothing without the other, poet, athlete, together they become great. And yet each, athlete, poet, is also weakened by this interdependence. The athlete is suppose to free himself from external praise, from dependence on others for his self-image; this is the meaning of the poet's injunction to become what he is. Be what *you* are *to and for only yourself.* "An ape is beautiful to children,"[28] the poet chides. Only one who knows himself can avoid pretense, flattery, and deceit, that is, can avoid mis-knowing himself in the gaze of others. And yet, the poem enjoins its subject and addressee not to be himself, but to become like his depiction. Become what you are, having learned what you are from me. This is the conflict as Pindar lays it out and lives it: you must come to be an ideal through a representation and a maxim. Perhaps poetry, in its care for fame and preservation of ideals, is the origin of morality.

In a second context in which Nietzsche quotes the Pindar phrase, we don't know quite what is intended. The phrase has no outward connection to Diogenes Laertius, Nietzsche's study of whom, as we've said, displays the line as motto in 1868. Still there are hints to its purpose there. Diogenes' *Lives and Opinions of Eminent Philosophers* can be taken as a set of models for emulation, and so the motto might well be an injunction to become as great as the philosophers. Become who you are, that is, who you could be, that is: be like these men. Indeed, Nietzsche's teacher, the philologist Friedrich Ritschl, defined the task of philology as the restoration of living models. The philologist gathers an herbiary of ancient texts to be read and understood by contemporaries, a library for moderns' personal development. So, since the Ritschlian Nietzsche appends this phrase as motto onto a study of Diogenes Laertius's sources, it might well mean "become who we were." Strip yourself of modern trappings and reveal the ancients buried within you. It might mean, additionally, in a personal register, become a philologist, as Nietzsche did in one stroke with this text.

Already the next quotation of the phrase is different. When Nietzsche returns to the Pindaric phrase in *The Gay Science* (1882), what comes to the fore is another tension, an inner pull between a social command and a rigorously separated, asocial self. Your conscience speaks to you: "270. *What does your conscience say?* 'You should become who you are.'"[29] One thing is clear: the force under which you become who you are is still emitted by another, in this case your conscience. Do you trust this internal other to speak for you yourself? and when it tells you, virtually, to ignore all other models? Is your conscience more you than you, or worse: are there grades or ranks of "you" extending in an unbroken chain of moral authorities, each one you, each more you than the previous? The "should" in this phrase comes from the you that always stands beyond yourself, beckoning to it to move to another stage. For Nietzsche, as he begins to acknowledge the irony of building a rigorous "individualism" on the basis of moral injunctions like this—they must be, they cannot be its foundation—the paradox that ensues is about the nature of following. Follow yourself—this is the famous formula for autonomy. There must be at least two of you then, a first and a second, an I and a you (a completely reversible relation, of course, I you, you I), *Herr und Knecht*—this is also obviously the structure of the will to power, telegraphed in the conflict or tension within the phrase "become who you are." Become who you are, instrument and lesson about self-overcoming.

The first two appearances of the injunction have one thing in common. They both to some extent present the maxim as potentially salvific, even if there are still difficulties with carrying it out. The rueful self-critique that sounds in the second title to *Ecce Homo—Wie Man Wird Was Man Ist*—makes it *e contrario* obvious that by the time he wrote that text, Nietzsche's hopes for becoming himself were pretty small, and perhaps his hopes for "becoming" were equally reduced. Appearing at the head of this rueful catalogue of disappointments, the phrase "how one becomes what one is" can only be a joke. Nietzsche may have had in mind to become an "exemplary man," as he once may have thought Diogenes Laertius taught him and his contemporaries, or as he once fantasized was possible when reading Emerson, or as he once strived to do in the shadow of Wagner (a perfect encounter in which to discover the paradoxes of learning to lead by following).

In a passage, dense with allusions to the philosophical tradition, to the biblical origin story, to descriptive psychology's claims about inner observation, and to Nietzsche, one feels the weight of his paradoxical injunction. *Know yourself does not mean: observe yourself* [beobachte dich]. *Ob-*

serve yourself is what the snake says. It means: make yourself into the master of your actions [zum Herrn deiner Handlungen]. *Now you are this already, are the master of your actions. What the snake says therefore means: unknow yourself* [Verkenne Dich, mistake yourself]*! Destroy yourself! and so something evil, and only when one bends down very low, does one hear the good in this as well, which says: "in order to make yourself into who you are."* [30]

One thing is certain: the Nietzschean injunction is the good element within this confusion, the one single good within the Socratic tendency at the heart of the Judaic story of creation. In contrast to "know yourself," the injunction "become who you are" is good despite its paradoxes. Kafka spells it out, the conflict within the idea of morality as Genesis and Socrates develop it and as Nietzsche satirizes it. "Become," this is an action, a making, an intention, a not yet, an absence, an "ought." "Are," this is a status, a being, a now, a presence, a fulfilled positivity. The phrase is tainted with a paradisal logic, Kafka realizes. It seduces you into thinking you can do something you are by nature unable to do. And yet this is not a problem with the Nietzschean phrase itself, only with the way it is understood.

The phrase had such a career across Nietzsche's trajectory and beyond it, as an effect of his writings, but it also functioned in a special way for Nietzsche, as something like his highest hope. What could Kafka do to it or with it? Like so many Nietzscheans of his age and ages since, he could have made it into his own project, to try to do it better than Nietzsche, to try to overcome himself or worse, to overcome Nietzsche by means of Nietzsche. Kafka is too sensitive to the inner tensions of the phrase. You might say he was the first to hear the symphony of the phrase's dissonance.

Socrates was in the Garden. Know yourself, he says, and slithers off. At this extreme height of intellectual syncretism that is typical of the treatise in thoughts, Kafka discovers a fact or two. Nietzsche was the one, before himself, to imagine rebuffing the Socrates snake. And secondly, despite Nietzsche or because of his irony, the tensions in the phrase cannot be surpassed, but they can be exploited. Socrates, Descartes, Brentano—Genesis. In each of them we are offered knowledge and alongside it the promise that we can "live up to" this knowledge; that is, we can become what we know. Like the two trees of the Garden, the maxim splits into knowledge and life and the means for fulfilling the promise are not given. In Genesis this is explicit—the tree of life is forbidden us. In philosophy the missing means are hidden but obvious in the structure of the science, divided as it is into metaphysics and ethics. Knowledge of the good is not itself good. Truth is not the just city. Will to power is not a means to becoming what you are.

The question of knowledge, from the beginning, from before the beginning, was already a question of power. This is in the injunction form—it is what it *wills*: that the injunction cease to be knowledge and become what it is not. Kafka admits: knowledge of the good is a promise and as such it can only be evil. Why would someone who was good need to know the good? This is obviously the meaning of the traditional Judaic figures, the tzadikim, whose goodness was predicated on their ignorance of it.[31] *Evil knows about the Good, but the good does not know about evil.*[32] The good is also ignorant about itself and the stupidity of the good clearly invalidates any rational morality, and it also obviates any morality that uses maxims to present the idea of the good as enactable.

"Know yourself," Kafka says—with Nietzsche—is the deception by which we unknow ourselves as ones who already live, act, are. It is the primary deception, the knowledge seduction, the seduction to striving, promises, time, world-flight, and messianic expectations—to a "beyond" of you, regardless whether it is within you or without. Yet if you bend down to the lowest possible perspective, the perspective in which anything higher disappears, when comparison is impossible, "become what you are" means abandoning "you" and the hope and violence that attends it.

"You," which always implies a command, an invitation to self-betterment, a call to be who you aren't but ought to be—is a matter, for Kafka, of being a master (*Herrsein*). In this he is not far from Zarathustra: "Wherever I found the living, there I found the will to power; and even in the will of the serving I found the will to be master [*den Willen Herr zu sein*]. The weaker is persuaded by its own will to serve the stronger, because it wants to be master over what is still weaker: this is the only pleasure it is incapable of renouncing."[33] Kafka picks up this Nietzschean problematic, the inescapable appetite for power as domination; his assertion that being is equivalent to possession is an effect of this problematic; for what is possession but the assertion of mastery of a stronger over a weaker. Like Nietzsche, he sees ontological relations as fundamentally power relations. Yet for Kafka they are always evil even so, unless they can be depotentized, made small, that is, let be no more than what they happen to be. There must be a kind of being or a way of being without

power, he supposes, that cannot be enjoined to become or promised anything. Although he looks for an alternative, Kafka nevertheless understands power in a manner similar to Nietzsche: its true name is "will."

34. Yielding

Kafka's question could be formulated this way: how can one imagine a
life—or live a life, *a* life and not "life" in general—when that life's organ
or the source for its dynamism is something other than willing; in this
respect he hews closely to Nietzsche's question adapted from Schopenhauer,[34] and yet he does not seek to battle Schopenhauerian nihilism in
the way Nietzsche does, although of course he also does not accept it.
Nietzsche's strident antipathy to forms of inaction, calling them, as he
does, alternately ascetic, nihilistic, submissive, slavish, Jewish, Christian,
or German, with the attendant preference for greatness, mountains, war,
struggle, and overcoming, irritates Kafka and conflicts with his political
intuition. Nietzsche very often rejects gestures that look like yielding,
and his rejections are fraught with a logical problem that may have bothered Kafka as much if not more than Nietzsche's frequent triumphalism.
Will to power, willing to will, does not in fact produce a world without
nihilism. The *nihil* is the sine qua non of willing itself, and the *nihil*
grows exponentially the more the will wills to will. Will to power produces a world, first of all, where a few great wills overcome themselves,
while the rest, the weaker, are dominated and forced to deny themselves
in order to keep living. Since this is the structure of the will—it always
needs a victim; no, a multitude of victims—even the great figures within
themselves will be 99 percent denial, submission, askesis, and only 1
percent victory. How can you will on, and on and on, if the renewed
appetite, want, wish, or struggle does not respond to and reproduce an
ever-renewed oppression, failure, and retreat? Power, as Nietzsche often
points out, seeks inequality. It produces an image of the world as total
imbalance, a world inequitable right down to its fundament. Nietzsche
hates equality as much as he loves difference conceived of as struggle—as
domination and subordination, as continual striving to overcome and
to become. This commitment inheres also in his famous perspectivism,
which enshrines a type of inequality—no perspective is equal to another—and it also seems to enshrine an inequity, a balance where higher
perspectives are better than others. If the will to power is the world's

fundament, there are only two basic perspectives: that of victors and that of the vanquished. The dynamism of the multiplicity of wills expresses itself each time in this duality. Within the dualism, whatever profusion of shades and grades of success, whatever other qualities are always hidden among the losers, since only the victor is ever victorious and the victor is simply victorious. Each sub-par position, each secondary, each thing that is not to the point or power, is already a kind of surrender.

A set of nodes or pivotal thoughts in the treatise open up the richness of the subordinated, presenting modes of surrender, even where they appear as the opposite of this. To say that being means "belonging-to," for example, whispers also that being involves a variety of yielding. Not far behind being, creation involves another variety, all the huge variety of modes of resting, that is of "not work." *On the seventh day he rests; then we fill the earth.*[35] While perhaps this thought signals a limitation of human beings, it would be wrong to interpret it as simply an assertion of lessness. There is more than a little hint of the Kabbalic motif of *tsimtsum* here, though the medium is different. One would expect a contraction of the infinite to make room for finitude; indeed, this is one definition of finitude, a constraint placed on an originally unconstrained being or arena. Although a divine removal is the basis for this thought, Kafka nevertheless shifts to the medium of work. Furthermore, when God in Lurianic *tsimtsum* contracts, what is left, what is yielded, is space. When a working god rests from creating the earth, a different type of creature, not in this case created but merely *allowed to proliferate*, emerges. "We" emerge, we are abandoned, let go, we issue from divine cessation of work and our mise en scène is allowance and burgeoning.

From these two examples a succinct formula can be derived that expresses the spirit of Kafka's "reductions" in the treatise in thoughts. It is not so much that positive claims or truths are negated, denied, or rejected; much the converse: truths have their yield restored to them. Creation needs its yield; being needs its yield. Possession is not built out of acts of possession. For possession to take place, it has to negate a full background of possessionlessnesses, out of which and against which possession asserts itself. You have to give up the richest, most extensive— more than infinite—pleroma of the unpossessed in order to acquire a single thing. With a small abandonment derived from the greater one but already turned against it, one gives up pure abandon. The yield is a result of a yielding of yielding, and the reverse is not the case. How weak abandonment is! One small gesture annihilates it. It is defenseless, it does not resist and it certainly doesn't struggle. For what reason, to what end? Striving likes to go places, but abandonment, to use a term not usually associated with Kafka, is happy, *glücklich*. The word refers tangentially, in German as in English, to the luck of what befalls you, the hap in happening. The "luck" or "happiness," the *Glück to grasp that the ground on which you stand can be no bigger than the two feet that cover it.*[36] This is so only when you have yielded ground as *Grund*, as fundament, as reason, as supportive and sturdy, as the greater sufficiency, and so forth. So yielding is precarious and needs to be cared for, practiced; to a great extent this is why Kafka's *pensées* range across and take on the entire conceptual world of European capitalism, philosophy, and theology; the inner harmlessness of these practices needs to be exposed, in order to renew the abandonments that allowed them at first to take shape.

Yielding yields both itself and its suspension. This is its bounty as well as its continued poverty. Like the German *lassen*, it speaks of both a bounty offered, something left behind, something submitted, left to others, and at the same time it speaks of a retreat, a self-abnegating tendency. Like *lassen*, whatever it gives, it gives by taking itself away, yet "yield" is more affirmative than *lassen*.[37] It affirms both of its senses, which are probably inseparable. Withdrawal, allowing another to go first, "yield" is an affirmation of a letting, a positive *détente*. Furthermore it is the harvest seen from the perspective of the dirt, the plant, the process. It is the product, before a commodity, seen not as the fruit of labor but as the give of the earth. This non-labor, the happening of nature, but also, and more important for us, exactly the same in the happening of culture, unlike the "laboring power" that Hannah Arendt objected to in Marx's theory, is a depotentized labor, not equivalent to effort or toil. And so it is not equivalent to suffering. Work—*Arbeit*—is one of Kafka's prime targets in the treatise.

Three vectors in the fourfold schema of Kafka's atheological analysis can now be reinterpreted. Being, faith, and art turn out to be functions of the fourth, the yield. Being is, as we have seen, a refusal to yield, a willful possession that involves suspension or giving up of yielding, a yielding turned against itself. In turning against itself, in yielding itself first and foremost, the yield gives itself up so thoroughly that it looks as though it has nothing to do with itself.[38] This self-distancing movement is what allows the yield to have a yield, to produce, to give over, to deliver up anything that could be taken, and thus to masquerade as possession. Another vector of its self-distancing is faith. From one perspective, faith is disappointment that the promise of possession has not been fulfilled, yet. It is the reaction, as has often been noted, of a community dispossessed of what they consider rightfully theirs. Dispossession is a reflex of the general interpretation of everything as possessable, insofar that is that every human thing, including action, thought, and language, *deals only with possession and its relationships.*[39] Faith is born out of the feeling of a right to possess and disappointment at being unable to exercise this right. And, too, it is the beginning of a return of the yield, although in the form of waiting. For in faith, one is asked to wait, and waiting invents the superstructure of directional time as the mark of impatience, which for Kafka is the only cardinal sin. *There are two cardinal human sins from which all others derive: impatience and indolence* [Lässigkeit]. *Because of impatience they were driven out of paradise, because of indolence they do not come back. But perhaps there is only one cardinal sin: impatience. Because of impatience they were driven out, because of impatience they do not return.*[40] This is an early thought, and it sets the tone for many of the others. Kafka discovers a grave error in his reasoning, or he sets a trap, or stages a lesson for readers. For it is of course only *Lässigkeit*, the tendency toward *lassen*, toward leaving and letting, whose cognates in English, laziness and lassitude, still bespeak a retardation of the will with no clear source. Impatience is the first cardinal sin, the one that leads to expulsion from the Garden. Kafka comes to realize, perhaps in the course of writing down this thought, that whatever it is that keeps humanity from returning also has to be impatience. The very idea that humanity does or should want to return is itself highly impatient. This leaves *Lässigkeit* as one possible mode in which life is not a clambering back up into the Garden.

Faith and its reification as the temporal continuum are impatient, and yet as soon as you make faith into an obstacle to be overcome, you intensify the impatience; unfaith in the form of doubt or knowledge is faith that has become intractable. We might say, on the relationship of time to faith, the continuum is born of disappointment that we have not been able to exercise the right to possess the world, and the arrow of time, its directionality, is the sign of the deepest impatience. Disappointment and impatience only dissimulate themselves as hope and waiting. Faith doesn't give an inch. Those most deviously determined to possess the world, despite all appearances, possess faith. It makes specific use of yielding; it is, if you will, a possessive yield, a willed suspension. In service of every act of faith is an image. A practice of making images that cannot be used in service of faith is one way to allow this deceptive form of possessiveness to subside a little.

Art improvises ever-new modes of abandonment. When the motive comes from an artwork, one can freely submit to the darkened image, the cloudy parable, the theologoumenon or other principle that has been returned to its confused ground. In this light, under the aegis of "darkening," the set of thoughts that make up the treatise might be characterized as an artwork. There is an overall image, but it is blurry. Or perhaps we could say that the thoughts are a blur, which, as we know, is not a form. Any thought by itself suffices to be called a "text" or a "work." Yet the thoughts cannot be taken individually and the whole does not cohere into anything like a justification for the imperfections of the parts. Unlike with a mere collection of aphorisms, a reader turns to Kafka's treatise in thoughts in search of answers, yet they are as tentative, experimenting, and poorly formed as the world whose jumble of principles they represent. The Treatise, or whatever it is, is akin to a painting in which most if not all the fundamental elements of European intellectual history are depicted, that is, from this perspective, they are in a jumble. It is a confused picture of a set of confusions.

If we hang this image on the wall in place of Altdorfer's *The Battle of Alexander at Issus* we find little justification for an ideology or a plan of action. Nothing in the thoughts individually or in their disjointed synthesis would lead us to look beyond them, except the very principles that it sets out, quite methodically and openly, to confuse, and whose confusions it shows to have originated with them. Insofar as it can show the confusions to be both originary and irreducible, the proper response is (a) to leave off thinking, where thinking means deriving truths from principles, and (b) to let go of action, where it relies on justification:

A   *In what does your justification consist?*
B   *I don't have any.*
A   *And you are able to live[?]*
B   *Precisely for that reason, since with justification I couldn't live. How could I justify the multiplicity of my acts and living conditions[?]*[41]

In short, justification is a confused principle, at least with regards to life. One cannot separate the two implications of the principle, that life is insufficient without it, and that it—the principle that justifies—is insufficient for the multiplicity of life. The confused principle, which both is and is not sufficient, however, this is no justification, but it is the reason, the lack of which allows true multiplicity, or whatever you want to call it, "living" to begin. It is of the utmost importance that the confusion of principles itself be clear and distinct, for those who accept only clarity and distinctness; that is to say, for those who expect justifications for ways of living, let them have at least the lack of a justification to serve that purpose, for a while. For those who do not need such a thing, there is no need to read the treatise at all.

35. Pressure to Act

A common denominator among Zionism, Kierkegaardianism, industrial capital, war, and some Nietzscheanisms is deed-ism—Kafka knew this. Everyone was hotly prescribing this or that action on this or that ground, but action it had to be. The only one in Kafka's own circle who questioned the emphasis on the deed (*Tat*) was Felix Weltsch, who warned for instance: "The present-day situation of the Jews is so complicated, that an all-embracing judgment which does not take into consideration all the individual facts is hardly possible."[42] An account of each individual fact would be necessary, Weltsch felt, before an appropriate plan of action could be decided on. Weltsch's attitude reflected the theory of action developed in his book *Gnade und Freiheit* (*Grace and Freedom*), and he was in this regard unique among the cultural Zionists in Prague, and very different from Brod. On the one hand, the only actions that count as true acts are "foundational" (*grundlegende*) ones; in other words, they establish new grounds for acting. On the other hand, foundational acts are free, imitating as they do divine creation. And so they are not really acts at all, since they do not respond or contribute to a historical situation, issue from an agent, solve a problem, and so forth. You might say that if Weltsch's concept of an act *was* in fact a response to "the present-day situation of the Jews," it was a response insofar as the dream of a fundamental, creative, total act recognizes the impossibility of acting in the present.[43]

In conceiving of "acts" as metaphysically suspect, Weltsch is closest to Kafka's own perception that there was no way out of (*Ausgang*) the "situation." He is farthest from Kafka, however, when, like his friend Brod, he regards the highest human capacity as the capacity to act. More than this, Weltschian action is transcendent. Out of this conviction springs the founding dichotomy: freedom means a great and total spiritual action; in contrast "grace" means submission, suppression, and waiting.[44] Grace is given, freedom is an infinite task.[45] Weltsch's is not the infinite task of Kant, however. Taking his cues from Schelling and Böhme, he places the source of action in the soul. Soul-action creates God in the soul,[46] and the soul carries out creation in, or of—it is hard to say which—a world. Weltsch develops his idea of God within the creative soul from a paradox he sees in the Schellingian and Böhmian "absolute." The absolute, God or nature, is the telos toward which all good action tends; yet if the absolute already exists before any human action, human action is not real, has no activity in it, since action is creation, and the end has already been created. If the absolute exists already, there is no real movement, no real becoming, and thus no freedom and no need for faith. Faith, Weltsch emphasizes at the very beginning of the book, is not a submissive attitude, but an imposing one. The *Grundlegung* that is real action is equivalent to faith, which Weltsch understands as "a free decision, a settlement" (*eine freie Entscheidung, eine Setzung*).[47] Faith is a free act of, in, and for the soul, and its highest achievement is the "redemption of God" through humanity.[48]

Weltsch's concept of a redeemed God is of a sufficiently idealist cast that it stands head and shoulders above the common contemporary stances toward "the present-day situation." Many of the intellectual positions, Weltsch's too, as is evident in this phrase, derive from the general Nietzscheanism or Kierkegaardianism that had become part of the "situation." Kierkegaard's "The Present Moment" was a much-read model for the kind of thinking that saw established institutions, intellectual and practical, as the problem. "Let this junk heap tumble down, get rid of it," thus Kierkegaard.[49]

Kafka's response to the substance of Weltsch's argument in the book has not been found, although he apparently wrote one. All that remains is a list of editorial suggestions from his proofreading the manuscript.[50] Yet we can imagine his feeling: exhortations to action were closing in on him. Programs for change, congresses, military maneuvers, rallies in the streets filled his corner of Europe, and calls to join the fight shouted from almost every page of the Jewish journals Kafka read religiously, even in Zürau. When the Balfour Declaration was published in the *Jü-*

dische Rundschau on December 23, 1917, a declaration welcoming it titled "Aufnahme der Erklärung" by Chaim Weizmann and Nahum Sokolow, secretary-general of the World Zionist Congress, appeared directly after it, commending the world-historical nature of the declaration and expressing the hope "that with the consent of all nations and governments our organization will succeed in realizing what the Jewish people have been yearning for two thousand years."[51] Celebration of the imminent realization of a two-thousand-year-old wish was merely the most grandiose form in which the pressure to act took shape. Significantly, too, Weizmann and Sokolow represent the "act" as the fulfillment of an ancient desire. Weltsch sturdily refused that fateful formulation. True acts for him were without sources in the past.

The aura of fate, in this coarse form, is also refused by Brod; yet he does not give up all elements of a messianic project, as Weltsch seems to do. In his novel *Tycho Brahe's Path to God*, which has been shown to be an allegory of his relationship with Kafka,[52] Brod has Brahe pass the torch of action to Kepler: "One thing alone: carry out my work; don't let this tremendous labor utterly perish . . . "[53] The labor of thought is what is meant here, but this labor is conceived of as helping God keep the world on track. "God has established a connection of deep import between my happiness and the laws of heaven and I must hold in my hand the law of these two, the law that governs the world, as well as the law that governs heaven."[54] Brod partially rejects this idea, that "God is in need of help," in his theo-political treatise, *Paganism–Christianity–Judaism*, but only partially.[55] Like Weltsch, and perhaps from conversations with him, Brod fashions "God" as a task for human beings. Instead of Kierkegaard and Nietzsche, Schelling or German mystics, Brod turns to Jewish scripture for a basic teaching, Rabbi Simon bar Yochai for a model, and Schmuel Bergmann, who was an acquaintance and fellow member of the Brentanist circle, for a contemporary theorization. From the Torah and the Talmud, Brod recalls teachings about man as contributor to the redemption of the world. The obvious redemptive man is the messiah, but in the Bible there is, Brod reminds us, more than one legendary messiah. There are two: the son of Joseph, who falls in battle and the son of David, the perfected messiah.[56] The former is a messiah who dwells in time and battles misfortune;[57] the other is a mythical figure who comes at the end of the world to nullify time. The first is the only true messiah for Brod. And when he rejects the mythical messiah, he also rejects, or tries to reject, the very idealism that characterizes Weltsch's treatise. The first messiah who acts in the world appears not as freedom but as a kind of grace. Obviously this is not the Lutheran grace that coincides with an ex-temporal redeemer. Rather, Brod cites the worldly grace of the first-century Tannaic sage Simon bar Yochai; not through his decisions on the law or the legal treatises attributed to the rabbi, but because of the life he led. Ben Yochai is the Zarathustra of the Jews. He becomes a model after withdrawing from the world and returning back to live within it, saying: "A miracle has occurred to me, therefore I shall do something useful." Brod makes a scholastic distinction between *gratia sufficiens* and *gratia efficax*,[58] identifying the latter as a "this-worldly miracle," "the miracle of the lost and regained world."[59] The messiah of the lost and regained world returns to fight "ignoble misfortune,"[60] and doctrines about him do not celebrate the "noble misfortune" of Protestantism, which would await a higher redemption. The this-worldly miracle of Judaism exhorts us to perform small tasks, not the infinite ones of Hermann Cohen, whom Brod singles out for criticism. The success of an infinite task remains infinitely distant, Brod argues.[61] Against Cohen Brod pits Bergmann, whose concept of work for the present (*Gegenwartsarbeit*) must have seemed like the fulfillment of ben Yochai's dictum.[62]

It is hard to imagine how Tycho Brahe would have felt if he found that his young Kepler had given up the redemptive work and advocated, if you can call what Kafka was writing advocacy, that we retire into the cave, this time not to create the world anew, but to live out of reach of great world forces. Brod's blindness to this aspect of Kafka's "thoughts" when he read them after Kafka's death is testimony to his greater blindness to the true tasks as Kafka saw them. *You are the task. No student far and wide.*[63] And: *Two tasks of the beginning of life: to constrict your circle ever more severely and to check over and over again if you are not hiding somewhere outside your circle.*[64] Compared to Weltsch, an idealist, Brod is almost a materialist, restricting his "act" to small cultural works in the present.

Bergmann's "cultural work" (*Kulturarbeit*) is quite humble, to be sure. He found another aspect of the Pentateuch salient, the work of Moses that did not achieve the goal but prepared the way. Action, for Bergmann in his article on *Gegenwartsarbeit*, means "preparation" for others to come who will benefit. "Our lot can be compared to the fate of Moses, all of whose work was only the preparation for the occupation of the land

and who was only allowed to see the promised land but not to live in it. This is the fate of all our work in the diaspora [*im Galuth*]. We always work for something. Our work produces a frame, but others should fill it in and enjoy the image as it develops."[65] Like Brod's, Bergmann's pivotal word is "work," and the milieu, as it is for all these action theorists, is diaspora. In one form of work, cultural work, a strong similarity also obtains between Bergmann and Franz Rosenzweig. The main example of cultural work that prepares the framework for a Jewish future is education.[66] Among the Prague intellectuals it was standard to reject the political rhetoric of the Zionist leaders who imagined a unified and total front of action that would succeed in completely actualizing the promise of the British declaration of support. In place of a consolidated political campaign, both Brod and his model Bergmann conceive of limited social action originating with individuals in an interpersonal sphere.

To contemporary responses to the "present-day situation of the Jews," ranging from demagogic Zionist rhetoric to the spiritual idealism of Weltsch and the moral work program of Brod and Bergmann, we must add the "mythic" approach expressed in Buber's 1920 *Drei Reden über das Judentum* (*Three Addresses on Judaism*).[67] The organ of action is feeling (*Gefühl*) for Buber, because action originates with "the people in me," and the inner people is not known but "felt."[68] The biblical moment Buber chooses is the most spectacular and the most equivocal. At the expulsion from the Garden, the Jews are marked as beings who act. The Fall is presented "as a decision [*Entscheidung*]."[69] What is the decision and what is the task? "The people in me [*Das Volk in mir*]," Buber says, was created to act, and the people is undoubtedly "in me" because I am not within my people at home in a native land.[70] A people not "naturally" living together in its community has to do more than think about community; it has to activate its "acting" nature and strive "toward true belonging, to living together and working together"[71] The watcher at the gates of Rome for the messiah who, when asked whom he awaits, responds, "for You," is a Buberian.[72] Nietzsche's dictum "Be who you are" is transformed by Buber into "Redeem yourself and your neighbors," meaning: form a natural community. That Judaism is "in us" makes it into a task of renaturalizing, turning the inside out, becoming authentically Jewish, regardless of what the nationalists or the diasporists want.

Whatever the content of "Judaism" for Buber here, its form is action. In keeping with his essentialist tendencies, Buber argues in the last of the three addresses that every *Volk* has its own inclinations; that of the Jews is toward "unity," "act," and the "future."[73] In this speech he develops a picture of the proper Jewish act. Whether he draws the idea from Hasidism or from his penchant for ecstatic practice and parabolic logic, either way, Hasidism is authentic Judaism for Buber because it is the essence of Jews, as compared to other "peoples," to act. His inclination toward action becomes biopolitical when he claims a Jew has better motor skills than sensory skills. This is also why Jewish art is more gestural,[74] and it is, somewhat counterintuitively, the explanation of Jewish legalism. This is just because law is for the purpose of regulating action, and as such it comes after the act (*Tat*) and tries to control it. In the battle between legal Judaism and the Judaism of the act, however, it is time for a return to the latter. Jesus was in this sense more a Jew than the Rabbis. Jesus was something like the first Hasid, whose acts preceded the new law. The act unites with the law in Hasidism, and the "idea of action" (*Tatidee*) triumphs.[75]

36. Subservience

A variety of attempts to define the yield cross Kafka's *pensées*. On one of these trajectories, Kafka moves from "ihm gehören" (belonging to him/ it) as the meaning of being to "gehorsam sein"(being obedient) as a possible meaning of "yielding." Obedience is a form of not-possessing that depends on the meager and quizzical gesture of acquiescence. Already our hackles are rising, since everything we have been taught cautions us against giving in to another in a way that is not an expression of our will to self-determination. Listen to Kafka as he toys with a perverse idea: *freedom and bondage are in an essential sense one. In which essential sense? Not in the sense that the slave can't lose his freedom, and so in a certain respect is freer than the free.*[76] Here Kafka is looking for a way in which freedom and bondage are the same, or, if you will, for a freedom that is not the overcoming of bondage.[77]

The first thing that crosses his mind, but he doesn't let it cross over into the fair copy, is an inkling about a kind of freedom that is not free in any sense we recognize, in which the most bound thing remains in its bonds. He toys with the idea that slaves are free because they cannot have anything further taken away from them. This does not satisfy the criterion that freedom and bondage are one, since a slave's bondage is still thought of as the ultimate degree of freedomlessness. However, the respect in which the slave is freer than the free, being the most totally destitute, having the least agency and "power to act" is nonetheless suggestive. The problem with this picture is not so much the oppression of slaves, but the continued unfreedom of masters, their enslavement to the will, and slavery so obviously supports and perpetuates the acts of masters that it can't possibly be the freedom Kafka is after. And yet no matter how distasteful it may be to assert the freedom of the one who is harshly fettered and subjugated, the critique of freedom as unfetteredness still stands. Unfetteredness is a weak form of freedom; and indeed it might not be freedom at all. And the inkling occurs within this perverse thought Kafka will pursue further. In some as yet unknown respect to be bound is to be free.

Slavery and servitude are not the same, precisely in their relationship to power. One could develop a theory of servitude out of Kafka, with reference to Robert Walser. In the special theory of servitude out of Kafkan sources, the suffering servant from *Isaiah* who is taken to foreshadow Christ would give way to the happy and willing servant who foreshadows nothing. The more ready, willing, and able, the freer. "Willingness" may look like an effect of the will, but it is not. It is, rather, the readiness at every minute to subordinate your will. Other people's possessions, other people's faith, other people's projects and striving, other people's suffering, these may concern the servant, but she does not suffer, strive, believe, or own along with the master, or at least she doesn't have to. Serving is a way to live in a world of will and representation without either. The will is not for her, even if it is in some sense directed toward her. But how is the servant's will to be reconciled with the master's? Provisionally, we might say that the servant, once she has willed herself to obey, to become an instrument of another's will, can safely cease to exercise her will. A servant's implacable face has been washed clean of the marks of joy and suffering that desire and disappointment bring. This is perhaps why servants in Kafka stories do not age.

At Robert Walser's Institut Benjamenta, the "apelike [*affenähnliche*]"[78] student Kraus is a "masterly"[79] servant and the recipient of admiring praise from the title character Jakob von Gunten. Walser's novel gives us a young Jakob who is much less than a perfect servant, and in this consists something like his freedom. His attraction to the uniforms worn by the students of servitude makes Jakob wonder whether he might rather have aristocratic blood in his veins.[80] With this and other observations he shows the remarkable similarity between servants and masters. Generals of a humble realm but not necessarily of a humble demeanor, servants are masters of their domains. Every master except the highest is indeed servant to someone. Only the last master is not also a servant. In contrast, every servant except the lowest servant is servant to some and master to others. Only the last servant is not also a master. If we cannot see the highest master because he is too big or too distant, we cannot see the last servant because he is too small and too near. Jakob flirts with the idea of becoming the very last servant who has the privilege of being master to none.

"One learns very little here, there is a shortage of teachers, and none of us boys from the Benjamenta Institute will come to anything, that is to say, we shall all be something very small and subordinate later in life."[81] Learning is not what is wanted when the dictum to be followed is "be small and stay small,"[82] because learning makes anyone big, and so servitude cannot be taught. In Walser's book, a servant gains no consciousness from the work; in fact it cannot even be called work, since it is done automatically, borrowing the intelligence, will, and ingenuity of the employer. This servant is an *acéphale*, a marionette, far from a *Knecht* in Hegel's sense. And, in addition, as Jakob discovers when he explores the forbidden inner rooms of the house, the teacher of servants himself has no secret source for his authority. The "Inner Chambers [*innere Gemächer*]"[83] are laughable, as are the fears and desires of anyone who commences a training in servitude. The career brings no riches, the principles are ridiculous, and even the beating that the master gives Jakob early in his training "only hurt." "It has only hurt me, and not for myself, for him, for the Herr Vorsteher."[84] Everything that happens to a servant as low as Jakob redounds on the master. A servant doesn't teach, she can only learn—but not about herself, only about the other, for the other, in the other's language. The final, lowest servant is thus without principle for her actions. In effect she can only react, but her reactivity says nothing about her; it says something only about the one who acts. "It only hurt me, and not for my sake, but for his, for Herr Master." The last servant has a superior (*Vorsteher*) but no subordinate (*Nachsteher*) and so can never experience the pleasure of violence. Thus Jakob interprets the violence against him as exercised by the master against himself. It is only pain, then: the last servant cannot suffer, since whatever he undergoes is not a passage to future gain. And since all his striving is on behalf of someone else, the setbacks and frustrations are also not his.

By this measure it was not in fact the slave revolt in morality that brought suffering to the world, as Nietzsche sometimes contends. It would be more accurate to say that suffering was born with the blond beast, since, although he discharges his will immediately, the expected quotient of pleasure is not always immediately provided by the world. Only in paradise, in other words, would a blond beast be able to will continually and be continually satisfied. Under any other conditions, natural, social, intellectual, historical, the blond beast would have to temper his beastliness in view of, out of faith in, a more distant goal. This eventuality produces the need for servants, who fulfill the ever-greater needs and fill the world.

The ideal community would be akin to a monastic community but with a different kind of subordination, with no ideology or higher agenda. In the totally subordinated community, the members serve each other, with no place for masters. In the briefest of charters for such a community, Kafka attempts to construct a community of pure servitude, by writing down a set of founding duties that fulfill the needs of all its members. The numbered precepts are divided into "duties" (*Pflichten*) and "rights" (*Rechte*). We may want to imagine this charter, written in late winter or early spring 1918, as not belonging to the treatise per se, although it is written in the same notebook. Instead we might think of it as the first consequence of the thoughts, the polity that results after the reduction of moral thinking of animals and humans to their founding precepts. Once he has accomplished his reduction in the treatise and demonstrated that the precepts are confused and thus impossible to follow, and that this impossibility of following has generated "Europe," Kafka writes his own brief litany of better precepts. It should be clear that these are the minimum number of precepts necessary for life, for what we might call a "small" life, and they presuppose a group whose instincts are more servile than domineering.

THE POSSESSIONLESS WORKFORCE

Duties: (1) Receive or possess no money, no valuables. Only the following possessions are permitted: the simplest dress (to be prescribed in detail), things needed for work, books, food for one's own use. Everything else belongs to the poor.

(2) Acquire a livelihood only through work. Eschew no kind of work for which one's strength suffices without adverse effects on health. Choose the kind of work either oneself or if this is not possible submit oneself to the direction of the work council, which is responsible to the government.

(3) Work for no other wages than two days' livelihood (to be prescribed in detail according to district).

(4) As moderate a life as possible. Eat only what is absolutely necessary, that is, a minimal payment that in a certain sense is a maximal payment, bread, water, dates. The poorest's food, the poorest's mattress.

(5) Relation to the employer to be treated as relation of trust, never demand the intercession of the courts. Carry out to completion any work undertaken no matter the circumstances, unless prevented by serious health considerations.

Rights: (1) Maximum work time six hours; for physical work, four to five.

(2) In case of illness and incapacity for work due to age, admission into state homes for the aged and into hospitals.

Working life as an affair of conscience and an affair of faith in fellow human beings.[85]

It is worth reading this founding document carefully. For our purposes a few facts about the duties listed in the charter will have to suffice. One can decide that the setting is Palestine, but it is not necessary in order to comprehend the community envisioned here. Nowhere does Kafka say this is a Jewish community; the group at issue is workers—a special class of workers: those who do not own the products of their labors, although they are (a) not alienated, and (b) may consume some of them. This is a picture of a community without alienation and without property, but also without labor power. Instead they have and exploit a special labor weakness. Throughout the charter, Kafka tries to mitigate the possibility of domination by owners, employers, governors. There is a dominant group, if you will, but it is the poor, for whose sake extra labor can be done. To be truthful, all work is done for the poor; before anything else the impoverished among us are cared for and preserved at the brink of poverty. That is because only use-value is recognized; but this is already too economical a term. It is not "use" but "consumption" that replaces "possession" as the carrier of rights. One has the right to consume, and what one cannot consume one has no right to. Likewise one cannot "consume" a worker more than hampers her consumption. To be corporeally thin, existentially unburdened of stores, stocks, money, or even of the potential for any of these things, for anything—is to consume without desire. A society that does not recognize surplus also does not recognize any earthly purpose for excess potential. The harvest (the yield) is a product of yielding and the economy is not one of effort (will) but a yielding economy. Rather than being a naturally occurring power that spills over from the mystical into the physical body, and from the physical into the psychological, from there to nature, and from nature into culture, and from culture into history, where it all eventually circles back, labor is, quite the contrary, a limited response to limited needs.

In the charter the duties set out maximums beyond which you cannot produce, consume, carry, keep—limit points of having, they might be called. The maximums, the content of the duties, are established not by the poor but by the very poorest. The poorest of us shall be the measure, shall be for all intents and purposes masters. We shall be mastered by those who cannot master and we shall become servants of their needs, whether the poorest be within or without us. Furthermore, this will not be for the sake of ourselves, but for the sake of our impoverished neighbors, who include ourselves. That is, even the care for the self is not selfish, but is done in view of continuing to serve those who cannot serve themselves.

This leads to another insight. As much as some of the precepts here, especially the rights, might correspond to Kant's "kingdom of ends," and as much as "duties" may also sound like a Prussian preoccupation, and if indeed this charter is, shall we say, Kafka's table of maxims, all of which could consistently be willed by the human (and animal) community for itself, it is not the freedom to oblige yourself to carry out the duties that Kafka emphasizes, but the other freedom, the one involved in obeying. Freedom of movement is not the goal but freedom from movement may be a result. As the ape in "A Report to an Academy" tells the committee, "In passing may I say that all too often men are betrayed by the word freedom. And as freedom is counted among the most sublime feelings, so the corresponding disillusionment can be also sublime. In variety theaters I have often watched, before my turn came on, a couple of acrobats performing on trapezes high in the roof. They swung themselves, they rocked to and fro, they sprang into the air, they floated into each other's arms, one hung by the hair from the teeth of the other. 'And that too is human freedom,' I thought, 'self-controlled movement.'"[86]

Not derived from autonomy but from pure obedience, subsistence is the mode that Kafka substitutes for the excessive, transcendental arrogance of "freedom." It remains to say what kind of mode subsistence is, yet we know that it is less than "existence," the state of standing beyond, of transcending. Existence, that is transcendental freedom, can be traced to an error in the understanding of bondage. *He is a free and secure citizen of the earth, since he is set on a chain that is long enough to freely give him [ihm frei zu geben] all earthly spaces and still only so long that nothing can drag him across the earth's borders. But simultaneously he is also a free and secure citizen of heaven, since he is set on a similarly calculated heavenly chain. If he wants to walk the earth, heaven's collar chokes him, if he wants heaven, earth's does the same. And nevertheless he has all possibilities and feels it, since he refuses to trace the whole thing back to an error in the original fettering.*[87]

37. Ontological Freedom

Subservience is a version of yielding that leads, however, to paradoxes of power. The slave is freer than the master in a sense we have become used to from reading Hegel and Marx, and in another way Nietzsche. What interests Kafka is less the inevitable inversions to which power is prone, less the hope or fiction that the slave will make a better master and paradoxically then also one day dissolve the structure of domination, and not the beast who wields a kind of power that is not domination; what interests Kafka is the freedom of bondage, a freedom from movement and all the strictures that the movement-will-struggle complex imposes. The kind of thing human beings call "freedom" identified by the ape as "self-controlled movement," in other words autonomous movement, is still deeply fettered, insofar as it remains in the cage of the self and its kind of internal control. And yet Kafka cannot answer the question about the slave's kind of freedom in bondage positively, at least not yet. How can he conceive of this highly and perhaps completely bound freedom in positive terms?

In response to his predicament another, more peculiar question asks to be posed: Does the world have corners? It won't be immediately clear why this is a response to Kafka's predicament over the meaning of freedom, or what kind of answer this question, in turn, might be seeking. To clarify, we shall have to take a few detours. We can say preliminarily, however, that the corner is an image of freedom in bondage, a place—no place—where a room gives no room.[88] Nonetheless, Kafka picks just this architectural and ontological feature as a site for experiments in the concept of freedom.

Despite his reputation as a psychologist, for ten years Franz Brentano worked on a grand ontological theory. That Brentano was an important inspiration for "fundamental ontology" and the Heideggerian *Seinsfrage* is well known. In 1907, his Gymnasium teacher, Conrad Gröber, gave Heidegger Brentano's 1862 dissertation "Von der mannigfachen Bedeutung des Seienden nach Aristoteles" (*On the Several Senses of Being in Aristotle*) as a birthday present. Heidegger said later that he worked through this book again and again in the 1910s,[89] and out of this reading, we are to surmise, sprang the *Seinsfrage*. In the epigraph to Brentano's thesis you can see the embryo of the question that drives *Being and Time*: "what *is* is said in many ways," *to on legetai pollachōs*. During the time Heidegger was first reading the dissertation, Brentano, having become one of the most consequential philosophy teachers in Central Europe, with a diaspora of students developing and modifying the project of descriptive psychology, in offshoots as various as phenomenology, psychoanalysis, Gestalt psychology, Polish logic, and other methods and schools—Brentano at this time was rethinking his position on being, stepping beyond the history of being, at least beyond Aristotle, if hesitantly, and beyond his own early brand of phenomenology. For ten years, from about 1910 until his death in 1917, Brentano dictated a growing collection of essays amounting to a theory of things, *res* and *realia*, which now fill two volumes in English translation.

One important essay in the collection discusses the part of a thing that delimits it from another, its boundary, *die Grenze*. This word might make it seem that Brentano has a spatial theory of *res* and *realia*, but we could say rather that in fact he has a thingy theory of space. Without explaining further here, let me say that his aim, to avoid "space" altogether, was in order to avoid any of the pitfalls, or "fictions" as he called them, of infinity theory, from Zeno to Cantor. Boundaries limited things, not space or spaces, and things were in themselves continuous extensions, though not because they were infinitely divisible. Things were continua because they could be bounded by a boundary, which made whatever aggregate or amorphic stuff within the boundary into a thing continuous with itself. Now this leaves the problem of what a boundary is, since it has to be both continuous with the thing it bounds and different or possibly even separate from it. Before we address the bipolar concept of the boundary in Brentano's ontological writings, one more fact about these things that are continuous with themselves but not infinitely divisible is of interest. Brentano does not sever the continuum from all ideas of infinity. That would destroy the possibility of a continuum. He does however change the object of infinity, substituting something new for the feature or aspect that is traditionally infinitized in a continuum. Mathematical-ontological theories of the continuum whether by Zeno or Cantor or Poincaré focused on the infinite division of space. The problem with this is that unless you can actually divide a continuum infinitely not just at one point but at all points and all at once, that is to make it totally divided or marked with all possible divisions, you cannot say that the continuum is complete, and an incomplete continuum is a contradiction in terms.[90] The false image of dividing any division in half and then in half again is much too limited a procedure to capture the total operation of division at all points at once that would be needed to demonstrate continuity by infinite division. Any attempt to "construct" a continuum in the total way is bound to fail, since one can add all numbers simultaneously even less than one can add them successively.[91] Another note: Brentano later suggests that a continuum is better conceived as infinite differentiation.[92] Such a conception avoids classic paradoxes of motion and the need for different orders of infinity. Even the Aristotelian solution, making infinite divisibility a potential rather than an actual mode, remains, in Brentano's estimation, a clever solution to a non-problem, when it is seen in the light of infinite differentiation.

Infinite qualitative differentiation is the route Brentano takes in his second approach to the continuum problem, when he formulates a new concept of the continuum itself. The first approach to the problem, written a little earlier, moves via the concept of boundaries. It is this approach that we want to understand. In the dictated essay "On What is Continuous," dated November 22, 1914, he writes: "One sees that in this entire putative construction of the concept of what is continuous [namely, the infinitely divisible] the goal has been entirely missed; for that which is above all else characteristic of a continuum, namely, the idea of a boundary in the strict sense (to which belongs the possibility of a coincidence of boundaries), will be sought after entirely in vain."[93] You can see already that one mechanism for guaranteeing the continuity of things, not to mention also the continuity of the whole of everything, will be the concept of a "coincidence of boundaries." To understand that, we have to ask what is strict about the "strict sense" of Brentano's boundary idea.

An explanation of the strictness is given in the following passage: "Because a boundary, even when itself continuous, can never exist except as belonging to something continuous of more dimensions (indeed receives its fully determinate and exactly specific character only through the manner of this belongingness), it is, considered for itself, nothing other than a universal, to which—as to other universals—more than one thing can correspond."[94] A boundary can never exist except as belonging to something continuous of more dimensions. The "never . . . except" indicates the sine qua non of the strict definition, which says: the meaning of a boundary depends on the dimensions that terminate at it. At a boundary a continuum of a larger cardinal dimensionality meets a smaller one. The three-dimensional meets the two-dimensional and this is its boundary; the two-dimensional meets its boundary in the one-dimensional, and the one-dimensional, believe it or not, meets its *Grenze* in the zero-dimensional. Here begins Brentano's late understanding of time. Whereas a cube is bounded by a surface, a surface by a line, and a line by a point, since Brentano accepts the idea of four dimensional space-time, a point is ultimately bounded by a discontinuity, and this confrontation of a point with dimensionlessness makes up an instant, what he calls "a mere boundary," the temporal instant.[95] Through combinations of the strict boundary and the mere boundary, every type of thing can be determined.

Another notion we have to understand is the "manner of belongingness" of a boundary to a continuum. This is what gives the continuum its specific character and full determination, Brentano says. In other words this notion makes it, in its concept, a complete and not a paradoxically incomplete continuum. Very briefly, manner of belongingness is a matter of direction. The "manner" in which a boundary belongs to a continuum and thus bounds a thing answers the question "which way does the continuum issue from its boundary?" The manner tells you as well to which continuum a boundary belongs. Brentano calls this directional aspect the "plerosis" of a boundary. Each boundary has a relative fullness, depending how it belongs to a continuum. A point, for example, is totally plerotic. It gives forth or issues continua on all sides; because of this too, its work as a boundary is highly limited, limited by being too full and so too vague. A line, in contrast, is bilaterally plerotic. It can issue continua on two sides. An example of the point's total plerosis is the center point of a disk, which is an internal boundary of the disk's total extension. The center point is a boundary in this way, a single quadrant of the disk cannot go any farther inward once it reaches the center point. From the point thus issues the whole inner expanse of the disk, which comes to another end in the circumference. A particularly complicated example, which Brentano does not address per se, is the kind of point that bounds three lines, the three lines that bound two surfaces, the surfaces that bound a part of a polyhedron. Another word for this is corner.

Without abandoning his study of psychic events, Brentano neverthe-less turned from presenting the structure and modes of the psyche to-ward intentional objects, toward beings and their constitution. Soon af-ter this, another Franz turned away from the psyche entirely—from the Brentanian psyche in particular that his friends and teachers had studied and believed in—toward his own thought of a polyhedron. On March 17, 1917, Brentano died, leaving his ontological writings unpublished. On October 19, 1917, Kafka wrote the following in his notebook, which also remained unpublished until after his death: *How pitiful is my self-knowl-edge when compared for instance with my knowledge of my room. (Evening). Why? There is no observation of the inner world in the same manner that there is observation of the outer world. Psychology is probably on the whole an anthropomorphism, a [nibbling away] at the boundaries.*[96] The shift here is putatively from an inside to an outside sphere, but it is noteworthy that the outside takes the form of a room, which is outside the soul perhaps, but also withdrawn from the public, well inside the broad boundaries of what is. It is not only now in 1917 that Kafka has problems with psychol-ogy—by which he means Brentanian descriptive psychology (the term he uses, before striking it out). And yet he makes an express point of leaving descriptions of the psyche behind. *Zum letztenmal Psychologie!*[97] Kafka had already been experimenting with nonpsychological, that is nonphe-nomenological situations and modes, and, it should be said, also with limits to ontology, with boundaries, and with a special kind of boundary, corners.

One finds the suggestion that the world is best described as a room all over the fictions. Gregor Samsa's world becomes his room, and the rooms of the creature of the late fragment "Der Bau" become his world. World and room are completely convertible in the fictions, as much in "The Judgment" as in the final stories.

Again, our question asks to be posed. If it is a peculiar question we can see now that is followed by a rather banal answer: the question, Does the world have corners? The answer, Yes, when it is equivalent to a room.

From all reports, we are supposed to think of doors when we read Kafka. Doors that open but cannot be entered, doors that appear as if from out of nowhere (in a corner, at times), doors that communicate with faraway places, abrogating distance—Kafkan doors have been made famous, on the one hand, because of their promise to be "before" something else, in front of and blocking, while still communicating with what exceeds, and, on the other hand, because of their ability to connect spaces that are not contiguous. These two aspects are intimately related. The front door, the door "before," is claimed by Derrida in his famous reading of the door parable. Although he reads it as a parable about the law, it is, one might argue, also about the door and the kind of space or better the kind of ontology that the portal presupposes. The back door, the one that works like a wormhole, is part of the captivating if not altogether accurate revolutionary reading by Deleuze and Guattari. These two French doors share the room of which they are a feature. Their powers to suggest a beyond to a room or to annul the distance to that beyond are a function of the room-ness of the room, its domesticity, closed-offness, and, as Brentano would say, the coincidence of its boundaries with other rooms.

Rooms have other important features in Kafka besides boundaries: windows, tables, walls, peepholes, as well as the set of all possible relations to adjoining rooms (*Nebenzimmer*). In truth, however, there is only ever one room. "The" room is always the reference point for any other. In the parable "Before the Law," we focus, with the doorkeeper and the man from the country, on the terminus, the rooms beyond the door. Unbeknownst to him, and it must be said also to the doorkeeper, these rooms are themselves only in function of the room-character of the primary room. They are places of escape from, next to, higher than, freer, however phantasmatically, in comparison to "the" room. Endless *Nebenzimmer* help conceal the importance of the room qua room, displacing attention into a wish to cross into a zone whose problems will, it is hoped, be different and not room-like.

Another oddity should be noted: the emphasis on rooms and corners is not peculiar to Kafka. Rather, although Kafka may indeed name it and bring it to light and eventually, perhaps, allow us to inhabit the room-ish world in a different way, the preoccupation with rooms and corners is typical of the era. The obstacles to a specifically Kafkan theory of rooms and corners have been that in his stories they are too deeply buried in the everyday. They contribute nothing to an existential viewpoint; they have little to do with the law; they are ontological in Brentano's sense, and not part of a direct critique of power politics or ethnic identitarianism. What do they do, these corners, these rooms? We shall have to let one example stand for the range of possible functions and meanings. This is a fragment written down sometime between 1917 and 1920.

> "Ach," said the mouse, "the world gets narrower with every passing day. First it was so wide that it made me anxious, then I ran on farther and walls started to rise up right and left in the distance, and now—it hasn't been very long at all since I started running—I am in the room appointed for me [*in dem mir bestimmten Zimmer*] and there in the corner stands the trap into which I run." "You only have to change direction," said the cat and gobbled it up.[98]

The complaining mouse is caught between two pitfalls, or imagines it is. The well-known parable, or "fable" as it was called, though not by Kafka, is written from the mouse's perspective. This fact is paramount. Narrator and reader may hear irony in these lines; to the mouse, however, the situation is serious and there is no way out, "no exit." Exit (*Ausgang*) is a term that, rather ironically in *The Trial* (*Der Prozess*), a story with no end to corridors and doors, refers there in the main to a legal result, *der Ausgang des Prozesses*. After 1917, however, something changes and the word *Ausgang* comes to refer in Kafka's fictions almost exclusively to an escape route and to the desires that drive you to seek one. All the ape Rotpeter wants is a "way out." In the mouse's intuition of its situation, it is clear there is no escape—a trap in front, a cat behind—yet a way out is what it seeks.

A more distant look at the text shows us that its logic is counterfactual: if the mouse had not turned around, he would not have been eaten. If the mouse had not tried to escape the *Angst* of the free open room (called *die Freie* in "Der Bau") and had not run toward the corner, an escape would not have been necessary. And, more generally, if the world didn't have the character of either-or, either bewildering to one who is in the open or comforting when it narrows to a point, the mouse wouldn't have been forced to make such a fatal decision. The open and the corner: yes, the world is decidedly a room.

All sorts of events happen in corners in Kafka's writings. People and occurrences conceal themselves. A corner is the outer-inner and the open secret in the room-shaped world, the closest thing to being out of reach and view while remaining unremarkable and public. In "Das Urteil" when he discovers how long a reach into his private life his father actually

has, Georg Bendemann stands "in a corner, as far as possible from his father."[99] Gregor Samsa retreats into a darkened corner when his bedroom
door is left open to onlookers.[100] Georg and Gregor may both be what
Kafka elsewhere calls "useless corner-standers and air breathers [*unnützen
Eckensteher und Lufteinatmer*]."[101] This sounds like a criticism, but it is
not. The position of corner-stander and the occupation of air-breather
repeat themselves in one of the more forceful Kafkan self-observations.
Already in 1914, the corner is a real possibility, this time for a withdrawal
from group belonging and identity grubbing. "What do I have in common with Jews? I hardly have anything in common with myself and I
should stand totally still in a corner, satisfied that I can breathe."[102] In
the quotidian corner, a quotidian thing happens. You breathe. Breathing
happens, which is to say, *ex silentio*, nothing more. The corner reduces
worldly experience to respiration, a rather drastic limitation (phenomenology calls it an *epochè*), to being able to stand and breathe. It is also
likely, according to this diary entry, that one could and *should* be satisfied
in this condition, having stepped out of the game of cat-and-mouse with
its deceptive offers of escape and even more deceptive dead ends.

There are other astonishing things about corners in Kafka. Many
people and things can fit in a single corner. In *Der Prozess* three youths
appear out of a corner while Joseph K. is being arrested; the *Advokat* and
his bed emerge from a corner when Joseph K. seeks them; his Uncle sits
at a table wholly lodged within a corner.[103] If one withdraws into a corner, one can whisper and not be heard.[104] In short one can enter, dwell in,
and exit from a corner with a kind of freedom that is totally unknown in
other parts of rooms. A corner, in this sense, is more open than any door.
Yet its openness is still that of a complete reduction of possibilities. It is
probable that Odradek who dwells nowhere dwells in one.

If the poor beleaguered mouse had only run a little farther, all the way
into . . . the corner . . .

One marked difference between the concept of world in Heidegger
and Husserl and world in Kafka is that the latter makes room, so to
speak, for narrowness, and at the same time it shows how the most narrow, the infinitely narrow, may offer no space but is freer than the open
middle. Heidegger and Husserl are concerned with the total science of
the wholeness of the world; they lay out the public arenas of the *Da*, the
lifeworld, *Mitsein*, and history, not to forget "the open" in which beings
can be encountered as they are. The difference is not merely thematic;

the differences from Husserl and Heidegger tie Kafka back into his Brentanian involvements, as peripheral or deniable as they may have been for him at times. The corner that is not a dead end ties Kafka to Brentano, insofar as Brentano's theory of boundaries is an ontology of narrowness, and further, speaking of boundaries, a narrowing to a point beyond a point, to a one-dimensional and then a nondimensional part of being, from which and out of which being is defined. A boundary allows a being to be a continuum with itself. Brentano's *principium individuationis* depends on the boundary function. The boundary of the world lies, one would expect if one extends his logic, where the boundaries coincide, at the confluence of all boundaries, inner and outer, of beings, states, nature, constructions, and so on. This must form part of the "strict sense" of boundary, the actual coincidence of individual boundaries and the final coincidence of individuals with an ultimate boundary, which, if one were speculating, might be called a corner. The continuum for Brentano thus emerges from a corner, a point, a discontinuum, whereas, in contrast, the cosmos for Aristotle is "caused" by an outermost circle. And yet, even if this or that being is constituted from its boundary for Brentano, distinguished from another being as this or that, even if it becomes continuous with itself from its boundary, and thus, as a result becomes individuated—even where the boundary, as a narrowing of dimensions, reduces ultimately to a point, world is still a summary aggregate of all boundaries and overlaps. Narrownesses for Brentano add up to a broad, fundamental, and encompassing whole. There really isn't a thought of corners there. Corners are neither wholes nor parts; they cannot be added up. Although a mereological argument could be made that they are constitutive of rooms, this is much truer of walls. Walls are the Brentanian boundaries of a roomish world. What then are corners? In Brentanian ontological terms, not a wholly inappropriate starting point, it seems, for looking at late Kafka as an ontological thinker, corners are the ends of boundaries, points at which the boundary logic of ontology may reach its limit.

One similarity between Brentano's thought of boundaries and Kafka's corner logic is that both are ontological and neither is spatial or geometrical. Boundary gives the enabling limit of a being, even if that being is the world. Space, on the other hand, is an abstraction that generalizes the boundary logic into a largest possible thing, a container, but the relationship with its contents is abstract and that abstractness conceals its ontological and not physical nature. There is no empty space within which there are material-physical beings; there are continuous and coincident beings, nothing more. The special noncontinuity and noncoincidence, the corner, lies at the boundary of the ontological. There (nowhere) being as a continuum with a boundary, being as the potential confluence of boundaries with other beings, becomes impossible. This is just to say that in a corner there are no identifiable beings. A mode of freedom happens then, ontological freedom it might be called. Its description is negative: the license not to be a being, not to possess, the freedom not to be in a world. A caution is in order however. Let us quote the very last lines of Kafka's late story "Investigations of a Dog" (Forschungen eines Hundes): "Freedom! Certainly such freedom as is possible today is a wretched business. But nevertheless freedom, nevertheless a possession."[105] Freedom can easily come to be a possession in its own right, especially when you have nothing else—this is the problem with the freedom of a slave. There is however a positive expression of this freedom that is harder to envision as a possession. In 1922, Kafka writes to Oskar Baum that instead of traveling "freely under the great sky," he would rather stay in his room. "So beautiful, so beautiful it is to be unnoticed [so schön, so schön ist es, unbeachtet zu sein]."[106] In this case the room itself is a corner of the world, and the freedom that arises in this constraint is beautiful in the extreme.

Kafka expresses the beauty of going unnoticed in several ways. One has to press oneself into a corner, and this activity is much more like a withdrawal or retreat, a giving of ground, an abandonment of space as organizing principle or expression of power. The Trial frequently tells the story of corners: "K. only saw that a man had dragged her into a corner by the door and there held her pressed against himself."[107] To be dragged completely into the corner, is this violence or salvation?

In the novel there is a joke about how you find a corner. Joseph K. is having little success obtaining the outcome (Ausgang) he wants in his case, and the trial is occupying more and more of his mind. His advocate, Herr Huld, a name with devotional overtones, in the middle of one of his long reproachful speeches, warns K. against doing what everyone does, that is, acquiring a "hack lawyer," a Winkeladvokat.[108] The question of whether the world has corners comes down to this: corners are noncoincident with the world and beings that enter them take on this attribute and this challenge. They cease being worldly without becoming otherworldly. What a *Winkeladvokat*—an advocate for or from corners—might tell you is that the world does not *have* corners, at least not as proper parts of itself, notwithstanding that they are to be found everywhere.[109]

38. Struggle, Will, Power, Strength

From the perspective of yielding, struggle or fighting looks like giving up. You tried to hold out, you wished to yield, but you could not, and so you began to struggle and strive. From this perspective yielding appears as a branch of the will. In the minds and words of its pugnacious advocates, it looks as though there is struggle and nothing but struggle. This does a disservice to yielding, which is humble and allows itself to be overrun. When one agonist is pitted against another, the strong and active one calls the outcome "victory." And yet victory is the yield from a false perspective; in every victory someone gives up their place, their weapons, their rights, their life. Without the yielding of one side or at times many other sides, without giving up the will to win, without giving in to specific demands, without giving over a body, without something that cedes, victory cannot take place. Force can only be measured at the moment the opponent gives way. More—force becomes itself not against a counterforce; for if one side does not cede, the result is stasis and force remains invisible. A way is given to force by yielding; force moves at the behest of the vanquished. If this is really so, why does the agonic-type theory remain blind to its dependency on yielding, to its weak underside and enabling possibility? Somehow it came to be in the nature of struggle to look as though it describes the whole of life.

Struggle, fight, contention, *agon*—*Kampf, Streit*—are bywords of Nietzsche's social and moral writings. His youthful "preface" "Homers Wettkampf" (Homer's Contest) depicts a society so totally determined by struggle that there can be no other principle of organization. Struggle is the victor, so to speak, and the only good. Any victor who wins too often or too thoroughly will be ostracized for the sake of the continuation of the fight.[110] The mode of struggle that interested Nietzsche seems to have been contest, agon. Although it may be a question of life or death for either or both of the contenders, a *Wettkampf* nevertheless lives off of the lively life of chance, the betting between contenders, *das Wetten*. A more ambitious type of combat marks the slave morality in its struggle against authentic, healthy power. Later the mode of struggle whose aim is dominance slowly begins to determine all relations in Nietzsche's social arena: struggle for dominance takes place between men and women, between epochs, between ideas:—truth and lies fight an age-old battle, as do truth and beauty, belief and knowledge, good and evil, and countless other pairs of opponents.[111] The great thinker fights the Church and in the same gesture enters the "play and struggle of forces [*Spiel und Kampf der Kräfte*]" in Europe,[112] to lead it "toward great politics [*zur großen Politik*]." When Nietzsche writes about politics, battle is often the analogy, and his polemical tone also evokes it: "the time for small politics is over: the next century will bring the *struggle* [*Kampf*, Nietzsche's italics] over the dominance of the earth,—the compulsion to large politics."[113] History is the largest set of such battles, whether they take place intellectually in polemical writings (*Streitschriften*) or in physical confrontations. Nietzsche's own interventions in European intellectual and moral history are battles as well. In a set of notes from 1887, he lists each of his intellectual engagements as "mein Kampf" against this or against that.[114]

Struggle is by no means only external, clashes between persons. External struggle springs from the deepest, most fundamental internal condition, the soul answering to the will to power. To some extent we think that the image of the self-struggling will derives from Nietzsche's interpretation of Darwinian evolution. Aphorism no. 349 of *The Gay Science* (*Die fröhliche Wissenschaft*) initiates us into the problem. Scholars who are committed to self-preservation as the *primum principium* of philosophical explanation are stridently attacked there. Nietzsche is upset, or so it seems, with the dogma of self-preservation because in it the principle of struggle is subordinated to the principle of sufficiency. Such a subordinated theory of struggle, which is "at its coarsest in Darwinism with its incomprehensibly one-sided doctrine of "the battle for existence,"[115] is the product of minor minds, scholars who have never liberated themselves from their own "struggle for existence"; that is, the scholars who support such a theory are children of a class who had to struggle for its means of existence, and this experience and temperament colors their theories. Scholars whose chief consideration was their own survival make mere survival the principle of nature. Along with the scent of class-ism that never leaves his writings, we also smell blood, the blood of a more permanent struggle. Nietzsche argues: "The battle for existence is only one exception, a temporary restriction of the life will. The large and the small battle everywhere pivots around excess, around growth and proliferation, around power [*Macht*], under the terms of the will to power, which is the very will of life."[116] The battle over the means for survival is the lesser battle; the greater battle is for power.[117] One could depict the lesser and greater *Kämpfe* in the following manner: the former is about *Kräfte*, the merest energies to show up at the fight; the latter is about *Macht*, the exercise of one's will over another's, the capacity to dominate.[118]

Will, or so it seems however, is not the origin and end of struggle; it itself is a function of struggle. This is an important insight that will inform Kafka's reflections on struggle.[119] Will is an effect of struggle and not its cause. The inverted priority of the faculty and the experience has an origin in Schopenhauer, and it is a pattern that Nietzsche, even in his most anti-Schopenhauerian moments, doesn't really abandon, although he seldom acknowledges it. Nietzsche recognizes the central position of struggle for life already in 1873, and quotes Schopenhauer as support:

> That struggle [*Jenen Kampf*] which is peculiar to all coming-to-be, that everlasting alternation of victory, is again something also described by Schopenhauer (*Welt als Wille und Vorstellung*, Vol. I, Book 2, §27):
>
> Persisting matter must continually change its form, since according to causality, mechanical, physical, chemical and organic phenomena greedily push to the fore, snatching matter from one another, for each would reveal its own inherent idea. We can follow this strife throughout the whole of nature. In fact we might say that nature exists but by virtue of it.[120]

The best example of the natural antagonism in struggle is matter, since it seems to consist in anything but will. If matter can be shown to be at base struggle, those things that are obviously will, form and force, for example, can easily be too. Schopenhauer peers into nature and sees the eternal clash (*Streit*)—in this case, of matter and form—that makes up all "organic phenomena." The ultimate victor is not matter or form, and it is neither one will nor another, but instead, as it is in Nietzsche, the victor is the clash itself; dead matter becomes "nature" in its continual tearing itself (*entreißend*) from itself. Willing emerges from the ripping; to will is to recognize the resistance of matter (*die beharrende Materie*) to form. Resistance gives birth to the "will to form." Since matter is not willing and form is of a different order than matter, because they are not one, that is, because they oppose one another, will arises to make a dynamic unity out of them. While thinking about the being of nature and constructing a critique of Darwinism in 1873, Nietzsche chooses to quote the above passage from Schopenhauer. There are other points in *The World as Will and Representation* in which Schopenhauer comes close to divulging the fact that the will, specifically the will to overcome, to dominate—is this the only nature the will can have?—depends on and arises out of natural strife or struggle. For instance—

> When a magnet lifts a piece of iron it is engaged in an ongoing struggle against gravity which, as the lowest objectivation of the will, has a more original right to the matter in the iron; the magnet even gathers strength through this constant struggle, since resistance spurs it on to greater efforts, as it were. This is how it is with all of them, even the appearance of the will that presents itself in the human organism: an ongoing struggle against the many physical and chemical forces which, as lower Ideas, have a prior right to that matter. [121]

—Schopenhauer makes the banal and definitional comment that victory depends on struggle. Yet he also sketches the internal relationships between supposed wills in the world as will. The relationship between the lower wills designated as "material" and the higher wills that Schopenhauer calls "organic" is the same as that in the original or "prior" (*frühere*) relationship between force and matter. In every event of willing there is one element that plays the matter and one that plays the force, one that pushes and one that resists, but what is between them is neither; force (*Kraft*) and resistance (*Widerstand*, which is but another force, always in the end the lesser, the loser) become power, or will, when brought together in struggle. In other words "will" is an epiphenomenon of *Kampf*.

This is why will can be equated with power by Nietzsche: an opponent is wanted who will enter into the circle: one you can overpower and who, the longer you keep him in a lower position, the longer his resistance, the greater your power grows. To be sure, will refers to the source of an activity or the beginning of a series, as Hannah Arendt describes it. The secret of will, however, is that without an opponent or an object, without something external to it that provides a counterforce, it could not be recognized as willing. In this Schopenhauerian vein, power, *Macht*, is in the relationship between forces, whose relative value as stronger and weaker is determined by the struggle, which alone turns forces into power.

Beyond power, which gets more entrenched the longer the struggle goes on, and which depends on and arises from hopes that the struggle will one day come to a final end—beyond actual power this is a matter of *the conservation of the feeling of power*. Power does not have to be real; it can be a representation. In fact, it may only ever be one. In a note from 1881, Nietzsche writes:

> The feeling of power [*Das Machtgefühl*] first conquering, then commanding (organizing)—it governs [*regulirt*] the conquered ones so that they conserve for it the feeling of power, and for this reason the feeling of power conserves [*erhält*] the conquered as conquered.—Even the function arises out of the feeling of power, in the struggle [*Kampf*] with weaker forces. The function conserves itself in the subduing and sovereignty [*Überwältigung und Herrschaft*] over lower functions—therein the lower function is maintained by the higher power![122]

Let us add at least a second exclamation point to Nietzsche's first: !!

What we have to look for are people, or better—for the designation is already to bound to struggle, the struggle for personhood, for recognition, rights—we have to look for positions, clines, points of no return, or better still, infinitesimals, where you can give up the struggle without resisting it. Nietzsche writes:

> The freest human being has the greatest *feeling of power* [*Machtgefühl*] over himself, the greatest *knowledge* about himself, the greatest *order* in the necessary battle of his powers [*Kräfte*], the relatively greatest *independence* of his individual powers, the relatively greatest *battle* in himself: he is the *most conflicted* [*zwieträchtigste*] being and the *richest in changes* and the *most long-lived* and the abundantly desiring, self-nourishing, the most diverging from himself and self-renewing.[123]

Kafka notes down a thought: *A human being has free will and it is in fact threefold. First, he was free when he willed this life; now he can admittedly not reverse it, since he is no longer the one who at that time willed it; it would then be the case that he is only "living" insofar as he carries out his earlier will. Second, he is free to the extent that he can choose this life's gait and path. Third, he is free to the extent that, as the one who he will at some point once again be, he has the will under every condition to let himself go through this life and in this way to let himself come to himself and in fact on a fully choosable, but still in any event thus labyrinthine path, so that he leaves no tiny speck of this life untouched. That is the threefold [nature] of the free will; it is also, since it is simultaneous, a unifold [or "monotony"—ein Einerlei] and it is at bottom so very uniform that it has no place for a will, whether a free or an unfree one.*[124]

There is too much to say about the differences between these two accounts of human freedom, not to mention their relative congeniality to metaphysical operators such as "change," "choice," "power," and "battle." Although presented in different terms, Kafka's tiny treatise on the freedom of the will belongs to his long-standing personal struggle against the metaphor of struggle. His early story "Description of a Struggle (*Beschreibung eines Kampfes*) begins when two "acquaintances" sink into a contention so inextricable and indeed also so inexplicable that the girl around whom the struggle seems to germinate cannot be the reason for their all-night race through the city. "But yes, my acquaintance still walked behind me, yes he quickened his pace when he noticed that he was being left behind, and acted as though it was natural."[125] The battle between the agonists drags on in silence until you come to understand that the struggle is without reason, just something "natural," and as such extending to every single thing they do or say; rather than to victory, it leads to a total stalemate. *One of evil's most effective means of seduction is the invitation to a struggle. It is like the struggle with women that ends in bed.*[126] That is, the seduction is to struggle in another form. Between the description of a struggle in 1907–8 and the invitation to a struggle ten years later, the motif has not changed, nor has the attitude toward it, but the objective and method are now quite different. The target is now clear: the invitation, glossed here as seduction. The invitation to struggle is a promise of pleasure, and this may ultimately be the pleasure in victory, similar to the great "feeling of power" as Nietzsche calls it. Yet, as Kafka recognizes, whoever accepts the invitation ends up in bed with the antagonist, that is, one is converted to belief in struggle as the proper mode of existence. Is there a position outside existence as struggle? In "Description" it is the warm room where the boy eats a sweet bun. He too is seduced by a woman, but it is more than that. At the beginning of the first draft of the story, the boy is lured away from his pleasant eating by the "acquaintance," who sets up a triangle—he has kissed a girl, he says, or she has kissed him, and he will tell the boy about it as they walk. From the start, the "struggle" is the seduction to desire. Thus the landscape of desire has also changed over those ten years: from a struggle over a woman, it has become a struggle against a woman and perhaps against all women—as symbols of seducers. And yet there is a position outside this struggle too. On one hand it is in Zürau, where the long war against Felice—

their "relationship" can only be called this, and it is certainly neither to Kafka's credit nor to Felice's shame—has ended. Skewed as the conflation of women with evil is, Kafka's *Kampf* had many other fronts. In 1919, he characterizes his siblings' involvement with their father and their father's involvement with his children as a battle.[127] He himself was quickly vanquished—it was never a "real battle" for Franz.[128] He didn't have the strength that Ottla had for maintaining perpetual hostilities. Undoubtedly, his friendship with Max Brod was as much an enmity (*Feindschaft*); from the very moment they met they clashed, Brod representing Schopenhauer, Kafka representing Nietzsche and even perhaps winning, certainly winning over a "friend" with whom he would enter into an agon to the death, beyond his own death, over his existence and his prestige as a thinker and writer, Brod at times surreptitiously making use of Kafka's "strengths" for his own purposes, good ones mostly. Zürau was a place of détente with Felice, with his parents, with the office, and with Brod, a pause in the engagements. For the one who does not accept the invitation there may be a place outside the struggle.

39. Heidegger, Letting and Leaving

A distinction, or most probably a pseudo-distinction, graces one of the early lectures in the group of courses Heidegger gave in the late 1930s and early 1940s on Nietzsche's philosophy. The distinction, and the fact that it may in the end not be a distinction or not a thoroughgoing one, helps us see some differences between Kafkan yielding and Heideggerian calm composure or "releasement" as it is sometimes translated—*Gelassenheit*. In the great lectures in which Nietzsche first came to have a "philosophy," Heidegger's unique synthesizing treatment of the oeuvre as an articulated whole with particular emphasis on the book *The Will to Power*—never accomplished by Nietzsche as a book, only as a plan, as multiple sketches and repeated promises—Heidegger works backward, as it were, from the apparent chaos of the Nietzschean corpus, made up of unpublished notes and sketches, lists and reminders to himself, and letters, as much as of published and republished works, which almost to a line come to be layered over with critical reevaluations by Nietzsche himself—Heidegger works backward from this chaos to something more unified, something like the "soul" of Nietzsche's thinking. In keeping with Heidegger's diagnosis of Nietzsche as Platonic, the "soul" of his philosophy is viewed as tripartite, comprising the death of God, the eternal return, and the will to power.

It will be uncontroversial I think to say about these three concepts or processes that they exhibit more than a passing resemblance to the temporal ecstasies of Dasein—*Geworfenheit, Verfallenheit, Sein zum Ende* or *Möglichkeit (thrownness, fallenness, being-toward-the-end or possibility)*—a decade earlier Heidegger offered these three as simultaneous, equiprimordial, and constructed out of one another with no other ground but each other. To remind ourselves, Kafka's schema, in contradistinction, appears to have four "dimensions" (as Heidegger called the ecstases in the late lecture "Time and Being"). First they are: being, time, death, and the will; then these four vectors or key concepts are reduced, drawn back across the thoughts to the following attitudes or practices: belonging-to, faith in, image-blurring, and yielding. Although the first three Kafkan attitudes have strong echoes of the trio past, present, and future, seen together as a figure, the fourfold does not correspond to either triptych, Nietzsche's or Heidegger's, for one obvious reason. Time is dropped as a category. Nietzsche and Heidegger, as far as they go with their critiques of "being," hold onto a trace of substance in time or temporality; they account for change either as overcoming or as phenomenological modification or as event. Nietzsche does this through "becoming" and Heidegger rightly I think accuses Nietzsche in these lectures of presenting "becoming" as the thinnest veil over permanence—the permanence of change, following a cartoonish version of Heraclitus. In Heidegger the trace of substance drifts in and out of the vocabulary of pertinence, mineness, owning, and possession, but also in the permanence of the ecstases themselves. In contrast, where Kafka's yield cuts across the trio death, time, and being, it opens an imbalance in the temporal dialectic, and suggests a counterposition to these traces of a time-thing.

The distinction or pseudo-distinction graces the Nietzsche lectures when Heidegger presents the will to power, one of the three Nietzschean ecstases. The distinction, which will help, I think, to illuminate the differences between yielding and being composed and being as letting be (*gelassen-sein*), is supposed to erupt within the meaning of willing. "To will" can mean either to dominate a submissor or to wish for something. Within this pair, something like not-willing makes an indirect appearance, but it takes Heidegger some years to return to the theme directly.

The question "is there something like yielding in Heidegger" could be answered in two ways, with reference to two pulses of thinking that emerge in the 1930s but are already present *in nuce* in *Being and Time.*

On the one hand, there is truthing, on the other, willing. Truthing as the withdrawal of being and opening of a world is a species of giving over—and Heidegger toys with *geben* words all over—*sich ergeben, es gibt,* and so on. To say that as "unforgetting," the movement of truth—*alētheia*—"gives" a world does not seem far from saying that yielding yields a yield. Yet, whereas being may withdraw into forgetfulness, it never yields—that is, it is never affected in its essence by anything.

Moreover, as Derrida and others have shown, Heidegger's rhetoric is often polemical, polemarchical, warlike, and not seldom domineering. He undoubtedly found sympathy for this stance in Nietzsche's *Kampf* rhetoric. *Being and Time* urges that Dasein should become powerful (*mächtig*) with respect to its everyday dissipated dispersion; it should take a stand, become resolute, decide, face finitude, open a world. Although it may have little to do with power, *potestas,* even the vocabulary of *Möglichkeit,* tied as it is to *mögen,* preference, involves putting oneself before others, liking and indeed wanting for oneself, at the expense of the multitude. Far be it from Heidegger not to recognize this in some way, and so sometime in the 1930s, alongside his designation of truth as *alētheia,* there arises a questioning of the will and willing that is almost absent from *Being and Time.* Bret Davis calls the attitude toward willing in *Being and Time* "profound ambivalence"[129] and I think this is right. Davis's book *Heidegger and the Will* uncovers the path, previously obscured by other interests, from ambivalence toward willing to acceptance, then a turn around and a critique, and finally to the thought of an alternative to willing, or what looks like an alternative. Davis's subtitle names the destination: *On the Way to Gelassenheit.*[130] The search for "the yield" in Heidegger, if it is there, should take place along this way as well.

The distinction that Heidegger makes in his reading of Nietzsche's will to power, where willing means either dominance or wishing, must have at first obscured for him the path toward *Gelassenheit,* a term Heidegger associates explicitly in 1944–45 with "not willing" and sometimes with "non-willing." In the distinction between dominance and wishing there is no place for abandonment, capitulation, giving over, up, in. There is no place for laid-backness—*gelassen-sein*—in the early stages of Heidegger's thinking about will. The distinction that seems all important to Heidegger—the choice between will as wish or will as power—claims all the attention and leaves the other distinction, the one between willing and not willing, in the shadows. Will as will to power is, for Nietzsche according to Heidegger, the "essence of being"; in a strong sense for Nietzsche, there is nothing but the will or wills, and will is always a matter of dominance.[131] We must remember that there is no "will itself," in the Leibnizian sense, an *appetitus* that would be equal in prominence and permanence to *perceptio*. Will is not a faculty, a capacity, a power, or anything localizable as an organ or organic part of a human being. In a particularly alluring phrase Heidegger describes the vortex that is the will: "But because for Nietzsche will as will to power designates the essence of Being, it remains forever the actual object of his search, the thing to be determined."[132] A thing that was already determined simply could not be the will, since the innovation of Nietzsche's view of will over Leibniz's, bringing him closer, in Heidegger's estimation, to Schelling,[133] consists in the fact that the only constitutive fact of the will is willing, and since willing is what gives determination, it seems unable to determine itself. It can determine but is itself "to be determined." Yet this logic of the indeterminacy of the will is quickly turned around. Will does in fact determine itself, and thoroughly: it determines itself in and by its activity as the giver of determination. This is its determination. "Will wills willing" is the proper formulation—the "to" in will to power also means "will," in the sense of being outside itself toward something else.

And this is the heart of the matter. Why insist so emphatically on this distinction in the meaning of willing? Willing cannot be equal to wishing in Heidegger's account of Nietzsche because will would not then be toward itself but toward another; there would be a kind of dissipation at the heart of things; will would not be a power in and by its own strength, an overcoming of and for itself, a movement toward itself, and a self-appropriation. Wishing means not being able to fulfill, by yourself, the demand you place on yourself, and in this way the concept of the wish is too close, Heidegger says, to "representation," which is also a movement toward a non-self, an intentional relation but without the means for self-fulfillment. "Is willing then a wishing to which we add our own initiative? No, willing is not wishing at all. It is the submission of ourselves to our own command, and the resoluteness of such self-command, which already implies our carrying out the command."[134] How Heidegger feels about this power-will-concept is not made explicit here, but his feeling about wishing is unmistakable. Wishing is too cognitive, too weak; it is but the desire for a will and the acknowledgement that no present power is sufficient to it. Wishing ends when willing begins. The wish's reach for the object, like that of representation, leaves the object as it is and untouched by power, which is to say, wishing does not make the object "mine," and so it also has no power to transform the one who wishes into an owner. These possessive transformations are "decisive" in Heidegger's question of the will, as this key passage should demonstrate:

> The decisive question is this: how, and on what grounds, do the willed and the one who wills belong to the willing to will? Answer: on the grounds of willing and by means of willing. Willing wills the one who wills, as such a one; and willing posits the willed as such. Willing is resoluteness toward oneself, but as the one who wills what is posited in the willing as willed. In each case will itself furnishes thoroughgoing determinateness to its willing.[135]

In short, willing is the preeminent form of self-ownership. From willing one gains a continual transformability of the self, of existence, and of being, but by means of a greedy appropriativeness. As the new name for "self-determination" (*Entschlossenheit*), will may provide what *Being and Time* could only hint at: a revolutionary potential emerging from the question of being (*Seinsfrage*). Truthing becomes productive in willing. The apophantic "as," it turns out, is first of all a function of willing, an effect of power, the power to "take" something as something—and is this power of "taking as" not, in its simplest form, already the power to "take" what one wants in the way one wants to, to "possess" it at every stage of a thing's existence? Isn't this what Heidegger means by "hermeneusis"? And the other side: leaving something behind, letting alone, leaving out, aside—these non-acts are not addressed here. Their place is marked by the unappreciated act, very close to a non-act, of "wishing," which abandons the thing and the self too much and provides little transformational gain for the one who wishes.

Now the two meanings of willing that Heidegger wants to distinguish absolutely from one another, wishing and dominance, may not be as distinct as he implies. Wishing he puts in a column with representational schemata, alongside the subject/object interpretation and the dethroned monarch "disinterested knowledge," curiosity, and the other "disowning" attitudes and acts. Wishing is not sufficiently appropriative. Yet what is wishing but a will to have what one does not presently have? What is will, then, but a wish to be able at last to assert possession over something? Is will so much a fact of power and wish so much a fact of cognition that they do not influence each other in essential ways? Nietzsche is not interested in wishing, perhaps—but he is also more interested in dominance by itself than in dominance as a route to possession-taking and ownership, ergo his depictions of will are very different from Heidegger's in one respect. At least for the blonde beast, willing is but a momentary release of energy. Heidegger is more interested in the constitution and continuation of a self through the will. In his great synthesis of the Nietzschean philosophy, willing becomes the "essence of being,"[136] a procurement of power through self-excess, which, let us remember, "belongs" to the self. If we are frank, it is no surprise that two of Heidegger's own tendencies, the tendency to prefer, if you will, modification or event as the climax of the hermeneutic process, and the tendency to think these as inseparable from a taking and holding and belonging, with the further step to owning your own self—these two tendencies seem to be mirrored in the distinction Heidegger makes in Nietzsche's formulas for the will. Heidegger prefers dominance to wishing. He asserts this in the name of Nietzsche, but it is clearly also for his own purposes. Yet there are problems with this, even just conceptually. Wishing has to put itself in service of willing, or else the will would have no object. Willing's object by definition has to be distant, unpossessed, undominated, free, available, yes, but also willing (in the sense of yielding) in order for power to have any effect at all. You wish for the object before you will it as yours. To exert power over what is already under your sway is not power but weakness, tyranny, abuse. Moreover, willing itself, in order to become itself, should begin with a wish. There must be a moment at which dominance is still a projection and a project. That is, wishing does not only present the object of willing, it also presents willing. A wish to will would have to precede willing, if willing is to be at all "free." In other words, when you will, when you dominate, you must wish to dominate and wish for a particular object of domination. Domination is riven by wishes; will needs the wish and its tendency to posit the free, the far off, the barely imaginable, the future. In its wish, which is also obviously not just any wish but the will's wish, a wish for power, the will locates its future, outlines the arena in which it will discharge itself, and pursues its hoped-for victim with single-minded purpose.

The will wishes, the will commands, the will dominates—but what does the will ultimately want? In a certainly overly laconic formula, we can say: will wants to possess. This is the most basic wish of the will.

It yearns for "belonging," well before it incites itself into operation. In Heidegger's reading of Nietzsche, the will doesn't only want belongings, it intends in the process to procure the coveted self-belonging for itself. "The decisive question is this: how, and on what grounds, do the willed and the one who wills belong to the willing to will? Answer: on the grounds of willing and by means of willing."[137] One way in which Heidegger overshoots Nietzsche, let's say, despite and because of how well he reads him, is his insistence that belonging be the internal bond and essence of willing.

Never a mere blast of energy, a release, an impulsive move beyond, *über sich hinaus*, willing is rather a sophisticated gathering point for the belonging together of elements. The priority of belonging does not begin in the Nietzsche lectures; it obviously is the spine of *Being and Time*. But by the time of the work on Nietzsche, it comes strongly to the fore. Belonging is transcendentally prior to will. The drive to possession is so intense that all its contraries are either expressed by Heidegger as negatives or else they are quickly discarded. As in *Being and Time*, you have to work very hard to find figures in Heidegger's Nietzsche lectures in which loss, privation, alienation, falling, distraction, dissipation, and chaos are not refused or restituted immediately through forms of belonging.

Before we turn to another assumption underlying his interpretation of will to power, let us listen to Heidegger's song of strength and power and mastery and resoluteness: "Because will is resolute openness toward itself, as mastery out beyond itself, because will is a willing beyond itself, it is the strength that is able to bring itself to power."[138] The pleasure he takes in the crescendo of intensifications is unmistakable, even if this isn't his pleasure he is describing but Nietzsche's, as he sees it, and even if he doesn't take this power talk over wholesale, this mood and this power-hungry rhetoric does mark a limit point of Heidegger's conception of willing in the late 1930s. Aware of this limit, Bret Davis opens a window onto Heidegger's period of "voluntarism," involvement in the Nazi Party, and enthusiastic embrace of the Führer Principle. "Resoluteness" (*Entschlossenheit*) in *Being and Time* we may suspect at times belongs to a misdirected, conservative revolutionarism; Davis shows how this figure gets expanded, deepened, and given a source in Schelling's text on human freedom, and then reaches a dangerous climax in Heidegger's inaugural address as rector of Freiburg University.[139] Davis also outlines the route along which Heidegger then retreats from the will, and how "dominance" soon comes to be associated with the ills of the modern age, a process of cultural critique that is undoubtedly already taking place across the Nietzsche lectures, but which intensifies and becomes most explicit after the war. As an example of this, look at the astounding turnaround in the statement made by the youth in Heidegger's "Evening Conversation in a Russian Prisoner of War Camp Between a Younger and an Older Man". "Maybe," the youth tells the older man, "maybe the will is itself actually the evil thing."[140]

A position closer to Kafka (and farther from Heidegger's Nietzsche) is hard to imagine. Davis contends that arriving at a frame of mind in which such an insight was possible cost Heidegger much time and thought and many "turns" in his commitments, not to mention also downturns in his friendships and his reputation.[141] Non-willing may be the major weapon with which the postwar Heidegger tries to slay the Heidegger of the 1930s. It would have to be a self-overcoming too, just as much as it is a protest against the era of *Machenschaft* and domination that he comes to think has eclipsed being and the question of being. Heidegger apprehends—Davis localizes the event of this apprehension between the third and fourth Nietzsche courses[142]—that the forgetting of being was never innocent. Being had been forced aside by willing, indeed by force, and his own accentuation of willing, the pragmatic side of his early thought, had been fully contaminated by this same bullying force and forcefulness. Being, and thus also human being in its essential ontological openness, would have to be more like not-willing or some fundamental motive unrelated to the will, a non-willing.

Proceeding once again by way of conceptual distinctions, in a "conversation" first written down in 1944–45 and then condensed and abbreviated more than a decade later for publication in the volume published under the name *Gelassenheit*, Heidegger separates "willing not to will" from "not willing at all, outside the will." We should assume, knowing Heidegger's liking for consistency, mainly conceptual consistency but often also performative consistency, an effect he preserves sometimes at a rather high cost to individual concepts, we should assume that the presentation of this distinction in a "conversation" is an effort to present not-willing without the appearance of an authorial will. One of the participants expresses the status of the conversation that takes place beyond will and power as "this restless to and fro between yes and no," and this should be understood not as intellectual indifference but as a

way to circumvent the two options, willing (yes) and willing not (no).[143]
Affirmation and rejection are minor acts of domination. Between a scientist (the translators' rendering of *Forscher*), a scholar (*Gelehrter*), and a
teacher (*Lehrer*, replacing *ein Weiser* in the original conversation written
in 1944–45), the matter of not willing takes shape without saying yes or
no, that is, in a milieu not dominated by anyone, in an interval between
individual wills that is not agonic, where no one has ultimate authority,
in the main because the scene is not an encounter between two wills, as,
for example, Socratic dialogues often were.

Lasciate ogne volontà . . . ! Abandon the will, all ye who enter here!
This imperative, hard as it is to imagine how it could be carried out, is
Kafka's. We ought to let the differences between Kafka and Heidegger
emerge now by making a list, and exemplify the differences with quotations from "Conversation on a Country Path," a somewhat foreshortened
translation of the German "Zur Erörterung der Gelassenheit: Aus einem
Feldweggespräch über das Denken" in *Gelassenheit*, published in 1959.

> **First difference:** the imperative. Kafka enjoins "don't wait." The Heideg-
> gerian ecstasis, the persona "teacher" admonishes in stark contrast "wait!"
>
> TEACHER   . . . perhaps the nature of thinking we are seeking is fixed in re-
> leasement [Gelassenheit].
> SCIENTIST With the best of will, I cannot re-present to myself this nature
> of thinking.
> TEACHER Precisely because this will of yours and your mode of thinking as
> re-presenting prevent it.
> SCIENTIST But then, what in the world am I to do?
> SCHOLAR I am asking myself that too.
> TEACHER We are to do nothing but wait.[144]

Thinking as willing—spontaneity, representation, inner perception, apperception, consciousness, intentional structure—has led us to narrow
our manner of being to forms of domination. A special sort of disposition
or act can save us, *Gelassenheit*, translated in this edition as "releasement."
And still, the translation doesn't take a clear stand on the most important
question: what kind of act is *Gelassenheit* and is it an act at all? However
it should be translated, it corresponds, as the scientist's plaintive question
indicates, to a not-doing, interpreted at first by the teacher as "waiting."

To understand the not willing or non-willing implied here, we have to
explore the word and concept *lassen*. It is a verb, no doubt, but it should

have an odd effect for a verb, if it can do what it proposes, that is, "to let and to leave," if it can invite another verb to action by a sort of inaction on its part. Linguistically, it yields its verbal force to another word, and so it is hard to pinpoint what action or even what passion corresponds to the phenomenon of *lassen*. It seems to stand at a limit of what we usually understand by a verb, at the limit of what we usually do or think we can do, and at the limit, perhaps also, of what words can do for us or to us.

This is the word in *Being and Time*, in the key methodological section on the meaning of phenomenology, §7, through which Heidegger describes the apophantic operation of language. "Der λόγος läßt sehen (φαίνεσθαι) . . . "[145] The logos is the instrument of a "pure" letting-be-seen.[146] In 1944–45, and again in the later redaction and publication in 1959, Heidegger reaches back to the *Sehenlassen*, the letting be seen, as much as to the *bewenden lassen* of inner-worldly beings, the letting ready-to-hand things turn toward each other, which operates prior to purposive activities in the workaday world.[147] He reaches back for these but now he has to make what was implicit in these usages explicit. In reaching back, he also takes command of that very facet of *lassen* that marked it as silent, operative, unthematized and nonetheless a very powerful word in *Being and Time*, more powerful for its *zuhandenen* quality than if it had been brought under the theoretical gaze there. *Lassen* operates in 1926–27 under a prohibition: it is never to be confused with *verlassen or überlassen*, abandonment or surrendering.[148] Heidegger leans toward letting and away from leaving, in other words. The double meaning is another curious conceptual distinction.[149] Heidegger definitely prefers one of its parts. He prefers *lassen* as an *intentio*, a letting of something, a granting of permission to do something, a certification of a distinction, a sanctioning, and as such an empowerment over something, even we might say with a trace of willing and domination still at work in it. This is because *lassen* as letting signifies the removal of a restriction, and this links *lassen* with the rhetoric of delimitation, horizoning, deconcealment, truthing, and will. Moreover, *lassen* is not merely synonymous with deconcealment, the opening of access to a thing or the opening of a world; it is that and yet it is also much more technical and you might say fundamental for the argument. What letting lets in, lets through, and lets loose on the world is deconcealment itself, the structure of world, the phenomeno-hermeneutic as such; not just a phenomenon but phenomenality itself comes forward in it. *Being and Time* already says: "*Lassen* means therefore: to allow/admit into [*zulassen*], give, hand to and suffice [*reichen*], send, let-belong [*gehören-lassen*]. In and through this *Lassen* is presencing/property [*Das Anwesen*] let in [*zugelassen*] where it belongs."[150]

It is time for the *lassen* to come forward. Things can be encountered, our way of encountering can be encountered, world as a network of these ways of meaningful activity can be encountered, but encountering, presencing/property, the being of *Dasein* has to be . . . let.

> **Second difference**: Heideggerian letting is not dominance; yet it is still a conduit for power, for ability, a *können*. This fact doesn't change between 1927 and 1959.

> SCHOLAR We can hardly come to releasement more fittingly than through an occasion of letting ourselves in [*durch eine Veranlassung zum Sicheinlassen*].[151]

The habitual avoidance of *verlassen* (abandoning, letting go, giving up) in 1926–27 is anything but abandoned in the *Veranlassung* (inducing, instigating, provoking) and *einlassen* (letting in) in 1944–45/1959 and the *zulassen* (admitting, giving permission to) in 1962, in the talk "Time and Being." The reflexive character of *Sicheinlassen*, letting yourself in, reminds us of the metaphysically powerful reflexive willing to will which Heidegger makes the center of Nietzsche's various meanings of willing. The conversation on the country path goes on to describe how "letting" is both a path and a movement, not a rest, a rest at times but only for a time, never absolute rest, rather a waiting, and waiting—it is easy to see waiting as a path, as *the* path to the open, because in waiting we grow powerful by being slowly de-hindered, let in, granted access, having our limitations lifted with respect to something.

> **Third difference**: if there is a yield in Heidegger it is a yield only in the productive sense; withdrawal gives way almost immediately to productivity. Letting lets in to something. If there is a yield in Heidegger, it is a "giving to" with a corresponding "taking" rather than a "giving up."

> SCIENTIST Finally I must now go back and ask, how far is it really releasement [*Gelassenheit*] into which I tried to let myself?
> SCHOLAR This question causes us great embarrassment.[152]

This is an embarrassing question: have we arrived, the scientist asks, at *Gelassenheit* when we ourselves have "let" ourselves into it? Can this way of being be brought about by the "self-controlled movement" mentioned by the ape in "A Report to an Academy"? The suggestion here is that *Sicheinlassen* letting oneself in to this special form of laxity may be at odds with the laxity. The scientist hints that there is already too much will. In *Gelassenheit* we are possessed by another, by the world. The stance is surely different: we do not take a resolute position—we are not *entschlossen*—but we also cannot "try" to let, we can only let ourselves, and with this "can" the residue of willing in letting becomes apparent.[153]

> **Fourth difference**: "letting" inverts the order of belonging, from taking ownership of the world (*Being and Time*) to being owned by the world (*Gelassenheit*), and nevertheless it does not yet exit the zone of belonging. Even being-owned now has to be shown to belong to us.

> SCHOLAR In fact (supposing that it is waiting which is Essential [sic], that is, all-decisive), waiting upon something [*warten auf etwas*] is based on our belonging in that upon which we wait [*daß wir in das gehören, worauf wir warten*].[154]

We belong to—this means equally: it is ours. *Lassen* is just the kind of thing that Heidegger was looking for in state of being or mood (*Befindlichkeit*) and speech (*Rede*), and if it suits us in "care" itself, then later in the will, and in "thinking." Heidegger was looking for a general milieu of belonging in which one could accept a place in a larger zone of belonging without overpowering that zone or things in it. Being let, having a "letting" attitude, welcomes a thing greater than any individual involvement; letting allows me, without the paradoxes and, truth be told, the emptiness of "Jemeinigkeit" (always-mine-ness), "Eigentlichkeit" (owningness), or "Entschlossenheit" (resoluteness), to be possessed by the horizon, to be seized by the world, to gain access to the worlding of world over and beyond my narrowness. Letting leaves the individual will behind, though still for the sake of belonging. At this point it seems as if Heidegger has managed to rid himself of domination while remaining gripped by belonging.

But the domination comes back. The tension in Heidegger's thought can only be called schizoid, where *Verfallenheit* can be modified and at the same time it can never be fully overcome, where disowningness can be owned, and yet dissipation and distraction are still the main marks of me. This schizoid tension plaques the desire to be rid of willing and no doubt has deep roots in either Heidegger's personality or his project or both. And then, as if his thinking had a mind of its own, as if it wished to keep traveling onward even after the destination—*Gelassenheit*—had been reached, in Heidegger's 1962 lecture "Zeit und Sein" ("Time and Being") belonging encounters its "own" counterforce. "Leaving" comes back to haunt the "letting" in its essential characteristic: owning. Possessiveness itself becomes schizoid. The specter of disowning arises again, though in a much more central and virulent way than it did in *Being and Time*. In the discussion of the event—*das Ereignis*—the issue of "expropriating" [*enteignen*] arises almost perforce, and also without any real conceptual resolution.

The lecture "Zeit und Sein" is something like the last blow in the struggle, internal to Heidegger's thinking, between willing and not-willing or the non-will. It is also the moment where the pseudo-distinction between wishing and willing is abandoned and the real distinction at issue is taken up with full force. Now the distinction between willing and non-willing or not willing takes its most refined form—as a conceptual struggle between appropriation and expropriation, words that roughly translate *ereignen* and *enteignen*. All the reticence and circumlocution and problem-setting of the dialogue on the country path are now gone. As unfailing as his ear is for the colors of rhetoric, Heidegger excuses the inconsistency of the performance of the lecture with the contents of the lecture in this way: "The lecture's risk lies in the fact that it speaks in propositional statements about something essentially incommensurable with this kind of saying."[155] That may be true—the saying of these formulas may not be a "letting" saying. And yet he feels some need for apodictic speech. Heidegger not only gives the lecture this way but openly and obviously revels in the formulation of these utterances, in a style one could only call the greedy hoarding of truths. In one of these formulations, the inner belonging—I don't know what else to call it—of appropriating and expropriating is expressed in the strongest terms possible. "Appropriation withdraws what is most fully its own from boundless unconcealment. Thought in terms of Appropriating, this means: it expropriates itself of itself. Expropriation [*Enteignis*] belongs to Appropriation [*Ereignis*] as such. By this expropriation, Appropriation does not abandon itself [*gibt das Ereignis sich nicht auf*]—rather it conserves what is its own [*sein Eigentum*]."[156] A more conspicuous, unyielding, categorical and final-sounding statement is hard to imagine. The statement avers: *enteignen* belongs to *ereignen*. And although we know that *Ereignis* is often translated as "event," we also know Heidegger is interested in the morphology of the German word, which implies something that is appropriated, taken possession of, had and owned. "Appropriation" is the dominant connotation, and the translation exploits this. "Expropriation" is subordinate to it, works in its service, in order to enhance its operation. The figure of *Enteignis* remains at a disadvantage in the sentence, although Heidegger does not remark on this. The sentence is about the appropriative event, its proper "self" and the ways in which it loses nothing through expropriation. The scientist's embarrassment about whether, through the will, he had actually entered into *Gelassenheit* is not in evidence. That dialogue and its ambivalences is left far behind. The lecture "Time and Being" was followed by a seminar. It was left to the student who transcribed the seminar to note some unease about the rushed treatment of *enteignen,* and also to record Heidegger's response: " . . . we must never forget that expropriation belongs essentially to Appropriation. But this includes the question: Expropriation in what direction?" The student then remarks, perhaps ironically: "The direction and meaning of this question was not discussed any further."[157]

No further discussion by Heidegger of the intentionality of expropriation. Why? The arc of his reasoning hangs on this silence. Being, giving, the gift, taking ownership, appropriating, withdrawal, truthing—each of the concepts discussed in the 1962 lecture and expanded in the accompanying seminar marks a move away from his position in *Being and Time*, that being is the being of beings. These concepts move toward— the historical movement of being, which depends on being's withdrawal, on its *leaving* in order that being can be *let*. The opening of a world in an event shows precisely this: the belonging of an event to itself happens when being leaves. So he returns to *lassen*. The leaving in *lassen* is ontologically prior to the letting, just as, it may be admitted, forgetting is prior in *alētheia*, and disowning and expropriation are prior in appropriational events. "The sole purpose of this lecture was to bring before our eyes Being itself as the event of Appropriation," Heidegger tells his listeners.[158] Yet *ereignen* has an outsized but underacknowledged investment in its contrary, *enteignen*. Several times in the course of the lecture and the seminar Heidegger explicitly equates this evential pair—*ereignen/ enteignen*—with the important fundamental-phenomenological pair— *alētheia/lēthē* (truth/forgetfulness).[159]

The will that wanders through Heidegger's writings from the late 1920s through the early 1960s comes to a landing place, if not a destination, in a set of terms where, although the will is conspicuously missing, one of its companions or components still lives on, a concept that grounds the will's character of powerful world-opening out of a closure and holding back (*epochē*). The version of willing that lives on even after Heidegger turns away from the will is the event. Willing had always been a route to possession anyway. Now possession has come out from willing's shadow as its main intention. But Heidegger also sees here that appropriation has to emerge from and fall back into its contrary in order for there to be history. He doesn't say it this way, but he does recognize that the greedy, gathering appropriative movement has to carry with it its own releasement, some part of it with some give, otherwise it would rigidify and die. The give, as is its wont, threatens to balloon out and swallow up everything before it. Too much give or releasement, withdrawal or concealment, and nothing will have been given, opened, or deconcealed. And therefore: "Expropriation [*Enteignis*] belongs to Appropriation [*Ereignis*] as such. By this expropriation, Appropriation does not abandon itself [*gibt das Ereignis sich nicht auf*]—rather it conserves what is its own [*sein Eigentum*]."[160]

Conserving what is its own—*sein/Sein*—is the main gesture that we find in Heidegger's reading of *lassen*. Even his openness to the double movement of *lassen* as letting and leaving leaves out the third possibility, an extreme leaving, abandonment without conservation. And abandonment seems to be precisely his worry here. Appropriation never gives itself up.

> **Fifth difference**: whether it says "leave behind" as in suspend possession of a thing or "let" as in permit, *lassen* means to *remove a restriction*. Contrariwise, yield means to *cede to a restriction* by finding room within its fetters that does not belong to it, in Kafkan terms to be a servant, to enter a corner, not to touch your limits, not to be who you are rumored to be, not to mistake the image of death for death, which has no image but also no substance and no meaning, to pursue neither illusions nor the end of illusions, not to believe and not to wait.

40. Childish Measures

Everybody knows it isn't true but it works anyway, whether through the force of conviction or some other magic. An emblem of this strange power whose source is impossible to divine is the household deity. The little figurine seems to come with the power to divert attention, to make the family believe that the fault and the authority lies not with them but with the gods. Rachel steals her family's household gods (*teraphim*) and this causes such confusion that Jacob is able to escape with his flocks and his wives.[161] Instead of trying to recapture Jacob, his livestock, and his daughter, when he finds their camp, Laban searches furiously for the idols, without a thought for family or property (Gen. 31:33–35). The idols take over responsibility and the children are able to escape, and this is the best outcome. There are many stories in Genesis of children trying to evade fathers, confronting taboos and attempting, sometimes with success, sometimes not, to stay out of reach of paternal power, and we know just how central this aspect of familial power politics was for Kafka. After the prison dance of sons and fathers comes the wisdom of Rachel. It is not hard to see how remote Rachel is from Jacob's line in this arena. She doesn't sacrifice the son for the sake of the father or the father for the sake of the son; she doesn't need or want faith; she plays on the faith or quasi-faith of others in order to free the children. She makes good use of the fear of destruction, however, that has been sublimated into the protective god, the little figurine that shields the house from greater powers. With his tiny shield removed, the father is exposed to destruction, exposed, that is, to his own weakness. Rachel hides the figurine under her on the camel cushion and prohibits her father from looking there, saying she is menstruating (Gen. 31:35).

The question you are left with, once you think you know what yield means, is how to put it into practice. Practicing the yield is not possible where *prattein* is a transaction, a manner of procuring possessions, a mode of using a capacity or power. Because the yield has no direct effects—whatever effects arise around it are not due to it—it gives away even this basic, most natural of privileges, the right to be a cause. The yield does not do any work. There are, however, things that work for no reason, without any active principle or special powers or, indeed, without being in possession of anything. There are things that work even in total dispossession, a state which Kafka calls *Fröhlichkeit* or *Glück*. *What is more jubilant* [fröhlicher] *than faith in a household god*. Kafka proposes that this is because *it is an under-through beneath true knowledge and a childish and happy getting to your feet.*[162] A knight would leap; you duck down, crawl through, and get to your feet again happily, evading the obstacle. The next thought that comes to Kafka extends and clarifies the theological context of this slapstick. *Theoretically there is a perfect possibility of happiness* [eine vollkommene Glücksmöglichkeit]: *to believe in the indestructible and not to strive for it.*[163] The goal is the indestructible, but goals are the causes of suffering qua suffering. Faith in the indestructible can lead to happiness, he argues, but only if you do not strive for it. Don't strive! And don't wait! This is the impossible double imperative. They come together in another: give in! This is why the possibility of perfect happiness, Kafka writes, is theoretical and not practical. Do not strive is the right command, but it cannot be followed without breaking it.

In the current fanaticism for happiness, different from the fanaticism of forty years ago because our current fanaticism is directed first toward the knowledge of happiness, toward *finding out what happiness is,* it is taken for granted that the meaning of living is pursuit of the good, interpreted as the good life, interpreted as happiness, interpreted as satisfaction, interpreted as a minimum of dissatisfaction. Some may take issue with this interpretation of happiness, saying that it should not be understood as personal satisfaction alone but rather as helping others, or pursuing the good of the environment or world populations. Some may take issue still with the interpretation of the good as the good life, saying that the good may be bigger than the framework of domestic pleasures or the lack of wants; it might be political or historical, or intellectual, knowledge for its own sake. Some may already say that the good is not to be had through striving. Kafka sometimes says this and in this way he may sound like a mystic or a stoic or a Buddhist. At times he seems to say that the good consists in the non-activity of not-striving. And yet, it is exceptionally rare to find an interpretation of life, not only as not a pursuit, but also as not in want of the good, however it may be defined. "Good," Kafka argues, is always the fulfillment of a pursuit. In this way even Good "for its own sake" still involves pursuit, requiring an active will to purposelessness or virtue. Kafka's nearest accomplice in the rejection of the "good" may well be Nietzsche. In any case, an important mode of happiness without "the good" for Kafka is a child's glee at evading capture.

Faith in a household god gets around the good by creeping underneath it. The little god of the house is obviously not a solution to any grand paradoxes. A lowly undergod, remnant of a forgotten pantheon, mundane representation, idol, a god whose scope is limited to a single household, emblem of a single family's worry, a figment with little or no power, except perhaps the power to deflect a modicum of the divine will to destruction—the little contentment that goes along with it is nothing like perfect happiness. Furthermore, this faith is without belief; for no one believes that this little figurine can save their house. It is the strong message of the new monotheism that indeed it cannot. The figurine is a monument to ridiculousness, the childishness of incredulity, which is its good, a small burst of joy.

What is to be done?" with the yield. "How are we to live?" with yielding as a first principle. "How are we to act in accordance with yielding?" if one cannot enact, perform, do, or practice it. What would life look like or mean and how are we to think about not only the important decisions but also day-to-day goings on if we do not use power?

A type of happiness occurs in yielding, *Glück* interpreted as *Fröhlichkeit*. Leaving achievement, comfort, satisfaction, luck, and yes, consolation, aside, the believer in a household god, this almost-unbeliever, holder of a minor faith without certainty, is overtaken by mirth. Even Nietzsche's *Heiterkeit*, cheerfulness, can't approach this sudden glee, since the former belongs to the clear conscience of the Greeks, who are reported not to know the unhappy consciousness of the moderns. Untroubled Greece is a projection of that unhappy consciousness anyway— at times Nietzsche intuits that the whole construction of the Greek way out is a fantasy indulged in by those sunk deepest into the slave mentality.

You sidestep, tease, dress up, hide, drag your feet, sing, evade a parental summons, stay up under the covers with a flashlight, nap during lessons, ask again "But why?" and "But why?" and "Why?" until the questioner becomes exhausted, plug your ears . . . something trivial distracts you . . . you lose your train of thought. If we wanted we could imagine these non-acts as counterparts, under the aegis of yielding instead of acting, to responsibility, love, identity, obedience, learning, working, waking, daytime awareness, truth. You might imagine the modes of yielding practice as a set of antipodes to philosophical attitudes: instead of ethics, silly games and evasions; instead of epistemology, pretending; instead of metaphysics, excuses; instead of politics, diffidence; instead of redemption, a hideout; instead of truth, fibs.

A catalogue of gestures like this in Kafka's fictions could be useful. The earlier fictions, from this perspective, seem overly adult, but the later are rich in silliness. Georg Bendemann retreats into a corner, but it does not occur to him, or he is unwilling, to hide. Gregor Samsa takes everything much too seriously, although you could argue that he was already playing a hilarious game in being a bug, and before that a salesman. Karl Rossmann wants to play adult, although he is perhaps the only one in New York or in his family who would pursue this ridiculous activity. Joseph K. is humorless, which is a major lesson of *The Trial* and quite a foolish thing given the circumstances. The schoolteacher in the giant mole story "teaches" an incredible legend as truth. Scientists scoff at his tale, and their scoffing is proof of its effectiveness as an "under-through-beneath" the legs of the plausible. In "Der Bau" when the burrowing creature, probably a mole, constructs a "labyrinth" at the entrance to his burrow, even he acknowledges it is a lame trick. An invader would crush it immediately: it is made of earth. And yet it wards off the creature's fears and in most cases his enemies as well, and that is the real trick.[164]

It is not that these things are purposeless, or even that they are purposive without a "real" purpose; they are to be distinguished rigorously from "play." They may well be purposive, yet the purposes are all within the game; they are excuses, excuses to one end, glee. To keep this end in sight, the rules have to be changed frequently. "No one wishes to undertake as many reforms as children do."[165]

Every adult act has a childish counterpart. The act of accepting a call or responding to a name has the counterpart "Who me?" or "It wasn't me!" In saying "Here I am" (*hineni*), Abraham had forgotten his youthful "Not me!" This silly and incredible evasion of responsibility, deflecting guilt, is how Kafka envisions "another" Abraham responding to God's call. Kierkegaard "paints the monstrous [*ungeheueren*] Abraham in the clouds."[166] To think that the way to drag this theologoumenon out of the sky was simply to imagine another Abraham, "*Ich könnte mir einen andern Abraham denken*",[167] this is itself jejune. The *akedah* is full of metaphysical horrors and theological subtleties, but Kafka thinks he can skirt around them all, the Kierkegaardian ones and others, by thinking up a set of alternatives. He asks, first, who would say *hineni*, "Here I am," who wasn't already certain, by some other means, from an earlier or a priori event, that the call was meant for him. Kafka's Abraham says "Wasn't me," and because of this the binding of Isaac, indeed the whole logic of domination, liberation, and genesis can't get started. In no way does this settle the paradox or annul the absurdity of the sacrifice of hope for the sake of hope. It does, however, point out a misunderstanding on the basis of which the paradox comes to be seen as paradoxical. If God is absolutely distant, then the call is not for us. Kafka does not say that a God absolutely different could not communicate with us, and thus this call must be false; that would be too much of a theological challenge and would undoubtedly lead to a struggle with and within theo-logic that might end in the naïve topos of atheism, that is, in a renewed faith in a not-god. The impulse of a child to refuse the call in order not to have to live up to whatever it implies cuts quicker and lighter, in this case, than any refutation or anti-logic.[168]

Proof that inadequate, even childish measures can also be used for salvation [Rettung]. . . .[169] Thus begins Kafka's famous parable, often called the "Silence of the Sirens." To puzzle out the logic of the parable as if it were a riddle is already to have fallen into the sirens' clutches. A four-year-old doesn't understand, a five-year-old makes up an answer to the riddle and it works just as well as the true one, a six-year-old gives the most rational explanation in the world why there is no answer, a seven-year-old has better things to do . . . There is something profound in Homeric legend, all the more profound for not once betraying its celebrated naïveté. The profundity comes in the obvious difference between *mythos* and *logos*. And this difference is signaled in the form of Kafka's first sentence. For what kind of "proof" is myth, legend, literature—?

Odysseus's "childish measure" is to stick his fingers in his ears. "I can't hear you," says the child, when everyone knows she has heard, and still she is protected as if in a magic circle of the parents' . . . one can only call it suspension of adult criteria. This measure might be called: "the false defense against the real attack." It may also appear as the false defense against the false attack that everyone believes is real. With this measure, illusions are preserved on all sides, above all the parents' illusion of their own authority, and it is not even necessary that the childish actor know that she moves in a milieu of disingenuousness. *To protect himself from the Sirens Odysseus stopped his ears with wax and had himself bound to the mast of his ship. Naturally any and every traveler before him could have done something similar (except those whom the Sirens lured from a great distance) but it was known throughout all the world that such things were of no help whatever.*[170] It is noteworthy in this passage that the one who behaves childishly does so in ignorance of the world's knowledge. All the permutations of the parable, like the permutations of Kafka's "thought Abrahams" in his letter to Klopstock a few years later, run on the same

basic assumption: they are charitable reactions and sympathetic self-de-
ceptions, by the sirens and by the world, to the stupidity of his reasons
and the at least apparent naïveté of his actions. In the final but by no
means of course ultimate interpretation, Odysseus uses his own ruse to
keep the world spinning. *Odysseus, it is said, was so full of guile, was such
a fox, that not even the goddess of fate could penetrate into his innermost
part. Perhaps he had really noticed, although this can no longer be grasped
by human understanding, that the Sirens were silent, and held up to them
and to the gods the aforementioned pretense* [Scheinvorgang] *merely as a sort
of shield.*[171] Those who are subject to fate, *moira*, and to the other gods
depend on Odysseus's trick to hold onto their faith and preserve their
beliefs about the power of the sirens and the vulnerability of humanity.
This means several things. First of all it means that childish measures
are not only a tool for avoiding the struggles in which no one has good
reason to participate anyway; they are also, and perhaps this is the more
important outcome, the foundation of all beliefs in substantial divisions,
hierarchies, things. Whatever the object of our faith, someone, through
deviousness and trickery, keeps up the pretense on our behalf, so we are
free to believe in fate, as the parable puts it. Thus, furthermore, it means
that the only one with a measure of freedom is the deceiver who does not
need to believe or disbelieve. Without entering into the struggle between
heroes and gods, childish Odysseus maintains the pretense without divulging he is doing so. Kafka returns here by a circuitous route to the
second source of modernity, to a Greek Genesis with a Greek Moses,[172]
Homer's Odysseus, whose tablets give birth to a history of suffering—the
name Achilles is often associated in folk etymologies and by contemporary classicists with *achos*, "grief or pain," and the name Odysseus has
ancient and modern supporters for a connection to *oduromai*, "lament,
bewail"[173]—for the pleasure of the non-sufferers, the gods. In Kafka's rewriting, the legend of Odysseus becomes a legend of suffering that is only
real for its spectators, because it assures them of an ordered cosmos and
their place in it. Odysseus has his fingers in his ears but his feet firmly in
the chaos beneath the fictive song and fictive silence of the sirens. This
is presumably what Kafka means when he includes the parenthetical remark (*außer jenen welche die Sirenen schon aus der Ferne verlockten*). The
ones whom the sirens entice out of an absolute distance, the ones who
know nothing in advance about what the gods and the world expect and
so cannot pretend, have no place in this legend or in the logic of childish

measures. These are purely expedients and they only make sense from within the established strictures and power relations of this world.

"Who me?" and "I can't hear you"—both are refusals to use power in response to power acts, and thus they drain them of their effects. One is a refusal to be the one summoned, the other a refusal to react, but both amount to the same thing. Refusal is too confrontational: they yield but do not thereby acquiesce. Not taking possession of what is offered to you yields in such a way that a new modality enters the world. Let us call it the useful weakness of pretense, which is the main mode of childish activities. The reason childish measures work, we might surmise, is the costless delight they produce in those used to suffering. This would be delight in the fact that it is still possible for pretending to be victorious over reasoning and reasonableness, and that anything, even the most serious life and reason-threatening activities, may in fact only be playacting in essence—pretend events (*Scheinvorgänge*). This is part of the delight given by the thoughts as well—everything adult, the most adult—faith, being, death—can be shown to be pretend.

That said, the useful weakness of pretense has a particular temporal structure. Against all appearances, childish measures cannot be carried out by children. It is precisely the survival of those unknowing and ineffectively tricky attempts of children to avoid duty, pressure, violence, identity, responsibility, and so forth that makes them so effective. One can believe that a child would do this, but no one could believe that an Odysseus would. It is as unbelievable, to coin a phrase, as truth. The childish hero is more than a child, he is superstitious or in some way acts on superstitions, which should be rigorously distinguished from beliefs. This is of course a matter of history. A superstition is a belief that outlives its context and objects. It may have the form of belief, but its contents or rituals have become difficult to take seriously, at least in the dominant systems.[174] There may be people, groups, whose existence depends on these beliefs: it doesn't affect the superstition as seen from the dominant systems. It is as if it were a different belief, a belief within another belief, a counterbelief—*Aberglaube*, a word incidentally that is hardly used in Kafka's oeuvre. If we let this silence speak, it may become a thread that connects the early and late texts, and weaves delicate patterns in the thoughts.

What survives beyond its own age into another age—the Latin for this is *superstes*—later, in Luther, for instance, comes to mean "false religion."

At the end of the Enlightenment, it means cultic or unreasoning religion as opposed to moral religion.[175] The *superstes* has cycled through its uses as a critical term within and without religion; in Kafka it comes into its own as a phenomenon. "How superstitious these people are!" Joseph K. shouts.[176] He is led to believe, as I think the reader is, that acting like "these people" is to be avoided. How different things are in Kafka's treatise and, later, in *The Castle*. Odysseus allows gods and men to continue their little superstition, the credulity that their power is reflected in his actions. Kafka's Abraham refuses to believe: "He is afraid that he will, to be sure, ride out as Abraham and his son, but on the way will turn into Don Quixote. The whole world would have been horrified, back then, had it been looking on, but this Abraham is afraid that the world will laugh itself sick over him. But it is not being laughable in itself that he fears—though he also fears that, above all he fears that he will join in the laughter—but chiefly he fears that this ridiculousness will make him still older and more repulsive, his son dirtier, more unworthy to be really summoned."[177] What is here described as a fear—not fear and trembling; fear and withdrawal, yielding from belief—is this superstition, now become his salvation, his rescue (*Rettung*). Because of this small counter-faith he does not go to Mount Moriah. Perhaps he is saved by a burning suspicion: that one day the real Abraham will come along and show him to have been the victim of vain fantasies.

It is hard to say when exactly Kafka decided that the obviously futile struggle in *The Trial* was the problem, was in fact a huge hint to struggle better, and that his task would have to be counteracting these sorts of hints. This would come to involve embracing superstition, without in the least challenging it. It would require taking it as a belief without content, a tiny ungrounded fear that wards off the larger complexes of being, faith, and death. What do you believe in? Rabbits' feet? Perhaps the change occurred with the hemorrhage Kafka experienced that summer, or in the fall with the final demise of his plans for marrying Felice; perhaps it grew out of his ripening critique of patriarchy and his search for an alternative to nationalist and ethnic Zionisms. Wherever it emerged, it is hard to imagine *The Castle* as anything other than a lesson on how to accept the smallest, crudest, silliest, most outmoded conviction, in order to protect oneself from the larger beliefs that drive K. to distraction.[178]

Superstition is the ecstasy of old or small or discredited beliefs that cannot possibly be believed, and so they become shields against adult commitments, against anything as grand as faith. From one perspective, the milieu of *The Castle* is a wasteland of shattered faith, everyone grasping, in the aftermath of a second fall, for their favorite superstitions. It is a world, too, in which "faith" is only the greatest superstition, another relic of a medieval moment in which a count administered the state. K.'s mistake is to seek and to see true belief everywhere he looks, when all that is left is a ritual warding-off, a set of minor obsessions, fears attached to minor figures, gestures by which the castle, the whole idea of the castle, is kept at a distance, and so pushed toward oblivion. K. might doubtless have given up on his desires and yielded to his most risible impulses in accord with the "childishness that seemed to be at home here."[179]

Notes

Preface

1. A legend from the rabbinical tradition holds that the earth refuses to be pliable once, for the angel Gabriel who has been sent to gather it for God's project of making Adam. See Louis Ginzberg, *Legends of the Jews, Vol. 1: Bible Times and Characters from the Creation to Moses in the Wilderness*, trans. Henrietta Szold and Paul Radi (Philadelphia: Jewish Publication Society, 2003), 53.

2. Anthony Adler, "Labyrinthine Dances: Choreography, Economy, and the Politics of Gesture in Hölderlin's *Hyperion*" (MS), 200.

3. Friedrich Nietzsche, *The Gay Science*, trans. Josefine Nauckhoff (Cambridge: Cambridge University Press, 2001), 94.

4. Friedrich Nietzsche, *Ecce Homo*, in *The Anti-Christ, Ecce Homo, Twilight of the Idols, and Other Writings*, trans. Judith Norman (Cambridge: Cambridge University Press, 2005), 345.

5. Ibid., 124. Friedrich Nietzsche, *Kritische Studien Ausgabe (KSA)*, 6: 337.

6. Nietzsche, *KSA*, 4, 179. *Thus Spoke Zarathustra: A Book for All and None*, trans. Adrian del Caro (Cambridge: Cambridge University Press, 2006), 110.

Introduction

1. David Suchoff, *Kafka's Jewish Languages: The Hidden Openness of Tradition* (Philadelphia: University of Pennsylvania Press, 2012).

2. Iris Bruce, *Kafka and Cultural Zionism: Dates in Palestine* (Madison: University of Wisconsin Press, 2007), 33, captures the idiosyncrasies of Kafka's Jewish upbringing amid the Zionist, socialist, and anti-Semitic movements in Prague. For the crucial background, see chap. 1, "Kafka's Jewish Prague," 12–33.

3. For a description of the irony with which Kafka viewed religious practices, moods, and attitudes, see ibid., 88–91.

4. Spinoza's theological politics seeks to free politics from the grip of institutional revealed religion by substituting natural theology.

5. This position is related to what Christopher Watkin calls "post-theological integration," which he sees as a movement that follows, on one hand, "imitative" atheist writers (e.g., Feuerbach and Camus) who build on theological structures, concepts, and modes, and, on the other hand, "ascetic" atheists (e.g., Nietzsche and Derrida) who openly reject theology. The problems of theology identified in the Enlightenment and by natural science thus become surmountable "after God," that is, after the imitation of theology and its strenuous rejection. See Watkin, *Difficult Atheism: Post-Theological Thinking in Alan Badiou, Jean-Luc Nancy, and Quentin Meillassoux* (Edinburgh: Edinburgh University Press, 2011), 11–16, and esp. 114–21 on Nancy's *atheologie*.

6. Manfred Engel bemoans the critical oblivion into which Kafka's "Zürau Aphorisms" have fallen in *Kafka-Handbuch: Leben–Werk–Wirkung* (Stuttgart: J. B. Metzler, 2010), ed. Manfred Engel and Bernd Auerochs, 287. Engel attributes this critical lacuna to the texts' incompatibility with current research agendas, although without elaborating. Nevertheless, a few books focus on them, including Werner Hoffmann, *Kafkas Aphorismen* (Bern: Francke, 1975), a mildly interpretive text that takes a "religious" side to the *pensées* seriously; Sabina Kienlechner, *Negativität der Erkenntnis im Werk Franz Kafkas: Eine Untersuchung zu seinem Denken anhand einiger später Texte* (Tübingen: Max Niemeyer, 1981), a complex analysis of the negative epistemology of the thoughts; Konrad Dietzfelbinger, *Kafkas Geheimnis: Eine Interpretation von Franz Kafkas "Betrachtungen über Sünde, Leid, Hoffnung und den Wahren Weg"* (Freiburg im Breisgau: Aurum, 1987), a commentary organized by thought that almost completely avoids theology and religion in favor of a quasi-psychological and Feuerbachian-mystical "revelation and development of the authentic essence of human beings, which is still a secret to them" (42); and Richard T. Gray, *Constructive Destruction: Kafka's Aphorisms, Literary Tradition, and Literary Transformation* (Tübingen: Max Niemeyer, 1987), a reconstruction of a European aphoristic tradition into which Kafka's *pensées* are placed, showing Kafka's

shortest texts to be compatible with the "crises" of modernity experienced by Austrian authors from Musil to Rilke. Gray suggests a fascinating "hypothetical, experimental" (215) method for interpreting Kafka based on a principle of "the productivity of the inconclusive" (291), whose spirit I hope inhabits this book.

7. Shaul Magid, "Subversion as Return: Scripture, Dissent, Renewal, and the Future of Judaism," in *Subverting Scriptures: Critical Reflections on the Use of the Bible*, ed. Beth Hawkins Benedix (New York: Palgrave Macmillan, 2009), argues strongly for "subversive biblicism" as the origin of the Abrahamic religions and the substance of their respective Bibles. For Magid, religions function by means of texts that are largely self-contradictory and continually dissent from their own propositions. He advocates a return to the Bible as it was "before Judaism and Christianity made it seamless" (223). This is similar to Kafka's stance in his *pensées*, except that Kafka does not think that religion is strengthened by its inner self-subversion.

8. The patron saint of Prague philosophy, Franz Brentano, by 1864 already a Catholic priest, nevertheless took the Spinozan side in his habilitation defense in 1866. Brentano saw philosophy as antithetical to theology and its assumptions and method as akin to natural science. "Philosophy must protest against the presumption of taking its principles from theology and against the assertion that it is only through the existence of a supernatural revelation that a fruitful philosophy becomes possible." Quoted in Barry Smith, *Austrian Philosophy: The Legacy of Franz Brentano* (Chicago: Open Court, 1994), 29.

9. Here I follow Ritchie Robertson: "It would be misleading, therefore, to discuss Kafka's thoughts in theological terms, for he had no belief in God and hence no theology. Martin Buber's claim that he had a characteristically Jewish faith in a *deus absconditus* can hardly be reconciled with Kafka's own utterances. Still less is there any foundation for the strange notion, which crops up now and again in Kafka studies, that he had some sort of Manichean belief in an evil god. It would be more accurate to associate Kafka with Feuerbach's view that God, with his omnipotence, perfection, etc., is a projection of the human potential from which man is at present estranged." Robertson, *Kafka: Judaism, Politics, and Literature* (Oxford: Oxford University Press, 1985), 201.

10. Georges Bataille, *The Unfinished System of Non-Knowledge*, trans. Michelle Kendall and Stuart Kendall (Minneapolis: University of Minnesota Press, 2001), 166.

11. Jean-Luc Nancy, *Dis-Enclosure: The Deconstruction of Christianity* (New York: Fordham University Press, 2008), 177n15, credits Bataille as the "creator and sole user of the word" "atheology" and criticizes Michel Onfray for ignoring this important source.

12. Ibid., 18. We should nonetheless distinguish this "nothing" from the

"nothing" in Derrida's remark: "nothing gets decided at the source." Jacques Derrida, "Faith and Knowledge: The Two Sources of 'Religion' at the Limits of Reason Alone," in *Acts of Religion* (New York: Routledge, 2002), 74. Gershom Scholem's "nothing" (*Nichts*) of revelation might also be noted. In a poem he sent to Benjamin in 1934, Scholem writes: "So allein strahlt Offenbarung / in die Zeit, die dich verwarf. / Nur dein Nichts ist die Erfahrung, / die sie von dir haben darf." Cited in Walter Benjamin, *Benjamin über Kafka: Texte, Briefzeugnisse, Aufzeichnungen*, ed. Hermann Schweppenhäuser (Frankfurt am Main: Suhrkamp, 1981), 73.

13. Nancy, *Dis-Enclosure*, 26.

14. Ibid., 12.

15. The way Nancy turns the death of God and the end of metaphysics into the highest possibility is neatly described by Watkin in *Difficult Atheism*: Nancy is "faithful to something in Christianity that is deeper than Christianity itself" (40).

16. Felix Weltsch, *Gnade und Freiheit: Untersuchungen zum Problem des schöpferischen Willens in Religion und Ethik* (Munich: Kurt Wolff, 1920), 10.

17. Ibid., 13–14, 112.

18. The details of Weltsch's philosophical training at the Charles University in Prague and involvement in the Fanta salon are given in Carsten Schmidt, *Kafkas fast unbekannter Freund. Das Leben und Werk von Felix Weltsch (1884–1964)* (Würzburg: Königshausen & Neumann, 2010), 96–103.

19. See Martin Heidegger, *Metaphysische Anfangsgründe der Logik im Ausgang von Leibniz, GA 26* (Frankfurt am Main: Klostermann, 1978), 70, 277–83.

20. *NS*, 2: 55 (November 31 or December 1, 1917); *FKA*, 7.95. All quotations are from the 1992 critical edition, Franz Kafka, *Nachgelassene Schriften II (NS, 2)*, ed. Malcolm Pasley (Frankfurt am Main: S. Fischer, 1992), unless a reading of the 2011 Stroemfeld facsimile edition, Franz Kafka, *Oxforder Oktavhefte 7 & 8 (FKA, 7–8)*, ed. Roland Reuß and Peter Staengle (Basel: Stroemfeld / Roter Stern, 2011), is decisive for an interpretive decision. For readers' reference, both editions are cited. Since this is a reconstruction of the thoughts as they were written down, I generally quote and interpret passages from the notebooks, even if they have been crossed out at a later stage. However, since this is also an attempt to draw out the implicit and esoteric inner conversation of the thoughts, I sometimes emphasize the edited version, if the underlying idea is more accessible or more precise there. In the notes, the quoted version is cited first, followed by the probable date on which it was written down in the notebook, and then an alternate edition is cited, should the reader want to compare editions. Dates are deduced from Kafka's own notations in the notebooks, so they should be taken as approximations. Quotations from Kafka's *pensées* are always in italics; quotations from other texts by Kafka and from texts by others

are between quotation marks. The "Zürau Aphorisms" have been translated into English again recently by Michael Hoffmann (London: Harvill Secker, 2006), but the translations here are mine. All other translations from German are also mine unless otherwise indicated.

21. Nancy, *Dis-Enclosure*, 36.

22. Ibid., 55.

23. Ibid., 58–59.

24. *NS*, 2: 55; *FKA*, 7.95.

25. Zettel #50; *NS*, 2: 124. Compare the notebook entry, which is missing "in sich," *NS*, 2: 58 (December 7, 1917) and *FKA* 7.100.

26. One can associate the indestructible with the will, as does Robertson, *Kafka*, 200, on analogy with Schopenhauer. See also T. J. Reed, "Kafka and Schopenhauer: Philosophisches Denken und dichterisches Bild," in *Euphorion: Zeitschrift für Literaturgeschichte* 59 (1965): 165–66.

27. *NS*, 2: 139–40; *FKA*, 8.87.

28. Bataille, *Unfinished System of Non-Knowledge*, 152.

29. *NS*, 2: 76 (between January 22 and 24, 1918); *FKA*, 7.148.

30. *NS*, 2: 49 (November 21 or 22, 1917); *FKA*, 7.76.

31. The desire to work the earth was not special to Kafka. Another Kafka, his sister, Ottla, moved to Zürau to rent a house in order to work a small subsistence garden. Moreover, gardening as good work for Jews, even in the Diaspora, was a frequent topic in the journals Kafka read regularly. The first line of Davis Trietsch's article "Die Gartenstadt als Konzentrationsform," *Jüdische Rundschau* 25 (1917), 207–8, asserts: "The main task of the Jewish world lies in the area of organization and concentration," both of which one achieves best through gardening. Iris Bruce identifies Kafka's interest in gardening with his cultural Zionism (*Kafka and Cultural Zionism*, 167–69).

32. There have been several attempts to class Kafka's *pensées* in a traditional genre of writing. Most significantly, Gray in *Constructive Destruction* tries to show how they respond to and continue the tradition of European aphoristics. Karl Erich Grözinger, *Kafka und die Kabbala: Das Jüdische im Werk und Denken von Franz Kafka* (Berlin: Philo, 2003), 184, argues, with the same intention but a different conclusion, that the genre originates with the mystical "topoi" of Meister Eckhart and in the sayings of the Belzer Rebbe collected and translated by Kafka's friend George Langer. Grözinger goes on to compare Kafka's thoughts with the Maggid's *dicta*, passage by passage (184–95). A list of the different possibilities for the mysterious genre can be found in the *Kafka-Handbuch*, 287. In Franz Kafka, *Beim Bau der Chinesischen Mauer: Ungedruckte Erzählungen und Prosa aus dem Nachlaß*, ed. Max Brod and Hans Joachim Schoeps (Berlin: Gustav Kiepenheuer, 1931), 253–54, the editors insist that the "thoughts" are closest to Pascal's *Pensées*, and for more than stylistic reasons.

33. W. R. Bion, "The Psycho-Analytic Study of Thinking," *International Journal of Psychoanalysis* 43 (1962): 306.

34. What to do about the order of the thoughts and how to assess their varied intensity or "value," as he calls it, were questions that plagued their first editor, Hans Joachim Schoeps, to whom in 1931 some of them seemed not even worth publishing. See Julius H. Schoeps, *Im Streit um Kafka und das Judentum: Max Brod, Hans-Joachim Schoeps Briefwechsel* (Königstein: Jüdischer Verlag bei Athenäum, 1985), 55.

35. Gray, *Constructive Destruction*, 210, argues that we have to read the thoughts in such a way that "a single text or sub-set of texts are not taken as representative of the whole . . . the dynamics of the aphoristic group configuration is one characterized by counterpoint, one in which texts supplement, correct, retract, and contradict one another." He goes on to name "interaction and dialogue" as their internal modality and their external relationship to tradition. An allusive way of describing the selective, asymmetrical inter-attraction of thoughts to one another is as a "conceptual community" (213). Writing about the late story "Der Bau," Henry Sussman, in "The Calculable, the Incalculable, and the Rest: Kafka's Virtual Environment," *MLN* 127, no. 5 (December 2012): 1144–70, speaks of an "inventory of isomorphic interfaces and translations" (1151), which could just as well apply to Kafka's treatise in thoughts.

36. The focus on internal relations here differs entirely from the theory of "thinking" proposed by Max Brod and Felix Weltsch, *Anschauung und Begriff* [*Intuition and Concept*] (Leipzig: Kurt Wolff, 1913). In their derivation of thinking from perceptual intuition, thinking means making the inauthentically conscious—i.e., you think you have an idea present but really do not—authentically conscious, by turning your inner attention on it in the mind (170–71). Thinking occurs for them in a continuum of grades of consciousness, from inauthentic to authentic, distraction to attention. In short, thinking is a variable psychological attention-state (*Aufmerksamkeitszustand*) that takes place totally within the psyche (169). For an exposition of their concept of "ostensive ideas," see Arnold Heidsieck, *The Intellectual Contexts of Kafka's Fiction: Philosophy, Law, Religion* (Columbia, SC: Camden House, 1994), 41–43.

37. In "Geisterschrift: Kafkas Spiritismus," in *Schrift und Zeit in Franz Kafkas Oktavheften*, ed. Caspar Battegay et al. (Göttingen: Wallstein, 2010), Andreas Kilcher, who has explored Kafka's engagement with the spiritualism popular in his circles, says of the writing that emerged from a "psychograph," an instrument that purportedly recorded the speech of spirits: "The one who writes is hence no author but a medium, his writing happens not deliberately but involuntarily, and what is written is not narrative, but disruptive and extemporal" (226–27). This also describes Kafka's catching and scribbling down thoughts that winter.

38. Roland Reuß, "Die Oxforder Oktavhefte 7 & 8 und die Zürauer Zettel Zur Einführung," in *Franz Kafka*, vol. 8, ed. id. and Peter Staengle (Frankfurt am Main: Stroemfeld, 2011), 4n12.

39. The conclusion Reuß comes to about the meaning of the occurrent order is not supportable *ex negativo*. Of the numbers on the Zettel, he writes: "their significance is neutral with regard to weighting the contents, a result only of the history of its composition." This may be factually correct, but it is not correct to assume that the order of occurrence and the meaningful order have to be two different things (ibid., 5).

40. Franz Kafka, *Briefe 1914–1917*, ed. Hans-Gerd Koch (Frankfurt am Main: S. Fischer, 2005), 368.

41. Franz Kafka, *Tagebücher*, ed. Hans-Gerd Koch et al. (Frankfurt am Main: S. Fischer, 1990), 569.

42. Kafka to Felice, August 14, 1913, in id., *Letters to Felice*, trans. James Stern and Elisabeth Duckworth (New York: Schocken Books, 1973), 304.

43. Otto Neurath, quoted in Smith, *Austrian Philosophy*, 15.

44. Kafka, *Briefe 1914–1917*, 372.

45. Weltsch, *Gnade und Freiheit*, 170.

46. Ibid., 55.

47. Max Brod, *Paganism—Christianity—Judaism: A Confession of Faith* (Tuscaloosa: University of Alabama Press, 1970), 4. Kafka writes to Brod about his book: "At the same time I cannot at all say that I agree with you or better said [*richtiger gesagt*]: the sympathy with "paganism" that for you is wholly private, I perhaps wear publicly. In general, where you speak from yourself, I am very close to you; where you begin to polemicize, I often also catch the desire to polemicize (as well as I can obviously)" (August 6, 1920). Franz Kafka, *Briefe 1918–1920*, ed. Hans-Gerd Koch (Frankfurt am Main: S. Fischer, 2013), 285.

48. Pascal, *Pensées*, trans. Honor Levi (Oxford: Oxford University Press, 1995), no. 513.

49. Kafka, *Tagebücher*, 816.

50. See Gray's reading in *Constructive Destruction*, 195, of Kafka's "profounder skepticism" than Pascal's, whose terrible doubt was "mollified by [his] faith in the Christian redeemer" (196).

51. "Descartes had already established for himself the rules of the method. Among these one reads the second rule, to unravel every question to be investigated into as many simpler questions as possible and to move toward the better answer where appropriate. The third rule prescribes that order be maintained in the chain of thoughts, such that one begins with the simplest and easiest objects and ascends little by little to the complicated," Kafka's teacher Anton Marty writes in *Deskriptive Psychologie*, ed. Mauro Antonelli and Johann Christian Marek (Würzburg: Königshausen & Neumann, 2011), 6.

52. Pascal, *Pensées*, no. 575.

53. With skepticism, Ritchie Robertson notes that "the system of thought that can be pieced together from Kafka's aphorisms" is just that, piecework that stands outside the thoughts themselves (Robertson, *Kafka*, 198).

54. There are two potential pitfalls to considering the composition of the thoughts significant for understanding them; one is formalism and the other is thematism. The latter asks the question how the "fragments" relate to one another thematically. Does a passage continue the previous passage's theme or does it diverge from it? In essence this is also a formalism, since it asks whether there is "coherence" or "continuity," and so in effect there is only one pitfall: formalism. One mark symbolizes this pitfall: the horizontal line that Kafka begins to use in the small notebooks, the *Oktavhefte*, and which becomes more frequent and more furious as the writing of the thoughts goes on. In order to discuss the marks—as lines, demarcations, separators, borders—we already have to presume an aesthetic schema to which we are committed: marks do this or that, mean thus. Interpreting the marks as interruptions, making the main concern a question of continuity, belies a general longing that infuses these traditional aesthetic categories. Discontinuity, it should go without saying, only makes sense with reference to a continuum.

55. *NS*, 2: 31 (October 19, 1917); *FKA*, 7.12.

56. To a great extent what Werner Hamacher writes about Kafkan parables in his interpretation of Walter Benjamin's sayings about them is also true of Kafka's *pensées*: "They are preparers and hinderers at the same time—and they prepare by hindering" (294). This means that it is to be expected that they produce a stop in thought, and that this stop is valuable for its own sake. Werner Hamacher, "Die Geste im Namen: Benjamin und Kafka," in *Entferntes Verstehen: Studien zu Philosophie und Literatur von Kant bis Celan* (Frankfurt am Main: Suhrkamp, 1998).

57. *NS*, 2: 31 (October 19, 1917); *FKA*, 7.12.

58. Friedrich Nietzsche, *The Birth of Tragedy and other Writings*, trans. Ronald Speirs (Cambridge: Cambridge University Press, 1999), 12.

59. Pascal, *Pensées*, no. 33.

60. Martin Luther, "The Fourteen Consolations," in *Luther's Works*, vol. 42, ed. Martin O. Dietrich (Philadelphia: Fortress Press, 1969), 124.

61. *NS*, 2: 31 (October 19, 1917); *FKA*, 7.12.

62. For all his traditionalism, Max Brod insists that Kafka was opposed to the consolatory aspects of religion. This was part of Brod's response to Hans-Joachim Schoeps and the theology of crisis that the latter adopted from Barth and ultimately from Kierkegaard. On the one hand, Brod pushed Kafka to read Kierkegaard and interprets his atheological thoughts as Kierkegaardian (as Hans-Joachim Schoeps does later, writing: "All of those for whom the fig-

ure of Kierkegaard means something should not pass by their contemporary Kafka" [cited in *Im Streit um Kafka und das Judentum*, ed. Julius H. Schoeps, 36]); on the other hand, Brod rejected the idea that theology could be a balm for the wounds of war, as it was in Gogarten, Barth, and Tillich. Max Brod, *Über Franz Kafka* (Frankfurt am Main: Fischer, 1966), 158. On the responses of Protestant theologians to the death of God issue and the modernists' crisis mentality, see John H. Smith, chap. 8, "Dialectical Theology," in *Dialogues Between Faith and Reason: The Death and Return of God in Modern German Thought* (Ithaca, NY: Cornell University Press, 2011), where the discussion of Barth makes clear how important time as "falling" is to these thinkers (223–25).

63. *NS*, 2: 83 (February 4, 1918); *FKA*, 8.15. Cf. Zettel no. 97. The passages about suffering in the New Testament that Kafka probably had in mind are listed in Bertram Rohde, *Studien zu Franz Kafkas Bibellektüre und ihren Auswirkungen auf sein Werk* (Würzburg: Königshausen & Neumann, 2002), 114–20.

64. "The diversion is best effected through the Word, by which our present thought is turned from the thing that moves us at the present moment to something that is either absent or does not move us at the moment" (*Luther*, "*Fourteen Consolations*," 124).

65. Kafka, *Tagebücher*, 858.

66. *NS*, 2: 31 (October 19, 1917); *FKA*, 7.12.

67. Ibid.

68. Kafka, *Tagebücher*, 851.

69. On Kafka's numerous encounters with Bibles and on the edition of the Luther translation he most likely worked with, see the Introduction to Rohde, *"Und blätterte ein wenig in der Bibel"* (20–31). Rohde reminds us in many places how central motifs from the New Testament also were to Kafka in this period, and how thoroughly forgotten nominally Christian topoi have been in Kafka criticism.

70. Kafka, *Tagebücher*, 1063. See discussion of this moment in Bruce, *Kafka and Cultural Zionism*, 74–77.

71. E.g., Anon., "Eine Erklärung der englischen Regierung für den Zionismus" (A Declaration by the English Government on Behalf of Zionism), *Jüdische Rundschau*, no. 46 (November 16, 1917), 1. On the ripple effects of the declaration, see Leonard Stein, *The Balfour Declaration* (New York: Simon & Schuster, 1961), "The Response to the Declaration I and II," 559–604.

72. An encompassing encyclopedia of Kafkan strategies, among which "producing confusion" is mentioned, can be found in Henry Sussman, "Kafka's Aesthetics: A Primer: From the Fragments to the Novels," in *A Companion to the Works of Franz Kafka*, ed. James Rolleston (Rochester, NY: Camden House, 2002). The strategies include: fragmentation, inversion, doubling, confusion,

proliferation, suspension, transformation, and inscription. Sussman calls these "art-games" (142).

73. The contention that Kafka "found the hypothesis of Scripture as revealed truth alluring," but had a tendency to "radical skepticism" is Robert Alter's in "Franz Kafka: Wrenching Scripture," *New England Review* 21, no. 3 (Summer 2000), an article on Kafka's way of reading the Bibles. Although the remark is not directly about the "thoughts," the contention that Kafka is writing "heretical midrash" is nonetheless alluring (8).

74. Walter Benjamin, *Gesammelte Schriften*, 2.3 (Frankfurt am Main: Suhrkamp, 1977), 1200.

75. Ibid., 1210.

Refutation of What Being Never Was

1. This marks a difference from Derrida's and Heidegger's concerns with "presence." The attributes of presence—some of which are hereness, nowness, immediacy, fullness, and exclusion of the distant or alien—are different in kind, though not perhaps different in their political-historical intentions, from the yield and its contraries. Contrary to the yield is obdurateness, an unwillingness to give way.

2. Few mentions does not mean few thoughts about or in philosophy. In addition to his philosophy classes at university and his participation in the Louvre Circle and the Fanta salon into the early 1910s and perhaps longer, Kafka took walks with Brod and his friend Albrecht Hellmann (Sigmund Kaznelson) between 1915 and 1917 where the talks, according to the latter's memoir of Brod, "Erinnerungen an gemeinsame Kampfjahre," in *Jüdischer Almanach auf das Jahr 5695* (1934–35), ed. Felix Weltsch, were of an "essentially philosophical nature" (167).

3. Belonging is also, in ontologies such as Brentano's that are essentially mereologies, the way one talks about how parts relate to the whole. See Arkadiusz Chrudzimski and Barry Smith, "Brentano's Ontology: From Conceptualism to Reism," in *The Cambridge Companion to Brentano*, ed. Dale Jacquette (Cambridge: Cambridge University Press, 2004), 201–4.

4. Feuerbach's *Das Wesen des Christentums* (Leipzig: Otto Weigand, 1848) is full of references to power and strength, *Macht* and *Kraft*. The reason for this is given in pt. 1, chap. 3, "Religion is the splitting into two [*Entzweiung*] of the human being from itself: it places God over against itself as oppositional being" (48). This means that God is "all powerful [*allmächtig*]; human being powerless [*ohnmächtig*]" (48). Feuerbach then goes on to show that all qualities attributed to God—e.g., understanding and love—are "mightier" than God. Since these are human powers, *Mächte*, the most human thing must be *Macht* itself.

5. *NS*, 2: 56 (November 31 or December 1, 1917); *FKA*, 7.95.

6. It is by no means an explicit theme in descriptive psychology, but belonging-to is implied in the intentional structure of mind. Objects are immanent "in" the mind and not alienable from its intentions. See Chrudzimski and Smith, "Brentano's Ontology: From Conceptualism to Reism" (204–5).

7. The rhetoric of belonging-to and having, and most expressly later the Latinate term "property," which became one of several philosophical technical terms for predicables, came to prominence as recently as medieval philosophy. In the *Categories*, Aristotle distinguishes between "being in" and "said of" as the main modalities of what later gets described as belonging with respect to a substance. Man is "said of" an individual substance, Socrates, for instance, but "man" is not in him, meaning a part of or constitutive of Socrates' being, whereas "tall" would "be in" him. There is no doubt that at points in their history these different ways of attributing within categorial thinking have been put in terms of belonging or possession. A thing belongs to a category; a property belongs to a substance. Aristotle does not directly use the metaphor of a master-servant relationship. Yet what is "being in"? On one hand, it is the correction to his teacher's teaching about appearances' "participation" (*methexis*) in ideas. "Being in" signals the rejection of an apparent world whose being is held outside it. Indeed, the opposite of "being in" is "being-outside" (*Categ.* 1a24–5). Rejecting an outside is as close as "being in" comes to revealing its affinity with belonging-to. Aristotle, *Categories and De Interpretatione*, ed. J. L. Ackrill (Oxford: Oxford University Press, 1963).

8. Martin Heidegger, *Einführung in die Metaphysik. GA 40* (Frankfurt am Main: Klostermann, 1983), 65.

9. See, e.g., the discussion of "participation" and "partaking" (*metexein*) that begins at *Phaedo* 100c5f.

10. See entry for ἔχω in Georg Autenrieth, *A Homeric Dictionary*, trans. Robert Keep (Norman: University of Oklahoma Press, 1958).

11. It goes without saying that *knowledge* is thought of as a possession in Plato. See *Phaedo* 75c6–7 and *Theaetetus*, 197bf, among many other paradigmatic passages. Here we are talking about ontology, where possession is less visible and less intuitive. Being is not thought to fly in from the outside, like Theaetetus's birds of knowledge. Plato, *Complete Works*, ed. John M. Cooper (Indianapolis, IN: Hackett, 1997).

12. Kafka is not the only one to find in everyday language a serious play on words holding the secret of being, the secret that it is equivalent to possession. In the *Phenomenology of Spirit* (1807), trans. A. V. Miller (Oxford: Oxford University Press, 1977), e.g., Hegel associates the verb *meinen* with the possessive adjective *mein*, to indicate that what I mean belongs to me and me alone, that is, that this type of possessiveness is the being of the naïve subject in subjective,

not yet dialecticized, idealism (66). Heidegger works in a similar fashion with many words, but especially relevant are the group *hören, gehören, zugehören, das Angehörige*. For a discussion of these puns, see Jacques Derrida, "Heidegger's Ear: Philopolemology (Geschlecht IV)," in *Reading Heidegger: Commemorations*, ed. John Sallis (Bloomington, IN: Indiana University Press, 1993), 174–79, 187–89. Kafka's *Sein/sein* joins an illustrious lineage, together with *meinen/mein* and *hören/gehören*.

13. Gabriel Marcel, "Outlines of a Phenomenology of Having," in *Being and Having*, trans. Katharine Farrer (London: Dacre, 1949), 157.

14. I take the protestations that substance "has no parts" as an indication *ex negativo* that this is precisely the way being looks when it is divided up in categorical thinking. See Arist. *Categ.* 3a29–32.

15. The word *hyparchein* is often synonymous with the verb *einai* in Attic prose, in Plato and Aristotle as well as elsewhere. As a verb it takes the same structure as the verb *einai* (to be): to wit, with a dative object it can be used to express belonging-to. It is not its semantics alone or its common usages that make it the word of choice to express belonging-to in certain situations for Aristotle. Perhaps it is its ability, as a secondary or tertiary word for being, to be separated out and become the marked term for the possessive aspect (held by Kafka to be primary).

16. Arist. *Categ.* 6ff. *passim.*

17. See Ackrill's note to 2a34 on 82 in *Categories* for some of the complexities of these different words and their potential interrelations.

18. It seems as though in Homer and Pindar, the word *hyparchein* is used to mean "to begin" something. See the entries in Autenrieth and Slater. In Plato *Crito* 45b1, Crito says to Socrates that he, Socrates, has (*hyparchein*) his, Crito's, money at his disposal. Here the verb communicates the power of disposition over something rather than a legal claim to ownership of it. At *Philebus* 33b, the verb governs the life a human being lives—an *anthrōpos* "has" this life, *hyparchein*. These are two of many examples of contexts in which the verb swings between a practical power over possessions without ownership and a more intellectual or metaphysical disposition. Frequently, however, *hyparchein* is used interchangeably with *einai*.

19. *Hyparchein* appears most frequently by far in the *Prior Analytics*, in propositions without a modal qualifier, assertoric premises. See the headnote in the commentary by Robin Smith in his translation of the *Prior Analytics*, 119–20 (Aristotle, *Prior Analytics*, in *The Complete Works of Aristotle*, vol. 1, ed. Julian Barnes [Princeton, NJ: Princeton University Press, 1984], 39–113). Smith also notes the high frequency of *hyparchein* to indicate the relationship of predicate to subject.

20. Aristotle, *Metaphysics* (Greek), ed. W. D. Ross (Oxford: Oxford University Press, 1924), 1005a15–18. *Metaphysics (English)*, in *The Complete Works of*

Aristotle, vol. 2, ed. Julian Barnes (Princeton, NJ: Princeton University Press, 1984), 1552–1728.

21. Arist. *Metaph.*, ed. Barnes, 1005b26–34.

22. Ibid., 1005b34.

23. Kant, *Critique of Pure Reason*, trans. Paul Guyer and Allen W. Wood (Cambridge: Cambridge University Press, 1998), 114.

24. Ibid., 131. Here is Gabriel Marcel on the dependence of containment on "having": "I should be told here that having is often apt to reduce itself to the fact of containing. But even if we admit that this is so, the important point must still be made, that the containing itself cannot be defined in purely spatial terms. It seems to me always to imply the idea of a potentiality. To contain is to enclose; but to enclose is to prevent, to resist, and to oppose the tendency of the content towards spreading, spilling out, and escaping" (Marcel, "Outlines of Phenomenology of Having," 159).

25. Kant, *Critique of Pure Reason*, B134.

26. Ibid., B131.

27. Ibid., B132.

28. Arist. *Nic. Eth.* 1103b.

29. Arist. *Categ.* 15b23, trans. Ackrill.

30. Ibid., 15b25. Franz Brentano notes the consensus among commentators that Aristotle eventually drops the category having, *hexis*, along with posture, *keisthai*, which it must be admitted looks like a subtype of *hexis*. See Brentano, *On the Several Senses of Being in Aristotle*, trans. Rolf George (Berkeley: University of California Press, 1975), 50–51. Later Brentano attempts to show that Aristotle subsumed *hexis* into the class of "motion," *kinesis* (108–9).

31. More than half of Brentano's *On the Several Senses of Being* (i.e., 49–148) is devoted to categorical being, but no serious examination of *hexis* takes place there.

32. Heidegger discusses the ways in which "being *belongs* to beings" (his italics) in *Basic Problems of Phenomenology* (Bloomington: Indiana University Press, 1982), 17–19.

33. See infra §39 in this volume, "Heidegger, Letting and Leaving."

34. Jacques Derrida, *Aporias*, trans. Thomas Dutoit (Stanford, CA: Stanford University Press, 1993), 38–40, 44–45, 59, 61, 64, 77.

35. Jacques Derrida, "Différance," in *Margins of Philosophy*, trans. Alan Bass (Chicago: University of Chicago Press, 1982), 26n26.

36. *NS*, 2: 34 (October 20, 1917); *FKA*, 7.24.

37. Jacques Derrida, *The Beast and the Sovereign*, vol. 1, trans. Geoffrey Bennington (Chicago: University of Chicago Press, 2009), 15, 42, 45, 50, 53, 56–9, 68–71, 83, and so on. The phrase "proper to man" is ubiquitous across the seminar, and it remains to be deconstructed.

38. Derrida, "The Ends of Man," in *Margins of Philosophy*, 121. See also 129n25 and 131–32n35.

39. Ibid., 133.

40. Derrida, *Aporias* 77.

41. Ibid., 76.

42. Ibid., 3.

43. Kafka, *Briefe 1918–1920*, 70 (February 2, 1919).

44. Adolf Damaschke, *Die Bodenreform: Grundsätzliches und Geschichtliches zur Erkenntnis und Überwindung der sozialen Not* (Berlin-Schöneberg: Buchverlag der "Hilfe," 1907), see esp. bk. 2, chap. 3, on "Community Land Possession and Hereditary Building Rights."

45. Ibid., 157.

46. Ibid., 157.

47. Ibid., 157.

48. *Jewish Study Bible* (Oxford: Oxford University Press, 2004), ed. Adele Berlin and Marc Zvi Brettler, 271. See note 24 on the meaning of Redemption: "In the Bible this term retains its literal, commercial sense, as in reclaiming a pawned item or mortgaged property."

49. *NS*, 2: 61 (December 9 or 10, 1917); *FKA*, 7.111.

50. *NS*, 2: 59 (December 18, 1917); *FKA*, 7.107.

51. Immanuel Kant, *Religion Within the Boundaries of Mere Reason*, trans. Allen Wood and George di Giovanni (Cambridge: Cambridge University Press, 1998), 71.

52. *NS*, 2: 58 (December 7, 1917); *FKA*, 7.100.

53. Kafka identifies the "suitcase story [*Koffergeschichte*]" as central to the novel and one of the comedic elements that proves it a "bald-faced imitation of Dickens." Diary entry from October 8, 1917, in *Tagebücher*, ed. Hans-Gerd Koch et al. (Frankfurt am Main: S. Fischer, 1990), 841.

54. Franz Kafka, *Der Verschollene*, ed. Jost Schillemeit (Frankfurt am Main: S. Fischer, 1983), 130.

55. Franz Brentano's assertion that "Every mental phenomenon includes something as object within itself" in *Psychologie vom empirischen Standpunkt* (1924), trans. Antos C. Rancurello, D. B. Terrell, and Linda L. McAlister as *Psychology from an Empirical Standpoint* (London: Routledge, 1995), 68, might be regarded as the "suitcase theory of mind."

56. Kafka, *Verschollene*, 11.

57. Ibid., 130.

58. Ibid., 14.

59. Ibid., 14.

60. Gesa Schneider, *Das andere Schreiben: Kafkas fotografische Poetik* (Würzburg: Königshausen & Neumann, 2008), talks about the photograph as a mat-

ter of feeling and as corresponding to Rossmann's "inner image" (83). Even in this psychological light it is a question of "possessing" the image.

61. Kafka, *Verschollene* 320.

62. On the centrality of possession in Walter Benjamin's political thought, see Peter Fenves, *The Messianic Reduction: Walter Benjamin and the Shape of Time* (Stanford, CA: Stanford University Press, 2011), 187–226. Fenves quotes Scholem's diary entry that records Benjamin's remark: "To every good, limited as it is in the temporal and spatial order, there accrues a possession-character as an expression of its transience." Benjamin is one of very few to see the intention of "possession" as inverting or at least repressing transience—and perhaps by *Da-sein*, Kafka means something like transience. Fenves writes: "With remarkable concision he [Benjamin] adds: 'But the possession, caught as it is in the same finitude, is always unjust.'" Kant, by contrast, proposes a *lex permissiva* that permits a wrong, possession, to be right for a time. And yet, Fenves argues, following Benjamin: "no order of possession, however it may be articulated, leads to justice" (ibid., 196–97). This line of reasoning was continued and extended in Fenves's Gauss lectures in the fall of 2006 on the Roman legal concept of *res nullius*, "no one's thing," the third part of which was dedicated to Kafka and a reading of "The Hunter Gracchus." To date this has been published only in German. Peter Fenves, "Niemands Sache: Die Idee der 'res nullius' und die Suche nach einer Kritik der Gewalt," in *philo:xenia*, 1st ser. (Bern: Urs Engeler, 2009), 123–205.

63. For a reading of this fragment in the context of the peculiar Roman legal topos *res nullius*, the thing of no one, see Peter Fenves, "'Workforce Without Possessions': Kafka, 'Social Justice,' and the Word *Religion*," in *Freedom and Confinement in Modernity: Kafka's Cages*, ed. A. Kiarina Kordela and Dimitris Vardoulakis (New York: Palgrave Macmillan, 2011), 107–26. In this interpretation, "religious" comes to mean the higher law by which members of a group lose their power to possess (122–26). This fragment can also easily be associated with the socialist-Zionist project, as Iris Bruce does in *Kafka and Cultural Zionism: Dates in Palestine* (Madison: University of Wisconsin Press, 2007), 170–73.

64. *NS*, 2: 105; *FKA*, 8.91–6.

65. Franz Kafka, *Der Prozess* (Berlin: Die Schmiede, 1925), ed. Malcolm Pasley (Frankfurt am Main: S. Fischer, 1990), 202; trans. Mike Mitchell as *The Trial* (Oxford: Oxford University Press, 2009), 107.

66. Kafka, *Der Prozess*, 222; *The Trial*, 117, trans. modified to reflect the vocabulary of the original.

67. Franz Kafka, *The Castle*, trans. Anthea Bell (Oxford: Oxford University Press, 2009), 5.

68. *NS*, 2: 78 (between January 28 and January 30, 1918); *FKA*, 7.159. Marcel comes close to identifying existence with "having," thus threatening the very

"existentialism" he wants to support by means of his critique of possessiveness. In "Outlines of a Phenomenology of Having," he recognizes the reciprocal lending of endurance by the possessor to the possessed and vice versa, calling it "a two-fold permanency" (162), and he also notes how precarious that permanence actually is, since its roots lie in desire and desperation. "I hug to myself this thing which may be torn from me, and I desperately try to incorporate it in myself, to form myself and it into a single and indissoluble complex. A desperate, hopeless struggle" (163). The primary thing one has, for Marcel, is the body, and this signals the dialectical inverse, that the body tyrannizes me in proportion to the dependence I have on it (164). You can see how this could lead to the kind of spiritualism and negative freedom of some existentialisms, crystalized in this statement: "Our possessions eat us up" (165).

69. *NS*, 2: 91 (between February 11 and 18, 1918); *FKA*, 8.39–40.

70. *NS*, 2: 90 (February 10, 1918); *FKA*, 8.36.

71. Job is also Gershom Scholem's recommendation for anyone interested in understanding Kafka, not just theologically, but at all. His early advice runs: "I would also advise you to begin any investigation about Kafka with the Book of Job or at least with a consideration of the possibility of divine judgment, which I see as the single object of Kafka's production" (Scholem to Benjamin, August 1, 1931, in Scholem, *Die Geschichte einer Freundschaft* [Frankfurt am Main: Suhrkamp, 1975], cited in *Benjamin über Kafka: Texte, Briefzeugnisse, Aufzeichnungen*, ed. Hermann Schweppenhäuser [Frankfurt am Main: Suhrkamp, 1981], 64).

72. *NS*, 2: 83 (February 5, 1918); *FKA*, 8.15–16.

73. Kafka, *Briefe, April 1914–1917*, 333.

74. *NS*, 2: 52 (November 24, 1917); *FKA*, 7.87–88.

75. Benedict de Spinoza, *Theological-Political Treatise*, trans. Michael Silverthorne and Jonathan Israel, ed. Jonathan Israel (Cambridge: Cambridge University Press, 2007), 7.

76. Kant, *Religion Within the Boundaries of Mere Reason*, 71. Kafka would have been familiar with the idea of moral religion from reading journals such as *Der Jude*, which were filled with references to Hermann Cohen and Kantianism. A good example of this is Jakob Klatzkin's article "Deutschtum und Judentum: Eine Besprechung," *Der Jude* 2, no. 4 (1917): 245–52. Written two years after Cohen's essay of the same title, Klatzkin's article systematically translates the theologoumena of Judaisms and Christianities (God, messiah, etc.) into "guarantees of the reality of ethics [*Sittlichkeit*]" (17).

77. *NS*, 2: 52 (November 24, 1917); *FKA*, 7.84–85.

78. *NS*, 2: 53 (November 24, 1917); *FKA*, 7.91.

79. René Descartes, *Principles of Philosophy* (1644), trans. Valentine Rodger Miller and Reese P. Miller (Dordrecht: D. Reidel, 1983) pt. 1, art. 7.

80. *NS*, 2: 93 (February 21, 1918); *FKA*, 8.48.

81. *NS*, 2: 134; Zettel no. 92. Cf. the notebook at *NS*, 2: 79; *FKA*, 8.4.

82. Kafka, *Tagebücher*, 788.

83. Perhaps this is why animals do not make gods for themselves or at least appear not to: because they have much less need for things.

84. For all Felix Weltsch's clear-sightedness about his friend Kafka's thought-world, he still believes that everything, including Kafka, takes its departure from "the ur-fact of humanity . . . from consciousness." Weltsch, *Religion und Humor im Leben und Werk Franz Kafkas* (Berlin: F. A. Herbig, 1957), 50.

85. Zettel no. 92, *NS*, 2: 134. Cf. the notebook at *NS*, 2: 79; *FKA*, 8.4.

86. Kafka, *Briefe 1914–1917*, 297 (April 22, 1917).

87. Franz Kafka, *Nachgelassene Schriften*, ed. Malcolm Pasley (Frankfurt am Main: S. Fischer, 1992), 1: 311.

88. Franz Kafka, *Drucke zu Lebzeiten*, ed. Hans-Gerd Koch (Frankfurt am Main: S. Fischer, 1994), 261.

89. *NS*, 1: 14.

90. Gabriel Marcel also wonders if the self might be a function of possession, like a kind of second body. "We should then realize that, contrary to the belief of many idealists, particularly the philosophers of consciousness, the self is always a thickening, a sclerosis, and perhaps—who knows?—a sort of apparently spiritualized expression (an expression of an expression) of the body, not taken in the objective sense but in the sense of my body in as far as it is mine, in so far as my body is something I have" ("Outlines of a Phenomenology of Having," 167).

91. Brentano: "To claim that our present consciousness does not belong to one thing, but that it is distributed across a multitude of things, means that it does not fully consist in a real thing [*in einem Realen*] or in a collective of real things. This, however, is completely inconceivable." Franz Brentano, *Descriptive Psychology*, trans. Benito Müller (London: Routledge, 1995), 14.

92. *NS*, 2: 81 (February 1, 1918); *FKA*, 8.8.

93. Kafka attended the lectures in the summer semester of 1902. See Barry Smith, "Brentano and Kafka," *Axiomathes* 8 (1997): 88.

94. Anton Marty, *Deskriptive Psychologie*, ed. Mauro Antonelli and Johann Christian Marek (Würzburg: Königshausen & Neumann, 2011), 21.

95. Ibid., 29.

96. Ibid.

97. Max Brod and Felix Weltsch *Anschauung und Begriff: Grundzüge eines Systems der Begriffsbuidung* (Leipzig: Kurt Wolff, 1913), 90–94, and see also chap. 3, "*Verschwommenheit* [Blurriness]." For an investigation of *The Trial* using the categories of Brod and Weltsch's analysis in this book, see Joel Morris, "Josef K.'s (A + x) Problem: Kafka on the Moment of Awakening," *German Quarterly* 82, no. 4 (Fall 2009): 469–82.

98. Marty, *Deskriptive Psychologie*, 30.

99. Ibid., 32.

100. Ibid., 35.

101. *NS*, 2: 32 (October 19, 1917); *FKA*, 7.16.

102. Ibid., 5.

103. *NS*, 2: 100 (February 25, 1918); *FKA*, 8.72.

104. *NS*, 2: 61 (December 9 or 10, 1917); *FKA*, 7.111–12.

105. One possible model for the multitude of subjects would have been the popular notion of an "inner diaspora." In the collection *Vom Judentum: Ein Sammelbuch* (Leipzig: Kurt Wolff, 1914), to which his friends Brod and Weltsch contributed, the Foreword by the editor, Hans Kohn, identified the master to the Prague Zionists as Ahad Ha'am, who taught that "Before any outer emancipation a liberation from the inner Diaspora [*Galuth*], from inner slavery must occur" (viii).

106. *NS*, 2: 66 (December 24, 1917); *FKA*, 7.127. Before crossing this thought out on Zettel no. 72, Kafka changed "can" to "must," making it read "so that it *must* be inferred" (*NS*, 2: 129).

107. This deduction is a step beyond the Brentanian psyche with its intentional manifold. In Marty's description: "inner experience shows in fact at the same time a manifold consciousness, and indeed manifold in a double sense: multiple objects at the same time and multiple manners of intentional relation" (*Deskriptive Psychologie*, 32).

108. In *Psychology from an Empirical Standpoint*, chap. 4, and *Descriptive Psychology*, chap. 2, "The Elements of Consciousness, " Brentano distinguishes a consciousness with manifold cognitions and modes of cognition from a Humean "bundle" of ideas with no frame.

109. *NS*, 2: 39 (October 22, 1917); *FKA*, 7.44.

110. Similarities between this parable and the theory of simultaneity in special relativity may not be fortuitous. Kafka most likely heard Einstein speak in the Fanta Salon and perhaps even knew him personally (Smith, "Brentano and Kafka," 86n16).

111. *NS*, 2: 35–36 (October 21, 1917); *FKA*, 7.27–32.

112. *NS*, 2: 78 (between January 28 and 30, 1918); *FKA*, 7.159.

113. Cf. Martin Heidegger, *Sein und Zeit* (Tübingen: Max Niemeyer, 1967), §46–§48.

114. John Zilcosky, *Kafka's Travels: Exoticism, Colonialism, and the Traffic of Writing* (New York: Palgrave Macmillan, 2003), analyzes Kafka's travel diaries, reading of travel narratives, and "vehement personal resistance to travel" (7), showing that foreign travel in Kafka's day tended to perpetuate the worst parts of the European oppressive imagination, and that he resisted this in many ways, one of which was by not traveling.

115. *NS*, 2: 84–85 (February 7, 1918); *FKA*, 8.19–24.
116. *NS*, 2: 57 (December 6, 1917); *FKA*, 7.100.

Better Weapons than Faith and Hope

1. Max Brod, *Paganism—Christianity—Judaism: A Confession of Faith* (Tuscaloosa: University of Alabama Press, 1970), see esp. chap. 7. Hugo Bergmann, "Die zionistische Kulturarbeit im Westen," in *Jawne und Jerusalem* (Berlin: Jüdischer Verlag, 1919), 12–15. Iris Bruce discusses Bergmann's sources for these ideas, Ahad Ha'am and bin Gorion (Micha Josef Berdyczewski), in *Kafka and Cultural Zionism: Dates in Palestine* (Madison: University of Wisconsin Press, 2007), 113–15.

2. Brod, *Paganism—Christianity—Judaism*, 181.

3. For this phenomenological reason, faith could not be dismissed out of hand in the way that Spinoza dismisses it in his *Theological-Political Treatise*, trans. Michael Silverthorne and Jonathan Israel, ed. Israel (Cambridge: Cambridge University Press, 2007), saying that it "amounts to nothing more than credulity and prejudices" (7).

4. When Spinoza writes "faith aims at obedience," he indicates the primary relationship of faith to power as opposed to truth (ibid., 184).

5. *NS*, 2: 58 (December 7, 1917); *FKA*, 7.100.

6. In "Outlines of a Phenomenology of Having," in *Being and Having*, trans. Katharine Farrer (London: Dacre, 1949), 159–60, Gabriel Marcel notes the transcendence of the *qui* of having over the *quid*. But this leads to a kind of concealment. "At the heart of having, then, we can discern a kind of suppressed dynamic, and suppression is certainly the key-word here. It is this which lights up what I call the transcendence of the qui. It is significant that the relation embodied in having is, grammatically, found to be intransitive. The verb 'to have' is only used in the passive in exceptional and specialized ways. It is as though we saw passing before us a kind of irreversible progress from the qui towards the quid." What Marcel is getting at here is critical. The sense of power moving in one direction, a one-sided domination of things, conceals the dynamic that makes it possible, which Marcel likens later to the Hegelian master-slave dynamic (163–64).

7. What is personal about this God? The term "personal" is equivocal, meaning potentially anthropomorphic or relative to a person. Most probably it recalls Luther's God, who is no less universal although he visits each person alone. This reading is strengthened by the letter Kafka sends Brod in August 1920: "You couldn't think the decisively god-like distant enough from itself, the entire world of the gods was only a means to hold the decisive factor away from the earthly body, in order to leave air for humans to breathe" (Kafka, *Briefe 1918–1920*, ed. Hans-Gerd Koch [Frankfurt am Main: S. Fischer, 2013], 285).

8. *NS*, 2: 66 (December 24, 1917); *HKA*, 7.124.

9. No doubt there are multiple affinities between Kafka's "indestructible" and Derrida's "unscathed" (id., "Faith and Knowledge: The Two Sources of 'Religion' at the Limits of Reason Alone," in *Acts of Religion* [New York: Routledge, 2002], 42, 48, 61, 61n16, 63, etc.). Yet what interests Derrida in this word—*indemne* and its etymologies—is its relationship to immunity and ultimately to the auto-immune reactions that a society undergoes and produces, in order, or so it thinks, to indemnify itself against destruction (61n16, 78–80). The difference between the two concepts can be seen in their negatives: for Derrida, it is imperative to think of a social unit based on the ability to be harmed, to be and remain vulnerable; for Kafka, it is imperative to think of a self and a social unit that does not lend itself trust through self-deception. Near the end of his essay, Derrida brings up the matter of trust, naming the "two sources of religion" (so many sources are named in the essay that we can only hear this "two" as a joke) "unscathedness" and now also "fiduciarity" (93).

10. See John 5:24, "He that heareth my word, and believeth him that sent me, hath eternal life."

11. See 1. Rom. 15:13

12. *NS*, 2: 49 (November 21 or 22 1917); *FKA*, 7.76.

13. Martin Luther, "Von der Freiheit eines Christenmenschen," in *D. Martin Luthers Werke: Kritische Gesamtausgabe* (Weimarer Ausgabe), vol. 7, ed. Paul Peitsch (Weimar: Hermann Böhlhaus, 1897), 12–38, Latin 53; German 24. English: "The Freedom of a Christian," in *Martin Luther: Selections from his Writings*, ed. John Dillenberger (Garden City, NY: Anchor Books, 1962), 57.

14. To mention not the least of them, Paul of Tarsus often talks of faith, *pistis*, as something that is had or held, often using the verb *echein* (see, e.g., Rom. 14:22).

15. See Rom. 1:15.

16. That Kafka's readings of Kierkegaard don't have exactly formative force on the thoughts is clear now, since although he announced his plan to read Kierkegaard in November 1917, he didn't actually begin in earnest until late February (see *Kafka-Handbuch: Leben–Werk–Wirkung*, ed. Manfred Engel and Bernd Auerochs [Stuttgart: J. B. Metzler, 2010], 284). Ritchie Robertson concurs with this conclusion (Robertson, *Kafka: Judaism, Politics, and Literature* [Oxford: Oxford University Press, 1985], 195).

17. Ernst Troeltsch, "Luther und der Protestantismus," *Neue Rundschau* 2 (1917) (Berlin: S. Fischer, 1917): 1300.

18. On the influence of Troeltsch's Luther on Kafka's thoughts, see Bertram Rohde, *"Und blätterte ein wenig in der Bibel": Studien zu Franz Kafkas Bibellektüre und ihren Auswirkungen auf sein Werk* (Würzburg: Königshausen & Neumann, 2002), 106–8.

19. Troeltsch, "Luther und der Protestantismus," 1321.

20. Ibid., 1302.

21. Ibid.

22. Ibid., 1318.

23. Ibid.

24. Ibid., 1315.

25. Ibid., 1314.

26. Ibid., 1313.

27. *NS*, 2: 49; *FKA*, 7.76.

28. Luther to Melanchthon, August 1, 1521, in *Luther's Works*, vol. 48: *Letters 1*, ed. Gottfried G. Krodel (Philadelphia: Fortress Press, 1963), 281–82.

29. Troeltsch, "Luther und der Protestantismus," 1309.

30. Ibid., 1325.

31. Kafka did not differ in this respect from Spinoza; indeed, they shared a project, though with vastly different sensibilities and results. "I resolved in all seriousness to make a fresh examination of scripture with a free and unprejudiced mind, and to assert nothing about it, and to accept nothing as its teaching, which I did not quite clearly derive from it" (Spinoza, *Theological-Political Treatise*, 8–9). It would likely seem to those familiar with Spinoza's *Treatise* that his skepticism of interpretation and his preference for the facts of nature (and where he does concede "facts" of scripture, he does so on analogue with the self-evident facts of nature) make Spinoza and Kafka incompatible (see ibid., 26, 45). Yet Kafka was as extremely literal as Spinoza and would have agreed that language was ineradicably polysemous. It is only that he thought nature was as polynatural as the *seme* was polysemous. And yet their literalisms differ in other respects too. "To formulate the matter succinctly, I hold that the method of interpreting Scripture [*sic*], does not differ from the [correct] method of interpreting nature, but rather is wholly constant with it," Spinoza writes (ibid., 98). By this he means that one can rationalize the confusing parts of scripture by seeing them as an allegory of the political situation of its authors, that is, as masking empirical facts. This is not what Kafka thinks. His literalism is more in line with Augustine, whose *Literal Interpretation of Genesis*, for all its claims to rationalize scripture, goes deeply into the confusions in the text. Augustine's unfinished work, a commentary on the minutiae of Genesis similar to Kafka's that breaks off at Genesis 1:27, is made up almost entirely of questions of understanding. The difference from Kafka would be that Augustine, when confronted with confusions in the text, seeks an understanding that makes the various assertions seem consistent with themselves and with each other. Augustine, *Two Books on Genesis: Against the Manichees and On the Literal Interpretation of Genesis, an Unfinished Book*, trans. Roland J. Teske, S.J. (Washington, DC: Catholic University of America Press, 1991).

32. Troeltsch, "Luther und der Protestantismus," 1310.

33. It seems redundant to say that this view is as remote as possible from Kant's Spinozan view of miracles : "If a moral religion (to be cast not in dogmas and observances but in the heart's disposition to observe all human duties as divine commands) must be established, eventually all the miracles which history connects with its inception must themselves render faith in miracles in general dispensable" (Kant, *Religion Within the Boundaries of Mere Reason*, trans. Allen Wood and George di Giovanni [Cambridge: Cambridge University Press, 1998], 122).

34. Felix Weltsch, *Gnade und Freiheit: Untersuchungen zum Problem des schöpferischen Willens in Religion und Ethik* (Munich: Kurt Wolff, 1920), 9.

35. Ibid., 10.

36. Weltsch writes to Kafka in November that he is in a dispute with Brod on this topic, to which Kafka replies "In any event I don't know where to begin with your remark about faith and grace and the divergence from Max or even from me" (Kafka, *Briefe 1914–17*, 367). The remarks on grace and faith in Weltsch's letter are reprinted in the appendix (ibid., 772).

37. Weltsch, *Gnade und Freiheit*, 12.

38. Ibid., 18.

39. *NS*, 2: 49 (November 21 or 22, 1917); *FKA*, 7.76.

40. *NS*, 2: 55 (November 31 or December 1, 1917); *FKA*, 7.95.

41. Weltsch, *Gnade und Freiheit*, 131.

42. Ibid., 74.

43. One point of reference for this kind of faith in the self and in the will is a famous section in Rousseau's *Emile*. The Savoyard Vicar spells out this faith: "I shall be me without contradiction or division and shall need only myself in order to be happy. . . . In joining my will to Yours, I do what you do; I acquiesce in Your goodness; I believe that I share beforehand in the supreme felicity which is its reward" (Jean-Jacques Rousseau, "Profession of Faith of the Savoyard Vicar," in *Emile, or On Education*, trans. Allan Bloom [New York: Basic Books, 1979], 293).

44. Weltsch, *Gnade und Freiheit*, 7.

45. *NS*, 2: 91–92 (between February 11 and 18, 1918); *FKA* 8.40–43.

46. *NS*, 2: 62, 70, 71, 81, 91–92.

47. An extreme thought of a time without transitions is outlined by Michael Levine in *A Weak Messianic Power: Figures of a Time to Come in Benjamin, Derrida, and Celan* (New York: Fordham University Press, 2013), 6–7, 29–30.

48. *NS*, 2: 65 (December 19 or 20, 1917); *FKA*, 7.123.

49. Kafka distances himself somewhat from the cheeriness of this thought when he quotes it in a letter to Brod on August 6, 1920 (*Briefe 1918–20*, 285) about the latter's book *Paganism—Christianity—Judaism*. Happiness, even the

actual kind, is doomed to fail. "The closest approach to your conception might be to say: There exists a theoretical possibility of perfect human happiness, that is, to believe in the determining divine principle and not to strive toward it. This possibility of happiness is as blasphemous as it is unattainable, but the Greeks perhaps were closer to it than many others. But not even this is paganism in your sense."

50. Kierkegaard, *Fear and Trembling and Repetition*, trans. Howard V. Hong and Edna H. Hong (Princeton, NJ: Princeton University Press, 1983), 41.

51. *NS*, 2: 93 (December 21, 1918); *FKA* 8.48.

52. Kierkegaard, *Fear and Trembling*, trans. Hong and Hong, 38 (cf. the version Kafka probably read: *Furcht und Zittern: Wiederholung*, trans. H. C. Ketels, in Kierkegaard, *Gesammelte Werke*, ed. H. Gottsched (Jena: Diederichs, 1909), 31).

53. Kierkegaard, *Fear and Trembling*, trans. Hong and Hong, 38 (cf. Ketels trans., 31).

54. *NS*, 2: 46 (between November 12 and 17, 1917); *FKA* 7.71.

55. See infra §32 in this volume, "No More Than."

56. Kierkegaard, *Fear and Trembling*, Hong and Hong trans., 36 (cf. *Furcht und Zittern*, Ketels trans., 30).

57. Zettel no. 1, *NS*, 2: 113. Cf. *NS*, 2: 30 (October 19, 1917); *FKA*, 7.8.

58. "I can make the great trampoline-leap through which I cross over [*übergehe*] into infinity; my back, like that of a tightrope walker, was dislocated and twisted in my childhood, and so it is easy for me" (Kierkegaard, *Furcht und Zittern*, Ketels trans., 30; cf. *Fear and Trembling*, Hong and Hong, trans., 36).

59. Following the more or less general latent Kierkegaardian reading of Kafka to which Brod also subscribed, Beth Hawkins identifies the position of the faithful as "this condition of separation, division, and rupture—what Kafka views as the human condition—that forms the basis of the kind of covenantal relationship that Kafka promotes" (Hawkins, *Reluctant Theologians: Kafka, Celan, Jabès* [New York: Fordham University Press, 2003], 35). She continues the Kierkegaardian reading of Kafka in her discussion of the "ethical aesthetic," in which God is a void (reading the thought on "truth" as a thought on "God") and human beings are obliged to decide on the basis of nothing how to be good with respect to it (see 57–65). A similar interpretation is offered by Walter Sokel in "Between Gnosticism and Jehova: The Dilemma in Kafka's Religious Attitude," in *The Myth of Power and the Self: Essays on Franz Kafka* (Detroit: Wayne State University, 2002), under the rubric of "Kafka's basic *religio*" (293). He takes the separation in the relationship to be a "paradox within the God of Genesis" (294) that puts human beings in a double bind: to wit, there are two laws, the law of a God that could communicate with humans and a law of God that can never do so. Sokel's doubleness is "the moment of God's

utmost estrangement from His world, prior to the Covenant with Abraham";
he calls it the "the proto-Gnostic phase or aspect of God" (294). Whether it
is covenantal or pre-covenantal, in God or between God and humanity, the
separation thesis is precisely what Kafka, in these thoughts, sets out to de-
bunk. Earlier, however, he might have found consolation in it. On December
17, 1913, Kafka praises "the beautiful robust schisms [*Sonderungen*] in Judaism.
One is given room. One sees oneself better, one judges oneself better" (*Tagebücher*, ed. Hans-Gerd Koch et al. [Frankfurt am Main: S. Fischer, 1990], 617).
An account of Gnostic-like strands in Kafka's oeuvre can be found in Stanley
Corngold, *Lambent Traces* (Princeton, NJ: Princeton University Press, 2004),
passim. The relation of Kafkan Gnosis to Nietzsche is treated in Corngold and
Benno Wagner, *Franz Kafka: The Ghosts in the Machine* (Evanston, IL: North-
western University Press, 2011), 151–76.

60. Friedrich Nietzsche, *Thus Spoke Zarathustra*, trans. Adrian del Caro
(Cambridge: Cambridge University Press, 2006), "Prologue" §3–§4.

61. *NS*, 2: 58 (December 18, 1917); *FKA*, 103.

62. Zettel no. 109; *NS*, 2: 139–40. The thought is in the form of a dialogue,
which is only implicit in the notebook entry, *NS*, 2: 102 (February 26, 1918);
FKA, 8.80–83.

63. *NS*, 2: 58 (December 7, 1917); *FKA*, 7.100.

64. *NS*, 2: 72 (January 20 or 21, 1918); *FKA*, 7.139.

65. *NS*, 2: 71 (January 20 or 21, 1918); *FKA*, 7.139.

66. A contemporary complement to Kafka's thought is Rei Terada's *Looking Away: Phenomenality and Dissatisfaction, Kant to Adorno* (Cambridge, MA:
Harvard University Press, 2009). Like Kafka in this thought, Terada is interested in the moral and affective effects of the distinction between a phenomenal world and a true world. Like Terada, Kafka does not pose this as a
problem to be solved, but rather as a staunch commitment in the history of
European thought. One could take the majority of Kafka's *pensées*, indeed, to
be arguing that "looking away" is the very gesture, the apprehensive-defensive
mode of perception, by which this division becomes affirmed in the first place.
Terada: "I try to dwell in the space before the acceptance of any perceived
fact, and hope by doing so to make available a different kind of epistemological therapeutics" (5). This is very close to Kafka's nonconsoling nonmethod.
The emphasis on "therapeutics" corresponds to Terada's view that phenomenal
prejudices are at base psychological, not philosophical. Kafka treats the issue
of dissatisfaction with appearances and the devaluation of experience as conceptual and linguistic. But the two are not far apart in their desire to stop the
fact/appearance machine once and for all. The endless swings back and forth
between *phenomenomania* and *misophenomenia* can be stopped, both seem to
argue, by acknowledging that givens, facts, and images are not a matter of de-

grees of reality, but rather are blunt instruments in social practices for affirming or denying certain power relations.

67. *NS*, 2: 82 (February 4, 1918); *FKA*, 8.12.

68. *NS*, 2: 91 (between February 11 and 18, 1918); *FKA*, 8.39.

69. *NS*, 2: 81 (February 1, 1918); *FKA*, 8.8.

70. Martin Buber, "Erneuerung des Judentums," in id., *Drei Reden über das Judentum* (Frankfurt am Main: Rütten & Loening, 1920), 61.

71. Ibid., 60.

72. Ibid., 90.

73. Ibid., 91.

74. See ibid., 15–20, "Das Judentum und die Juden," on "Jew-substance."

75. Ibid., 74.

76. Ibid., 79.

77. *NS*, 2: 34; *FKA*, 7.23–24.

78. Buber, "Das Judentum und die Menschheit," in id., *Drei Reden*, 52.

79. Ibid., 52–55.

80. Brod and Weltsch and other friends and Zionists criticize the progress idea in industrial capitalism but hold onto it for Zionism. Writing about Taylorism in "Zwei Welten," *Der Jude* 2, no. 1 (1917): 48, Brod likens progress to hell, and yet he is not willing to remove time as a medium for improvement in moral and political matters.

81. *NS*, 2: 57 (December 4 or 5, 1917); *FKA* 7.99.

82. *NS*, 2: 318–19.

83. Buber, "Erneuerung des Judentums," in id., *Drei Reden*, 79.

84. Ibid., 87.

85. Ibid., 102.

86. Already crossed out in the notebook is *human history is the second between two steps of a wanderer. FKA*, 7.24.

87. Zettel 6, *NS*, 2: 114.

88. Read inter alia "The Perpetual Race of Achilles and the Tortoise," in Jorge Luis Borges, *Selected Non-Fictions*, trans. Esther Allen, Suzanne Jill Levine, and Eliot Weinberger (New York: Viking, 1999), 43–47.

89. *NS*, 2: 34 (October 20, 1917); *FKA*, 7.23.

90. *NS*, 2: 104 (February 27, 1918); *FKA*, 84–87.

91. *NS*, 2: 62 (December 12, 1917); *FKA*, 7.116.

92. Richard T. Gray in contrast attributes to Kafka a belief in "an endless process of change" (Gray, *Constructive Destruction: Kafka's Aphorisms, Literary Tradition, and Literary Transformation* [Tübingen: Max Niemeyer, 1987], 154).

93. *NS*, 2: 88; *FKA*, 8.32.

94. *NS*, 2: 53 (November 24, 1917); *FKA*, 7.88.

95. *NS*, 2: 83 (February 5, 1918); *FKA*, 8.16–19.

96. Kant to Stäudlin, March 4, 1793, in id., *Correspondence*, ed. and trans. Arnulf Zweig (Cambridge: Cambridge University Press, 1999), 458.

97. Kant, *Religion Within the Boundaries of Mere Reason*, trans. Allen Wood and George di Giovanni (Cambridge: Cambridge University Press, 1998), 105.

98. Kant, *Critique of Pure Reason*, trans. Paul Guyer and Allen W. Wood (Cambridge: Cambridge University Press, 1998), A808/B836.

99. See ibid., "Appendix to the Transcendental Dialectic," section entitled "On the Regulative Use of the Ideas of Pure Reason," esp. A642/B670–A647/B675.

100. Hegel, *Faith and Knowledge*, trans. Walter Cerf and H. S. Harris (Albany: State University of New York Press, 1977), 141.

101. *NS*, 2: 83–84 (February 5, 1918); *FKA*, 8.16–19.

102. The haggadic legend that the tree of knowledge forms a hedge around the tree of life, which, though infinitely bigger than it, is successfully obstructed and protected by the much smaller tree is recounted in Louis Ginzberg, *Legends of the Jews, vol. 1: Bible Times and Characters from the Creation to Moses in the Wilderness*, trans. Henrietta Szold and Paul Radi (Philadelphia: Jewish Publication Society, 2003), 69.

103. A tradition of interpreting the tree of life as a reward for good action is discussed in James L. Kugel, *Traditions of the Bible: A Guide to the Bible as It Was at the Start of the Common Era* (Cambridge, MA: Harvard University Press, 1998), 136–38.

104. *NS*, 2: 110; *FKA*, 8.103.

105. Ibid.

106. *NS*, 2: 110–11; *FKA*, 8.103–4.

107. *NS*, 2: 67 (between December 30, 1917 and January 1, 1918); *FKA*, 7.128 (cf. Zettel no. 74, 129). Kafka's first mentions of the Garden and the Fall come in his diaries in 1916. These passages are discussed along with their biblical sources in Rohde, *"Und blätterte ein wenig in der Bibel,"* 197–215.

108. Kafka reminds Brod in a letter in December 1917 (*Briefe 1914–17*, 383) that the impossibility of reversing the Fall is what makes him suffer.

109. This is an elaboration on a theme sketched by Kafka's friend Oskar Baum in his novel *Die böse Unschuld: Ein jüdischer Kleinstadtroman* (Frankfurt am Main: Rütten & Loenig, 1913), in which a Czech national, Julius Budweiser, although innocent of the charge that he caused a Jewish girl to become pregnant, is condemned by the national and familial, personal and social attitudes of the *Kleinstadt* (small town) of the title, which is a swamp of evil, practiced in every case without direct guilt by any party.

110. Spinoza accepts the antinomy and comes to a different conclusion. If Adam had been forbidden to eat the fruit, he obviously could not have done so. God is thus not God in the story but the projection onto a heavenly screen

of a fallible earthly ruler (Spinoza, *Theological-Political Treatise*, 62–65). On attempts to circumvent the logical antinomy and pinpoint a historical Garden of Eden in space and time, see chaps. 8 and 9 in Delumeau's *History of Paradise: The Garden of Eden in Myth and Tradition*, trans. Matthew O'Connell (Urbana: University of Illinois Press, 2000).

111. Zettel no. 84; *NS*, 2: 131. Cf. the notebook, *NS*, 2: 72 (January 20 or 21, 1918); *FKA*, 7.139–40.

112. *NS*, 2: 72 (January 20 or 21, 1918); *FKA*, 7.140.

113. "Adorno's 'inverse theology' entails not the concealment of the divine, but the revelation of our fallen reality," Elizabeth Pritchard notes in "*Bilderverbot* Meets Body in Theodor Adorno's Inverse Theology," *Harvard Theological Review* 95, no. 3 (July 2002): 295. On the difference between inverse and negative theology, see ibid., 291–92n2.

114. Max Brod, "Kafka: Eine Biographie," in *Über Franz Kafka* (Frankfurt am Main: Fischer, 1966), 152.

115. Kafka, *Tagebücher*, 792.

116. *NS*, 2: 62 (December 12, 1917); *FKA*, 7.115–16.

117. *NS*, 2: 58 (December 7, 1917); *FKA*, 7.103.

118. Evil is not a part of the subject; in this Kafka departs from the argument as Kant presents it in *Religion Within the Boundaries of Mere Reason*. Evil has two aspects in Kafka's thoughts about it: first, it is that toward which one strives (what previously was called good) or anything gained by striving, along with the impulse to strive. Striving for itself may be another matter. Second, it is the whole complex of good and evil, which also implies the need for striving. Kant explicitly agrees *avant la lettre* with Kafka, that the Fall narrative is the origin of the question of good and evil for philosophy. Kant transfers the Fall narrative into the moral soul: "Every evil action must be so considered, whenever we seek its rational origin, as if the human being had fallen into it directly from the state of innocence" (*Religion*, 86).

119. Kafka, *Tagebücher*, 789.

120. Ibid.

121. *NS*, 2: 65 (December 21, 1917); *FKA*, 7.124.

122. Augustine, "On Lying," in *Seventeen Short Treatises of St. Augustine of Hippo* (Oxford: John Henry Parker, 1847), 396–97.

123. Kafka, *Briefe 1918–1920*, 34.

124. Ibid.

125. Ibid., 34–35.

126. Ibid., 35.

127. Ibid.

128. Kafka, *Briefe 1918–1920*, 34.

129. Kierkegaard's counsel is not for just anyone; it is for the few with the

fortitude and the imagination to wait for their fantasy. This is, in fact, the problem Kafka has with Kierkegaard's reading of the Abraham story at Genesis 22. He writes of this in the previous letter to Brod. Far from being a purely negative thinker, as Brod asserts, Kierkegaard drives his "positivity into the monstrous"; he does not see "the ordinary person," and as a result "he paints the monstrous Abraham in the clouds" (Kafka, *Briefe 1918–1920*, 31).

130. Ibid., 35.

131. *NS*, 2: 73 (January 20 or 21, 1918); *FKA*, 7.143.

132. Ibid.

133. *NS*, 2: 75 (between January 22 and 24, 1918); *FKA*, 148–52. Cf. Zettel no. 86, *NS*, 2: 131–33.

134. This subsection is reprinted in abbreviated form from Paul North, "Messiahs and Principles," in Anna Glazova and Paul North, eds., *Messianic Thought Outside Theology* (New York: Fordham University Press, 2014, 195–220).

135. In *The Disenchantment of the World: A Political History of Religion* (Princeton, NJ: Princeton University Press, 1997), Marcel Gauchet calls this "organizing submission through dispossession" (13) under "the reign of the absolute past" (23). Gauchet's political understanding of messianic time does not repudiate, but also does not directly require the type of understanding suggested by Jacob Taubes in *The Political Theology of Paul* (Stanford, CA: Stanford University Press, 2004), which Taubes calls the "inner logic of the messianic." "Inner" here means psychological; Taubes is interested in the "high price to the human soul" that living messianically entails (10). Gauchet is interested in the specifically political activity, namely, the suppression of politics, that a psychological account masks.

136. In his book *A Secular Age* (Cambridge, MA: Belknap Press of Harvard University Press, 2007), Charles Taylor, invoking Bernard Williams, writes of the meantime in which "time is homogenized" as that which turns all extraordinary or legendary events into "what happened around here yesterday" (271). That is to say, without heroes and gods, and without faith, time becomes the medium of nothing much happening. In fact the dialectic at work in this case is the same, insofar as heroes and gods are those beings that are never around here today or yesterday, or even tomorrow, but in some inaccessible temporal remove. Everydayness is highly messianic: it is the time of faith, not of the arrival of faith's object.

137. *NS*, 2: 34 (October 20, 1917); *FKA*, 7.23–24.

138. *NS*, 2: 54 (November 25, 1917); *FKA*, 7.91.

139. *NS*, 2: 55 (November 31 or December 1, 1917); *FKA*, 7.92.

140. In *Paganism—Christianity—Judaism*, Brod broaches a similar subject, the singularity of Jesus: "My own Jewish way of thinking tells me that there are

as many ways to grace as there are human beings endowed with grace." Jesus's "sacrifice" was for Jesus alone, and it took Paul to universalize it, whereafter Jesus the idiosyncratic one became "the son of God." This was a result not of Jesus' teachings but of "Paul's idea to deprive his personal experience of grace of its individual character, and to force it upon all mankind" (218).

141. There is no "test" of faith for this plurality, insofar as a test is a narrow door through which only a few pass. The structure that Kierkegaard applies to Abraham, of a noble knight of faith who passes an ordeal, however ironic the tale may be, cannot apply here. Brod, however, assimilates Kafka to the Kierkegaardian Abraham when he says that Kafka is "a poet of the test [*Prüfung*] of faith, the test in faith" ("Kafkas Glauben und Lehre," in *Über Franz Kafka*, 5). In *The Intellectual Contexts of Kafka's Fiction: Philosophy, Law, Religion* (Columbia, SC: Camden House, 1994), Arnold Heidsieck contends that Kafka is affected by Kierkegaard's "ethical individualism" but goes further than the Dane because he does not have to fight against the Hegelian dialectic, and so he can reject not only mediation but the "general," against which Kierkegaard's single individual makes sense (132–37).

142. Kafka thinks *bis* can mean "when" in the sense of "as soon as," a limit that has to be reached in order to trigger an event, or the event that marks the limit. Toward the end of September 1917, Kafka writes Weltsch in Prague with a "library request." "You know our old *bis*-dispute," he writes, in regard to an exchange of letters on the topic with Felice. According to Felice, *bis* can only be used to mean "until" (*solange bis*), something valid for a time up to a terminus. Kafka asks Weltsch to look for evidence that *bis* can mean "as soon as" (*Briefe: April 1914–1917*, 327).

143. *NS*, 2: 56–57 (December 4 or 5, 1917); *FKA*, 7.99.

144. The final *erst* in the last clause is missing in the Fischer critical edition, and this is corrected in the Stroemfeld historical-critical edition. Contrast *NS*, 2: 57 with *FKA*, 7.99.

145. In contrast, Ritchie Robertson reads this condition, the subtraction of need from the messianic complex, as exactly the same as the condition set in the previous remark, the infinite plurality of faith (Robertson, *Kafka*, 231). While discussing the figure of K. in *Das Schloss*, Robertson reminds us of Kafka's reading in Jewish history that contained descriptions of messianisms and messianic events (228–35).

146. There is one proximal precedent for thinking an ecclesia that comes to be *after* the messiah comes. On September 30 or October 1, 1917, Kafka writes to Brod: "the hasidic stories in the Jewish Echo [*Das Jüdische Echo*, a Bavarian journal] are maybe not the best, but all these stories, I don't understand why, are the only Jewish things in which, independent of my own constitution, I immediately and always feel at home; in everything else I am only blown

in and then another puff of air carries me out again" (*Briefe 1914–1917*, 336).
The stories he is referring to were compiled and translated by Chaim Bloch
and published as "Aus der Welt der Chasidim," in *Das Jüdische Echo*, no. 38
(September 21, 1917): 421–24. These texts come hard after a full page ad that
declares in block letters "T," showing the wide variety of Jewish causes among
which Kafka could choose. He chooses the hasidic tales. One of them stands
out from the rest for its much smaller but perhaps more far-reaching headline:
"Erst erlösen, dann Buße." The story comprises a single passage. The Rabbi
of Ruzhin offers God a deal: since you destined us for diaspora (*Golus*) before
we had even sinned, you will get our penitence only on the same condition.
Redeem us and then we will become worthy. Only after redemption at any rate
can we "atone out of a full heart [*aus vollem Herzen*]" (423).

147. *NS*, 2: 34 (October 20, 1917); *FKA*, 7.23–24.

148. Contrast this with the "small door" messianism analyzed by Levine in
Weak Messianic Power, 24–26. Here the messiah does not so much arrive as
"enter" through one of the interstices of the discontinuum. Kafka is more concerned with the determining endpoints of time than with the historical and
ethical possibilities in the image of its infinite divisibility.

149. Franz Rosenzweig, *Der Stern der Erlösung* (Frankfurt am Main:
Suhrkamp, 1988), 16.

150. In this way Kafka prefigures, in the shift between these two notes,
something Walter Benjamin will formulate in 1921 in his "Theological-Political
Fragment." The messiah declares that nothing has yet happened; it all happens with and through him, "after" in an extratemporal sense. The messiah
is the one after whom there could exist something like messianicity. "Profana-
tion is messianic and nothing other than it" is one consequence drawn from
this belated messianicity, as articulated by Werner Hamacher in "Das Theologisch-politische Fragment," in *Benjamin Handbuch: Leben—Werk—Wirkung*,
ed. Burkhardt Lindner (Stuttgart: Metzler, 2006), 182. Here is the important
Benjamin passage: "Only the messiah himself consummates all historical happening, namely, in the sense that he alone redeems [*erlöst*], consummates [*vol-
lendet*], creates [*schafft*] its relation to the messianic" (Benjamin, "Theologisch-
politisches Fragment," in *Gesammelte Schriften II*, vol. 1 [Frankfurt am Main:
Suhrkamp, 1999], 203). The sources for Benjamin's reformation of the messianic mode are investigated by Peter Fenves in *The Messianic Reduction: Walter Benjamin and the Shape of Time* (Stanford, CA: Stanford University Press,
2011). In the earliest known instance in his oeuvre, Benjamin writes about a
"messianic" mode that corresponds to a child's experience of color in a picture
book, which "reduces children to their own condition—'reminding' them, so
to speak [in a Platonic sense—PN], who they are, namely children, who see
from the perspective of a child" (77). Fenves emphasizes that there is no point

of convergence between the child reduced to childhood and an adult; messianic means being a child for whom no adulthood is coming.

151. Weltsch to Kafka, November 26, 1917, letter 82 in Kafka, *Briefe 1914–17*, 774.

152. Brod, however, thinks of this as Kafka's "intensifying study of Kierkegaard," which contributes to his "religious and ethical development" (*Über Franz Kafka*, 145).

153. Kafka to Weltsch, November 15, 1917, letter 1088 in Kafka, *Briefe 1914–17*, 366.

154. *NS*, 2: 15.

155. Kafka to Weltsch, November 15, 1917, letter 1088 in Kafka, *Briefe 1914–17*, 366.

156. Kafka to Brod, November 23–24, 1917, letter 1089 in Kafka, *Briefe 1914–17*, 367.

157. Kafka to Brod, November 14, 1917, letter 1087 in Kafka, *Briefe 1914–17*, 364.

158. Ibid., 365.

159. *NS*, 2: 78 (between January 28 and 30, 1918); *FKA* 7.159.

160. Ibid.

161. Kafka to Brod, November 23–24, 1917, letter 1089 in Kafka, *Briefe 1914–17*, 369.

162. " . . . once I even woke up trembling" (Kafka to Weltsch, November 15, 1917, letter 1088 in Kafka, *Briefe 1914–17*, 365). "My health is quite good, assuming that the mouse fear does not take over from the tuberculosis" (367).

163. Kierkegaard, *Fear and Trembling*, trans. Hong and Hong, 121 (cf. *Furcht und Zittern*, Ketels trans., 114).

164. Nietzsche sees it not as a passion exactly, more as a *Gefühl*, a feeling. The profit from faith, he writes in an unpublished note, is *die Steigerung des Machtgefühls*, "a heightening of the feeling of power." The remark belongs to a critique of faith, no doubt, in the manner of theo-politics, insofar as it shows faith to be made out of a more basic impious blend of biology and will. The remark also, however, demonstrates Nietzsche's desire to take over the power of faith and use it for other purposes. Friedrich Nietzsche, *Kritische Studienausgabe*, ed. Giorgio Colli and Mazino Montinari (Berlin: De Gruyter, 1988), 10: 505.

165. Kafka, *Briefe 1918–1920*, 34–35.

166. *NS*, 2: 104 (after February 27, 1918); *FKA*, 8.87.

167. *NS*, 2: 103 (February 27, 1918); *FKA* 8.83–84. This note belongs to what looks like a series of reflections on and responses to *Fear and Trembling* written over two days at the end of February 1918. See Claude David, "Die Geschichte Abrahams: Zu Kafkas Auseinandersetzung mit Kierkegaard," in *Bild und Gedanke, Festschrift für Gerhard Baumann*, ed. Günther Schnitzler (Munich: Wilhelm Fink, 1980), 79–90.

168. See esp. the discussion of Agamemnon and the tragic hero's difference from the knight of faith in *Fear and Trembling*, trans. Hong and Hong, 79.

169. *NS*, 2: 103 (February 27, 1918); *FKA*, 8.83–84.

170. Kafka, *Briefe 1918–1920*, 34.

171. Ibid., 35.

172. Ibid.

173. On "meaning" in *Fear and Trembling*, see the chapter "Allegory, Meaning, 'Weaning'" in Peter Fenves, *Chatter: Language and History in Kierkegaard* (Stanford, CA: Stanford University Press, 1993), 184–90.

174. Kafka, *Briefe 1918–1920*, 35.

175. To address, briefly and unsatisfactorily, the question of religions: what counts as Jewish and what counts as Christian never comes up as such in Kafka's treatise—the differences between denominations, confessions, religions, be they historical or doctrinal, seem almost irrelevant to Kafka here. Kafka calls the *Tanakh* the Old Testament, he prefers Genesis to all the other books in the Bible, his messianic thoughts tend toward the Christological, his theological reading leans toward classical texts in a deeply problematic and negative rethinking of Christianity: Augustine (whom he wants to read), Pascal (whom he read), and Kierkegaard, whose position he passes through more by accident than by plan. Yet the integrity of a single "religion" is never a pressing issue, except, perhaps, if it should falter or threaten to disappear. Kafka's flirtations with a vanishing or indeed vanished Judaism include critical remarks about his father's generation of Bohemian Jews, a visit to the rabbi of Groddek, and his reading of "the shorter Graetz" (Heinrich Graetz's *Volkstümliche Geschichte der Juden* [3 vols.; Leipzig: Oskar Leiner, 1888–89], an abbreviated version of Graetz's eleven-volume *History of the Jews*, originally published between 1853 and 1876). Of the rare references to "faiths" in the Central Europe of his day, the most interesting references to concepts that nominally belong to one or the other seem to collapse difference, without at the same time omitting details or begging the question by referring to "Judeo-Christianity." While there is no support given to either "religion" *qua* faith, there are many questions about both. In "Kafka as Anti-Christian: 'Das Urteil,' 'Die Verwandlung,' and The Aphorisms," in *A Companion to the Works of Franz Kafka*, ed. James Rolleston (Rochester, NY: Camden House, 2002), 101–22, Ritchie Robertson demonstrates Kafka's critique of Christianity in the early stories "The Judgment" and "The Metamorphosis," as well as in the treatise. In the earlier fictions, Kafka "deploys Christian imagery to question the values of Christianity" (106), but in the treatise he is working with Christian theologoumena in a different way, affirming the individuality of faith and questioning the senses, with—according to Robertson—a positive belief in the indestructible, even if he alters the Christ figure beyond recognition (110–20).

Excursus: For a Kafkan Logic

1. In *The Infinite Conversation*, trans. Susan Hanson (Minneapolis: University of Minnesota Press, 1993), chap. 14, Maurice Blanchot discusses the special modalities of the "he" narration in Kafka's fictions (379–87). Where Blanchot thinks the third person is the key to the narrator of Kafka's novels, he also explicitly shifts the gender and, let's say, the organicism of the pronoun to the "neutral" "it." Whereas Blanchot thinks the third person is the key to the narrator of Kafka's novels, Joseph Vogl invents a new position, a collective fourth person, in "Vierte Person. Kafkas Erzählstimme," *Deutsche Vierteljahrsschrift für Literaturwissenschaft und Geistesgeschichte* 68, no. 4 (December 1994): 45–56.

2. I largely accept the label "double dialogicality" adopted by Per Linell in *Approaching Dialogue: Talk, Interaction and Contexts in Dialogical Perspectives* (Amsterdam: John Benjamins, 2001), although the question will always be poseable, what the relationship between the two halves of his "quatrologue," between dialogues in "situations" and dialogues in "traditions" precisely is (54, 132–33). It is hard to imagine a "situation" that is not so thoroughly determined, positively or negatively, by traditions (language, gesture, stance, expression, mind, etc.) as to make the relationship highly asymmetrical in favor of the tradition. A situation happens within a tradition, but, in Kafka's sense, it also happens to a tradition, and so it can become the limit point. Beyond this there is no independence of a "situation."

3. A preliminary description of the "second-person standpoint" is given in Stephen Darwall, *The Second-Person Standpoint: Morality, Respect, Accountability* (Cambridge, MA: Harvard University Press, 2009), 3–25.

4. See Darwall's "Second-Personal Interpretation" of the categorical imperative (ibid., 35).

5. A basic error (*Grundfehler*) can be exposed, and it is usually a matter of the mode of presentation (*Darstellung*) to begin with. See the fragment at Kafka, *Tagebücher*, 861–62.

6. Franz Kafka, *The Castle*, trans. Anthea Bell (Oxford: Oxford University Press, 2009), 56; *Das Schloss* (Frankfurt am Main: S. Fischer, 1982), 96.

7. "I am reading *Iphigenia in Tauris*," Kafka notes on November 16, 1910. "In it, apart from some passages that are obviously wrong, one almost has to marvel at the dried-up German language coming from the mouth of a pure lad" (Kafka, *Tagebücher*, 126). See also Kafka to Brod in December 1910: "The bit of the novel that is enclosed I wrote yesterday and already I leave it at that. It is already old and surely not without errors" (Kafka, *Briefe 1902–1922*, ed. Max Brod [Frankfurt am Main: S. Fischer, 1966], 85–86).

8. Around March 26, 1911 (*Tagebücher*, 159–61), Kafka notes three defects (*Mängel*) in Brod's novel *Die Jüdinnen*.

9. Kafka, *Tagebücher*, 160 (around March 26, 1911).

10. Ibid., 703 (December 2, 1914).

11. Ibid.

12. See Kafka to Hedwig W. in 1908 (*Briefe 1902–1924*, 54), to Brod on August 14, 1912 (ibid., 102), and various letters to his editors at Wolff.

13. Wagenbach, *Franz Kafka*, 83–89.

14. Students are legion in Kafka's fictions and diaries. See "Ein älterer Student" a fragment from 1911, in Kafka's *Tagebücher*, 151–58. In 1912, Kafka writes notes about Taldmud students in yeshivas (*Tagebücher*, 352–56). A group of story beginnings follow this fragment that open with the words "Der Student. . . . " See also the story fragment, "Der Dorfschullehrer" from 1915 (*NS*, 1: 194–216) and the 1914–15 story about the horse from Ebersfeld that fascinated a young student (*NS*, 1: 225–29). See also the multiple drafts, in the diary, of a polemic about Kafka's own education, which all begin with the sentence: "Wenn ich es bedenke, so muß ich sagen, daß mir meine Erziehung in mancher Richtung sehr geschadet hat" (*Tagebücher*, 17–28).

15. Kafka, *Tagebücher*, 839–40.

16. Of the intellectual description he had composed about himself, Kafka also writes: "It would make a good epitaph" (Kafka to Brod, October 7 or 8, 1917, in *Briefe 1914–1917*, 342).

17. *Briefe, April 1914–1917*, 333.

18. *NS*, 2: 47 (between November 18 and 20, 1917); *FKA*, 7.71.

19. Kafka, *Tagebücher*, 861.

20. "It is a universal rule that each pair of opposites of this type has reference to that to which the particular 'habit' is natural" (Arist. *Categ.* 10.12a27–29, trans. Ackrill). "Now no one can think a negation determinately without grounding it on the opposed affirmation" (Kant, *Critique of Pure Reason*, B603).

21. In this sense Rosenzweig's double negative does not escape the Hegelian font from which it springs, wanting a dynamism that itself does not change, on the back of a negative that if it negates itself, the second negation is the same as the first, exactly equal to it; only thus can the negation of nothing (*Verneinung des Nichts*) become the affirmation of not-nothing (*Bejahung des Nichtnichts*), only where, that is, the two are already fully convertible (Rosenzweig, *Stern der Erlösung*, 26–27, 124).

22. Georg Friedrich Wilhelm Hegel, *Encyclopedia of the Philosophical Sciences in Basic Outline. Part 1: Logic*, trans. Klaus Brinkmann and Daniel O. Dahlstrom (Cambridge: Cambridge University Press, 2010), 78.

23. Ibid., 116.

24. Kafka to Brod, February 8, 1919, in Kafka, *Briefe 1918–1920*, 70.

25. There were less subtle and less interesting interpretations of these mar-

ginal identities. Buber identifies one, the *Trotzjude*, one who is a Jew because denounced as a Jew by others. About the *Trotzjude* Buber judges that "his Judaism" has no "living substance" (Buber, *Drei Reden*, 15). The not and not-not is something other than a judgment on the inner substance of Milena's Jewishness.

26. Refer to the discussion in the "Vienna Logic" in Immanuel Kant, *Lectures on Logic*, trans. J. Michael Young (Cambridge: Cambridge University Press, 1992), 370.

27. See Kant, *Critique of Pure Reason*, §2, "On the Logical Function in Judgments," B97/A71–72.

28. A discussion of the translation of Aristotle's *aoristos* with *infinitus* that explains the migration of the Aristotelian judgment, which fell under number (universal, particular, singular, unbounded), ultimately into a judgment of quality in Kant (previously almost exclusively divided into two kinds, negative and positive), can be found in A. Menne, "Das unendliche Urteil Kants," *Philosophia Naturalis* 19 (1982): 151–62). On pp. 157–58, Menne cites the first-century Roman historian Quintus Curtius Rufus as the likely source for the transposition of the "indefinite name" into an "infinite judgment" in Kant. "The infinite judgment 'S is non-A', asserts that the sphere of the subject-concept 'S' is included in the infinite sphere external to that of the concept 'A', whose negation, 'non-A', is the predicate of the judgment," Béatrice Longuenesse states in *Kant and the Capacity to Judge: Sensibility and Discursivity in the Transcendental Analytic of The Critique of Pure Reason*, trans. Charles T. Wolfe (Princeton, NJ: Princeton University Press, 1998). "[W]hereas rationalist metaphysicians of the Wolffian school, and the precritical Kant himself, believed that with the idea of the *ens realissimum* they had a 'concept of what possesses all reality' (A576/B604) as the purely intelligible ground of all possible realities in things, the later Kant analyzes the act of understanding in infinite judgment as merely positing the thing, reflected under the subject-concept, in the 'infinite sphere of all possible determinations' outside the sphere of the concept whose negation is the predicate. An infinite judgment is thus essentially *indeterminate*" (296).

29. Menne, "Das unendliche Urteil Kants," 162.

30. Kant, *Critique of Pure Reason*, B97–98.

31. Ibid., A574/B602.

32. Longuenesse, *Kant and the Capacity to Judge*, 297.

33. Kant, *Critique of Pure Reason*, A571/B599.

34. Ibid., A573/B 601.

35. Ibid., A574/B 602.

36. Ibid., A573/B601.

37. Ibid., A576/B604.

38. *NS*, 2: 78 (between January 28 and 30, 1918); *FKA*, 7.159.

39. *NS*, 2: 67 (between December 30, 1917, and January 1, 1918); *FKA* 7.128.

40. The impossibility of a "first sin" is discussed in chaps. 1 and 2 (25–34) of Søren Kierkegaard, *The Concept of Anxiety: A Simple Psychologically Orienting Deliberation on the Dogmatic Issue of Hereditary Sin*, trans. Reidar Thomte and Albert B. Anderson (Princeton, NJ: Princeton University Press, 1980).

41. Kafka, "Konvolut 1920," in *NS*, 2: 334.

42. *NS*, 2: 46 (between November 12 and 17, 1917); *FKA*, 7.68.

43. Something like this is intuited by Bakhtin, who argues that a pronoun is a lexical marker of address. To label *du* a pronoun is to articulate its place in a formal descriptive system, but not in events of speech. Addressivity, which is carried in and put into effect through *du*, is in the whole utterance, which is only "whole" in its movement, that is, in its ability to find and interrupt a second person (99). Michael Bakhtin, "The Problem of Speech Genres," in *Speech Genres and Other Late Essays*, trans. Vern W. McGee (Austin: University of Texas, 1986), 60–102.

44. Vivian Liska marks out the difficult task of articulating Kafkan criteria for a communal "we" in the essays in *When Kafka Says We*. Kafka is shown to be both a trendsetter and an extreme thinker of community (portrayed as less extreme only perhaps than Paul Celan) in an era in which European Jews writing in German were incessantly reflecting on the topic. The paucity of we's in Kafka indicates a growing loss of innocence about the hopeful use of the pronoun before World War II, and the special uses of "we" indicate the resistances to using it afterward, because of the easy reconciliation it implies. The paradigm of an uncommon community—taking the term "uncommon" not from Jean-Luc Nancy but from Kafka himself (whom Liska, 1, quotes as remarking, "What have I in common with Jews? I have hardly anything in common with myself . . . ")—the paradigm of not-in-common for Liska is something like a group permeated by foreign elements: asymmetrical spools, fleas, women. Vivian Liska, *When Kafka Says We: Uncommon Communities in German Jewish Literature* (Bloomington: Indiana University Press, 2009).

45. *NS*, 2: 101 (February 26, 1918); *FKA*, 8.76–79.

46. In this sentence, Kafka might be seen to take leave of the "free indirect discourse" (*erlebte Rede*) that is the central mode of narration in his stories according to Hartmut Binder's careful analysis in *Motiv und Gestaltung bei Franz Kafka* (Bonn: H. Bouvier, 1966), 201–31.

47. In *Theory of Language: The Representational Structure of Language* (1931), trans. Donald Fraser Goodwin (Amsterdam: John Benjamins, 2011), 37–39, Karl Bühler expressly connects his notion of language as organon, tool, with the language philosophy of Kafka's teacher Anton Marty (Bühler, 1). On the relationship between Bühler and Marty, see Barry Smith, *Austrian Philosophy: The Legacy of Franz Brentano* (Chicago: Open Court, 1994), 20.

48. This would be the difference between Kafka's second-person, secondary address, and the dialogicisms envisioned by Cohen, Buber, and Rosenzweig. Kafka did not perhaps know anything about Cohen until Felix Weltsch's profile of him, "Hermann Cohen," *Prager Tagblatt*, no. 85 (April 12, 1918): 2, in which Weltsch accorded Cohen "world-historical significance" (2), and even then there is no evidence that Kafka read Cohen. In Cohen's formulation, the *ich* is indeed a derivative of the *du*, but that does not mean they are any less co-dependent. See Hermann Cohen, *Die Religion der Vernunft aus den Quellen des Judentums* (Leipzig: Gustav Fock, 1919), 22–23. See also the account by Kafka and Brod's friend, Schmuel Hugo Bergmann, of Cohen's turn from transcendental to dialogical philosophy in *Dialogical Philosophy from Kierkegaard to Buber*, trans. Arnold A. Gerstein (Albany: State University of New York Press, 1991). Bergmann attributes the shift to dialogue to a turn away from a philosophy of a single principle—reason—to a philosophy with two principles—reason and history. Thereafter "becoming" is the watchword, and the concept of God has to be abandoned for an ongoing conversation with God about what God is and wills (151–55). Roland Reuß, editor of the *Historisch-kritische Ausgabe* of Kafka's works, mentions "The immanent movement of the Kafkan microtext" ("Die Oxforder Oktavhefte 7 & 8 und die Zürauer Zettel. Zur Einführung," in *Franz Kafka–Heft 8*, ed. Roland Reuß and Peter Staengle [Frankfurt am Main: Stroemfeld, 2011], 14). By calling it a conversation, it becomes an exorbitant movement instead of an immanent, concentric one.

49. Kafka, *Tagebücher*, 831.

50. *NS*, 2: 46 (between January 28 and 30, 1918); *FKA*, 159–60.

51. I must first be a you to somebody before I can be an I. This may be considered a feature of being as having. Gabriel Marcel: "The statement 'I have' can only be made over against another which is felt to be other. In so far as I conceive myself as having in myself, or more exactly, as mine, certain characteristics, certain trappings, I consider myself from the point of view of another but I do not separate myself from this other except after having first implicitly identified myself with him" ("Outlines of a Phenomenology of Having," 161). The difference between having and speaking is a difference between otherness, considered as third-personal, and second-personal relations.

52. Kafka, *Tagebücher*, 837–38 (September 25, 1917).

53. *NS*, 2: 97 (February 24, 1918); *FKA*, 8.63–64.

54. Kafka, *Tagebücher*, 818–19 (August 4, 1917).

55. Address and appeal are only secondary concerns in the Brentano-inspired language theory of Anton Marty, Kafka's teacher, who in his *On the Origins of Language* (1875) faces the problem that, after defining language as an "announcement of the inner life" (62), communication has to be given an external, derivative foundation and a secondary role. Marty also talks about language

often in the text as a "possession [*Besitz*]" (1, 8, 36, 63, 76), and as such it is only a reflection of the "inner life" that it conveys. Anton Marty, *Ueber den Ursprung der Sprache* (Würzburg: A. Stuber, 1875). On Marty's mentalist view of language, see Neil Alan, "The Brentanist School," *Pli* 10 (2000): 249–52. Marty adopted a Humboldtian view of language, whereby it was a "formative organ of thought." The development of this view into a "general semasiology" is described by Liliana Albertazzi in "Anton Marty," in *The School of Franz Brentano*, ed. Albertazzi et al. (Dordrecht: Kluwer, 1996). Even the pragmatic operations of language are subordinated to the in-formation by language of thinking (92–93).

56. *NS*, 2: 42 (October 23 or 24, 1917); *FKA*, 7.55–56.

57. *NS*, 2: 79–80 (between January 28 and 30, 1918); *FKA*, 8.7.

58. For a description of this movement of talk and truth as the proper mode of a general philology that corresponds to speech itself, see Werner Hamacher, *Minima Philologica* (New York: Fordham University Press, 2015).

59. Bakhtin distinguishes between conventional and real units of language. Real units become units because of what cuts them off; that is, they have their end not in themselves but in a subsequent unit. You cannot say that their completion is either internal or external to them; it is made up by the overall movement of speech, that is to say, by indeterminacy (71–72). The ways in which a rejoinder may complete an utterance—raising an issue, expanding it with a question, answer, assertion, objection, broaching simply or complicating, describing, stating a thesis, adding an elaboration, abbreviation, formulation, reformulation, and so forth—are thus the linguistic, retortative, moving replacements for the intentional vectors of consciousness: thinking, feeling, willing (on these see Brod and Weltsch, *Anschauung und Begriff*, chap. 8, "Das Denken"). Language shares with mind an act-oriented ontology. There is no repository of thoughts or of words, only acts of thinking or speaking. Bakhtin adds to this the stipulation that words come from the "conversation," drawn not from a universal treasury but from what was recently said (87). The social linguist Per Linell develops this anti-foundationalist trend in dialogism in which there is no language outside the dialogue and where the dialogue is not an event between two a priori constituted persons but is the structure of the social per se. See Linell, *Approaching Dialogue*, esp. chap. 1.3 "Dialogism, Dialogicality and Dialogue" and 1.4 "The Traditional Conflation of 'Dialogism' and 'Dialogue'" (8–12).

60. *NS*, 2: 69 (January 14, 1918); *FKA*, 7.131.

61. *NS*, 2: 38 (October 21, 1917); *FKA*, 7.39–40.

62. Among psychoanalytic theorists, Christopher Bollas proposes a theory of intrasubjective self-address as *du* in *The Shadow of the Object: Psychoanalysis of the Unthought Known* (New York: Columbia University Press, 1987). This

must be part of the Freudian topography, he argues, which is of course already organized by pronouns. Bollas discovers the origins of you-ness in the infantile "holding environment" that allows a recognition of the self as an object for the mother, and subsequently as an object for the parents as a unit, which the person then carries with her through life. "Through the experience of being the other's object, which we internalize, we establish a sense of two-ness in our being, and this subject-object paradigm further allows us to address our inherited disposition, or true self, as other" (51).

63. *NS*, 2: 58 (December 18, 1917); *FKA*, 103.

64. *NS*, 2: 90 (February 10, 1918); *FKA*, 8.36.

65. *NS*, 2: 138–39 (February 23, 1918); *FKA*, 8.59.

66. In his essay "Kafkas Fürsprache," in *Kafkas Institutionen*, ed. Arne Höcker and Oliver Simons (Bielefeld: Transcript, 2007), 189–212, Rüdiger Campe argues that "intercession" or "advocating," "speaking-for" (*Fürsprechen*) is a central structure in the pragmatics of language within legal procedure and other formalized social events, and that Kafkan fiction makes use of it but also exposes its centrality and its pitfalls. Obviously "speaking for" has a long history as well in religion and in imagining theological scenes, especially scenes of revelation.

The Problem of Our Art

1. This is why Heidegger can write that "the being of life is simultaneously death" (*Einführung in die Metaphysik, Gesamtausgabe, vol. 40* [Frankfurt am Main: Klostermann, 1983], 16). And when Derrida takes issue with this statement, it is because it limits death to *Dasein* and excludes animals, who merely "perish" (Derrida, *The Beast and the Sovereign*, vol. 1, trans. Geoffrey Bennington. [Chicago: University of Chicago Press, 2009], 307–8). As though anticipating Heidegger's position, Kafka writes in 1920, "even the most conservative ones muster the radicality of death!" (*NS, 2:* 340).

2. *NS*, 2: 78 (between January 28 and 30, 1918); *FKA*, 7.159–60.

3. Ibid.

4. Ibid.

5. In *Lambent Traces: Franz Kafka* (Princeton, NJ: Princeton University Press, 2004), 94–110, Stanley Corngold hypothesizes that Nietzsche is Kafka's father. Earlier, in *Franz Kafka: The Necessity of Form* (Ithaca, NY: Cornell University Press, 1988), Corngold finds great affinities between the two writers' modes of critique, aphoristic styles, and notions of self and power (139–64). *Für Alle und Keinen: Lektüre, Schrift und Leben bei Nietzsche und Kafka*, ed. Friedrich Balke et al. (Zurich: diaphanes, 2008), explores the relationship between the two writer-thinkers: the final section, "Kafkas Nietzsche-Spiel" (201–94),

deals directly with Kafka's silence about Nietzsche; the underlying Nietzschean themes in Kafka's discussions of assimilation are discussed in Andreas Kilcher, "Das Theater der Assimilation: Kafka und der jüdische Nietzscheanismus" (201–29). Nietzsche's picture of the herd instinct and the revaluation of values are particularly present in Kafka's thinking. See also Patrick Bridgewater, *Kafka and Nietzsche* (Bonn: Bouvier, 1974).

6. *NS*, 2: 73 (January 20 or 21, 1918); *FKA*, 7.140–43.

7. Martin Heidegger, *Sein und Zeit* (Tübingen: Max Niemeyer, 1967), §45, 234.

8. Søren Kierkegaard, *Furcht und Zittern: Wiederholung*, trans. H. C. Ketels, in *Gesammelte Werke*, ed. H. Gottsched (Jena: Diederichs, 1909), 31.

9. Heidegger, *Sein und Zeit*, 250.

10. Ibid., 251–55, *passim*.

11. Ibid., §52, 258.

12. "With Kafka it is very strange: semblance [*der Schein*] does not cover over the essence [*das Wesen*] here but rather compromises it, since with Kafka precisely the essence turns into a semblant one [*zum Scheinenden wird*]," Benjamin notes (*GS*, 2.3: 1200).

13. The phenomenal, that is, imagistic, understanding of perception in Brentanist philosophy is explained in Arnold Heidsieck, *The Intellectual Contexts of Kafka's Fiction: Philosophy, Law, Religion* (Columbia, SC: Camden House, 1994), 21–28. See also Heidsieck's demonstration of Kafka's skepsis regarding sense experience (79–85).

14. *NS*, 2: 141–42 (written on a separate sheet; date uncertain, possibly 1917–18).

15. *NS*, 2: 101 (February 26, 1918); *FKA*, 8.76.

16. *NS*, 2: 100–101 (February 25, 1918); *FKA*, 75–76.

17. In *The Imperative to Write: Destitutions of the Sublime in Kafka, Blanchot, and Beckett* (New York: Fordham University Press, 2014), chap. 7, Jeff Fort discusses impossible images of death in Blanchot, writing: "The 'look' of the death mask [in Nancy remarking on Heidegger—PN], and of the corpse from which it was made, is in fact the *withdrawal* of the look, the occlusion of the gaze, and the infinite recession of the one who bore it" (252).

18. Kafka, *Tagebücher*, ed. Hans-Gerd Koch et al. (Frankfurt am Main: S. Fischer, 1990), 790 (entry made between June 19 and July 5, 1916). Bertram Rohde, *"Und blätterte ein wenig in der Bibel": Studien zu Franz Kafkas Bibellektüre und ihren Auswirkungen auf sein Werk* (Würzburg: Königshausen & Neumann, 2002), 31, locates this verse (Gen. 5:24) in a Luther Bible published after 1892.

19. Kafka, *Tagebücher*, 546.

20. *NS*, 2: 100 (February 25, 1918); *FKA*, 8.75.

21. *NS*, 2: 74 (February 20 or 21, 1918); *FKA*, 7.144–47.

22. Kafkan atheology draws its concepts resolutely from the sensible realm, rather than from the realm of freedom. Moral religion in contrast draws a sharp line between the transcendental and the empirical, even in the case of evil. The ground of evil is not in the senses for Kant; to think this confuses the natural with the moral spheres (*Religion Within the Boundaries of Mere Reason,* trans. Allen Wood and George di Giovanni [Cambridge: Cambridge University Press, 1998], 57). "*Sensuous nature* [*Sinnlichkeit*] therefore contains too little to provide a ground of moral evil in the human being, for, to the extent that it eliminates the incentives originating in freedom, it makes of the human a purely *animal* being; a reason exonerated from the moral law, an *evil reason* as it were (an absolutely evil will), would on the contrary contain too much, because resistance to the law would itself be thereby elevated to incentive (for without any incentive the power of choice cannot be determined), and so the subject would be made a *diabolical* being.—Neither of these two is however applicable to the human being" (58).

23. This alone should distinguish it from "radical evil" in moral religion, which means to incorporate a deviation from the maxim into a moral maxim (ibid., 55). It also makes no reference to the evil (*Böse*) in Nietzsche's critique of the slave mentality.

24. *NS*, 2: 47 (between November 18 and 20, 1917); *FKA*, 7.72.

25. *NS*, 2: 48 (November 21 or 22, 1917); *FKA*, 7.75.

26. *NS*, 2: 48 (November 21 or 22, 1917); *FKA*, 7.76.

27. Friedrich Nietzsche, *Thus Spoke Zarathustra*, trans. Adrian del Caro (Cambridge: Cambridge University Press, 2006), 18.

28. Beyond the truth/appearance doublet, however, is still a "beyond," and as such it involves an ideal, a wish, a semblance. With this in mind Rei Terada, in *Looking Away: Phenomenality and Dissatisfaction, Kant to Adorno* (Cambridge, MA: Harvard University Press, 2009), exposes the shortcomings in Nietzsche's strategy, his "hatred of the haters of reality" (115). Nietzsche only goes so far as to critique the appearance/truth pathology, even when it is he who is sick with it and he must in practice hate himself. Nietzsche becomes dissatisfied with dissatisfaction, and yet this, as Terada points out, also does not interrupt the wishing for a beyond to semblance—except at the end perhaps when the whole complex disappears into madness (117–18).

29. Ibid., 89.

30. Ibid.

31. Franz Kafka, *The Castle*, trans. Anthea Bell (Oxford: Oxford University Press, 2009), 88; *Das Schloss* (Frankfurt am Main: S. Fischer, 1982), 156.

32. I emphasize here the negative side of the light that slips through the barrier, what Stanley Corngold names "lambent traces," which he also says can be "a delusive glitter with the power to harm" (*Lambent Traces*, 113).

33. "No other writer has carried out the 'thou shalt make no graven image,' so exactly," Walter Benjamin writes (*GS*, 2.2: 428; *SW*, 2: 808). Brod was the first, as far as I know, to see the prohibition of graven images as Kafka's primary self-law.

34. *NS*, 2: 76 (between January 25 and 27, 1917); *FKA*, 7.155. As an afterthought, he added the words "noch in diesem Leben" (Zettel no. 88, *NS*, 2: 133).

35. Unless it is conceptual in the way Brod and Weltsch in *Anschauung und Begriff: Grundzüge eines Systems der Begriffsbildung* (Leipzig: Kurt Wolff, 1913) derive conceptuality from representability (*Vorstellbarkeit*), the capacity to be depicted. For them a concept is an image, though one with the details blurred. See their chaps. 4 and 5.

36. Another mark of resistance to his friend's intentions is Max Brod's insistence that this muddiness (*Undeutlichkeit*) in theological matters is an obstacle to be overcome. "Thus Kafka also sees not heteronomy coming between God and human beings, but only unclarity [*Undeutlichkeit*], in any case a nearly inconsolable complication brought about by the bureaucratic insertion of middlemen who, full of malice and poison, always hinder the good." The difference between Kafkan "muddy" (*trüb*) and Brodian *undeutlich* is significant. Brod's understanding of "unclarity" goes back to his work on Brentanian psychology with his colleague Weltsch. For them, there are only two types of indistinctness—seeing something from a distance as opposed to up close, and confusing something for something similar to it—i.e., physical indistinctness or indistinctness of identity (*Anschauung und Begriff*, 60–61). Once he has set up unclarity as an obstacle, without question or remorse, Brod then reverses what he records Kafka as saying emphatically in another conversation: "Kafka did not see the world of the absolute hopelessly closed for him and for us. Hope—also for us!" (Max Brod, *Über Franz Kafka* (Frankfurt am Main: Fischer, 1966], 162).

37. Friedrich Nietzsche, *Writings from the Late Notebooks*, trans. Kate Sturge (Cambridge: Cambridge University Press, 2003), 160.

38. Maurice Blanchot, *Friendship*, trans. Elizabeth Rottenberg (Stanford, CA: Stanford University Press, 1997), 252–53.

39. Ibid., 255.

40. Ibid., 261.

41. In quotation marks, part of a dialogue that erupts in the letter. Kafka to Brod, July 5, 1922, in Kafka, *Briefe 1902–1922*, 385.

42. Ibid.

43. Blanchot, *Friendship*, 261.

44. Nietzsche, *Writings from the Late Notebooks*, 160.

45. Blanchot, *Friendship*, 252.

46. Kafka to Brod, July 5, 1922, in Kafka, *Briefe 1902–1922*, 384.

47. Blanchot, *Friendship*, 264

48. Kafka to Brod, July 5, 1922, in Kafka, *Briefe 1902–1922*, 385.

49. Ibid., 384.

50. Ibid., 385.

51. See §17, "A Twofold Truth," above in this volume.

52. See Friedrich Nietzsche, *Philosophy and Truth: Selections from Nietzsche's Notebooks of the Early 1870s*, ed. Daniel Breazeale (Atlantic Highlands, NJ: Humanities Press, 1979), a collection of texts to do with truth written by Nietzsche around the project of a book on early Greek thinking.

53. Maudemarie Clark's influential study, *Nietzsche on Truth and Philosophy* (Cambridge: Cambridge University Press, 1990), pinpoints this shift. In the "history of an error" section, she writes: "I will argue that we have reason to interpret it instead as evidence that Nietzsche abandoned his denial of truth in his last works because of its dependence on the thing-in-itself" (109).

54. This is not a dilemma, to Maudemarie Clark, but rather the assertion of an empirical truth that is different from "Platonic" semblance. Nietzsche discovers that "To deny the true world is not to deny truth" (ibid., 114). Clark distinguishes herself explicitly from Heidegger in this; he does not see Nietzsche as departing from the exclusive Platonic categories of truth and semblance (see ibid., 115).

55. Friedrich Nietzsche, *Human All-Too Human*, trans. R. J. Hollingdale (Cambridge: Cambridge University Press, 1996), 301.

56. Nietzsche, *Twilight*, 168.

57. Ibid., 171.

58. Ibid.

59. *NS*, 2: 82 (February 4, 1918); *FKA*, 8.11.

60. Heidegger's discussion of the "reversal" (*Umdrehung*) of Plato is to be found in "Nietzsche's Overturning of Plato," in *Nietzsche*, trans. David Farrell Krell (San Francisco: Harper, 1991), 1: 200–210. Whether this is an inversion, such that the terms are simply reversed, or an overturning, as the English translation has it, such that it stands on its head, is still an important question.

61. Plato's *Phaedo*, trans. David Gallop (Oxford: Oxford University Press, 1975), gives a fully developed myth of the two worlds as "hollows in the earth" (109a–c) with complex passages to the surface, which, Socrates says (just before his execution) must have multiple forkings in them (107e–108a).

62. Ibid., 74cf. and *Republic* 476c–d, ed. G. R. F. Ferrari, trans. Tom Griffith (Cambridge: Cambridge University Press, 2000).

63. *NS*, 2: 69 (January 14, 1918); *FKA*, 7.131.

64. *NS*, 2: 51 (November 23, 1917); *FKA*, 7.80–83.

65. For a summary that does not sacrifice nuance for concision, see the introduction by G. R. F. Ferrari in Plato, *Republic*, trans. Griffith, xi–xxxi.

66. Plato *Rep.* 475e4.

67. See Nicole Loraux's extended meditation in *The Divided City: On Memory and Forgetting in Ancient Athens* (New York: Zone Books, 2006) on the power of what the Greeks called *stasis* (in this sense, civil war) to produce regimes of thought whose main figure becomes *diakrinein*, judgment. In arguing against the structuralist anthropologization of Greece into a set of signifying practices and for a "re-politicization," she writes: "Yet conflict is also something that is always yet to be overcome, on the uncertain border between vote and fratricide, where the law of the majority endlessly attempts to exorcise the threat of division" (57). That Plato attempts something similar by other means (and by Loraux's terms fails), by means of the analogy of the city with the individual *psuchē* and the turn away from politics to truth she demonstrates in a later section, "Of the Individual-City (72–86).

68. For one example of talk of "having" with regard to the forms, see Plato *Phaedo* 100c5f.

69. *NS*, 2: 82 (February 4, 1918); *FKA*, 8.11.

70. Zettel no. 63, *NS*, 2: 127. Note the significant change from the notebook entry, which has *Die Kunst ist*, and the thought, which has *Unsere Kunst ist*. *NS, 2:* 62 (December 11, 1917).

71. Nietzsche, *Philosophy and Truth*, 96.

72. *NS*, 2: 653.

73. *Ibid.*

74. Plato *Rep.* 518a–b.

75. *NS*, 2: 75–76 (between January 22 and 24, 1918); *FKA*, 7.148.

76. See "Zarathustra's Prologue" in Nietzsche, *Thus Spoke Zarathustra*, trans. del Caro, 3.

77. Here Kafka is closer to Kant than to the Bible or to Kierkegaard. Sin is a transcendental not an actual fact. Scripture, Kant says, misrepresents the order of reason as the order of time (*Religion Within the Boundaries of Mere Reason*, 63).

78. Zettel no. 101, *NS*, 2: 136. The Zettel in this case has a sketch on it as well, an image of roots that clarifies the somewhat undercooked thought (*NS, 2:* 93 [February 21, 1918]).

79. *NS*, 2: 66 (December 14, 1917); *FKA*, 7.124.

80. *NS*, 2: 72 (January 20 or 21, 1918). This thought was later added to Zettel no. 83, *NS*, 2: 131.

81. *NS*, 2: 73 (January 20 or 21, 1918); *FKA*, 7.140–43.

82. See *NS*, 2: 78.

83. In the *Textbibel des Alten und Neuen Testaments* one reads "die Schlange verführte mich," "the snake seduced me." In Luther's Bible, the post-1892 edition probably owned and used by Kafka, one reads "Die Schlange betrog

mich," "the snake deceived me." Emil Kautzsch and Carl Heinrich Weizsäcker, *Textbibel des Alten und Neuen Testaments* (Freiburg im Breisgau: J. C. B. Mohr, 1899).

84. Such as Is. 19:13.

85. Such as Is. 37:10 or Jer. 4:10.

86. Kafka, "Konvolut [Bundle] 1920," in *NS*, 2: 360.

87. In his obituary for Kafka, his friend Oskar Baum called him "a poet of very strong imagery" (*einen so bildkräftigen Dichter*). Oskar Baum, "Franz Kafka," *Der Jude* 8 (1924), 482.

88. Kafka, "Konvolut [Bundle] 1920," in *NS*, 2: 356.

89. Published in English as André Bazin, "The Ontology of the Photographic Image," trans. Hugh Gray, in *Film Quarterly* 13, no. 4 (Summer 1960): 4–9.

90. Ibid., 7.

91. Ibid., 8.

92. Ibid., 9.

93. Carolin Duttlinger's book *Kafka and Photography* (Oxford: Oxford University Press, 2007) argues for the centrality of photographic images to Kafka's entire oeuvre. Yet although she identifies the complex and ambiguous status of photographs for Kafka in his life and in his writing, namely, the hubris of their claims to present reality and the reality of their failures to do so, she avoids discussing the moral or theological function and value of images. At times the book comes close to seeing images as paradisal promises of knowledge that drive moral action, but for the most part it returns to their epistemological failings, a preoccupation that tends to perpetuate the seduction toward knowledge. "Indeed, the meaning of a photograph is rarely self-evident; Kafka portrays photographs as riddles to be resolved and finds himself drawn to incongruous or opaque details which undermine their overall 'message.' Paradoxically, however, his textual commentaries rarely reduce the pictures' ambiguity but only reinforce their inherent mystery" (4). The suggestion of increased ambiguity is deepened in chap. 7, which deals with some ways photographs depict and execute power. Epistemic questions are also the main concern of Gesa Schneider's *Das andere Schreiben: Kafkas fotografische Poetik* (Würzburg: Königshausen & Neumann, 2008).

94. Bazin, "Ontology," 9.

95. Kafka, *Tagebücher*, 831 (September 15, 1917).

96. Kafka, *The Castle*, 17, 88; *Das Schloss*, 29, 156.

97. Kafka, *Briefe 1918–1920*, 30 (around March 5, 1918).

98. Nietzsche, *Twilight*, 171.

99. Kafka, *Tagebücher*, 824–25.

100. *NS*, 2: 65 (December 21, 1917); *FKA*, 7.124.

101. *NS*, 2: 75 (between January 22 and 24, 1918); *FKA*, 7.152. This constitutes a slight but important variation on the very end of Kleist's essay "On the
Marionette Theater," in which the narrator promises a return to innocence for
those who eat a second time from the tree of knowledge. Then again, he adds,
this can only happen at the very end of the world. Heinrich von Kleist, *Selected
Writings*, trans. David Constantine (Indianapolis, IN: Hackett, 2004), 416.

102. Nietzsche, *Thus Spoke Zarathustra*, trans. del Caro, 127.

103. Ibid., 263.

The Yield: On Forgoing Power

1. Gabriel Marcel comes close to naming, though negatively, a freedom
outside of self-possession, outside being as belonging-to. He ends his 1933
lecture on "having," "Outlines of a Phenomenology of Having," in *Being and
Having*, trans. Katharine Farrer (London: Dacre, 1949), with a discussion
of "the distinction between autonomy and freedom" (173), autonomy being
a species, the highest perhaps, of self-having. Although he concentrates on
artistic production as the locus of a different kind of freedom (where one *has*
talent but *is* a genius), the freedom he envisions does not have to be so elitist;
it involves a general kind of abandonment. "The more I enter into the whole
of an activity with the whole of myself, the less legitimate it is to say that I
am autonomous. . . . It is rooted in Being, at a point either short of self or beyond self, and in a sphere which transcends all possible possession; the sphere,
indeed, which I reach in contemplation or worship. And, in my view, this
means that such non-autonomy is very freedom" (172–74). Yielding differs in
several ways from contemplation or worship. For one thing, in order to "give
up" and be short of itself, the yield does not have to subordinate itself to the
power of a god or of an object.

2. Gilles Deleuze and Felix Guattari, *Kafka: Toward a Minor Literature*,
trans. Dana Polan (Minneapolis: University of Minnesota Press, 1986), 3.

3. Jorge Luis Borges, *Selected Non-Fictions*, trans. Esther Allen et al. (New
York: Viking, 1999), 244, aligns Kafka with "unutterable and self-repeating
infinities," hinting that infinity itself can become a constraint.

4. Zettel no. 26, *NS*, 2: 118. Not in Kafka's notebook entry from November
18, 1917, that includes the first part of the thought, see *NS* 2: 47.

5. Franz Kafka, *Tagebücher*, ed. Hans-Gerd Koch et al. (Frankfurt am Main:
S. Fischer, 1990), 839; to Felice, September 30, 1917, in *Kafka, Briefe 1918–1920*,
333; to Brod, October 7 or 8, 1917, ibid., 342–43.

6. Faith corresponds precisely to willing in Luther's *"Preface to the Romans"
(1522)*, in *Martin Luther: Selections from His Writings*, ed. John Dillenberger
(Garden City, NY: Anchor Books, 1961). Luther sees the capacity in a dialec-

tic between compulsion and freedom. Compulsion is associated with law and law-following. Faith is free, the seat of freedom the heart, where spontaneity happens, welling up like a spring. Faith is the opposite of reluctance, unwillingness, and so faith is a kind of willing (22).

7. Deleuze and Guattari, *Kafka: Toward a Minor Literature*, 41.

8. Ibid., 35.

9. Ibid., 45.

10. Ibid., 51.

11. *NS*, 2: 84 (February 6, 1918); *FKA*, 8.19.

12. For a discussion of finite infinity as the "not finite" or "bad infinity," see G. W. F. Hegel, *Faith and Knowledge*, trans. Walter Cerf and H. S. Harris (Albany: State University of New York Press, 1977), 106–14, on Jacobi and Spinoza's infinities.

13. *NS*, 2: 71 (January 19, 1918); *FKA*, 7.136. Cf. Kierkegaard, *Furcht und Zittern: Wiederholung*, trans. H. C. Ketels, in id., *Gesammelte Werke*, ed. H. Gottsched (Jena: Diederichs, 1909), 114: "as soon as the generation only takes care of its task, which is its highest duty, it cannot tire, since the task always suffices [*reicht . . . aus*] for a human lifetime."

14. Ibid.

15. The combination of frustrated transcendence and a thereby strengthened will to transcendence is allotted to Kafka in much Kafka criticism. Brod and Schoeps take this stance in their correspondence of the late 1920s, reprinted in *Im Streit um Kafka und das Judentum: Max Brod, Hans-Joachim Schoeps Briefwechsel* (Königstein: Jüdischer Verlag bei Athenäum, 1985), passim, as does Robert Alter in "Franz Kafka: Wrenching Scripture," *New England Review* 21, no. 3 (Summer 2000): 7–19. A more complex view is expressed by Stanley Corngold in "Kafka's Later Stories and Aphorisms," in the *Cambridge Companion to Kafka*, ed. Julian Preece (Cambridge: Cambridge University Press, 2002): "Kafka requires a metaphysical orientation, which posits a division between this life and a higher life, all the time he demonstrates the impossibility of surveying the line between them" (96).

16. Kafka offers an alternative, in beings that do not have themselves, to the phenomenon that Eric Santner identifies in *The Royal Remains: The People's Two Bodies and the Endgames of Sovereignty* (Chicago: University of Chicago Press, 2011) as a post-theological "surplus of immanence." As Santner describes it, the surplus is what is left after divine sovereignty has melted into temporal sovereignty and after the temporal sovereignty of the monarch has scattered into the "people." Aura scatters in "flesh" that pulsates rather than emanating. Santner identifies fleshy theological remnants in the early Kafka, in "The Judgment": "one of the crucial moments in the story can be characterized as the revelation of the flesh that at some level sustains the final, lethal judg-

ment: "'Ah, Georg,' his father said and immediately went toward him. His heavy robe fell open as he walked, the sides flapping around him—'My father is still a giant, thought Georg to himself'" (27n31). The "surplus of immanence" results from an "investiture crisis" that Santner began tracking in *My Own Private Germany: Daniel Paul Schreber's Secret History of Modernity* (Princeton, NJ: Princeton University Press, 1996). For want of God, Schreber invested his own fantasies with the symbolic glory and power once reserved for other stand-ins—priests, rulers, fathers (*My Own Private Germany*, xii). This surplus is also known as "office" and what Santner discovers in Kantorowicz also applies to Kafka's bureaucratic creatures: "being human itself comes to appear as a kind of sacred office with which each member of the species is invested" (44).

17. *NS*, 2: 34 (October 20, 1917); *FKA*, 7.23.

18. Søren Kierkegaard, *Fear and Trembling*, trans. Howard V. Hong and Edna H. Hong (Princeton, NJ: Princeton University Press, 1983), 39.

19. *NS*, 2: 78 (between January 28 and 30, 1918); *FKA*, 7.156–59.

20. Hans Joachim Schoeps, the first editor of the Zürau Aphorisms, was convinced that they had been written in the wrong order and told Brod that he would correct it. "Aph. 90 is a logical impossibility: I have then turned it around again as K. surely meant it, so that it runs: "2 possibilities: to make yourself infinitely small or to be it. The *second* is fulfillment, therefore inactivity, the *first* beginning, therefore act" (Brod and Schoeps, *Im Streit*, 58). Schoeps's unapologetic assimilationism and nationalism shows through in this tiny change. See also his 1933 article "Wir gehen einen deutschen Weg," *Central-Verein-Zeitung: Blätter für Deutschtum und Judentum* 12, no. 23 (July 13, 1933): 275–76.

21. Although he doesn't mention it, it would have been possible for Kafka to have read Hugo Bergmann's book on the history of mathematical concepts of infinity, *Das Unendliche und die Zahl* (Halle: Max Niemeyer, 1913), which presents various attempts to come to terms with the paradoxical quality of a number series with no end.

22. There is a real struggle in Kafka and within Kafka, the boy, the man, the writer, to own up to being small and staying small. Avital Ronell's riffs on "miserliness" in *Loser Sons: Politics and Authority* (Urbana: University of Illinois Press, 2012) describe a version of this: he is miserly in his admonition to his father, and the ways he crafts his self-relation and love relations are stingy (132–33). "Miserliness is about wanting at another, ground level. It piles up on the want, grinding and recycling, hoarding the bits and pieces of provisional ownership" (133). Beyond this greedy clutching, Ronell sees Kafka as trying to be small, or really being small, in one way: as a "good loser," i.e., one familiar with "the posture of surrender, the syntax of a bow to the other" (144).

23. "Die Erklärung der englischen Regierung," *Jüdische Rundschau* 47 (December 23, 1917): 377, the lead article on the front page.

24. In *The Imperative to Write: Destitutions of the Sublime in Kafka, Blanchot, and Beckett* (New York: Fordham University Press, 2014), Jeff Fort follows the flights of destitution, diminishment, and degradation through Kafka's fictions, especially the violent ways they are produced by teeth that chew up and leave nothing recognizable behind (62).

25. George Berkeley, *De Motu and The Analyst*, trans. Douglas M. Joseph (Dordrecht: Springer, 1992), 199.

26. For more than a decade, Peter Fenves has been on and off holding a seminar at Northwestern University on Nietzsche and Kafka, in which a dialectic of willing, similar to the one Heidegger identifies in his Nietzsche lectures, is the central thought image tying the two writer-thinkers together. I first encountered the Nietzschean problematic in Kafka, and for that matter the occasional Kafkan moments in Nietzsche, in this seminar in fall 2002. Testimony to the theory that a very good seminar bears fruit about a decade later, the arguments about willing and alternatives in this book are indebted to Fenves and those intense sessions in Kresge Hall.

27. On Nietzsche's reading or potential misreading of the line and Pindar's irony, read John Hamilton, "Ecce Philologus: Nietzsche and Pindar's Second Pythian Ode," in *Nietzsche and Antiquity: His Reaction and Response to the Classical Tradition*, ed. Paul Bishop (Rochester, NY: Camden House, 2004), 54–69.

28. Pindar, "2nd Pythian Ode," in *The Odes of Pindar*, trans. John Sandys (Cambridge, MA: Harvard University Press, 1937), lines 72–73.

29. Friedrich Nietzsche, *The Gay Science*, trans. Josefine Nauckhoff (Cambridge: Cambridge University Press, 2001), 152.

30. *NS*, 2: 420 (October 23 or 24, 1917); *FKA*, 55–56.

31. On October 6, 1915, Kafka retells a story told him by Jiri Langer about the Bal Shem Tov, in which the latter, designated as "B.," confronts another, higher tsadik, the highest of all, who appears every hundred years. As is expected, this highest tzadik is totally without knowledge of his own goodness. It turns out, however, that the Bal Shem Tov is "higher" than this "highest" tsadik, who comes to his house and eats enough for thirty people. "I expected an angel of the first class, but I was not prepared for an angel of the second class," B. says (*Tagebücher*, 767). Here Kafka tries to envisage a role for an angel who is the best because not the highest but the second highest and with all-too-human appetites.

32. *NS*, 2: 48 (November 21 or 22, 1917); *FKA*, 7.75.

33. Friedrich Nietzsche, *Thus Spoke Zarathustra*, trans. Adrian del Caro (Cambridge: Cambridge University Press, 2006), 89; *Also Sprach Zarathustra*, *KSA*, 4: 147–48.

34. The ways in which the motifs of renunciation (*Entsagung*) and task (*Aufgabe*) bleed over from Schopenhauer into the treatise are outlined by T. J.

Reed in "Kafka und Schopenhauer: Philosophisches Denken und dichterisches Bild," *Euphorion: Zeitschrift für Literaturgeschichte* 59 (1965): 164.

35. *NS*, 2: 15.

36. *NS*, 2: 46 (between November 12 and 17, 1917); *FKA*, 7.71.

37. Gabriel Marcel, the "affirmative" existentialist, continues his thoughts on being and having in a later essay, "Belonging and Disposability," in *Creative Fidelity*, trans. Robert Rosthal (New York: Fordham University Press, 1964), 38–57. In order to explain having, it becomes apparent to him, he has to explain first its root power or disposition, "belonging-to," and in order to argue against the primary mode of belonging, the "autonomous self" and its modes—self-belonging and self-disposability—he has to expose several contradictions within it and present alternatives, which are, when compared to belonging, what he calls "affirmative" (57). The analysis of belonging-to in this essay is unparalleled. Belonging is first of all an "assertion" that constitutes a warning not to do something, to "make no claims on the object in question" (39). The warning to "make no claims" is the basic element of what, in aggregate, become social practices of exclusion. Social "belonging" is expressed in the third person; a *socius* emerges where "the I" is capable of being treated as a "him" (42). Although Marcel does not discuss Kant's practical philosophy except to dismiss it, he nevertheless argues that taking others as means, saying "he belongs to me" and "we belong to this," cannot have its evil diminished by saying "I belong only to me." Autonomy is not going to produce the Kingdom of Ends; it is not going to produce a good world. Autonomy says, negatively, I belong to nobody else and thus excludes everybody else (43). What is required is a reduction of "belonging" to its contradictions. A political sphere thoroughly determined by "belonging" is a form of total anarchism based in the "deification of self which is usually unavowed" (44). This is emphatically not freedom, nor is it very democratic. In fact it goes over into its opposite. The I that belongs only to itself maniacally holds onto a formal relation, the contents of which are free to change, as long as they do not seem to be the possessions of others. Marcel does not develop the thought further, except to point to an intermediate state of "radical indisposability" (53) that precedes artistic creation, which is a selfish act that is at the same time for others.

38. There is a way in which this yielding, and the dissimulation that goes along with it, incorporates and responds to Kafka's earlier fascination with spiritualism and theosophy. In a diary entry from 1911 in which Kafka describes his discussion with Rudolf Steiner, he claims that the "clairvoyant-like states" are close to him when he writes, but that he lacks "the tranquility of rapture [*Begeisterung*]" that the doctor has described as the basis of such states (*Tagebücher*, 34). Once the prophetic, visionary aspect of spiritualism is removed, it becomes an "other consciousness" without the promise of special knowledge or a new

birth out of the death of the old that Steiner promised, and one is left with "an experience that disorients the mind," as June Leavitt calls it in *The Mystical Life of Franz Kafka: Theosophy, Cabala, and the Modern Spiritual Revival* (Oxford: Oxford University Press, 2012), 25. Central aspects of his encounters with the spirit world are recorded by Andreas Kilcher in "Geisterschrift: Kafkas Spiritismus," in *Schrift und Zeit in Franz Kafkas Oktavheften*, ed. Caspar Battegay et al. (Göttingen: Wallstein, 2010), 223–44. In Leavitt's reading, the majority of "mystical" stories were written before 1917. Her account of Kafka's engagement with spiritualism reminds us that the origins of these ideas come from sources as various as Freemasonry; Buber's work on Hasidism; Kafka's formerly Hasidic friend Yitzhak Löwy; his friend George Langer who became a student of the Belz Rebbe; and Walter Köhler's book *Die Gnosis* (Leavitt, *Mystical Life*, 123–24). For another route by which Kabbalic motifs may have reached Kafka, see Paul Franks, "Rabbinic Idealism and Kabbalistic Realism: Jewish Dimensions of Idealism and Idealist Dimensions of Judaism," in *The Impact of Idealism*, vol. 4: *Religion*, ed. Nicholas Adams (Cambridge: Cambridge University Press, 2013), 232–41. *Tsimtsum*, the initial contraction of God that provides a negative space for creation, plays an important role in the negativities of idealism. How contraction, through Lessing and Jacobi, and later Hegel and Schelling, might have come to offer Kafka a solution or dissolution of theological problems remains to be worked out. Ritchie Robertson has discussed the notion of *tsimtsum* as a possible factor in Kafka's thought in *Kafka: Judaism, Politics, and Literature* (Oxford: Oxford University Press, 1985), 195–96.

39. *NS*, 2: 59 (December 18, 1917); *FKA*, 7.107.

40. *NS*, 2: 32–33 (October 20, 1917); *FKA*, 7.19.

41. *NS*, 2: 82 (February 4, 1918); *FKA*, 8.12. On the provenance of justification (*Rechtfertigung*) and Kafka's familiarity with Paul's "Letter to the Romans," see Bertram Rohde, *"Und blätterte ein wenig in der Bibel": Studien zu Franz Kafkas Bibellektüre und ihren Auswirkungen auf sein Werk* (Würzburg: Königshausen & Neumann, 2002), 126–34.

42. Felix Weltsch, "Masaryk and Zionism," in *Thomas G. Masaryk and the Jews*, ed. Ernst Rychnovsky, trans. B. R. Epstein (New York: B. Pollak, 1941), 78.

43. In an earlier text, "Erlebnis und Intention (Die aktivistische und die romantische Gefahr)," in *Tätiger Geist! Zweites der Ziel-Jahrbücher, 1917–1918*, ed. Kurt Hiller (Munich: Georg Müller, 1918): 254, Weltsch warns against too great a love for the experience of action, which has its place in ethics but should not be the only motivator. Loving the action and not the end is one of the dangers of activism (*Aktivismus*), which he calls "a weakening through the act."

44. Felix Weltsch, *Gnade und Freiheit*, ed. Hans-Gerd Koch (Düsseldorf: onomato, 2010), 136.

45. Ibid., 132.

46. Ibid., 160.

47. Ibid., 13.

48. Ibid., 170.

49. Søren Kierkegaard, *The Moment and Late Writings*, trans. Howard V. Hong and Edna H. Hong (Princeton, NJ: Princeton University Press, 2009), no. 4, 158.

50. See Hans-Gerd Koch's edition of Weltsch's *Gnade und Freiheit*, 187–93.

51. *Jüdische Rundschau* 47 (23 December 1917): 378.

52. This is insinuated in Peter Fenves's introduction to the English version of Brod's novel *Tycho Brahe's Path to God*, trans. Felix Warren Crosse (Evanston, IL: Northwestern University Press, 2007).

53. Ibid., 97.

54. Ibid., 79.

55. Max Brod, *Paganism—Christianity—Judaism: A Confession of Faith* (Tuscaloosa: University of Alabama Press, 1970), 28.

56. Ibid., 43.

57. The "doctrine" of noble and ignoble misfortune is discussed in the context of Brod's development from an "indifferentist" to a believer in belief in Claus-Ekkehard Bärsch, *Max Brod im Kampf um das Judentum* (Vienna: Passagen, 1992), 94–109, esp. 112–13.

58. Brod, *Paganism—Christianity—Judaism*, 181.

59. Ibid., 101.

60. Ibid., 29.

61. Ibid., 41.

62. Samuel (Schmuel) Hugo Bergmann, "Die zionistische Kulturarbeit im Westen," in *Jawne und Jerusalem* (Berlin: Jüdischer Verlag, 1919, 12–15), 13.

63. *NS*, 2: 46 (between November 12 and 17, 1917); *FKA*, 7.68.

64. *NS*, 2: 81 (February 1, 1918); *FKA*, 8.8.

65. Bergmann, "Die zionistische Kulturarbeit im Westen," 12.

66. Ibid., 15.

67. See Iris Bruce, *Kafka and Cultural Zionism: Dates in Palestine* (Madison: University of Wisconsin Press, 2007), 23–24, 28–29.

68. Martin Buber, *Drei Reden über das Judentum* (Frankfurt am Main: Rütten & Loening, 1920), 29.

69. Ibid., 42.

70. Ibid., 29.

71. Ibid., 35.

72. Ibid., 31.

73. Ibid., 71.

74. Ibid., 79.

75. Ibid., 89.

76. *NS*, 2: 89 (February 10, 1918); *FKA*, 8.35–36.

77. In "'The Fall Is the Proof of Our Freedom': Mediated Freedom in Kafka," in *Freedom and Confinement in Modernity: Kafka's Cages*, ed. A. Kiarina Kordela and Dimitris Vardoulakis (New York: Palgrave Macmillan, 2011), Vardoulakis writes that "absolute freedom and absolute imprisonment cannot sustain their separation" in Kafka's fictions (91). What Vardoulakis seems to be suggesting is that proving absolute freedom illusory is the first step to a more complex understanding of freedom. The ape in Kafka's story "A Report to an Academy" laughs at the idea of becoming totally free by becoming human (101). An alternative, however, remains illusive.

78. Robert Walser, *Jakob von Gunten*, trans. Christopher Middleton (New York: New York Review Books Classics, 1999), 9; *Jakob von Gunten* (Zurich: Suhrkamp, 1985), 11.

79. Ibid., English, 4; German, 7.

80. Ibid., English, 4; German, 7–8.

81. Ibid., English 3; German, 7.

82. Ibid., English, 155; German, 145.

83. Ibid., English, 18; German, 20.

84. Ibid., English, 17; German, 20.

85. *NS*, 2: 106–7 (around February 27, 1918); *FKA*, 8.91–96. Werner Hamacher, "Uncalled: A Commentary on Kafka's 'The Test,'" in *Reading Ronell*, ed. Diane Davis (Urbana: University of Illinois Press, 2009, 74–93), 89–90, construes this manifesto as a charter for a community without a special "vocation" (*Beruf*).

86. Franz Kafka, *The Complete Stories* (New York: Schocken Books, 1971), 253.

87. *NS*, 2: 63 (December 14, 1917); *FKA*, 7.119–20.

88. An allusive discussion on corners in Kafka's fictions can be found in Vivian Liska, *When Kafka Says We: Uncommon Communities in German Jewish Literature* (Bloomington, IN: Indiana University Press, 2009), 1–2.

89. Martin Heidegger, *Unterwegs zur Sprache* (Frankfurt am Main: Klostermann, 1985), 93.

90. Franz Brentano, *Philosophical Investigations on Space, Time, and the Continuum*, trans. Barry Smith (London: Croom Helm, 1988), 3–4.

91. Ibid., 5–6.

92. Ibid., 31.

93. Ibid., 3.

94. Ibid., 8.

95. Ibid., 11.

96. *NS*, 2: 31–32 (October 19, 1917); *FKA*, 7.15.

97. *NS*, 2: 81 (February 1, 1918); *FKA*, 8.8.

98. *NS*, 2: 343.

99. Franz Kafka, *Drucke zu Lebzeiten*, ed. Hans-Gerd Koch (Frankfurt am Main: S. Fischer, 1994), 57.

100. Ibid., 177, 182.

101. Ibid., 331.

102. Kafka, *Tagebücher*, 622 (January 8, 1914).

103. Kafka, *The Trial*, 11, 70, 73; *Der Prozess*, 20, 130–31, 137.

104. Kafka, *The Trial*, 25; *Der Prozess*, 46.

105. Kafka, *The Complete Stories*, 316.

106. Kafka to Oskar Baum, July 4, 1922, in Kafka, *Briefe 1902–1924*, 382.

107. Kafka, *The Trial*, 38; *Der Prozess*, 70.

108. Kafka, *The Trial*, 81–82; *Der Prozess*, 152.

109. Corners are nevertheless accessible from the world: "hiding places are innumerable," *Verstecke sind unzählige* . . . , goes a thought from November 19, 1917 (*NS*, 2: 47).

110. Friedrich Nietzsche, "Homers Wettkampf," *KSA*, 1: 783–92. On the expulsion of the "best," see Aristotle *Politics*, in *The Complete Works of Aristotle*, vol. 1, ed. Julian Barnes (Princeton, NJ: Princeton University Press, 1984), bk. 3, 1284a3f.

111. The "battle" between truth and beauty is staked out in Friedrich Nietzsche, "Die dionysische Weltanschauung." *KSA*, 1: 559–66. On the battle between truth and lies, see id., "Über Wahrheit und Lüge im aussermoralischen Sinne," 873–90. On the battle between faith and knowledge, see fragments from the *Nachlass* written in late 1872 or early 1873 (*KSA*, 7: 429–30). On the battle between good and evil, see *Zur Genealogie der Moral*, *KSA*, 5: 285.

112. Friedrich Nietzsche, *Jenseits von Gut und Böse*, *KSA*, 5: 194.

113. Ibid., *KSA*, 5: 140.

114. Friedrich Nietzsche, "Meine fünf 'Neins,'" *KSA*, 12: 453–54.

115. Friedrich Nietzsche, *Die fröhliche Wissenschaft*, *KSA*, 3: 585–86.

116. Ibid.

117. A secret channel cuts between power, a worldly concern, and the most spiritual and high, Luther's "faith." In "Freedom of a Christian," faith is thoroughly identified with power, which splits up into three vectors. Freedom in the heart is born of an alchemical power, on the metaphor of the transfer of heat that transforms the properties of a base material (58). Trust in God's promises is a species of indirect power: giving God what belongs to God, *reddens Deo suum*, one gets power in return (62). Finally, it is the power to unify the self and the ecclesia (see Luther, "Preface to the Romans," 29).

118. In *Loser Sons*, Ronell recasts the whole rhetoric of father and sons in

terms of a battle of wills: see chap. 5, "The Battle of Wills: On Being Cheap" (131–51).

119. A different account of the prominence of *Kampf* in Kafka attributes it to a pathetic goal rather than the operation of the will: Kafka teaches the lesson "that the horrific struggle to establish a human self results in a self whose humanity is inseparable from that horrific struggle" (David Foster Wallace, *Consider the Lobster and Other Essays* [New York: Little, Brown, 2006], 64). *Kampf* is an encompassing Kafkan motif according to Betiel Wasihun in *Gewollt—Nicht-Gewollt: Wettkampf bei Kafka, mit Blick auf Robert Walser und Samuel Beckett* (Heidelberg: Universitätsverlag Winter, 2010): "Kafka describes agonal structures that cross all regions of life, all realities of his 'heroes' (15). She reminds us that Kafka wrote to Felice that "overcoming the battle is *improbable*" (16).

120. Arthur Schopenhauer, *Philosophy in the Tragic Age of the Greeks*, trans. Marianne Cowan (Washington, DC: Regnery, 1962), 56 (trans. modified). Friedrich Nietzsche, *KSA*, 1: 822–26.

121. Arthur Schopenhauer, *The World as Will and Representation*, vol. 1, ed. and trans. Judith Norman et al. (Cambridge: Cambridge University Press, 2010), 170–71.

122. Nietzsche, fragments from the *Nachlass*, 1881, *KSA*, 9: 550.

123. Ibid., 487–88.

124. *NS*, 2: 94–95 (February 22, 1918); *FKA*, 8.52–56.

125. *NS*, 1: 59.

126. Zettel no. 7, *NS*, 2: 114. Compare the notebook entry, which includes the line *Die wahren Seitensprünge des Ehemanns, die, richtig verstanden, niemals lustig sind*, excised in the fair copy (*NS*, 2: 34–35 (October 20, 1917); *FKA*, 7: 24–27.

127. *NS*, 2: 176.

128. *NS*, 2: 179.

129. Bret W. Davis, *Heidegger and the Will: On the Way to Gelassenheit* (Evanston, IL: Northwestern University Press, 2007), Intro., xxx.

130. Here is Davis's description, ibid., 193, of that way: "In 1959 Heidegger published two texts in a small volume entitled *Gelassenheit*: a memorial address for the composer Conradin Kreutzer (1780–1849) given in 1955, also entitled 'Gelassenheit'; and a "conversation" (*Gespräch*) between three characters, a Scientist (*Forscher*), a Scholar (*Gelehrter*), and a Teacher (*Lehrer*), entitled 'Toward an Explication of Gelassenheit: From a Conversation on a Country Path about Thinking.' The latter text ([*Gelassenheit*] 29–71) was excerpted and reworked from a much longer unpublished conversation (*GA* 77:3–157) written fifteen years earlier in 1944–45. In other words, the conversation—Heidegger's most explicit and sustained meditation on *Gelassenheit* as *Nicht-Wollen*—was origi-

nally composed precisely at the end of his prolonged *Auseinandersetzung* with Nietzsche's philosophy of the will to power. The portion published in 1959 is a slightly revised version of most of the last third of the earlier unpublished version (see *GA* 77:105–23, 138–57), which has now appeared in full in volume 77 of the *Gesamtausgabe*."

131. Heidegger, *Nietzsche*, 1: 39.

132. Ibid.

133. Ibid., 34.

134. Ibid., 40.

135. Ibid., 40–41.

136. Ibid., 39.

137. Ibid., 40.

138. Ibid., 42.

139. Davis, *Heidegger and the Will*, "Between Voluntarism and Deference of Will: A Politics of Self-Assertion and Sacrifice" and "Thinking the Affair: On Relating Heidegger's Nazism to His Philosophy," 71–84.

140. Martin Heidegger, *Feldweg-Gespräche (1944/45)*, *GA*, 77 (Frankfurt am Main: Klostermann, 1995), 208.

141. "Heidegger's turn from the will is not merely a matter of a change in terminology; it signals a fundamental change in thought inasmuch as it is precisely this characteristic of man "stationing himself abroad among beings in order to keep them within his field of action" that becomes the target of Heidegger's critique of the will as a matter of what I am calling 'ecstatic-incorporation'" (Davis, *Heidegger and the Will*, 148).

142. Ibid.

143. Martin Heidegger, "Conversation on a Country Path About Thinking," in *Discourse on Thinking: A Translation of* Gelassenheit, trans. John M. Anderson and E. Hans Freund (New York: Harper & Row, 1966, 58–90), 75.

144. Ibid., 62.

145. Heidegger, *Sein und Zeit*, 32.

146. Ibid., 32–35, passim.

147. Ibid., §18, 84.

148. Ibid., §57, 277.

149. Stefan Lorenzer captures the double movement of *lassen* in "Notiz über das Lassen," in *Babel: Für Werner Hamacher* (Basel: Urs Engeler, 2009). Rosenzweig mentions the two linguistic instruments of creation from the Book of Genesis. For him they are the *Gut!* and the *lassen* (*Stern der Erlösung*, 166–73).

150. Heidegger, "Zeit und Sein," 46.

151. Heidegger, "Conversation," trans. Anderson and Freund, 69; "Feldweggespräch" in *Gelassenheit* (Pfullingen: Günther Neske, 1959), 46.

152. Heidegger, "Conversation," 70; "Feldweggespräch," 52.

153. Heidegger, "Conversation," 72–74; "Feldweggespräch," 49–52.

154. Heidegger, "Conversation," 74; "Feldweggespräch," 52.

155. Heidegger, *On Time and Being*, trans. Joan Stambaugh (New York: Harper & Row, 1972), 25.

156. Ibid., 22–23; Heidegger, "Zeit und Sein," in *Zur Sache des Denkens, GA 14* (Frankfurt am Main: Vittorio Klostermann, 2007), 28.

157. Heidegger, *On Time and Being*, 43.

158. Ibid., 21.

159. Ibid., 24 and 41.

160. Ibid., 22–23. Heidegger, "Zeit und Sein," 28.

161. Gen. 31:19–21. The association of two sentences—"Meanwhile Laban had gone to shear his sheep, and Rachel stole her father's household idols. Jacob kept Laban the Aramean in the dark, not telling him that he was fleeing, and fled with all that he had" (*Jewish Study Bible*, ed. Adele Berlin and Marc Zvi Brettler [Oxford: Oxford University Press, 2004], 64)—indicates a connection between the disappearance of household gods and a disappearance of sense.

162. *NS*, 2: 64 (December 19 or 20, 1917); *FKA*, 7.123.

163. *NS*, 2: 65 (December 19 or 20, 1917); *FKA*, 7.123.

164. An exemplary reading of the mole's story can be found in John T. Hamilton, *Security: Politics, Humanity, and the Philology of Care* (Princeton, NJ: Princeton University Press, 2013), 25–28. The paradox of security is that "the animal is secure only as long as he remains insecure" (28).

165. *NS*, 2: 8.

166. Kafka, *Briefe 1918–1920*, 31 (around March 5, 1918).

167. Kafka to Robert Klopstock, June 1921, in *Briefe 1902–1922*, 333.

168. Here I rely on some of Hamacher's arguments in "Uncalled."

169. *NS*, 2: 40 (October 23, 1917); *FKA*, 7.47.

170. Ibid. Trans. modified from that by Willa and Edwin Muir in Kafka, *The Complete Stories*, ed. Nahum N. Glatzer (New York: Schocken Books, 1971), 430–31.

171. Ibid.: 41–42; *FKA*, 7.55. Trans. modified from ibid., 432.

172. Walter Benjamin reminds us that the Greek and not just the Jewish past shows up in Kafka (*GS*, 2.2: 415; *SW*, 2: 799).

173. For a critical view of the linguistic evidence for these traditional associations, see Gary B. Holland, "The Name of Achilles: A Revised Etymology," *Glotta* 71 (Göttingen: Vandenhoeck & Ruprecht, 1993): 17–27.

174. Benjamin addresses this historical-temporal structure in his concept of "the Forgotten" in Kafka (*GS*, 2.2: 430–32; *SW*, 2: 809–12).

175. Kant, *Critique of Pure Reason*, B34: "Through criticism alone can we sever the very root of materialism, fatalism, atheism, of freethinking unbelief, of enthusiasm and superstition, which can become generally injurious."

176. Kafka, *The Trial,* 125; *Der Prozess,* 237.

177. Kafka to Robert Klopstock, June 1921, in Kafka, *Briefe 1902–1922,* 334.

178. K. could have learned this from the assistants, whose "childish-clownish conduct" is a constant source of consternation for him (218).

179. Kafka, *The Castle,* 26; *Das Schloss,* 45.

Select Bibliography

Abelson, J. "Maimonides on the Jewish Creed." *Jewish Quarterly Review* 19, no. 1 (1906): 24–58.

Adler, Anthony. *"Labyrinthine Dances: Choreography, Economy, and the Politics of Gesture in Hölderlin's Hyperion."* MS.

Alan, Neil. "The Brentanist School." *Pli* 10 (2000): 244–59.

Albertazzi, Liliana. "Anton Marty." In *The School of Franz Brentano*, ed. id., Massimo Libardi, and Roberto Poli. Dordrecht: Kluwer, 1996.

Allemann, Beda. *Zeit und Geschichte im Werk Kafkas*. Ed. Diethelm Kaiser and Nikolaus Lohse. Göttingen: Wallstein, 1998.

Alter, Robert. "Franz Kafka: Wrenching Scripture." *New England Review* 21, no. 3 (Summer 2000): 7–19.

Aristotle. *Categories and De Interpretatione*. Trans. and ed. J. L. Ackrill. Oxford: Oxford University Press, 1963.

——. *Ethica Nicomachea*. Ed. Ingram Bywater. Oxford: Oxford University Press, 1920.

——. *Metaphysics*. Vol. 1. Ed. W. D. Ross. Oxford: Oxford University Press, 1924.

——. *Metaphysics*. In *The Complete Works of Aristotle*, ed. Julian Barnes, 2: 1552–1728. Princeton, NJ: Princeton University Press, 1984.

——. *Politics*. In *The Complete Works of Aristotle*, ed. Julian Barnes 1: 1986–2129. Princeton, NJ: Princeton University Press, 1984.

——. *Prior Analytic*. In *The Complete Works of Aristotle*, ed. Julian Barnes, 1: 39–113. Princeton, NJ: Princeton University Press, 1984.

Augustine, Saint, Bishop of Hippo. *Confessions*. Trans. Henry Chadwick. Oxford: Oxford University Press, 1991.

——. *On Genesis (Two Books on Genesis: Against the Manichees and On the*

Literal Interpretation of Genesis, an Unfinished Book). Trans. Roland J. Teske, S.J. Washington, DC: Catholic University of America Press, 1991.

———. "On Lying." In *Seventeen Short Treatises of S. Augustine, Bishop of Hippo*, 382–425. Oxford: J. H. Parker; London: F. and J. Rivington, 1847.

Autenrieth, Georg. *A Homeric Dictionary*. Trans. Robert Keep. Norman: University of Oklahoma Press, 1958.

Bakhtin, Michael. "The Problem of Speech Genres." *Speech Genres and Other Late Essays*. Trans. Vern W. McGee. Austin: University of Texas, 1986.

Balke, Friedrich, Joseph Vogl, and Benno Wagner, eds. *Für Alle und Keinen: Lektüre, Schrift und Leben bei Nietzsche und Kafka*. Zurich: diaphanes, 2008.

Bärsch, Claus-Ekkehard. *Max Brod im Kampf um das Judentum*. Vienna: Passagen, 1992.

Bataille, Georges. *The Unfinished System of Non-Knowledge*. Trans. Michelle Kendall and Stuart Kendall. Minneapolis: University of Minnesota Press, 2001.

Baum, Oskar. *Die böse Unschuld: Ein jüdischer Kleinstadtroman*. Frankfurt am Main: Rütten & Loenig, 1913.

———. "Franz Kafka." *Der Jude* 8 (1924): 482–83.

Bazin, André. "The Ontology of the Photographic Image." Trans. Hugh Gray. *Film Quarterly*, 13, no. 4 (Summer 1960): 4–9.

Benjamin, Walter. *Benjamin über Kafka: Texte, Briefzeugnisse, Aufzeichnungen*. Ed. Hermann Schweppenhäuser. Frankfurt am Main: Suhrkamp, 1981.

———. "Franz Kafka: Zur zehnten Wiederkehr seines Todestages." *GS* (1972), 2.1: 409–38.

———. *Gesammelte Schriften*. Ed. Rolf Tiedemann and Hermann Schweppenhäuser. 17 vols. Frankfurt am Main: Suhrkamp, 1972–89. Cited as *GS*.

———. *Selected Writings*. Ed. Marcus Bullock and Michael W. Jennings. 4 vols. Cambridge, MA: Belknap Press, 1996–2003. Cited as *SW*.

Bergmann, Samuel (Schmuel) Hugo. *Dialectical Philosophy from Kierkegaard to Buber*. Trans. Arnold A. Gerstein. Albany: State University of New York Press, 1991.

———. *Das Unendliche und die Zahl*. Halle: Max Niemeyer, 1913.

———. "Die zionistische Kulturarbeit im Westen." In *Jawne und Jerusalem*, 12–15. Berlin: Jüdischer Verlag, 1919.

Berkeley, George. *De Motu and The Analyst*. Trans. Douglas M. Joseph. Dordrecht: Springer, 1992.

Binder, Hartmut. *Motiv und Gestaltung bei Franz Kafka*. Bonn: H. Bouvier, 1966.

Bion, W. R. "The Psycho-Analytic Study of Thinking." *International Journal of Psychoanalysis*, 43 (1962): 306–10.

Blanchot, Maurice. *De Kafka à Kafka*. Paris: Gallimard, 1981.

———. *Friendship*. Trans. Elizabeth Rottenberg. Stanford, CA: Stanford University Press, 1997. Originally published as *L'amitié* (Paris: Gallimard, 1992).

———. *The Infinite Conversation*. Trans. Susan Hanson. Minneapolis: University of Minnesota Press, 1993.

Bloch, Chaim. "Aus der Welt der Chassidim." *Jüdische Echo*, no. 38 (September 21, 1917): 421–24.

Boethius, Anicius Manlius Severinus. *The Consolation of Philosophy*. Trans. David R. Slavitt. Cambridge, MA: Harvard University Press, 2008.

Bollas, Christopher. *The Shadow of the Object: Psychoanalysis of the Unthought Known*. New York: Columbia University Press, 1987.

Borges, Jorge Luis. *Selected Non-Fictions*. Trans. Esther Allen, Suzanne Jill Levine, and Eliot Weinberger. New York: Viking, 1999.

Brentano, Franz. *Descriptive Psychology*. Trans. Benito Müller. London: Routledge, 1995.

———. *Philosophical Investigations on Space, Time, and the Continuum*. Trans. Barry Smith. London: Croom Helm, 1988.

———. *Psychology from an Empirical Standpoint*. Trans. Antos C. Rancurello, D. B. Terrell, and Linda L. McAlister. London: Routledge, 1995.

———. *Psychologie vom empirischen Standpunkt*. Leipzig: Duncker & Humblot, 1874.

———. *On the Several Senses of Being in Aristotle*. Trans. Rolf George. Berkeley: University of California Press, 1975.

Bridgewater, Patrick. *Kafka and Nietzsche*. Bonn: Bouvier, 1974

Brod, Max. "Die jüdische Kolonisation in Palästina." *Die Neue Rundschau: XXVII. Jahrgang der freien Bühne*, 2: 1267–76. Berlin: S. Fischer, 1917.

———. *"Kafka: Eine Biographie."* In *Über Franz Kafka*. Frankfurt am Main: Fischer, 1966.

———. *"Kafkas Glauben und Lehre."* In *Über Franz Kafka*. Frankfurt am Main: Fischer, 1966.

———. *Paganism—Christianity—Judaism: A Confession of Faith*. Tuscaloosa: University of Alabama Press, 1970.

———. *Tycho Brahe's Path to God*. Trans. Felix Warren Crosse. Evanston, IL: Northwestern University Press, 2007.

———. "Zwei Welten." *Der Jude* 2, no. 1 (1917): 47–51.

Brod, Max, and Felix Weltsch. *Anschauung und Begriff: Grundzüge eines Systems der Begriffsbildung*. Leipzig: Kurt Wolff, 1913.

Bruce, Iris. *Kafka and Cultural Zionism: Dates in Palestine*. Madison: University of Wisconsin Press, 2007.

Buber, Martin. *Drei Reden über das Judentum*. Frankfurt am Main: Rütten

& Loening, 1920. Translated in *At the Turning: Three Addresses on Judaism* (New York: Farrar, Straus & Young 1952).

Bühler, Karl. *Theory of Language: The Representational Structure of Language.* Trans. Donald Fraser Goodwin. Amsterdam: John Benjamins, 2011.

Butler, Judith. *Giving an Account of Oneself.* New York: Fordham University Press, 2005.

Campe, Rüdiger. "Kafkas Fürsprache." In *Kafkas Institutionen,* ed. Arne Höcker and Oliver Simons, 189–212. Bielefeld: Transcript, 2007.

Chrudzimski, Arkadiusz, and Barry Smith. "Brentano's Ontology: From Conceptualism to Reism." In *The Cambridge Companion to Brentano,* ed. Dale Jacquette, 197–220. Cambridge: Cambridge University Press, 2004.

Clark, Maudemarie. *Nietzsche on Truth and Philosophy.* Cambridge: Cambridge University Press, 1990.

Cohen, Hermann. *Die Religion der Vernunft aus den Quellen des Judentums.* Leipzig: Gustav Fock, 1919.

Corngold, Stanley. *Franz Kafka: The Necessity of Form.* Ithaca, NY: Cornell University Press, 1988.

———. "Kafka's Later Stories and Aphorisms." In *The Cambridge Companion to Kafka,* ed. Julian Preece, 95–110. Cambridge: Cambridge University Press, 2002.

———. *Lambent Traces: Franz Kafka.* Princeton, NJ: Princeton University Press, 2004.

Corngold, Stanley, and Benno Wagner. *Franz Kafka: The Ghosts in the Machine.* Evanston, IL: Northwestern University Press, 2011.

Damaschke, Adolf. *Die Bodenreform: Grundsätzliches und Geschichtliches zur Erkenntnis und Überwindung der sozialen Not.* Berlin-Schöneberg: Buchverlag der "Hilfe," 1907.

Darwall, Stephen. *The Second-Person Standpoint: Morality, Respect, Accountability.* Cambridge, MA: Harvard University Press, 2009.

David, Claude. "Die Geschichte Abrahams: Zu Kafkas Auseinandersetzung mit Kierkegaard." In *Bild und Gedanke, Festschrift für Gerhard Baumann,* ed. Günther Schnitzler. Munich: Wilhelm Fink, 1980.

Davis, Bret W. *Heidegger and the Will: On the Way to Gelassenheit.* Evanston, IL: Northwestern University Press, 2007.

Deleuze, Gilles, and Felix Guattari. *Kafka: Toward a Minor Literature.* Trans. Dana Polan. Minneapolis: University of Minnesota Press, 1986.

Delumeau, Jean. *History of Paradise: The Garden of Eden in Myth and Tradition.* Trans. Matthew O'Connell. Urbana: University of Illinois Press, 2000.

Derrida, Jacques. *Aporias.* Trans. Thomas Dutoit. Stanford, CA: Stanford University Press, 1993.

————. *The Beast and the Sovereign. Vol. 1.* Trans. Geoffrey Bennington. Chicago: University of Chicago Press, 2009.

————. "Différance." In *Margins of Philosophy.* Trans. Alan Bass. Chicago: University of Chicago Press, 1982.

————. "Faith and Knowledge: The Two Sources of 'Religion' at the Limits of Reason Alone." In *Acts of Religion,* 40–101. New York: Routledge, 2002.

————. "Heidegger's Ear: Philopolemology (Geschlecht IV)." In *Reading Heidegger: Commemorations,* ed. John Sallis, 163–218. Bloomington, IN: Indiana University Press, 1993.

Descartes, René. *Principles of Philosophy.* 1644. Trans. Valentine Rodger Miller and Reese P. Miller. Dordrecht: D. Reidel, 1983.

Dietzfelbinger, Konrad. *Kafkas Geheimnis: Eine Interpretation von Franz Kafkas "Betrachtungen über Sünde, Leid, Hoffnung und den Wahren Weg."* Freiburg im Breisgau: Aurum, 1987.

Duttlinger, Carolin. *Kafka and Photography.* Oxford: Oxford University Press, 2007.

Edwards, Brian F. M. "Kafka and Kierkegaard: A Reassessment." *German Life and Letters* 20, no. 3 (April 1967): 218–25.

"Eine Erklärung der englischen Regierung für den Zionismus." *Jüdische Rundschau,* no. 46 (November 16, 1917): 1.

Engel, Manfred, and Bernd Auerochs, eds. *Kafka-Handbuch: Leben–Werk–Wirkung.* Stuttgart: J. B. Metzler, 2010.

Fenves, Peter. *"Chatter": Language and History in Kierkegaard.* Stanford, CA: Stanford University Press, 1993.

————. *The Messianic Reduction: Walter Benjamin and the Shape of Time.* Stanford, CA: Stanford University Press, 2011.

————. "Niemands Sache: Die Idee der 'res nullius' und die Suche nach einer Kritik der Gewalt." In *philo:xenia,* 1st ser., 123–205. Bern: Urs Engeler, 2009.

————. "'Workforce Without Possessions': Kafka, 'Social Justice,' and the Word Religion." In *Freedom and Confinement in Modernity: Kafka's Cages,* ed. A. Kiarina Kordela and Dimitris Vardoulakis, 107–26. New York: Palgrave Macmillan, 2011.

Feuerbach, Ludwig. *Das Wesen des Christentums.* Leipzig: Otto Weigand, 1848.

Fleischacker, Samuel. *Divine Teaching and the Way of the World: A Defense of Revealed Religion.* Oxford: Oxford University Press, 2011.

Fort, Jeff. *The Imperative to Write: Destitutions of the Sublime in Kafka, Blanchot, and Beckett.* New York: Fordham University Press, 2014.

Franks, Paul. "Rabbinic Idealism and Kabbalistic Realism: Jewish Dimensions of Idealism and Idealist Dimensions of Judaism." In *The Impact of Idealism, vol. 4: Religion,* ed. Nicholas Adams, 219–45. Cambridge: Cambridge University Press, 2013.

Gauchet, Marcel. *The Disenchantment of the World: A Political History of Religion.* Princeton, NJ: Princeton University Press, 1997.

Ginzberg, Louis. *Legends of the Jews. Vol. 1: Bible Times and Characters from the Creation to Moses in the Wilderness.* Trans. Henrietta Szold and Paul Radi. Philadelphia: Jewish Publication Society, 2003.

Glazova, Anna, and Paul North, eds. *Messianic Thought Outside Theology.* New York: Fordham University Press, 2014.

Gray, Richard T. *Constructive Destruction: Kafka's Aphorisms, Literary Tradition, and Literary Transformation.* Tübingen: Max Niemeyer, 1987.

Grözinger, Karl Erich. *Kafka und die Kabbala: Das Jüdische im Werk und Denken von Franz Kafka.* Berlin: Philo, 2003.

Grözinger, Karl Erich, with Stéphane Mosès and Hans Dieter Zimmermann, eds. *Franz Kafka und das Judentum.* Frankfurt am Main: Jüdischer Verlag bei Athenäum, 1987.

Hamacher, Werner. "Die Geste im Namen: Benjamin und Kafka." In *Entferntes Verstehen: Studien zu Philosophie und Literatur von Kant bis Celan.* Frankfurt am Main: Suhrkamp, 1998.

———. *Minima Philologica.* New York: Fordham University Press, 2015.

———. "Das Theologisch-politische Fragment." In *Benjamin Handbuch: Leben—Werk—Wirkung,* ed. Burkhardt Lindner, 175–92. Stuttgart: Metzler, 2006.

———. "Uncalled: A Commentary on Kafka's 'The Test'." In *Reading Ronell,* ed. Diane Davis, 74–93. Urbana: University of Illinois Press, 2009.

Hamilton, John. "Ecce Philologus: Nietzsche and Pindar's Second Pythian Ode." In *Nietzsche and Antiquity: His Reaction and Response to the Classical Tradition,* ed. Paul Bishop, 54–69. Rochester, NY: Camden House, 2004.

———. *Security: Politics, Humanity, and the Philology of Care.* Princeton, NJ: Princeton University Press, 2013.

Hawkins, Beth. *Reluctant Theologians: Kafka, Celan, Jabès.* New York: Fordham University Press, 2003.

Hegel, Georg Wilhelm Friedrich. *Encyclopedia of the Philosophical Sciences in Basic Outline. Part 1: Logic.* Trans. Klaus Brinkmann and Daniel O. Dahlstrom. Cambridge: Cambridge University Press, 2010.

———. *Faith and Knowledge.* Trans. Walter Cerf and H. S. Harris. Albany: State University of New York Press, 1977.

———. *Phenomenology of Spirit.* 1807. Trans. A. V. Miller. Oxford: Oxford University Press, 1977.

Heidegger, Martin. *Basic Problems of Phenomenology.* Bloomington: Indiana University Press, 1982.

———. "Conversation on a Country Path About Thinking." In *Discourse on*

Thinking: A Translation of Gelassenheit, trans. John M. Anderson and E. Hans Freund, 58–90. New York: Harper & Row, 1966.

———. *Country Path Conversations.* Trans. Bret W. Davis. Bloomington: Indiana University Press, 2010.

———. *Einführung in die Metaphysik.* Gesamtausgabe, vol. 40. Frankfurt am Main: Klostermann, 1983.

———. *Feldweg-Gespräche (1944/45).* Gesamtausgabe, vol. 77. Frankfurt am Main: Klostermann, 1995.

———. *Gelassenheit.* Pfullingen: Günther Neske, 1959.

———. *Metaphysische Anfangsgründe der Logik im Ausgang von Leibniz.* Gesamtausgabe, vol. 26. Franfurt am Main: Klostermann, 1978.

———. *Nietzsche.* Vols. 1 and 2. Trans. David Farrell Krell. San Francisco: Harper, 1991.

———. *Sein und Zeit.* Tübingen: Max Niemeyer, 1967.

———. *On Time and Being.* Trans. Joan Stambaugh. New York: Harper & Row, 1972.

———. *Unterwegs zur Sprache.* Frankfurt am Main: Klostermann, 1985.

———. "Zeit und Sein" ("Time and Being"). Lecture reprinted in *Zur Sache des Denkens,* 3–30. *Gesamtausgabe, vol. 14.* Frankfurt am Main: Vittorio Klostermann, 2007.

Heidsieck, Arnold. *The Intellectual Contexts of Kafka's Fiction: Philosophy, Law, Religion.* Columbia, SC: Camden House, 1994.

———. "Kafka's Fictional and Non-Fictional Treatments of Administrative, Civil, and Criminal Law." www.usc.edu/dept/LAS/german/track/heidsiec/KafkaLawsources/KafkaLawsources.pdf. Accessed February 15, 2015.

———. "Kafka's Narrative Ontology." *Philosophy and Literature,* 11, no. 2 (October 1987): 242–57.

Hellmann, Albrecht (Sigmund Kaznelson). "Erinnerungen an gemeinsame Kampfjahre." *Jüdischer Almanach auf das Jahr 5695* (1934–35), ed. Felix Weltsch, 166–70.

Hoffmann, Werner. *Kafkas Aphorismen.* Bern: Francke, 1975.

Hyman, Arthur. "Maimonides' Thirteen Principles." In *Jewish Medieval and Renaissance Studies,* ed. Alexander Altmann, 119–44. Cambridge, MA: Harvard University Press, 1967.

James, William. *Varieties of Religious Experience: A Study in Human Nature.* 1902. London: Routledge, 2002.

Jewish Study Bible. Ed. Adele Berlin and Marc Zvi Brettler. Oxford: Oxford University Press, 2004.

Das Jüdische Echo: Bayrische Blätter für die jüdischen Angelegenheiten, no. 38 (September 21, 1917).

Kafka, Franz. *Beim Bau der chinesischen Mauer: Ungedruckte Erzählungen und*

Prosa aus dem Nachlaß. Ed. Max Brod and Hans Joachim Schoeps. Berlin: Gustav Kiepenheuer, 1931.

———. *Briefe 1902–1924*. Ed. Max Brod. Frankfurt am Main: S. Fischer, 1966.

———. *Briefe 1914–1917*. Ed. Hans-Gerd Koch. Frankfurt am Main: S. Fischer, 2005.

———. *Briefe 1918–1920*. Ed. Hans-Gerd Koch. Frankfurt am Main: S. Fischer, 2013.

———. *The Castle*. Trans. Anthea Bell. Oxford: Oxford University Press, 2009.

———. *The Complete Stories*. Ed. Nahum N. Glatzer. New York: Schocken Books, 1971.

———. *Drucke zu Lebzeiten*. Ed. Hans-Gerd Koch. Frankfurt am Main: S. Fischer, 1994.

———. *Historisch-kritische Franz-Kafka-Ausgabe*. Ed. Roland Reuß and Peter Staengle. 8 vols. and 4 supplements. Basel: Stroemfeld, 1995. Cited as *FKA*.

———. *Letters to Family, Friends, and Editors*. Trans. Richard and Clara Winston. New York: Schocken Books, 1977.

———. *Letters to Felice*. Trans. James Stern and Elisabeth Duckworth. New York: Schocken Books, 1973.

———. *Nachgelassene Schriften und Fragmente*. 2 vols. Ed. Malcolm Pasley. Frankfurt am Main: S. Fischer, 1992–93. Cited as *NS* 1 or 2.

———. *Der Prozess*. Berlin: Die Schmiede, 1925. Ed. Malcolm Pasley. Frankfurt am Main: S. Fischer, 1990.

———. *Das Schloss*. Ed. Malcolm Pasley. Frankfurt am Main: S. Fischer, 1982.

———. *Tagebücher*. Ed. Hans-Gerd Koch, Michael Müller, and Malcolm Pasley. Frankfurt am Main: S. Fischer, 1990.

———. *The Trial*. Trans. Mike Mitchell. Oxford: Oxford University Press, 2009.

———. *Der Verschollene*. Ed. Jost Schillemeit. Frankfurt am Main: S. Fischer, 1983.

———. *Zürau Aphorisms*. Trans. Michael Hoffmann. Introduction and afterword by Roberto Calasso. London: Harvill Secker, 2006.

Kant, Immanuel. *Correspondence*. Ed. and Trans. Arnulf Zweig. Cambridge: Cambridge University Press, 1999.

———. *Critique of Pure Reason*. Trans. Paul Guyer and Allen W. Wood. Cambridge: Cambridge University Press, 1998.

———. *Kritik der reinen Vernunft*. Ed. R. Schmidt. Hamburg: Felix Meiner, 1954.

———. *Lectures on Logic*. Trans. J. Michael Young. Cambridge: Cambridge University Press, 1992.

———. *Religion Within the Boundaries of Mere Reason*. Trans. Allen Wood and George di Giovanni. Cambridge: Cambridge University Press, 1998.

Kautzsch, Emil, and Carl Heinrich Weizsäcker. *Textbibel des Alten und Neuen Testaments*. Freiburg im Breisgau: J. C. B. Mohr, 1899.

Kienlechner, Sabina. *Negativität der Erkenntnis im Werk Franz Kafkas: Eine Untersuchung zu seinem Denken anhand einiger später Texte.* Tübingen: Max Niemeyer, 1981.

Kierkegaard, Søren. *The Concept of Anxiety: A Simple Psychologically Orienting Deliberation on the Dogmatic Issue of Hereditary Sin.* Trans. Reidar Thomte and Albert B. Anderson. Princeton, NJ: Princeton University Press, 1980.

———. *Fear and Trembling and Repetition.* Trans. Howard V. Hong and Edna H. Hong. Princeton, NJ: Princeton University Press, 1983.

———. *Furcht und Zittern: Wiederholung.* Trans. H. C. Ketels. In *Gesammelte Werke.* Ed. H. Gottsched. Jena: Diederichs, 1909.

———. *The Moment and Late Writings.* Trans. Howard V. Hong and Edna H. Hong. Princeton, NJ: Princeton University Press, 2009.

———. *The Sickness unto Death: A Christian Psychological Exposition for Upbuilding and Awakening.* Trans. Howard V. Hong and Edna H. Hong. Princeton, NJ: Princeton University Press, 1980.

Kilcher, Andreas B. "Das Theater der Assimilation: Kafka und der jüdische Nietzscheanismus." In *Für Alle und Keinen: Lektüre, Schrift und Leben bei Nietzsche und Kafka*, ed. Friedrich Balke, Joseph Vogl, and Benno Wagner, 201–29. Zurich: diaphanes, 2008.

———. "Geisterschrift: Kafkas Spiritismus." In *Schrift und Zeit in Franz Kafkas Oktavheften*, ed. Caspar Battegay, Felix Christen, and Wolfram Groddeck, 223–44. Göttingen: Wallstein, 2010.

Kisiel, Theodore. *The Genesis of Heidegger's "Being and Time."* Berkeley: University of California Press, 1993.

Klatzkin, Jakob. "Deutschtum und Judentum: Eine Besprechung." *Der Jude* 2, no. 4 (1917): 245–52.

Kleist, Heinrich von. *Selected Writings.* Trans. David Constantine. Indianapolis, IN: Hackett, 2004.

Kohn, Hans, ed. *Vom Judentum: Ein Sammelbuch.* Leipzig: Kurt Wolff, 1914.

Kugel, James L. *Traditions of the Bible: A Guide to the Bible as It Was at the Start of the Common Era.* Cambridge, MA: Harvard University Press, 1998.

Lange, Wolfgang. "Über Kafkas Kierkegaard-Lektüre und einige damit zusammenhängende Gegenstände." *Deutsche Vierteljahrsschrift für Literaturwissenschaft und Geistesgeschichte* 60, no. 2 (June 1986): 286–308.

Lawson, Richard H. "Kafka's Use of the Conjunction *Bis* in the Sense 'As Soon As.'" *German Quarterly* 35, no. 2 (1962): 165–70.

Leavitt, June O. *The Mystical Life of Franz Kafka: Theosophy, Cabala, and the Modern Spiritual Revival.* Oxford: Oxford University Press, 2012.

Levine, Michael. *A Weak Messianic Power: Figures of a Time to Come in Benjamin, Derrida, and Celan.* New York: Fordham University Press, 2013.

Linell, Per. *Approaching Dialogue: Talk, Interaction and Contexts in Dialogical Perspectives.* Amsterdam: John Benjamins, 2001.

Liska, Vivian. *When Kafka Says We: Uncommon Communities in German Jewish Literature.* Bloomington: Indiana University Press, 2009.

Longuenesse, Béatrice. *Kant and the Capacity to Judge: Sensibility and Discursivity in the Transcendental Analytic of "The Critique of Pure Reason."* Trans. Charles T. Wolfe. Princeton, NJ: Princeton University Press, 1998.

Loraux, Nicole. *The Divided City: On Memory and Forgetting in Ancient Athens.* New York: Zone Books, 2006.

Lorenzer, Stefan. "Notiz über das Lassen." In *Babel: Für Werner Hamacher.* Basel: Urs Engeler, 2009.

Luther, Martin. "The Fourteen Consolations." In *Luther's Works, vol. 42,* ed. Martin O. Dietrich, 119–66. Philadelphia: Fortress Press, 1969.

———. "The Freedom of a Christian." In *Martin Luther: Selections from His Writings.* Ed. John Dillenberger. Garden City, NY: Anchor Books, 1962.

———. "Von der Freiheit eines Christenmenschen." In *D. Martin Luthers Werke. Kritische Gesamtausgabe (Weimarer Ausgabe), vol. 7,* ed. Paul Peitsch, 12–38. Weimar: Hermann Böhlhaus, 1897.

———. *Luther's Works, vol. 48: Letters 1.* Ed. and trans. Gottfried G. Krodel. Philadelphia: Fortress Press, 1963.

———. "Preface to the Romans." In *Martin Luther: Selections from His Writings.* Ed. John Dillenberger. Garden City, NY: Anchor Books, 1961.

Magid, Shaul. "Subversion as Return: Scripture, Dissent, Renewal, and the Future of Judaism." In *Subverting Scriptures: Critical Reflections on the Use of the Bible.* Ed. Beth Hawkins Benedix. New York: Palgrave Macmillan, 2009.

Marcel, Gabriel. "Belonging and Disposability." In *Creative Fidelity,* trans. Robert Rosthal, 38–57. New York: Fordham University Press, 1964.

———. "Outlines of a Phenomenology of Having." In *Being and Having.* Trans. Katharine Farrer. London: Dacre, 1949.

Marty, Anton. *Deskriptive Psychologie.* Ed. Mauro Antonelli and Johann Christian Marek. Würzburg: Königshausen & Neumann, 2011.

———. *Ueber den Ursprung der Sprache.* Würzburg: A. Stuber, 1875.

Marx, Karl. *Capital: A Critique of Political Economy. Vol. 1.* Trans. Ben Fowkes. London: Penguin Books, 1976.

Menne, A. "Das unendliche Urteil Kants." *Philosophia Naturalis* 19 (1982): 151–62.

Miethe, Helge. *Sören Kierkegaards Wirkung auf Franz Kafka: Motivische und sprachliche Parallelen.* Marburg: Tectum, 2006.

Morris, Joel. "Josef K.'s (A + x) Problem: Kafka on the Moment of Awakening." *German Quarterly* 82, no. 4 (Fall 2009): 469–82.

Mosès, Stéphane. "Zur Frage des Gesetzes: Gershom Scholem's Kafka-Bild." In *Franz Kafka und das Judentum,* ed. Karl Erich Grözinger, with Stéphane Mosès and Hans Dieter Zimmermann, 13–34. Frankfurt am Main: Athenäum, 1987.

Müller, Ernst. "Übertragungen aus dem Buche Sohar." *Der Jude* 2, no. 1 (1917): 93–96.

Nancy, Jean-Luc. *Adoration*. New York: Fordham University Press, 2013.

———. *Dis-Enclosure: The Deconstruction of Christianity*. New York: Fordham University Press, 2008.

Neesen, Peter. *Vom Louvrezirkel zum Prozess: Franz Kafka und die Psychologie Franz Brentanos*. Göppingen: Alfred Kümmerle, 1972.

Neumann, Gerhard. "Umkehrung und Ablenkung: Franz Kafkas 'Gleitendes Paradox.'" *Deutsche Vierteljahrsschrift für Literaturwissenschaft und Geistesgeschichte* 42, special no. (November 1968): 702–44.

Neumann, Gerhard, ed. *Der Aphorismus: Zur Geschichte, zu den Formen und Möglichkeiten einer literarischen Gattung*. Darmstadt: Wissenschaftliche Buchgesellschaft, 1976.

Nietzsche, Friedrich. *The Anti-Christ, Ecce Homo, Twilight of the Idols, and Other Writings*. Trans. Judith Norman. Cambridge: Cambridge University Press, 2005.

———. *The Birth of Tragedy and other Writings*. Trans. Ronald Speirs. Cambridge: Cambridge University Press, 1999.

———. *The Gay Science*. Trans. Josefine Nauckhoff. Cambridge: Cambridge University Press, 2001.

———. *Human All-Too Human*. Trans. R. J. Hollingdale. Cambridge: Cambridge University Press, 1996.

———. *On the Genealogy of Morality*. Trans. Carol Diethe. Cambridge: Cambridge University Press, 2006.

———. *Philosophy in the Tragic Age of the Greeks*. Trans. Marianne Cowan. Washington, DC: Regnery, 1962.

———. *Philosophy and Truth: Selections from Nietzsche's Notebooks of the Early 1870s*. Ed. Daniel Breazeale. Atlantic Highlands, NJ: Humanities Press, 1979.

———. *Sämtliche Werke: Kritische Studienausgabe*. 15 vols. Ed. Giorgio Colli and Mazino Montinari. Berlin: De Gruyter, 1988. Cited as *KSA*.

———. *Thus Spoke Zarathustra: A Book for All and None*. Trans. Adrian del Caro. Cambridge: Cambridge University Press, 2006.

———. *Writings from the Late Notebooks*. Trans. Kate Sturge. Cambridge: Cambridge University Press, 2003.

North, Paul. *The Problem of Distraction*. Stanford, CA: Stanford University Press, 2012.

Pascal, Blaise. *Pensées*. Trans. Honor Levi. Oxford: Oxford University Press, 1995.

Pindar. *Second Pythian Ode*. In *The Odes of Pindar*. Trans. John Sandys. Cambridge, MA: Harvard University Press, 1937.

Plato. *Complete Works.* Ed. John M. Cooper. Indianapolis, IN: Hackett, 1997.

――――. *Platonis Opera, vol. 4: Clitopho, Respublica, Timaeus, Critias.* Ed. John Burnett. Oxford: Oxford University Press, 1962.

――――. *Phaedo.* Trans. David Gallop. Oxford: Oxford University Press, 1975.

――――. *The Republic.* Ed. G. R. F. Ferrari. Trans. Tom Griffith. Cambridge: Cambridge University Press, 2000.

Politzer, Heinz. *Franz Kafka: Parable and Paradox.* Ithaca, NY: Cornell University Press, 1962.

Pritchard, Elizabeth. "*Bilderverbot* Meets Body in Theodor Adorno's Inverse Theology." *Harvard Theological Review* 95, no. 3 (July 2002): 291–318.

Reed, T. J. "Kafka und Schopenhauer: Philosophisches Denken und dichterisches Bild." *Euphorion: Zeitschrift für Literaturgeschichte* 59 (1965): 160–72.

Reuß, Roland. "Die Oxforder Oktavhefte 7 & 8 und die Zürauer Zettel. Zur Einführung." In *Franz Kafka–Heft 8*, ed. id and Peter Staengle, 3–16. Frankfurt am Main: Stroemfeld, 2011.

Robertson, Ritchie. "Kafka as Anti-Christian: 'Das Urteil,' 'Die Verwandlung,' and The Aphorisms." In *A Companion to the Works of Franz Kafka*, ed. James Rolleston, 101–22. Rochester, NY: Camden House, 2002.

――――. *Kafka: Judaism, Politics, and Literature.* Oxford: Oxford University Press, 1985.

Rohde, Bertram. *"Und blätterte ein wenig in der Bibel": Studien zu Franz Kafkas Bibellektüre und ihren Auswirkungen auf sein Werk.* Würzburg: Königshausen & Neumann, 2002.

Ronell, Avital. *Loser Sons: Politics and Authority.* Urbana: University of Illinois Press, 2012.

Rosenzweig, Franz. *Der Stern der Erlösung.* Frankfurt am Main: Suhrkamp, 1988.

Rousseau, Jean-Jacques. "Profession of Faith of the Savoyard Vicar." In *Emile, or, On Education.* Trans. Allan Bloom. New York: Basic Books, 1979.

Rozenblit, Marsha L. *Reconstructing a National Identity: The Jews of Habsburg Austria During World War I.* Oxford: Oxford University Press, 2001.

Santner, Eric. *My Own Private Germany: Daniel Paul Schreber's Secret History of Modernity.* Princeton, NJ: Princeton University Press, 1996.

――――. *The Royal Remains: The People's Two Bodies and the Endgames of Sovereignty.* Chicago: University of Chicago Press, 2011.

Schillemeit, Jost. "Chancen und Grenzen der Willensfreiheit: Fragen der Ethik und Religionsphilosophie bei Max Brod, Felix Weltsch und Kafka (1920)." In *Kafka-Studien.* Ed. Rosemarie Schillemeit. Göttingen: Wallstein, 2004.

Schmidt, Carsten. *Kafkas fast unbekannter Freund. Das Leben und Werk von Felix Weltsch (1884–1964).* Würzburg: Königshausen & Neumann, 2010.

Schneider, Gesa. *Das andere Schreiben: Kafkas fotografische Poetik.* Würzburg: Königshausen & Neumann, 2008.

Schoeps, Hans-Joachim. "Wir gehen einen deutschen Weg." *Central-Verein-Zeitung: Blätter für Deutschtum und Judentum*, 12, no. 23 (July 13, 1933): 275–76.

Schoeps, Julius H., ed. *Im Streit um Kafka und das Judentum: Max Brod, Hans-Joachim Schoeps Briefwechsel*. Königstein: Jüdischer Verlag bei Athenäum, 1985.

Scholem, Gershom. *Die Geschichte einer Freundschaft*. Frankfurt am Main: Suhrkamp, 1975.

Schopenhauer, Arthur. *Die Welt als Wille und Vorstellung*. Ed. Luwig Berndl. Munich: Georg Müller, 1912.

———. *The World as Will and Representation*. Ed. and trans. by Judith Norman, Alistair Welchman, and Christopher Janaway. Cambridge: Cambridge University Press, 2010.

Skempton, Simon. *Alienation After Derrida*. London: Continuum, 2010.

Smith, Barry. *Austrian Philosophy: The Legacy of Franz Brentano*. Chicago: Open Court, 1994.

———. "Brentano and Kafka." *Axiomathes* 8 (1997): 83–104.

Smith, John H. *Dialogues Between Faith and Reason: The Death and Return of God in Modern German Thought*. Ithaca, NY: Cornell University Press, 2011.

Söderblom, Nathan. *Das Werden des Gottesglaubens: Untersuchungen über die Anfänge der Religion*. Trans. Rudolf Stübe. 1916. 2nd ed. Leipzig: J. C. Hinrichs, 1926.

Sokel, Walter. "Between Gnosticism and Jehova: The Dilemma in Kafka's Religious Attitude." In *The Myth of Power and the Self: Essays on Franz Kafka*. Detroit: Wayne State University, 2002.

Spinoza, Benedict de. *Theological-Political Treatise*. Trans. Michael Silverthorne and Jonathan Israel. Ed. Jonathan Israel. Cambridge: Cambridge University Press, 2007.

Stein, Leonard. *The Balfour Declaration*. New York: Simon & Schuster, 1961

Suchoff, David. *Kafka's Jewish Languages: The Hidden Openness of Tradition*. Philadelphia: University of Pennsylvania Press, 2012.

Sussman, Henry. "Kafka's Aesthetics: A Primer: From the Fragments to the Novels." In *A Companion to the Works of Franz Kafka*, ed. James Rolleston, 123–48. Rochester, NY: Camden House, 2002.

———. "The Calculable, the Incalculable, and the Rest: Kafka's Virtual Environment." *MLN* 127, no. 5 (December 2012): 1144–70.

Taubes, Jacob. *The Political Theology of Paul*. Stanford, CA: Stanford University Press, 2004.

Taylor, Charles. *A Secular Age*. Cambridge, MA: Belknap Press of Harvard University Press, 2007.

Terada, Rei. *Looking Away: Phenomenality and Dissatisfaction, Kant to Adorno*. Cambridge, MA: Harvard University Press, 2009.

Trietsch, Davis. "Die Gartenstadt als Konzentrationsform." *Jüdische Rundschau*, 25 (1917): 207–8.

Troeltsch, Ernst. "Luther und der Protestantismus." *Die Neue Rundschau*. Vol. 2. Berlin: S. Fischer, 1917.

Vardoulakis, Dimitris. "'The Fall Is the Proof of Our Freedom': Mediated Freedom in Kafka." In *Freedom and Confinement in Modernity: Kafka's Cages*, ed. A. Kiarina Kordela and Dimitris Vardoulakis, 87–106. New York: Palgrave Macmillan, 2011.

Vogl, Joseph. "Vierte Person. Kafkas Erzählstimme." *Deutsche Vierteljahrsschrift für Literaturwissenschaft und Geistesgeschichte* 68, no. 4 (December 1994): 745–56.

Wagenbach, Klaus. *Franz Kafka: Eine Biographie seiner Jugend, 1883–1912*. Bern: Francke, 1958.

Walser, Robert. *Jakob von Gunten*. Zurich: Suhrkamp, 1985.

―――. *Jakob von Gunten*. Trans. Christopher Middleton. New York: New York Review Books Classics, 1999.

Wasihun, Betiel. *Gewollt, Nicht-Gewollt: Wettkampf bei Kafka, mit Blick auf Robert Walser und Samuel Beckett*. Heidelberg: Winter, 2010.

Watkin, Christopher. *Difficult Atheism: Post-Theological Thinking in Alan Badiou, Jean-Luc Nancy, and Quentin Meillassoux*. Edinburgh: Edinburgh University Press, 2011.

Weltsch, Felix. "Erlebnis und Intention (Die aktivistische und die romantische Gefahr)." In *Tätiger Geist! Zweites der Ziel-Jahrbücher, 1917–1918*, ed. Kurt Hiller, 246–63. Munich: Georg Müller, 1918.

―――. *Gnade und Freiheit: Untersuchungen zum Problem des schöpferischen Willens in Religion und Ethik*. Munich: Kurt Wolff, 1920. Reprinted with an afterword by Hans-Gerd Koch (Düsseldorf: onomato, 2010).

―――. "Hermann Cohen." *Prager Tagblatt*, no. 85 (April 12, 1918): 2.

―――. "Masaryk and Zionism." In *Thomas G. Masaryk and the Jews*, ed. Ernst Rychnovsky, trans. B. R. Epstein. New York: B. Pollak, 1941.

―――. *Religion und Humor im Leben und Werk Franz Kafkas*. Berlin: F. A. Herbig, 1957.

Zilcosky, John. *Kafka's Travels: Exoticism, Colonialism, and the Traffic of Writing*. New York: Palgrave Macmillan, 2003.

Index

Crossing Aesthetics

Giorgio Agamben, *The Open: Man and Animal*

Jean Genet, *The Declared Enemy*

Shosana Felman, *Writing and Madness: (Literature/Philosophy/Psychoanalysis)*

Jean Genet, *Fragments of the Artwork*

Shoshana Felman, *The Scandal of the Speaking Body: Don Juan with J. L. Austin, or Seduction in Two Languages*

Peter Szondi, *Celan Studies*

Neil Hertz, *George Eliot's Pulse*

Maurice Blanchot, *The Book to Come*

Susannah Young-ah Gottlieb, *Regions of Sorrow: Anxiety and Messianism in Hannah Arendt and W. H. Auden*

Jacques Derrida, *Without Alibi*, edited by Peggy Kamuf

Cornelius Castoriadis, *On Plato's 'Statesman'*

Jacques Derrida, *Who's Afraid of Philosophy? Right to Philosophy 1*

Peter Szondi, *An Essay on the Tragic*

Peter Fenves, *Arresting Language: From Leibniz to Benjamin*

Jill Robbins, ed. *Is It Righteous to Be?: Interviews with Emmanuel Levinas*

Louis Marin, *Of Representation*

Daniel Payot, *The Architect and the Philosopher*

J. Hillis Miller, *Speech Acts in Literature*

Maurice Blanchot, *Faux pas*

Jean-Luc Nancy, *Being Singular Plural*

Maurice Blanchot / Jacques Derrida, *The Instant of My Death / Demeure: Fiction and Testimony*

Niklas Luhmann, *Art as a Social System*

Emmanual Levinas, *God, Death, and Time*

Ernst Bloch, *The Spirit of Utopia*

Made in the USA
Middletown, DE
09 November 2024

64197481R00239